EXPERT EVIDENCE IN CRIMINAL LAW: THE SCIENTIFIC APPROACH

SECOND EDITION

EXPERT EVIDENCE IN CRIMINAL LAW: THE SCIENTIFIC APPROACH

SECOND EDITION

Alan D. Gold

Expert Evidence in Criminal Law: The Scientific Approach, second edition
© Irwin Law Inc., 2009

Published in 2009 by

Irwin Law Inc.
14 Duncan Street
Suite 206
Toronto, ON
M5H 3G8

www.irwinlaw.com

ISBN: 978-1-55221-170-0

Library and Archives Canada Cataloguing in Publication

Gold, Alan D.
    Expert evidence in criminal law : the scientific approach / Alan D. Gold. — 2nd ed.

Includes ibibliographical references and index.
ISBN 978-1-55221-170-0

1. Evidence, Expert. I. Title.

KS485.G64 2009   345'.067   C2009-903718-1

The publisher acknowledges the financial support of the Government of Canada through the Book Publishing Industry Development Program (BPIDP) for its publishing activities.

We acknowledge the assistance of the OMDC Book Fund, an initiative of Ontario Media Development Corporation.

Printed and bound in Canada.

1 2 3 4 5   13 12 11 10 09

Mixed Sources
Product group from well-managed forests,
controlled sources and recycled wood or fiber
www.fsc.org Cert no. SW-COC-000952
© 1996 Forest Stewardship Council
FSC

Summary Table of Contents

Detailed Table of Contents

Foreword to the First Edition

IN ALAN GOLD'S excellent book on expert evidence in criminal law, someone notes that the age of the expert has truly arrived because great portions of trials are now consumed by expert testimony. I should know as I have played a part in this endeavour, having testified in over 250 trials during the last quarter-century. Although I make every effort to be scientifically accurate, I recognize that personal biases (for example, an abiding belief that a defendant is innocent) might occasionally affect my testimony, however subtly.

Expert Evidence in Criminal Law: The Scientific Approach makes clear the problems that courts have faced when dubious testimony about single cases, or about a study that involves multiple cases, is proffered. Lawyers and judges are not typically in a good position to scrutinize the testimony as thoroughly as it should be. One lesson from the examples that Gold provides is that it is important to continually ask not only "What is the evidence for your claim?" but to insist that the "expert" provide more than authors of the study and where it was published, and be able to describe precisely what form the evidence takes.

This book is an eye-opener to anyone who mistakenly believes all experts and their evidence can be trusted as the truth. Although Gold admits that expert scientific evidence has contributed greatly to the administration of justice, he points out the concerns about the quality of this evidence and the lack of scientific literacy of judges and lawyers — to say nothing of ordinary jury members whose scientific education is equally minimal. Gold gives many examples of "junk science" used in the justice system, and he shows you how to differentiate between the worthwhile and the worthless "expert" evidence, stating that the scientific perspective contains "the only reliable standard by which opinions can be judged." Reading this book will give you the necessary questions when considering scientific evidence, as Gold has listed many useful reports and books that debunk much of what has passed as expert evidence.

What I have also learned through courtroom experiences is that some experts are more than willing to testify in ways that are suspect, if not downright appalling. Consider the testimony of a psychologist in a criminal case in which a lawyer/politician defendant from Rhode Island was accused of sexual abuse. To bolster the complainant's claim of recovered memory, a psychologist testified about a published case history involving six-year-old Jane Doe who had accused her mother of sexual abuse. When Jane was seventeen, Dr. Corwin, a forensic psychiatrist, interviewed her again and published the case history in a "peer-reviewed" journal. The expert witness psychologist in the Rhode Island trial referred to Corwin's work as a "single subject study." He testified that Jane clearly "had no memory for this abuse that had happened 11 years earlier." The expert went on to testify that at age seventeen, Jane's memory came back, and he praised the work as "documentation of a recovered memory experience." He later called the research with Jane Doe "an 11-year prospective study of a single case of a documented recovered memory."

In other litigation, this time in Utah, Dr. Corwin himself testified about Jane's spontaneous return of a detailed recollection and called his work "remarkable in the kind of documentation" it provided. Corwin discussed his case study in the context of traumatic experiences and traumatic amnesia, and in the context of a widely cited published study that showed that about one-third of women who had apparently experienced sexual abuse in childhood did not mention it to interviewers seventeen years later. This expert testimony was clearly an effort to bolster the complainant's claims of recovered memory of sexual abuse in the Utah case. Thus, inside of courtrooms, and outside as well, "experts" were citing the Jane Doe case repeatedly, calling it up as proof that memories can be repressed, and then reliably recovered.

What is especially troubling about this testimony is that psychological science has shown that people can be unduly persuaded by vivid case histories that have a way of living long after the theories they engendered were put to rest. Vivid cases that are concrete and detailed have a disproportionate impact on beliefs in general, and on the outcome of cases in particular. But is the Jane Doe case even true? Along with Dr. Mel Guyer from the University of Michigan, I investigated the authenticity of the case of Jane Doe. Finding the identity of the individuals was a major hurdle, but once we did, we compiled a great deal of evidence — medical and legal documentation from the time — that threw significant doubt on Jane's story. And we even uncovered significant evidence that the abuse accusations had been planted in the mind of Jane during a vicious custody battle. There was so much doubt that we concluded the case had no place in the legal and scientific literature, and we published our exposé. If the case never surfaces again, and the (probably) falsely accused mother has some modicum of justice, that will be reward enough for us — reward enough to offset the wounds from the disgraceful treatment that our investigation caused us to endure at the hands of what Gold calls "fanatical opponents."[1]

Expert Evidence in Criminal Law: The Scientific Approach is an impressive attempt to bring some real science into the "expert" testimony that gets introduced at trial and to banish dangerous pseudo-science. Wonderfully written by one of Canada's most pre-eminent lawyers, it should play a role in fostering much-needed changes in what gets in and what stays out. The end result will be an enhanced level of justice that all citizens will receive from their legal system.

ELIZABETH F. LOFTUS, PH.D.

Distinguished Professor
University of California at Irvine
Department of Psychology and Social Behavior
Department of Criminology, Law and Society
Department of Cognitive Sciences
Fellow, Center for the Neurobiology of Learning and Memory
Past President of the American Psychological Society

---

1   See note 89 in chapter 7 for further commentary on this case.

Preface to the Second Edition

OVER HALF A decade has passed since the first edition. There have been some bright spots since then. Professor Loftus's undeserved forensic agony described in her foreword to the first edition had a happy ending.[1] The Supreme Court of Canada clearly embraced the scientific method in deciding upon the inadmissibility of hypnotically refreshed "memories."[2] The faith expressed in the preface to the first edition that "[t]he courtroom, when it is populated by scientifically literate lawyers and judges, is an excellent forum for the exposure of junk science" was amply vindicated in some remarkable cases: in *Kitzmiller et al. v. Dover Area School District et al.*,[3] Judge John E. Jones III, who was nominated by former U.S. President George W. Bush, made a very strong ruling against "intelligent design," holding that it was creationism and not science; and *Dimmock v. Secretary of State for Education & Skills*,[4] after extensive evidence, judicially exposed the "global warming" junk science in Al Gore's movie *An Inconvenient Truth*.

However, the highly anticipated paradigm shift in admissibility because of the *Daubert* trilogy has failed to materialize, at least for the criminally accused,[5] and the issues continue to bedevil courts.[6] Examples of "expert" evidence that have appeared in courtrooms recently include the following:

1 Carol Tavris, "Whatever Happened to Jane Doe?" *Skeptical Inquirer* (January–February 2008), online: www.csicop.org/si/2008-01/tavris.html.
2 *R. v. Trochym*, [2007] 1 S.C.R. 239.
3 400 F. Supp. 2d 707 (M.D. Pa. 2005), online: www.aclupa.org/downloads/Dec20opinion.pdf.
4 [2007] EWHC 2288 (Admin), online: www.bailii.org/ew/cases/EWHC/Admin/2007/2288.html.
5 See chapter 2, note 15 and accompanying text.
6 The Honourable Mr. Justice W. Ian C. Binnie, "Science in the Courtroom: The Mouse That Roared" (2008) 27:2 Advocates' Soc. J. 11.

- composition bullet lead analysis (CBLA) evidence that the lead in the fragments recovered from the decedent and the lead in bullets the defendant possessed were analytically indistinguishable, that both the lead fragments recovered from the decedent's body and the defendant's bullets came from the same source of lead, and both the fragments recovered from the decedent's body and the defendant's bullets came from the same box or boxes and were packaged on the same date by the manufacturer;[7]
- multiple unexplained infant deaths in the same family are so statistically unlikely it must be parental homicide;[8]
- a shirt found in the accused's possession "matches" the shirt worn by the bank robber on surveillance videos;[9]
- shaken baby syndrome is a reliable proof of homicide;[10]
- the physical findings from the examination of the complainant's genitalia show she was sexually abused;[11]
- forensic ballistics identification evidence is reliable evidence to link the accused's gun with the shooting;[12]
- a lip-reader purports to read the conversation of two alleged criminals caught soundlessly speaking on a surveillance video;[13]
- facial mapping and body mapping between photographs of the accused and videos of the perpetrator can identify the accused;[14]
- risk assessment of young offenders using the "Level of Service Inventory—Saskatchewan Youth Edition" can accurately identify the future dangerousness of an accused.[15]

Therefore, the need for scientifically literate defence counsel and judges, not to mention prosecutors, police officers, and expert witnesses continues unabated.

The first edition of this text was wonderfully well received and I cling to the belief, however unscientific, that it has made a contribution to the education of the bench and bar in this area. I hope this revised edition will continue that contribution in an equally enjoyable and readable fashion.

---

7 *State v. Behn*, 2005 N.J. Super. LEXIS 73; *Clemons v. State*, 2006 Md. LEXIS 192.
8 *R. v. Anthony*, [2005] EWCA Crim 952.
9 *United States v. McKreith*, 2005 U.S. App. LEXIS 14072.
10 *R. v. Harris*, [2005] EWCA Crim 1980.
11 *Gersten v. Senkowski*, 426 F.3d 588, 2005 U.S. App. LEXIS 22322.
12 *United States v. Green*, 2005 U.S. Dist. LEXIS 34273.
13 *R. v. Luttrell*, [2004] EWCA Crim 1344.
14 *R. v. Hien Puoc Tang*, [2006] NSWCCA 167.
15 *R. v. B.H.D.*, [2006] S.J. No. 345 (Prov. Ct.).

Preface to the First Edition

I HAPPILY ACCEPTED the publisher's suggestion to do a Canadian book on expert evidence in criminal cases from a scientific perspective for several reasons. For one thing, the time was clearly right. An explosion of expert evidence in the last several decades had brought an increasing concern about junk science and pseudo-science in our courtrooms. As described in the text, in 1993 the U.S. Supreme Court in a line of cases beginning with *Daubert v. Merrell Dow Pharmaceuticals*[1] mandated the scientific method as the obligatory standard for expert opinion evidence. Any doubt about the relevancy of *Daubert* for Canadian lawyers and judges was settled by *R. v. J-L.J.*[2] when the Supreme Court expressly referenced *Daubert* as a relevant authority and expressly adopted the same elements of analysis. According to our highest courts, expert evidence was now required to obey the rules of science to be admissible.

For another thing, the effort was clearly necessary. Although science knowledge for lawyers and judges had effectively been mandated by our highest courts, in truth there was a scarcity of legal reference works where that knowledge could be obtained in a format accessible to lawyers and judges approaching the topic for the first time, yet helpful and useful to others familiar with the basic concepts and issues.

Finally, and most important, such a book would be a most righteous effort. Modern society, for the scientifically literate, can be a depressing place. It is a frustrating paradox that amid a society blessed with exponentially increasing scientific knowledge accompanied by unimaginable technological achieve-

---

1   509 U.S. 79 (1993) [*Daubert*].
2   [2000] 2 S.C.R. 600.

ments, scientific illiteracy is growing and flowering to an extent that seemingly rivals the Middle Ages. Ubiquitous horoscopes, bogus alternative medicines, superstitious behaviours — including government-run lotteries and the apparent constitutional rights to reason as badly as one wants and to be as gullible as the most diabolical conman could wish for — offer little cause for optimism for anyone concerned about junk knowledge. It seems an overwhelming, almost impossible endeavour to seek to overthrow the grip that utter nonsense holds on much of contemporary society.

However, the criminal justice system offers an enclave where optimism can prevail. In addition to the judicial philosophical commitment that "science rules," there is also the actual feasibility of the enterprise. The courtroom, when it is populated by scientifically literate lawyers and judges, is an excellent forum for the exposure of junk science. When a knowledgeable lawyer confronts ignorance or beliefs masquerading as fact and knowledge, the result is almost inevitably a victory for truth. This lesson was learned in 1925 by William Jennings Bryan; it has been learned more recently, to their appropriate shame, by many clinical psychologists and other counsellors unaware of the basic principles of good science.

But the "big if" is clear: scientifically literate lawyers and judges. To aid in that most worthwhile cause was the motivation for this book: a book that I hope contains all the principles and knowledge needed to expose bogus experts and junk science and reduce inflated expert evidence to its proper valuation, a book that will assist in fostering the scientific literacy that is now judicially required in our court system. Of course, the reader will be left to judge the degree to which this book achieves its goals.

I would especially like to thank my indispensable assistant Cheryl Gafer for her immeasurable help in the preparation of this book. I also wish to thank an anonymous reviewer whose kind words and very helpful suggestions were instrumental in the final product. The people at Irwin Law were a pleasure to work with. My editor, Maraya Raduha, does not know the size of the "wow" she got when I saw all her hard work on the manuscript and the wise changes she made, and I am exceedingly grateful. I also wish to acknowledge and thank other members of my office, and especially my invaluable associate Maureen Mcguire. Families can make an important contribution to a project like this, and Ruth, Evan, Jessica, and Caitlin helped more than they will ever know. I hope they all are proud of this book.

Needless to say, I alone should be indicted for any and all errors, omissions, and other malfeasance that become apparent.

"Whatever knowledge is attainable, must be attained by scientific methods."

–Bertrand A.W. Russell, *Religion and Science* (1975)

"To sum up: it is wrong always, everywhere, and for anyone, to believe anything upon insufficient evidence."

–William Kingdon Clifford, *The Ethics of Belief* (1879)

CHAPTER 1

Introduction

EXPERT WITNESSES ARE granted a special licence by the courts of law.[1] While most witnesses called to assist the law in its fact-finding and decision-making enterprise are limited to recounting what they personally observed with their own senses, expert witnesses are allowed to opine. They are — subject to the rules of evidence in that regard — allowed to offer their beliefs and conclusions as substantive evidence. The law's relationship with this special category of witnesses has had an unsteady course.

Initially, the law was suspicious of experts and their evidence. One author wrote in 1906:

> The testimony of skilled witnesses is perhaps that which deserves least credit with a jury. These usually speak to opinions and not to facts; and it is often really surprising to see the facility and extent to which views can be made to coincide with wishes or interests. Skilled witnesses do not, indeed, wilfully misrepresent what they think: but their judgments have often become so warped by regarding the subject from only one point of view, that they are, in truth, not capable of forming an independent opinion even when they would conscientiously desire to do so. Being zealous partisans, their belief becomes synonymous with the Apostle's definition of Faith, "the substance of things

---

1   An expert witness is defined as someone who possesses "special skill or knowledge acquired through study or experience that entitles him or her to give an opinion or evidence concerning his or her area of expertise": John A. Yogis, *Canadian Law Dictionary*, 4th ed. (Hauppauge, NY: Barron's Educational Series, 1998) at 100.

hoped for, the evidence of things not seen." Lord Campbell once said, "Skilled witnesses come with such a bias on their minds to support the cause in which they are embarked, that hardly any weight should be given to their evidence."[2]

Wigmore, the leading American authority on the law of evidence, is quoted as having said: "It [the rule permitting expert opinion testimony] has done more than any one rule of procedure to reduce our litigation to a state of legalized gambling."[3] Another commentator stated:

> In the lush pastures of the Common Law a number of sacred cows graze and no-one dares to cull them or even try to make them healthier. One answers to the name of "expert evidence." ... It is a scraggy animal, despised by many, yet its continued existence is essential for the proper administration of justice. Properly cared for it could provide good progeny but the breeding would have to be selective as some strains may not be worth encouraging.[4]

The present Chief Justice of Canada, the Right Honourable Beverley McLachlin, has noted the much different attitude towards expert evidence that has developed in more recent times:

> By the 1980s the law had travelled a great distance indeed from its early suspicion of the dangers of expert evidence. Experts were allowed to testify on any subject, regardless of whether it was within the understanding and experience of the judge and jury. Experts were allowed to go beyond expert opinions and permitted to summarize complicated or ambiguous sets of facts. The hypothetical question was no longer to be insisted upon. And, in perhaps the most serious incursion on the traditional view, expert witnesses were to be allowed to testify and base their conclusions on what was admitted to be hearsay and inadmissible evidence, subject only to the rather ineffectual admonition that care should be given to the "weight" the evidence should be given.
>
> Newly freed from its old constraints, expert evidence burst on the courthouse scene with a startling vigour. The age of the expert had truly arrived. Increasingly, great portions of trials, simple and complex, were consumed by expert testimony. Litigation became not only a contest on the facts and the law, but a battle of experts. Each side raced to retain the best experts in the field before their opponent could hire them. Experts vied to put in longer and

2   J.P. Taylor, *A Treatise on the Law of Evidence*, 10th ed. by W.E. Hume-Williams (London: Sweet & Maxwell, 1906) at 63, quoted by The Honourable Chief Justice B.M. McLachlin in "The Role of the Expert Witness" (1990) 14:3 Prov. Judges J. 27.

3   Quoted in Welcome D. Pierson, "Abuses in the Use of Expert Testimony" (1961) 9 Defense L.J. 117 at 119.

4   L.J. Lawton, "The Limitations of Expert Scientific Evidence" (1981) 20 J. Forensic Sci. 237.

more learned reports. This occurred, not only in fields where a real assistance was required by the court — and they are many — but in situations where one would have thought a reasonably intelligent judge and jury could have made up their own minds. Perhaps the apotheosis of the expert revolution in this small corner of the world arrived when in a falling-down-the-steps case on Granville Mall an expert was flown all the way in from Ireland. His expertise? The fine art of falling down the steps.[5]

Chief Justice McLachlin "suspects" that "[f]rom an era when expert evidence was regarded with suspicion — perhaps too much suspicion — we have moved to an era where it has become the most important part of many lawsuits."[6]

Yet this ascendancy of expert evidence creating our modern forensic age of experts has generated a veritable mountain of critical commentary. Powerful arguments have been mounted that the time for substantially increased suspicion has returned.[7] Terms such as "junk science" and "pseudo-science" are familiar to anyone with even a passing knowledge of the area. The criticisms of these terms are not unfair. The concerns are valid and the problems are real. The licence granted to expert witnesses has clearly been abused.

Knowledge and expertise have grown exponentially in our society, and our courts' increased consumption of expert evidence reflects that reality of our modern world. But increased expertise and increased *claims* of expertise are not the same thing, and the business of the administration of justice is fundamentally too important to tolerate confusion between the two. The law wants and needs the benefit of any real and reliable expertise to assist it in its difficult job. Criminal law especially, with its ever more difficult assignment of discriminating the guilty from the innocent, requires real breakthroughs such as DNA evidence.[8]

---

5   McLachlin, "The Role of the Expert Witness," above note 2.

6   *Ibid.*

7   Erica Beecher-Monas, "Blinded by Science: How Judges Avoid the Science in Scientific Evidence" (1998) 71 Temp. L. Rev. 55; David L. Faigman *et al.*, "Check Your Crystal Ball at the Courthouse Door, Please: Exploring the Past, Understanding the Present, and Worrying about the Future of Scientific Evidence" (1994) 15 Cardozo L. Rev. 1799; Paul C. Giannelli, "The Abuse of Scientific Evidence in Criminal Cases: The Need for Independent Crime Labs" (1997) 4 Va. J. Soc. Pol'y & L. 439; Paul C. Giannelli, "Scientific Evidence in Criminal Prosecutions" (1992) 137 Mil. L. Rev. 167; Randolph N. Jonakait, "Forensic Science and the Need for Regulation" (1991) 4 Harv. J.L. & Tech. 109; Michael J. Saks, "Merlin and Solomon: Lessons from the Law's Formative Encounters with Forensic Identification Science" (1998) 49 Hastings L.J. 1069; Clive A. Stafford Smith & Patrick D. Goodman, "Forensic Hair Comparison Analysis: Nineteenth Century Science or Twentieth Century Snake Oil?" (1996) 27 Colum. H.R.L. Rev. 227.

8   A wealth of information about DNA can be found in *Federico and Rondinelli's DNA NetLetter*, available on Quicklaw in Commentary.

Although there is no doubt that DNA testing has been a major break-through in the detection of crime, issues still arise with DNA evidence.[9] For example, according to press reports a DNA identification with stated odds of one in 37 million was mistaken, where the suspect's alibi was confirmed.[10] The United Kingdom's Forensic Science Service (FSS) reported the mismatch during a meeting in January 2000 with members of the National Commission on the Future of DNA Evidence, the U.S. Justice Department's DNA task force. (The FSS maintains the United Kingdom's DNA database, reportedly the world's largest with 660,000 profiles on file.) In this case, the DNA evidence was left at the scene of a burglary in Manchester and was matched with a person who was in the national database because of a previous arrest. The DNA profiles matched at six points of identification, or loci, resulting in the "one in 37 million" claim. After the suspect provided an alibi, police asked for a retest. A new technique was used to examine ten loci, and the match failed on the additional loci. According to the FSS, the mismatch was probably caused by

---

9   "When DNA evidence was first introduced, a number of experts testified that false positives are impossible in DNA testing.... This claim is now broadly recognized as wrong in principle ... and it has repeatedly proven wrong in practice.... But it has been mentioned frequently, without skepticism, in appellate court opinions": W.C. Thompson, F. Taroni, & C.G. Aitken, "How the Probability of a False Positive Affects the Value of DNA Evidence" (2003) 48 J. Forensic Sci. 47. For other documented DNA testing errors, see online: http://darwin.bio.uci.edu/~mueller/error_rate.html [last updated 12 December 2006].

   See also William C. Thompson *et al.*, "Part 1: Evaluating Forensic DNA Evidence: Essential Elements of a Competent Defense Review" *The Champion* (April 2003) at 16, online: www.bioforensics.com/articles/champion1/champion1.html. This work is an amazingly readable primer on DNA evidence and all the respects in which it is less than perfect. See also William C. Thompson *et al.*, "Part 2: Evaluating Forensic DNA Evidence: Essential Elements of a Competent Defense Review" *The Champion* (May 2003) at 24, online: www.bioforensics.com/articles/Champion2.pdf; D. Krane *et al.*, "Sequential Unmasking: A Means of Minimizing Observer Effects in Forensic DNA Interpretation" (2008) 53:4 J. Forensic Sci. 1006, online: www.bioforensics.com/articles/sequential_unmasking.html; William C. Thompson, "Tarnish on the 'Gold Standard': Recent Problems in Forensic DNA Testing" *The Champion* (January/February 2006) at 10, online: www.bioforensics.com/articles/Thompson_Champion_Tarnish.pdf.

   See chapter 4, the text following note 48.

10 See R. Willing, "Mismatch Calls DNA Tests into Question" *USA Today* (8 February 2000). See also Paul C. Giannelli, "Book Review — *The DNA Story: An Alternative View*" (1998) 88 J. Crim. L. & Criminology 380 at 398; Ian W. Evett *et al.*, "DNA Profiling: A Discussion of Issues Relating to the Reporting of Very Small Match Probabilities" [2000] Crim. L. Rev. 341. See generally David L. Faigman *et al.*, *Modern Scientific Evidence*, 2 vols. (St. Paul, MN: West, 1997) vol. 2, cc. 15–19 regarding DNA evidence.

   See *R. v. Murrin*, [1999] B.C.J. No. 2715 (S.C.) dealing with a new form of DNA evidence — mitochondrial DNA as distinguished from nuclear DNA analysis.

the rapidly increasing size of the database: it reported that as more profiles are added, the possibility of suspects with very similar DNA increases. A German case involved an accused with a past record involving violence who was able to provide an "iron clad" alibi to the rape and murder to which he was linked by a database cold hit: he was confined in a maximum security mental institution before, during, and after the time when the crime was committed.[11] In another case, Gary Leiterman was convicted of the murder of Jane Mixer, after being identified as one of two persons whose DNA was found matching the DNA sample on the victim's clothing through a database search. This case is especially problematic because the second person who was identified by the DNA evidence was a four-year-old child at the time of the murder.[12] However, for every breakthrough of DNA's quality, there have unfortunately been many more disappointments along the lines of phrenology[13] and voiceprints.[14]

Although there can be no doubt that expert scientific evidence has contributed greatly to the administration of justice, it is also clear that the quality of expert evidence must be a concern, especially when it comes to bogus experts. Consider the story of Dr. Louise Robbins:[15]

> Louise Robbins had but one claim to fame: She could see things in a footprint that nobody else could see.
>
> Give her a ski boot and a sneaker, for instance, and Robbins contended that she could tell whether the two shoes had ever been worn by the same person.

---

11   Kristen Edwards, "Ten Things about DNA Contamination That Lawyers Should Know"(2005) 29 Criminal Law Journal 71 at 76.

12   Simon A. Cole & Michael Lynch, "The Social and Legal Construction of Suspects" (2006) 2 Ann. Rev. Law & Soc. Sci. 39 at 48–49; Thompson, "Tarnish on the 'Gold Standard,'" above note 9 at 14. See generally Kristen Edwards, "Ten Things about DNA Contamination That Lawyers Should Know," *ibid.*

13   See Pierre Schlag, "Commentary: Law and Phrenology" (1997) 110 Harv. L. Rev. 87 for a description of just how "scientific" and credible phrenology seemed to be in its heyday.

14   *United States v. Bahena*, 223 F.3d 797 (8th Cir. 2000); *People (California) v. Kelly*, 549 P.2d 1240 (Cal. 1976); *R. v. O'Doherty*, [2002] Crim. L.R. 761 (Irish C.A.); *R. v. Medvedew* (1978), 43 C.C.C. (2d) 434 at 448 (Man. C.A.), O'Sullivan J.A., dissenting; *People (New York) v. Collins*, 405 N.Y.S.2d 369 (1978); and *D'Arc v. D'Arc*, 385 A.2d 278 (N.J. Super. Ct., Ch. Div. 1978). Unfortunately, the battle continues: *State (Alaska) v. Coon*, 974 P.2d 386 (Alaska 1999). See generally *On the Theory and Practice of Voice Identification* (Washington, DC: National Research Council, Committee on Evaluation of Sound Spectrograms, 1979). See Michael J. Saks, "Merlin and Solomon: Lessons from the Law's Formative Encounters with Forensic Identification Science" (1998) 49 Hastings L.J. 1069 at 1112–19; Faigman *et al.*, above note 10, vol. 2, c. 25, "Talker Identification" at 188–226; David C. Ormerod, "Sounding Out Expert Voice Identification" [2000] Crim. L.R. 771.

15   M. Hanson, "Believe It or Not" (June 1993) 79 A.B.A. J. 64.

Show her even a portion of a shoe print on any surface, Robbins maintained, and she could identify the person who made it.

It might be amusing, coming as it did from an anthropology professor who once astounded her colleagues by describing a 3.5 million-year-old fossilized footprint in Tanzania as that of a prehistoric woman who was 5-1/2 months pregnant.

It might also be considered harmless, had it remained a subject of academic speculation at the University of North Carolina at Greensboro, where Robbins taught anthropology courses and collected footprints from her students for comparison.

By 1976, however, Robbins had taken her quirky ideas out of the classroom and into the courtroom, where her amazing feet-reading abilities seemed to dazzle juries and made her something of a celebrity on the criminal trial circuit. Newspapers called her a female "Quincy." She was profiled in the *ABA Journal*. Her techniques were even touted in the pages of *Time* magazine.

By her own account, Robbins appeared as an expert, mostly for the prosecution, in more than 20 criminal cases in 11 states and Canada over the next 10 years until a losing battle with brain cancer finally forced her off the witness stand. She died in 1987 at the age of 58. By then, her testimony had helped send at least a dozen people to prison. And it may have put one man on death row.

There's just one catch. Robbins was the only person in the world who claimed to do what she said she did. And her claims have now been thoroughly debunked by the rest of the scientific community.

Melvin Lewis, a John Marshall Law School professor who keeps track of more than 5,000 expert witnesses, dismisses Robbins' work as "complete hogwash."[16]

One law review article[17] gave the following description of one of her cases and appropriately shames the court involved:

Probably the most dramatic example of this criterion at work is *State v. Bullard*, a murder case in which the court admitted the testimony of a physical anthropologist to establish that a bare footprint found at the crime scene matched that of the defendant. The unknown footprints lacked ridge detail (the unique set of traits familiar from its use in fingerprint analysis), and the supervisor of the laboratory used by the Sheriff's Department in the case testi-

---

16 Robbins testified in Canada and one resulting murder conviction was upheld by a 2:1 majority: *R. v. Nielsen and Stolar* (1984), [1985] 16 C.C.C. (3d) 39 (Man. C.A.), rev'd as to Stolar (1988), 40 C.C.C. (3d) 1 (S.C.C.).

17 "Developments in the Law — Confronting the New Challenge of Scientific Evidence" (1994) 108 Harv. L. Rev. 1481 at 1502–3.

fied that, because of this lack of ridge detail, he could not match the unknown footprints with those of the defendant. However, the prosecution found a physical anthropologist who applied an unprecedented technique, which she claimed enabled her to identify footprints based solely on a visual comparison of their sizes and shapes. She had no formal training in footprint identification and admitted that she was the only person in the United States to attempt this kind of analysis. The court explained her methodology as follows:

> [S]he relies upon a technique of comparison pertaining to the size and shape of the footprint in four areas: namely, the heel, arch, ball, and toe regions. The footprint size and shape reflect the size and shape of the internal bone structure of the foot, so the bones indirectly play a major part in the analysis. . . . Dr. Robbins explains that since each person's foot size and shape are unique, she can identify a footprint represented by a clearly definable print of whatever part of the foot touches the ground. By examining the sides, front, and rear ends of each region of the foot, Dr. Robbins explains that she can compare known footprints with unknown footprints and determine if they are made by the same person.

Asked if there was some body of research upon which she based her footprint theories, Dr. Robbins pointed to nothing more substantial than a collection of information about footprints that was assembled by an English scientist and that had been used "in the development of shoes that would not hurt the feet of soldiers."

The reasoning by which the court decided to admit this evidence which would seem barely to pass the "giggle test," let alone one of the doctrinal tests — reflects the strong influence of the show-and-tell elements. The court seemed to be very impressed with the various media employed in the expert's presentation, pointing out that she "used photographs, models, slides and overlays that were before the court and verifiable by the jury."[18]

A Mississippi dentist by the name of Dr. Michael West, a self-described forensic odontologist, or bite-mark analyst, was Dr. Robbins' equivalent in that field:

> [I]n an already imprecise field, Dr. Michael West has taken forensic odontology to bizarre, megalomaniacal depths. West claims to have invented a system he

---

18   A complete discussion of this sorry episode in forensic science, and the appellate court cases dealing with this "technique," can be found in Andre A. Moenssens *et al.*, *Scientific Evidence in Civil and Criminal Cases*, 4th ed. (Mineola, NY: Foundation Press, 1995) at 614–20 and 1049–52.

modestly calls the "West Phenomenon." In it, he dons a pair of yellow goggles and with the aid of a blue laser, he says he can identify bite-marks, scratches, and other marks on a corpse that no one else can see — not even other forensics experts. Conveniently, he claims his unique method can't be photographed or reproduced, which he says makes his opinions unimpeachable by other experts. Using the "West Phenomenon," West once claimed to have found bite-marks on a decomposed woman's breast that previous pathologists had missed. In another case, he claimed to have positively traced a half-eaten bologna sandwich at the murder scene to the defendant's teeth based on bite-marks in the sandwich. The defendant was convicted, but the case was later tossed out when West admitted to disposing of the sandwich after studying it. Because no one can replicate his methods, West said, the sandwich was no longer necessary. In other cases, West claims to have found bite-marks on bodies that had been submerged in swamps for weeks, and on others that had been buried for well over a year.[19]

Another example involves Joyce Gilchrist, a forensic chemist in the Oklahoma City Police Department crime laboratory, who "appears to have used her lab tests to confirm the detectives' hunches rather than seek independent scientific results. She also tried to control the result . . . . She treated discovery requests with contempt and kept evidence from the defense. She systematically destroyed evidence at the very time when she knew that much of that evidence might be retested."[20]

Re Investigation of the West Virginia State Police Crime Laboratory, Serology Division,[21] describes the career of forensic scientist Fred Zain, whose conduct included (1) overstating results, (2) overstating the frequency of genetic matches, (3) representing that multiple items had been tested when only one had been done, (4) reporting inconclusive results as positive, (5) repeatedly altering laboratory records, (6) failing to report conflicting results, (7) implying a match with the suspect when testing supported only a match with the victim, and (8) reporting scientifically impossible or improbable results.

---

19   Radley Balko, "'Indeed, and Without a Doubt': How a Mississippi Dentist May Be Sending Innocent People to Jail" *ReasonOnline* (2 August 2007), online: www.reason.com/news/show/121671.html.

20   Mark Furman, "Death and Justice: An Expose of Oklahoma's Death Row Machine 232" (2003), quoted in Paul C. Giannelli, "Scientific Evidence: Alchemy, Magic, and Forensic Science" (2006) 21:3 Criminal Justice 50, where a number of cases of astounding malfeasance by Gilchrist are described.

21   438 S.E.2d 501 (W. Va. 1993) (with attached appendix).

State (Maine) v. Ruybal[22] and *State (Ohio) v. DeFronzo*[23] also involved cases of analysts reporting results of tests never conducted. *R. v. Kayretli*[24] describes Dr. Paula Lannas, a U.K. Home Office pathologist, whose professional work as described in the judgment left much to be desired.[25] In *R. v. Campbell*[26] the work of a toxicologist at Ontario's Centre of Forensic Sciences was roundly criticized.

A deplorable example of experts is found in *Ward v. The Queen*,[27] where the Court of Appeal was driven to state:

> Three senior RARDE [government forensic] scientists took the law into their own hands, and concealed from the prosecution, the defence and the court, matters which might have changed the course of the trial. The catalogue of lamentable omissions included failures to reveal actual test results, the failure to reveal discrepant Rf values, the suppression of the boot polish experimental data, the misrepresentation of the first firing cell test results, the concealment of subsequent positive firing cell test results, economical witness statements calculated to obstruct enquiry by the defence, and, most important of all, oral evidence at the trial in the course of which senior RARDE scientists knowingly placed a false and distorted scientific picture before the jury. It is in our judgment also a necessary inference that the three senior RARDE forensic scientists acted in concert in withholding material evidence.
>
> . . .
>
> For the future it is important to consider why scientists acted as they did. For lawyers, jurors and judges a forensic scientist conjures up the image of a man in a white coat working in a laboratory, approaching his task with cold neutrality, and dedicated only to the pursuit of scientific truth. It is a sombre thought that the reality is sometimes different. Forensic scientists may become partisan. The very fact that the police seek their assistance may create a relationship between the police and the forensic scientists. And the adversarial character of the proceedings tends to promote this process. Forensic scientists employed by the government may come to see their function as helping the police. They may lose their objectivity. That is what must have happened in this case.

22   408 A.2d 1284 at 1285 (Me. 1979).
23   N.E.2d 1027 at 1031 (Ohio C.P. 1978).
24   [1998] EWCA Crim 3445.
25   See also *R. v. Brooks*, [2002] EWCA Crim 2107 at para. 13: "Since the conviction it has transpired that Mr Turner's reliability as an expert witness in this field is in doubt."
26   [1998] O.J. No. 6299 (Gen. Div.), Chilcott J.
27   (1992), 96 Crim. App. R. 1 at 51 (U.K.C.A. (Crim. Div.)).

Other examples of forensic expert horrors can be found in "Incredible Forensic Reports, Testimony, and Textbooks, or 'Forget Science and Integrity, Get the Money!'" by Herbert Leon MacDonell.[28] Dr. MacDonell, a leading, world-recognized criminalist and authority on bloodstains and related forensic evidence issues, describes how

> [o]ver the past several years it has become apparent that there are individuals who prepare forensic reports, present testimony as an expert in some forensic discipline, author articles and textbooks, or some combination of these, when they really: 1) do not have an understanding of scientific methodology or even a basic knowledge of what science is really all about; and/or 2) do not explain their findings in clear and accurate terms; and/or 3) do not conduct as thorough an examination of the evidence as they should; and/or 4) are apparently incapable of designing a meaningful experiment to give them a better understanding of certain physical evidence in a case; and/or 5) are simply dishonest and will say just about anything the attorney who hires them wants them to say. The latter are *bona fide* liars-for-hire, however, all of these constitute a problem for the justice system both civil and criminal.

> Dr. MacDonell describes a dozen cases with inexcusable and unacceptable "expert" evidence, not to mention a professed textbook called *How to Solve a Murder: The Forensic Handbook*, which is, he sadly notes, "published by a most reputable company," but which contains "astounding information on blood drops, as well as other equally inaccurate statements on firearms."[29]

Eminence is no guarantee of the quality of expert opinions.

In the case of Sally Clark, the solicitor wrongly convicted of the murder of her two young children, the evidence of three medical experts helped to convict her. One of these experts was changeable in his opinions, another concealed or forgot to mention facts that did not support his conclusions, and a third relied upon erroneous statistical reasoning. And yet they were all eminent men, in one case world famous in his field: a Home Office pathologist, Dr. Alan Williams; a professor of forensic pathology, Michael Green; and a professor of paediatrics, Sir Roy Meadow.[30]

---

28 (Corning, NY: Laboratory of Forensic Science, 1999), ADGN/RP-096 (on Quicklaw in Commentary).
29 *Ibid.* at 15.
30 Dr. Theodore Dalrymple, "Expert Witnesses Are Not What They Seem — And I Should Know" *The Daily Telegraph* (2 February 2003); (2003) 27:1 Advocates' Q. 1. See also Dr. Michael Fitzpatrick, "The Cot Death Controversy" (10 February 2004), online: www.

The Inquiry into Pediatric Forensic Pathology in Ontario ("Goudge Inquiry") was a public inquiry established by the Government of Ontario to investigate dozens of cases that were corrupted by the intellectual failings of Dr. Charles Smith, who was, as the Inquiry's *Report* noted, "viewed as one of Canada's leading experts in pediatric forensic pathology, and the leading expert in Ontario."[31] The Inquiry detailed what it described as "the tragic story of pediatric forensic pathology in Ontario from 1981 to 2001."

Sometimes the rot lies not in the individual witness but in the alleged "scientific" test being carried out:

> For years defendants were convicted because a "paraffin" test detected nitrate residues, presumably from gunpowder, on their hands. Not until the test had been used for a quarter of a century did more comprehensive studies reveal that it suffers from an unacceptable number of false positives. These results may be caused by contamination from such common substances as tobacco or nail polish.[32]

Problematic expertise can also come to court in the form of claims for new kinds of expert evidence, forcing lawyers and judges to constantly evaluate novel science claims. For example, Cor van der Lugt of the Dutch Institute for Criminal Investigation and Crime Control in the Netherlands is an extremely vocal proponent of "earprint" evidence. He "strongly believes that ears are unique like everything in nature is unique and that the print of an ear which has enough characteristic features can be used to match individuals and is able to provide identity."[33]

How is the law to deal with matters such as this? Is the proponent's undoubted sincerity and unfaltering belief in the efficacy of a pet project sufficient for the law to grant admission into evidence? In *State (Washington) v. Kunze*,[34] the Court of Appeal rejected earprint evidence as proper expert evidence. In

---

spiked-online.com/Articles/000000CA3D8.htm: "Until last year Professor Sir Roy Meadow was one [of] the most respected doctors in Britain."

31   The complete proceedings, submissions, evidence, and report are online: www.goudgeinquiry.ca. An English case of incompetent forensic pathology evidence is *R. v. Puaca*, [2005] EWCA Crim 3001.

32   Jon P. Thames, "It's Not Bad Law — It's Bad Science: Problems with Expert Testimony in Trial Proceedings" (1995) 18 Am. J. Trial Advoc. 545 at 547.

33   See Cor van der Lugt, "(Ears and) Earprints, Individualising Crime Scene Marks?!" in (2006) Problems of Forensic Sciences 38, online: www.forensicscience.pl/pfs/46_lugut.pdf. See generally the articles on earprints (as well as related topics) on Andre A. Moenssens' website, online: www.forensic-evidence.com/site/MasterIndex.html.

34   97 Wash. App. 832 (Div. 2 1999).

the English murder case *R. v. Dallagher*,[35] the admissibility of earprint evidence went unchallenged at trial, and the defence was unsuccessful on appeal in raising the issue of admissibility for the first time in the appeal court; however, the appeal by the accused from conviction was ultimately successful because research showed the unreliability of the evidence. On appeal the defence introduced fresh evidence consisting of research demonstrating the unscientific nature of the evidence, as well as now objecting to the admissibility of the "expert" evidence. In rejecting the inadmissibility argument, the appeal court was quite unconcerned with issues of science, seeming to be satisfied simply with the fact that the earprint proponents were "experts," relying (ironically) on the earlier English decision in *R. v. Robb*,[36] which admitted voiceprint evidence without any concern about its scientific reliability. That case relied on a nineteenth-century precedent that put the English test for admissibility as whether "study and experience will give a witness's opinion an authority which the opinion of one not so qualified will lack, and (if so) whether the witness in question is skilled and has adequate knowledge." The court even acknowledged in the judgment that the technique (voiceprints) in *Robb* had subsequently been discredited and would not be admissible, without any apparent concern that maybe it should ensure the earprint evidence at issue was reliable enough to avoid a similar fate. Ultimately, the court set aside the accused's convictions because the "expert" evidence of match in light of the fresh evidence of unreliability made the convictions unsafe.[37]

"Brainwaves" as a lie-detector mechanism are now being touted and may appear in a courtroom soon (undoubtedly promoting itself as the greatest breakthrough since the last greatest breakthrough) if even a superficial plausibility surrounding the topic can be maintained.[38] Dr. Lawrence Farwell, a psychiatrist who heads the Human Brain Research Laboratory in Fairfield, Iowa, has developed a technique he calls "brain fingerprinting," which he likens to finding fingerprints or DNA traces at a crime scene.[39] "It's not actually a lie detec-

---

35 [2002] EWCA Crim 1903.
36 (1991), 93 Crim. App. R. 161 (U.K.C.A. (Crim. Div.)).
37 Earprint evidence was also considered in *R. v. Kempster*, [2003] EWCA Crim 3555 and the conviction upheld based upon the other evidence.
38 Such plausibility does not seem likely: see C.E. Grassley, *Investigative Techniques: Federal Agency Views on the Potential Application of "Brain Fingerprinting"* (Washington, DC: United States General Accounting Office, 2001), GAO-02-22, describing the whole matter more realistically.
39 Ronald Bailey, "A Truth Machine" (14 November 2001), online: www.reason.com/news/show/34911.html, describes the work of Dr. Farwell.

tor," explains Farwell. "Instead it detects whether or not certain information is stored in a person's brain." According to the explanation,

> ~~brain fingerprinting does not tell investigators whether a suspect is guilty or not, just that specific information is or is not present in his or her brain~~ . . . Brain fingerprinting works by flashing words or pictures relevant to a crime on a computer screen along with other, irrelevant, words or pictures. When a person recognizes information, specific electrical brain impulses that Farwell calls memory and encoding related multifaceted electroencephalographic responses (MERMERS) ~~are involuntarily elicited~~. MERMERS are measured using a headband equipped with sensors. When details of a crime that only the perpetrator and investigators would know are presented, the perpetrator's brain emits a MERMER, but the brain of an innocent person does not. Farwell claims that his MERMER device has been 100 percent accurate in tests.

Lawyers and judges must know how to deal with claimed breakthroughs such as this.

The issues surrounding expert evidence matter considerably because it is undoubtedly powerful evidence.[40] ~~By its nature and inherently persuasive method of presentation from an apparently learned authority, it stands out as more prestigious and demanding of acceptance than the mundane evidence of ordinary witnesses relating what they saw or heard~~. In consequence and not surprisingly, flawed expert evidence is the second-leading factor in miscarriages of justice.[41]

Its dangers have been recognized by the courts, and those dangers have led, at least in theory, to a rule of *exceptional* rather than routine admissibility. ~~This exceptional admissibility of expert opinion evidence is a reflection of the dangers that such evidence poses for the criminal justice system as we know it~~. In *R*.

---

40 "About one quarter of the citizens who had served on juries which were presented with scientific evidence believed that had such evidence been absent, they would have changed their verdicts — from guilty to not guilty": Joseph L. Peterson *et al.*, "The Use and Effects of Forensic Science in the Adjudication of Felony Cases" (1987) 32 J. Forensic Sci. 1730 at 1748. See also Stephen J. Ceci & Helene Hembrooke, eds., *Expert Witnesses in Child Abuse Cases: What Can and Should Be Said in Court* (Washington, DC: American Psychological Association, 1998) c. 9, concerning the strong effects of expert testimony, no matter how unscientific, on juries.

41 See, for example, Brandon L. Garrett, "Judging Innocence" (2008) 108 Colum. L. Rev. 55 at 81 (discussing how of the 200 exonerated defendants, 113 included erroneous forensic evidence; the second leading cause of wrongful conviction). Bruce A. MacFarlane, "'Convicting the Innocent' — A Triple Failure of the Justice System" at 63–69, online:www. canadiancriminallaw.com/articles/articles%20pdf/convicting_the_innocent.pdf. See also online: www.innocenceproject.org/understand/Forensic-Science-Misconduct.php.

v. D.D.,[42] the Supreme Court of Canada devotes a whole section of its judgment to the dangers of expert evidence, thus explaining its exceptional admissibility.

The primary danger arising from the admission of any opinion evidence is that the province of the jury might be usurped by that of the witness and the fact-finding process thereby distorted. Faced with an expert's impressive credentials and mastery of scientific jargon, which lay jurors do not easily understand, jurors are likely to overvalue the evidence, giving it more weight than it really deserves, or even to abdicate their role as fact-finders and simply attorn, or defer, to the opinion of the expert in their desire to reach a just result. The reality of "human fallibility in assessing the proper weight to be given to evidence cloaked under the mystique of science" was noted by La Forest J. in *R. v. Béland*[43] as a reason for exclusion with respect to the evidence of the results of a polygraph tendered by the accused. The inherent paradox in the contemporary expert evidence rule that can unfairly and improperly lead a jury to overvalue the evidence has been succinctly put as follows:

> In an insightful review of the use of expert evidence in litigation, University of Michigan Law Professor Samuel Gross outlined the "essential paradox" of expert testimony: "We call expert witnesses to testify about matters that are beyond the ordinary understanding of lay people (that is both the major practical justification and a formal legal requirement for expert testimony), and then we ask lay judges and jurors to judge their testimony."[44]

Such evidence not only begins with a psychological advantage favouring acceptance, it also comes with certain innate features that tend to shield the evidence from the critical examination that the opposing party is entitled to undertake. In the context of its concern about the danger of attornment, the Supreme Court noted "the fact that expert evidence is highly resistant to effective cross-examination by counsel who are not experts in that field. In cases where there is no competing expert evidence, this will have the effect of depriving the jury of an effective framework within which to evaluate the merit of the evidence."[45]

The Court further stated:

---

42 [2000] 2 S.C.R. 275.

43 [1987] 2 S.C.R. 398 at 434. See also *R. v. Walrath*, [2001] B.C.J. No. 1319 (S.C.), regarding the polygraph.

44 Sanja Kutnjak Ivkovic & Valerie P. Hans, "Jurors' Evaluations of Expert Testimony: Judging the Messenger and the Message" (2003) 28 Law & Soc. Inquiry 441.

45 *R. v. D.D.*, above note 42 at 300.

~~Additional dangers are created by the fact that expert opinions are usually derived from academic literature and out-of-court interviews, which material is unsworn and not available for cross-examination.~~ Though not properly admissible as evidence for the proof of its contents, this material generally finds its way into the proceedings because "~~if an expert is permitted to give his opinion, he ought to be permitted to give the circumstances upon which that opinion is based.~~"[46]

With a verbal exterior difficult for a cross-examiner to pierce and an obscured factual and theoretical foundation that can be immunized from direct attack, ~~expert evidence is clearly,~~ potentially, ~~a most dangerous threat to accurate fact-finding in the administration of justice.~~ To this must also be added that it is time-consuming and expensive, two other features generally regarded as inimicable to achieving justice. "The significance of the costs to the parties and the resulting strain upon judicial resources cannot be overstated. When the door to the admission of expert evidence is opened too widely, a trial has the tendency to degenerate into 'a contest of experts.'"[47]

No wonder that courts speak of this category of evidence being only "exceptionally" admissible. Yet, there remains apparent in our criminal courts such an abundance of expert evidence that it strains the normal understanding of the concept of "exceptional." And why, if the courts are so clearly alive to the dangers of expert evidence, has there been seen in the courts such a quantity of "expert" evidence about which there can be only immensely justified embarrassment?

In what follows, the reader will see that courts have exhibited both undue suspicion of expert evidence and undue gullibility. ~~Sometimes courts have travelled in the wrong direction because of the self-interested advocacy of counsel, and sometimes, because of the ineffectiveness or ill-preparedness of counsel.~~ For example, in *R. v. F.(D.S.)*,[48] "expert evidence" that should never have been allowed was held not to warrant setting aside the accused's conviction for the following reasons:

> Although it would have been preferable if these studies had been produced
> and evidence had been led with respect to the methodology employed and the
> specific conclusions reached, I am satisfied that there was a sufficient basis to
> find that the subject matter of the admitted evidence met the test for reliability
> discussed in *McIntosh*. That, it seems to me, was the fundamental difference

---

46 *Ibid.* at 301.
47 *Ibid.*
48 (1999), 23 C.R. (5th) 37 (Ont. C.A.).

between the evidence that was admitted and the excluded evidence. I find no inconsistency in the trial judge's reasoning in this respect.

Next, the appellant argues that the trial judge erred in admitting the evidence because the studies referred to by Ms. Sinclair had not been produced. Although, as I said above, it would have been preferable if those studies had been made available, that is a matter that went to the weight not the admissibility of Ms. Sinclair's evidence. At trial, it was open to the defence to challenge Ms. Sinclair's general statements about the empirical or scientific support for her opinions. It did not do so. I do not think the trial judge erred in this respect.

Thirdly, although the appellant accepts that the expert evidence was relevant, he argues that the evidence should have been excluded because its reliability was questionable, its probative value was minimal, and its probative value was outweighed by its prejudicial effect. The first difficulty with this argument is that at trial the defence did not seriously challenge the reliability of the admitted evidence; there is no basis in the evidence to support the submission that its reliability was questionable.[49]

In the sexual abuse case of *R. v. F.(P.S.)*,[50] the following appears:

That examination was said to have revealed certain relevant evidence. Dr Cahill, a doctor specialising in community paediatrics with a special interest in child protection, found evidence that, in her judgment, could indicate anal abuse of the complainant, but she did not suggest that such evidence was conclusive of the matter. She found two things that were significant and suggestive of abuse. First there was an area of peritonea, or redness with neat borders, which, in the doctor's opinion was likely to be caused by a transmitted fungal infection. Secondly, a zone of enous congestion, a small area of blue vein where blood had collected in a blood vessel at the 9 o'clock position around the anus. Such injuries to the blood vessels in the area was likely to have been caused by in and out movements and would usually last for several months before dispersion. The doctor conceded that there could be other physical reasons for this finding, but she thought them to be rarely found in a ten year old girl. A swab was taken which showed no infection and the doctor's evidence concluded at that point. . . . No medical expert evidence was called on behalf of the applicant.

One can only wonder whether this was anything more than the doctor's subjective opinion or whether it was supported by objective data. The concern becomes

---

49 *Ibid.* at 50–51.
50 [2002] EWCA Crim 2132 at paras. 7–11.

very real because the appeal from conviction was based upon fresh evidence as follows:

> The present situation is that three and a half years after his conviction this applicant, having changed his entire legal team at least once, now presents to this court a lengthy and carefully reasoned medical report, dated June 2001, by Dr Peter Dean who is an expert in forensic medicine. . . .
>
> His report fundamentally disagrees with the views expressed by the paediatrician called by the Crown at trial. The signs that she found he describes as being entirely non-specific and are widely recognised as being within the range of normal findings at least in young people of this girl's age. As such, he expresses the view strongly that it would be highly unsafe to rely or put any weight on these findings in respect of an allegation of anal abuse.

Nevertheless, the appeal was dismissed because of the lengthy time delay.

Sometimes unmeritorious claims of expertise have been fostered by the context being seen as "a good cause," such as cases of terrible political crimes,[51] or cases involving allegations of child abuse or domestic violence. But mainly courts have erred when they have failed to stay the course that science would set.

* * * * *

This book is about a consideration of expert evidence from the scientific perspective because that is the only reliable standard by which opinions can be judged. Whether the issue is admissibility or believability, there must be some external standard by which the proffered opinions will be measured. Whether the argument is one of admissibility — discriminating opinions worth hearing from those that are not — or one of believability — discriminating those opinions worth accepting from those that are not — the task at hand is the same: differentiation among the good, the bad, and the ugly. This requires some external criteria that are applied to the opinions being judged. The rules we know as science or the scientific method, the knowledge we refer to as scientific literacy, form the basis for those concepts and procedures, rules, and ideas that permit an accurate valuation of the worth of opinions.

The matter could be determined by some form of institutional authority, such as prevailed in Communist countries where science was made subject to Marxist doctrines. There, only expert opinions approved by some sort of Central Committee would be allowed to be expressed and, once expressed, were subject to mandatory acceptance because of presumed ideological validity. Al-

---

51 Such as cases in England involving the I.R.A.: see above note 27 and accompanying text regarding *Ward v. The Queen*.

ternatively, the rule of admissibility could be made virtually devoid of exclusionary content by allowing opinions from one and all, so long as the speaker had a certain minimum level of credentials or education or experience. Once admitted, acceptance could be left to the arbitrary whim, taste, or preference of the decision maker — much as the choice whether or not to read and believe horoscopes or bestow one's cash on psychics. In fact, some suggest this latter situation has come to prevail in some jurisdictions.

Any desirable rule providing for the admission of expert opinion evidence seeks to strike a proper, defensible, and intelligent balance between wholesale admission and wholesale exclusion, a balance that discriminates as much as possible between opinions that will assist the administration of justice and those that will not. Any subjective valuation of admissible expert evidence similarly seeks to discriminate the worthwhile from the worthless. Formulations based upon the status and prestige of the presenter, the glibness or lucidity of the presentation, the impressive or even "commonsensical" nature of the opinion, all of these approaches to ascertaining truth have historically been dismal failures.

It has come to be appreciated that rules of admission and valuation grounded upon the scientific method are demonstrably the only valid and reliable formulations that can consistently save the justice system from worthless, overstated, inflated, unfair, or misleading expert opinion evidence. This is the valuable lesson that the "junk science" experience has taught the legal system.

As a result, as will be seen later in this chapter, in contemporary formulations of the rules of evidence regarding expert opinion evidence, the justice system is having the excellent sense to increasingly demand compliance with the demands of good science as a requirement for the admission of expert evidence. Appellate courts in North America are recognizing that there is really only one relatively successful antidote for a system that has in recent times appeared to suffer a bad case of "junk science," of inadequate, unreliable, and even worthless opinions that have managed to beguile their way into courtrooms disguised as expertise. That remedy is scientific literacy: a knowledge of science and its methods sufficient to distinguish good science from bad and expose the latter. Because the system can only act through its participants — the judges and lawyers who apply its rules and enforce its requirements — it is scientific literacy on the part of lawyers and judges that is crucial to a justice system that does not want to be routinely embarrassed by a gullibility that countenances the likes of Louise Robbins.

Recognition of the desirability of scientific literacy in the justice system is not a new phenomenon. According to a report issued more than a decade ago by a committee set up by the British Council for Science and Society and the legal group Justice, lawyers need to know more about science and, in effect, require science lessons to ensure that justice is done. The report said that criminal lawyers should have "at least some basic training in scientific methodology, reasoning and language."[52]

As another author put it, "the most practical and effective method of dealing with the problem of junk science in the courts . . . is to undertake scientific education. . . . Law school education, and probably the tests for admission to the bar should include some requirements for showing of scientific literacy."[53]

Scientific literacy *is* essential for justice to be done. It is essential if it is to be the case that only probative opinions are to be admitted and only valid inferences to be drawn by a trier of fact. The structured questioning of a well-briefed and scientifically literate opposing counsel can be a searching and rigorous examination of expert evidence and an effective way to expose what the evidence can and cannot support, especially when accompanied by the quality logical reasoning of a scientifically literate fact-finder. Nothing else is as successful at excluding junk science and bogus experts from the courtroom.

Issues about junk science and scientific illiteracy in the justice system are a part of the larger problem that exists in every aspect of our society. We live in a time of ubiquitous lotteries and psychic hotlines ("Tired of those other phony psychics? Call a real psychic!"), a time when governments are investing millions in so-called alternative medicines (not just unproved medicines, but demonstrably useless ones), a time appropriately described as "The Flight from Science and Reason."[54]

As well, surveys show most people have little understanding of basic scientific concepts. It has been estimated that only a small percentage (approximately 10 percent) of U.S. adults were scientifically literate in the 1990s and this has perhaps increased to 28 percent by 2007. "A slightly higher proportion of American adults qualify as scientifically literate than European or Japanese adults, but the truth is that no major industrial nation in the world today has a sufficient number of scientifically literate adults."[55] Science education is arguably a spectacular failure, with basic principles of scientific method not being taught in a manner to allow otherwise well-educated people to apply them in

---

52 "Science Lessons Needed to Ensure Justice Is Done" *New Scientist* (21/28 December 1991) 6.

53 K. Loevinger, "'Review Essay': Science and the Legal Rules of Evidence" (1992) 32 Jurimetrics J. 487 at 501–2.

54 Paul R. Gross, Norman Levitt, & Martin W. Lewis, eds., *The Flight from Science and Reason*, vol. 775, *Annals of the New York Academy of Sciences* (New York: New York Academy of Sciences, 1996). This volume is a superb documentation of the many areas of contemporary life that have been swept over by an ever-rising tide of foolishness and irrationality. See Wallace Simpson, "Antiscience Trends in the Rise of the 'Alternative Medicine' Movement" in Gross *et al., ibid.* at 188–97.

55 "Scientific Literacy: How Do Americans Stack Up?" *Science Daily* (27 February 2007), online: www.sciencedaily.com/releases/2007/070218134322.htm.

everyday experiences.[56] It is no wonder that in such an overarching social reality the justice system suffers equally.

It was because of this very reality that the following was newsworthy enough to make *The New York Times*:[57]

Even as many other colleges and universities have abandoned their core curriculums, Columbia University has held fast. Established more than 80 years ago, the curriculum has remained firmly rooted in the humanities.

But university officials say that a sizable change may be in the offing: a new science course is under consideration as a requirement. The course, which does not yet have a name, is meant to introduce students to contemporary topics in science, from the brain to outer space. More important, said David J. Helfand, the Columbia astronomer who is leading the effort, is the need to teach students "scientific habits of mind."

"What struck me when I arrived here 25 years ago," he added, "was how we have this unfashionable but critically important notion that the faculty should specify some of what everyone should know. But I was horrified to find that our students take seven prescribed courses and none are in the sciences."

. . .

Although students are required to take three science courses, they are allowed to choose them from a sizable menu that includes mathematics, computer science, biology, physics and psychology. Until now, the faculty has not tried to define what every educated graduate should know about science; in the humanities, it does.

The legal system does not start with any immunizing advantage. Science has never been linked inexorably with a legal education. And as one judge has candidly written,

[j]udges, trial and appellate, generally are not recruited from within the ranks of behavioral research scientists. They tend to have little formal, post-secondary, science education, behavioral or otherwise, except as provided in continuing judicial education programs. They tend to have no particular training in statistical analysis as it relates to scientific research. In short they tend to be

56 "[I]t sometimes seems as if the world's most advanced society has collapsed utterly into the worship of pseudoscience, with people possessing just enough education to get everything spectacularly fouled up in their minds": Christopher Hitchens, "Review of 'Fairy Tale: A True Story'" *Vanity Fair* (October 1997).

57 Karen W. Arenson, "Science May Soon Join Core Courses at Columbia" *The New York Times* (26 September 2002) B3.

scientifically ignorant, which means they are not acquainted with, let alone conversant, with scientific practice or language.[58]

Another commentator put it this way:

The blame has often been placed upon the continued and pervasive scientific illiteracy of judges and lawyers, which has been termed "a disgrace to their profession." Many who pursue law as a career appear to do so in order to escape that "math and science stuff." Unfortunately for them in a technological world that "stuff" has pursued them into the courtroom itself, and their flight has only left them unprepared for the delayed confrontation.[59]

Yet, participants in the administration of justice have the capacity and ability to embrace scientific literacy.[60] And what is most important, it is their legal duty to do so to the extent that appellate courts forge an inexorable link between acceptable expert opinion evidence and the norms and methods of science. The law of expert opinion evidence in response to concerns and criticisms about "junk science" is becoming very much concerned with the ways of proper science, and it is no longer possible to understand the former without the latter. Those ways are essential to banishing bogus experts and junk science theories from our courtrooms, and even reassessing previously accepted forms of expert opinion evidence that may no longer be justified scientifically.

Reforms have been suggested to improve how courts handle expert evidence.[61] The obvious ones are increased judicial education and recruitment of

---

58   Alan G. Gless, "Some Post-*Daubert* Trial Tribulations of a Simple Country Judge: Behavioural Science in Trial Courts" (1995) 13 Behav. Sci. & L. 261 at 262–63.

59   Dan L. Burk, "When Scientists Act Like Lawyers: The Problem of Adversary Science" (1993) 33 Jurimetrics J. 363 at 365.

60   See *R. v. Clark* (2 October 2000), London 1999/07495/Y3 (U.K.C.A. (Crim. Div.)), a judgment replete with statistical analysis concerning the probability of two unexplained infant deaths in one family; *Kitzmiller et al. v. Dover Area School District et al.*, 400 F. Supp. 2d 707 (M.D. Pa. 2005), online: www.aclupa.org/downloads/Dec2oopinion.pdf, where Judge John E. Jones III, who was nominated by former U.S. President George W. Bush, made a very strong ruling against "intelligent design," holding that it was creationism and not science, and *Dimmock v. Secretary of State for Education & Skills*, [2007] EWHC 2288 (Admin), online: www.bailii.org/ew/cases/EWHC/Admin/2007/2288. html which, after extensive evidence, judicially exposed the "global warming" junk science in Al Gore's movie *An Inconvenient Truth*.

61   See, for example, The Honourable Mr. Justice W. Ian C. Binnie, "Science in the Courtroom: The Mouse That Roared" (2008) 27:2 Advocates' Soc. J. 11; "Developments in the Law — Confronting the New Challenge of Scientific Evidence," above note 17 at 1509–16 and 1583–1604, summarizing various proposed and adopted solutions to the problems posed by scientific evidence. The Honourable Fred Kaufman, Commissioner, *Report of the Kaufman Commission on Proceedings Involving Guy Paul Morin* (Toronto: Ministry of

appropriately trained judges;[62] others include allowing for out-of-court seminars for the trial judge,[63] requiring joint reports by opposing experts,[64] and establishing a "Science Court" with Court-Appointed Experts,[65] court-appointed expert advisors,[66] and scientific referees.[67] One author argued for court-appointed certified experts as follows:

> The scientific and legal communities have widely divergent norms of professional conduct, but proper adjudication of technologically complex disputes in the American legal system depends upon each community maintaining its respective norms. When scientists begin to adopt the norms of law, efficient dispute resolution is impeded. Several mechanisms have been proposed to discourage such shifts in professional ethics. The most viable of these options appears to be the use of court-appointed experts: many courts already have the authority to appoint such experts, so no major change in the structure of the legal system is required. What is required, however, is assistance from scientific professional societies in the form of a roster of certified or recommended experts. Thus, both the legal and scientific communities have important roles to play in minimizing the occurrence of adversary science.[68]

This book will later offer a further suggestion for reform — one that is a novel suggestion as far as I know — but one that I hope will be seen to follow logically and inevitably from a foundation of good science. Pending such reform, the primary defence against bogus expert evidence is a law that increas-

---

the Attorney General, 1998) at 328, online: www.attorneygeneral.jus.gov.on.ca/english/about/pubs/morin [Kaufman Commission Report], recommended instructions to the jury on science.

62 Binnie, *ibid.* at 18.

63 *Ibid.*

64 *Ibid.* at 20.

65 For example, *ibid.* at 19; not everyone thinks it is a good idea. M.N. Howard (editor of *Phipson on Evidence*) wrote that a system of court-appointed experts would be colonized by "the usual cabal of log-rollers, time-servers, self-publicists and friends with friends": M.N. Howard, "The Neutral Expert: A Plausible Threat to Justice" [1991] Crim. L. Rev. 98 at 103.

66 Andrew Roberts, "Drawing on Expertise: Legal Decision-making and the Reception of Expert Evidence" [2008] Crim. L. Rev. 443 at 461–62.

67 The Kaufman Commission Report, above note 61, considered the proposed solution of allowing expert witnesses an opportunity to speak unconstrained by the adversarial system, by asking them at the end of their evidence whether there was anything else they wished to add. The suggestion was found wanting: see pages 345–48. The Commission did recommend joint educational programs on forensic issues for prosecutors and defence counsel together: see pages 361–63.

68 Burk, above note 59 at 375–76, with the suggestions mentioned being discussed at 371–75.

ingly demands substantial congruence between the requirements for admissibility and the demands of good science. As well, scientifically literate lawyers and judges must both properly apply that body of law.

Every accused deserves a defence counsel that can expose overreaching expert evidence and a court that can appreciate the exercise, as were the necessary precursors to the following judicial condemnations (though one must be given pause that such witnesses still come to soil the witness box well into the 21st century):

> Before we summarize this evidence, we must comment on the evidence of the Crown's expert, Dr. Spitz, who has been a forensic pathologist for more than fifty years. Dr. Spitz provided the opinion that Dr. Penistan's determination that Lynne Harper died by 7:45 p.m. is "admirably accurate" and rests on "solid scientific foundation." It became abundantly clear during cross-examination, however, that the only basis for Dr. Spitz's opinion was his own experience in conducting autopsies and his belief arising from this experience that if stomach contents are readily identifiable at autopsy, then death must have occurred within two hours of the last meal. Dr. Spitz was unable to cite any recent scientific literature that would support this view. He refused to acknowledge obvious shortcomings in his opinion when these were pointed out to him in cross-examination. He refused to concede that his opinion rested on faulty assumptions and misperceptions of the available primary evidence in this case. These shortcomings could well explain why the Crown does not ask us to rely on his evidence other than in a few very minor respects. In the result, we have not placed any reliance on his evidence and we give it no further mention.
>
> ...

Credibility of the entomology experts

Before engaging in a detailed analysis of the substance of the expert evidence, it is appropriate to begin with general observations about the credibility of the entomology experts. Broadly speaking, all of the experts whose opinions were placed before the court, except one, offered at least some support for the appellant's claim that Lynne died hours after 8:00 p.m. on June 9 and probably some time the next morning. The sole exception was Dr. Neal Haskell, an expert called by the Crown. Dr. Haskell's opinion supported a finding that Lynne died before 8:00 p.m. on June 9. Dr. Sherah VanLaerhoven and Dr. Richard Merritt, who testified for the appellant, gave evidence in a careful and measured way. Their evidence was indicative of an objective consideration of the relevant factual data. The same cannot be said for Dr. Haskell. Despite what would appear to be impressive credentials, Dr. Haskell tended to overstate the effect of his opinion. He was dogmatic and reluctant to admit obvious errors. He assumed an adversarial position as revealed in correspondence with the Crown that Crown counsel disclosed to the appellant's counsel. Several critical elements of his opinion were based on nothing more than his purported experience, which could not be verified and was not supported by any empirical work. He was unable to demonstrate that his experience had been replicated by other scientists. At a hypothetical new trial, the absence of evidentiary support for the factual assumptions on which Dr. Haskell's opinion are based could potentially lead to the exclusion of his opinion by the trial judge. Even if the trial judge were to find that his opinion cleared the admissibility hurdle, we think it is unlikely that a reasonable jury would place any reliance on his opinion.[69]

There are at least two reasons why the administration of justice may be finally recognizing the role of science in the evaluation of expert evidence. The first is indirect: the ascendancy of DNA evidence. DNA evidence is grounded completely in science and produces highly reliable and useful results for the administration of justice. It is ideologically neutral, helping both to convict the guilty and to exonerate the innocent. But a subtle side effect of DNA's increased visibility has been the implied criticism of other kinds of purported expert evidence. In standing as a brilliant example of expert evidence because of its scientific foundation, DNA evidence has become a psychologically powerful testament against the many sorry examples of nonscientific expert evidence.[70]

The other reason is quite direct: the U.S. Supreme Court has expressly adopted the scientific method as the standard for all opinion evidence in U.S. federal courts. This trend has been echoed by the Supreme Court of Canada in *R. v. J-L.J.*,[71] which clearly followed the former's lead. Therefore, we are in a period of transition where the law of expert evidence is becoming, most justifiably, increasingly concerned with good science as the yardstick to measure expert opinion evidence. Three revolutionary decisions of the U.S. Supreme Court illustrate this. It is appropriate therefore to turn next to those decisions.

---

69 *R. v. Truscott*, [2007] O.J. No. 3221 at paras. 165, 166, and 312 (C.A.).

70 Michael J. Saks & Jonathan J. Koehler, "What DNA 'Fingerprinting' Can Teach the Law about the Rest of Forensic Science" (1991) 13 Cardozo L. Rev. 361.

71 [2000] 2 S.C.R. 600.

CHAPTER 2

The U.S. Revolution

U.S. DEVELOPMENTS

IN THE UNITED States the admissibility of expert evidence in federal courts appeared to undergo a sea change in the nineties when the U.S. Supreme Court, interpreting the Federal Rules of Evidence, mandated scientific validity as the hallmark of expert testimony. It was in 1993 in *Daubert v. Merrell Dow Pharmaceuticals*[1] that the Court settled the principles of admission of expert testimony under the Federal Rules of Evidence (Rules 702 through 706).

The Court implicitly adopted the foundational view that, as the physicist Richard Feynman put it, science is what we have learned about how to keep from fooling ourselves. Consequently, to be on solid epistemic ground, the Court in *Daubert* expressly held that the law would accept as expert opinion evidence only what good science would accept, and nothing less.[2] *Daubert* held as follows:

---

1   509 U.S. 579 (1993) [*Daubert*].
2   "A review of all the briefs, motions, and *amicus curiae* briefs submitted to the court in this case strongly suggests that the decision is primarily based on the *amicus* brief submitted by the Carnegie Commission on Science, Technology, and Government as *Amicus Curiae* in Support of Neither Party. . . . This is the only brief that contains reference to the principle of falsifiability, testability, and replication. It is the suggested framework of this brief as a replacement for the Frye Rule that is adopted by the Supreme Court in its decision": Ralph Underwager & Hollida Wakefield, "A Paradigm Shift for Expert Witnesses," online: www.tc.umn.edu/~under006/Library/Paradigm_Shift.html.

"Science is not an encyclopedic body of knowledge about the universe. Instead, it represents a process for proposing and refining theoretical explanations about the world that are subject to further testing and refinement". [Brief for American Association for the Advancement of Science and the National Academy of Sciences as *Amici Curiae* 7–8] . . . But, in order to qualify as "scientific knowledge," an inference or assertion must be derived by the scientific method. Proposed testimony must be supported by appropriate validation — i.e., "good grounds," based on what is known. In short, the requirement that an expert's testimony pertain to "scientific knowledge" establishes a standard of evidentiary reliability.[FN9]

[9] We note that scientists typically distinguish between "validity" (does the principle support what it purports to show?) and "reliability" (does application of the principle produce consistent results?). See Black, A Unified Theory of Scientific Evidence, 56 Ford. L. Rev. 595, 599 (1988).

. . .

Faced with a proffer of expert scientific testimony, then, the trial judge must determine at the outset . . . whether the expert is proposing to testify to (1) scientific knowledge that (2) will assist the trier of fact to understand or determine a fact in issue. . . . This entails a preliminary assessment of whether the reasoning or methodology underlying the testimony is scientifically valid and of whether that reasoning or methodology properly can be applied to the facts in issue. We are confident that federal judges possess the capacity to undertake this review. Many factors will bear on the inquiry, and we do not presume to set out a definitive checklist or test. But some general observations are appropriate.

Ordinarily, a key question to be answered in determining whether a theory or technique is scientific knowledge that will assist the trier of fact will be whether it can be (and has been) tested. "Scientific methodology today is based on generating hypotheses and testing them to see if they can be falsified; indeed, this methodology is what distinguishes science from other fields of human inquiry." Green, at 645. See also C. Hempel, Philosophy of Natural Science 49 (1966) ("[T]he statements constituting a scientific explanation must be capable of empirical test"); K. Popper, Conjectures and Refutations: The Growth of Scientific Knowledge 37 (5th ed. 1989) ("[T]he criterion of the scientific status of a theory is its falsifiability, or refutability, or testability"). Another pertinent consideration is whether the theory or technique has been subjected to peer review and publication. Publication (which is but one element of peer review) is not a *sine qua non* of admissibility; it does not necessarily correlate with reliability, see S. Jasanoff, The Fifth Branch: Science Advisors as Policymakers 61–76 (1990), and in some instances well-grounded but innovative theories will not have been published, see Horrobin, The Philosophical Basis of Peer Review and the Suppression of Innovation, 263 JAMA 1438 (1990). Some propositions, moreover, are too particular, too new, or of too limited interest to be published. But submission to the scrutiny of the scientific community is a component of "good science," in part because it increases the likelihood that substantive flaws in methodology will be detected. See J. Ziman, Reliable Knowledge: An Exploration of the Grounds for Belief in Science 130–133 (1978); Relman and Angell, How Good Is Peer Review?, 321 New Eng. J. Med. 827 (1989). The fact of publication (or lack thereof) in a peer-reviewed journal thus will be a relevant, though not dispositive, consideration in assessing the scientific validity of a particular technique or methodology on which an opinion is premised. Additionally, in the case of a particular scientific technique, the court ordinarily should consider the known or potential rate of error, see, e.g., *United States v. Smith*, 869 F.2d 348, 353–354 (CA7 1989) (surveying studies of the error rate of spectrographic voice identification technique), and the existence and maintenance of standards controlling the technique's operation. See *United States v. Williams*, 583 F.2d 1194, 1198 (CA2 1978) (noting professional organization's standard governing spectrographic analysis), cert. denied, 439 U.S. 1117, 99 S.Ct. 1025, 59 L.Ed.2d 77 (1979). Finally, "general acceptance" can yet have a bearing on the inquiry. A "reliability assessment does not require, although it does permit, explicit identification of a relevant scientific community and an express determination of a particular degree of acceptance within that community." *United States v. Downing*, 753 F.2d, at 1238. See also 3 Weinstein & Berger ¶ 702(03), pp. 702–41 to 702–42. Widespread acceptance can be an important factor in ruling particular evidence admissible, and "a known technique that has been able to attract only minimal support within the community," Downing, [*supra*], at 1238, may properly be viewed with skepticism.[3]

Four years later, the U.S. Supreme Court established the standards of appellate review of such testimony in *General Electric Co. v. Joiner*[4] and, two years after that, in 1999, in *Kumho Tire Co. v. Carmichael*,[5] it decided to subject both the scientific and nonscientific expert testimony to equal admission standards based on the *Daubert* test.

---

3   *Daubert*, above note 1 at 590–94.
4   522 U.S. 136 (1997) [*Joiner*].
5   526 U.S. 137 (1999) [*Kumho*].

In *Kumho*, the Supreme Court ruled that the general holding in *Daubert* — setting forth the trial judge's general "gatekeeping" obligation — applies not only to testimony based on "scientific" knowledge, but also to testimony based on "technical" and "other specialized" knowledge. The Court reasoned that the evidentiary rationale underlying the *Daubert* gatekeeping function was not limited to scientific knowledge. All expert witnesses are granted testimonial latitude unavailable to other witnesses on the "assumption that the expert's opinion will have a reliable basis in the knowledge and experience of his discipline," and accordingly, holding all experts to the same rigorous standards was appropriate. The Court also observed that requiring trial judges to administer evidentiary rules under which a gatekeeping obligation depended on distinguishing between scientific knowledge and technical or other specialized knowledge would be difficult, if not impossible. The Supreme Court further stated that a trial court "should" consider one or more of the specific *Daubert* factors when doing so will help determine the reliability of that testimony.

The *Daubert-Joiner-Kumho* trilogy provides a set of basic principles that now control expert testimony in U.S. federal courts. This framework has since been expressly codified by amendments to the U.S. Federal Rules of Evidence made in December 2000. Expert qualifications, conclusions, and *their* assurances of reliability are no longer sufficient. The Court has to examine the entire matter and obtain independent, objective assurances of reliability by assessing the expert opinion and how it was obtained against the dictates of good science. The expert's assurance of reliability was no longer sufficient; science's assurance was required.

The Court determined that under the Federal Rules, district courts should play a gatekeeping role to assure that the proffered evidence is both "reliable" and "relevant." Second, it held that expert scientific testimony can only be reliable if the judge finds its underlying methodology to be sound. Finally, to help the judge evaluate the soundness of the methodology and overall "reliability" of scientific theory advocated by an expert, the Court directed trial courts to consider the following factors (which the Court labelled as its "general observations"):

1. falsifiability of the theory;
2. peer review and publication of the theory;
3. known or potential rate of error and the existence of standards controlling the research on which the theory is based; and
4. general acceptance of the methodology underlying the theory in the scientific community.

The Court cautioned that the list of these four factors should not be considered exhaustive. More about these factors and other aspects of the scientific method will be considered later in this chapter. However, a more detailed general analysis of the holding in *Daubert* explains the technical meanings of validity and reliability as follows:[6]

> In defining evidentiary reliability as "trustworthiness," *Daubert* established that the test for legal reliability is whether an expert's inference or assertion was "derived by the scientific method." In a footnote defining legal reliability, the Supreme Court distinguished scientific reliability from scientific validity and directed judges to rely exclusively on the latter in their evaluation of the legal reliability prong. As *Daubert* recognized, reliability and validity differ as scientific measures. Whereas validity describes how well the scientific method reasons to its conclusion, reliability describes the ability of the scientific method to produce consistent results when replicated. For example, a new test for blood alcohol level may be invalid in that it grossly underestimates the amount of alcohol in one's bloodstream, and yet may be reliable in that it underestimates the blood alcohol level in one's bloodstream by the same amount every time.
>
> Despite the Court's insistence that judges focus on scientific validity when determining legal reliability, two of the four factors that the Court recommended as gauges for evidentiary reliability — whether a theory or technique has been tested and the technique's error rate — are in fact measures of scientific reliability, rather than validity. Accordingly, notwithstanding the *Daubert* footnote, application of the first prong of the *Daubert* test will require inquiry into issues of scientific reliability. The need for courts to examine effectively scientific reliability as well as scientific validity is consistent with *Daubert*'s test for evidentiary reliability. Scientific evidence can hardly be "trustworth[y]" unless it also is scientifically reliable — that is, unless it produced consistent results. Moreover testability, or falsifiability, is the premise of the scientific method, which accepts a scientific hypothesis as proven only if the hypothesis withstands attempts at falsification. If empirical studies attempting to falsify an underlying hypothesis fail to yield consistent results, these studies may be so unreliable as to be unhelpful to the trier of fact and thus should not be admitted.
>
> In considering scientific reliability, judges will often need to address the statistical significance of scientific studies. Although *Daubert* itself raised the issue whether scientific evidence must meet a threshold level of statistical significance for admissibility, the Court did not speak to statistical significance, perhaps because it concluded that legal reliability embraces only scientific

---

6 "Developments in the Law — Confronting the New Challenge of Scientific Evidence" (1994) 108 Harv. L. Rev. 1481 at 1504 and 1534–37.

validity. Yet because significance testing, too, is central to a large body of scientific research statistical inference will frequently factor into *Daubert*'s legal reliability prong. Statistical significance evaluates the probability that an observed difference between two populations would have occurred randomly if the populations compared were the same. For a given scientific study in which statistical significance can be determined, the threshold level of significance is discretionary. Still, at a chosen level of significance, the inability to reject the possibility that an observed difference occurred randomly must bear on the question whether such a difference would be observed in repeated studies. Judicial inquiry into statistical significance is, therefore, necessary in determinations of scientific, and hence evidentiary, reliability.

If the underlying methodology and reasoning have proved legally reliable, judges must then determine whether the evidence satisfies the second *Daubert* admissibility prong, relevancy. The relevancy prong requires that judges examine "the proffered connection between the scientific research or test result to be presented, and particular disputed factual issues in the case." For example, a scientifically valid study showing a significant association between the incidence of a certain type of injury and exposure to a given agent in laboratory animals would not necessarily be admissible to show that this same association existed for humans. Courts must assess the scientific validity of the hypothesis proffered to justify such an extrapolation. A court that has already analyzed the legal reliability of the reasoning and methodology underlying the animal study will be better able to determine whether the parameters of that study, such as the level and duration of exposure, sensibly describe human experience. If the proffering party fails to demonstrate that the hypothesis for extrapolation to humans is valid, the evidence is not relevant and hence is inadmissible.

Daubert specifically held, unravelling the words "scientific" and "knowledge" in Federal Rule 702 (as it then read), that expert testimony must be grounded "in the methods and procedures of science," be more than "subjective belief or unsupported speculation," and be supported by appropriate validation. The trial judge must focus "solely on principles and methodology,"[7] not on the conclusions they generate. The court must ensure that in each step, from initial premise to ultimate conclusion, the expert faithfully showed a valid scientific methodology.

Daubert and its follow-up cases assume that trial judges will be able to discern the scientific method with reasonable accuracy. This will be done by

---

7   See generally David L. Faigman *et al.*, *Modern Scientific Evidence*, 2 vols. (St. Paul, MN: West, 1997) vol. 1, c. 1, "The Legal Standards for the Admissibility of Scientific Evidence" 10–45.

means of a *"Daubert* hearing," a *voir dire* examination of an expert to investigate whether his or her methods were properly scientific.

The explicit significance of the *Daubert-Joiner-Kumho* trilogy lies in the mandating of science as the threshold for admissibility of expert opinion evidence. The principles of good science were always available to lawyers as weapons to attack expert witnesses and devalue their credibility and the probative value of their evidence. But the sentiment arose, not unfairly, that U.S. courts (especially in the torts arena) were awash with junk science and bogus experts deluding gullible jurors into awarding obscene amounts for all manner of nonculpable or even fictitious complaints. The adversary system was perceived as inadequate to the task of ensuring intellectual justice, so the admissibility bar had to be raised by the federal trial judge being assigned the gatekeeping function of safeguarding the scientific virtue of expert evidence. Federal judges were given a new power to control what would be allowed to be heard by a jury as expert evidence.

A complete version of the Uniform Rules of Evidence, including the official comments to the rules dealing with expert evidence in light of *Daubert*, is available on the Internet.[8]

In consequence of the *Daubert* trilogy, scientific literacy for American federal judges became a priority, leading to the publication of the *Reference Manual on Scientific Evidence* by the Federal Judicial Center. Now in a second edition, it is available for free on the Internet.[9]

The contents of the reference manual include the following:

+ Introduction by Stephen Breyer
+ The Supreme Court's Trilogy on the Admissibility of Expert Evidence by Margaret A. Berger
+ Management of Expert Evidence by William W. Schwarzer & Joe S. Cecil
+ How Science Works by David Goodstein
+ Reference Guide on Statistics by David H. Kaye & David A. Freedman
+ Reference Guide on Multiple Regression by Daniel L. Rubinfeld
+ Reference Guide on Survey Research by Shari Seidman Diamond

---

8   Online: www.law.upenn.edu/bll/archives/ulc/ure/evid1004.pdf.
9   Online: www.fjc.gov/public/pdf.nsf/lookup/scimanoo.pdf/$file/scimanoo.pdf. The Goudge Report recommended: "The National Judicial Institute should consider developing additional programs for judges on threshold reliability and the scientific method in the context of determining the admissibility of expert scientific evidence." Commissioner Stephen T. Goudge, *Report of the Inquiry into Pediatric Forensic Pathology in Ontario* (Toronto: Ministry of the Attorney General, 2008) Recommendation 135 at 502 [Goudge Report].

- Reference Guide on Estimation of Economic Losses in Damages Awards by Robert E. Hall & Victoria A. Lazear
- Reference Guide on Epidemiology by Michael D. Green, D. Mical Freedman, & Leon Gordis
- Reference Guide on Toxicology by Bernard D. Goldstein & Mary Sue Henifin
- Reference Guide on Medical Testimony by Mary Sue Henifin, Howard M. Kipen, & Susan R. Poulter
- Reference Guide on DNA Evidence by David H. Kaye & George F. Sensabaugh, Jr.
- Reference Guide on Engineering Practices and Methods by Henry Petroski

State judges have a similar manual: *A Judge's Deskbook on the Basic Philosophies and Methods of Science* by Sophia I. Gatowski & Shirley A. Dobbin.[10]

Daubert has been characterized by many as a "revolution" in expert evidence law.

> Twenty-five years from today, lawyers and judges will look back to this period of time and see it as a turning point in law's use of science.... *Daubert* and its progeny reflect the growing realization that in order to do justice in our technological society, judges must be trained in and fully understand the scientific method. The question is no longer whether this is necessarily so, only how, and how long before, it will become so.[11]
>
> *Daubert* ... signals a new receptivity to science as a functional component of American jurisprudence. This broader and more emblematic reading of the case will in time overshadow the technical importance of *Daubert* as a new "test" to be used for admitting scientific evidence. We predict that as a consequence of *Daubert*, a number of common practices of science will become common practices of law, [such as] ... the widespread adoption by the judiciary of an "empirical" approach to issues concerned with the legal process.... An empirical approach ... begins with the assumption that direct observation and experience provide the only firm basis for understanding nature.[12]

Daubert, and a concern about scientific illiteracy in our system of justice, is "thus helping to convert the law from a literary culture that is largely ignor-

---

10 (Reno, NV: University of Nevada, Reno, 1999).

11 David L. Faigman, "Making the Law Safe for Science: A Proposed Rule for the Admission of Expert Testimony" (1996) 35 Washburn L.J. 401.

12 Laurens Walker & John Monahan, "*Daubert* and the Reference Manual: An Essay on the Future of Science in Law" (1996) 82 Va. L. Rev. 837.

ant of scientific culture to a new culture, one that will integrate a sophisticated understanding of science into legal decision making.[13]

In essence, the *Daubert* trilogy adopts a changed perspective and relocates the axis of decision. With the old commercial marketplace test, judges piggy-backed onto what consumers seemed to think about a proffered expertise and expert. Under Frye's general acceptance test, judges took a rough nose count and deferred to what the producers of knowledge thought about the knowledge they had to offer. *Daubert* finally places the obligation to evaluate the evidence where one might have expected it to be all along—on the judges themselves. For empirical or scientific proffers, *Daubert* requires judges to evaluate the research findings and methods supporting expert evidence and the principles used to extrapolate from that research to the tasks at hand.

. . .

Daubert, in many respects, appeared to be a revolutionary decision. Certainly judges', scholars', and lawyers' reactions to it support this view. . . . The core principle of *Daubert* is its changed focus from Frye's deference to the experts to a more active judicial evaluation of a particular field's claims of expertise. Under Frye, judges did not need to understand professionals in the pertinent fields. *Daubert* mandates that judges query which methods support the scientific opinions that experts seek to offer as testimony and this requires that they understand those methods and data. In *Daubert v. Merrell Dow Pharmaceuticals*, for instance, questions about testing and error rate led to responses about comparison groups, standard deviations, relative risk, statistical significance, and many other concepts foreign to the average lawyer. The revolutionary core of *Daubert* is in this call for judges to become knowledgeable about basic research methods. *Daubert*, in effect, brought the scientific revolution into the courtroom.[14]

It is important to bear this in mind: *Daubert's* appreciation of science's intellectual primacy is important beyond simply setting a new U.S. standard for expert evidence admissibility. *Daubert* and the follow-up cases implicitly extolled science and its methods as the appropriate standard for the assessment

13   Faigman *et al.*, above note 7, vol. 1, Preface at vii. Other useful references include Jan Beyea & Daniel Berger, "Scientific Misconceptions among *Daubert* Gatekeepers: The Need for Reform of Expert Review Procedures" (2001) 64 Law & Contemp. Probs. 327, online: www.law.duke.edu/journals/64LCPBeyea; and Joseph Sanders, "*Kumho* and How We Know" (2001) 64 Law & Contemp. Probs. 373, online: www.law.duke.edu/journals/64LCPSanders.

14   Michael J. Saks & David L. Faigman, "Expert Evidence after *Daubert*" (2005) 1 Ann. Rev. Law & Soc. Sci. 105.

of all expert opinion evidence even beyond the issue of admissibility. Even after expert evidence is admitted, science provides guidance as to the proper respect that the evidence should be accorded. Its limitations, deficiencies, applicability, or inapplicability can be accurately gauged. In short, adherence to science improves legal decision making even in regard to admissible expert evidence. Recognition of this fact implicitly by *Daubert* is the other major significant benefit of that decision.

As matters now stand, in fact, using the standards of science to diminish the weight of proffered expert opinions rather than secure its inadmissibility may be the most favourable outcome practically available, as *Daubert*'s promise remains unfulfilled in American criminal cases. The years since *Daubert* have not been kind to those seeking to challenge prosecutorial expert evidence.[15] "[T]he expert evidence of criminal prosecutors is subject to less scrutiny tha[n] that of criminal defendants."[16] "[C]ourts have found a multitude of ways to avoid the outcomes *Daubert* would have led to, had it been applied conscientiously to the reality of the non-science forensic sciences."[17] Another author puts the issue: "'*Daubert*, schmaubert,' do criminal defendants get the short end of the science stick?"[18]

> Criminal defendants have not benefited from the more liberal admissibility standards for scientific testimony that *Daubert v. Merrell Dow Pharmaceuticals, Inc.* seemed to promise. Criminal defendants have their own proffers of scientific evidence rejected "almost always," and they rarely even raise, much less win, *Daubert* or state court *Daubert*-like motions against the prosecution's scientific evidence.[19]

* * * * *

15 Jane Campbell Moriarty, "Symposium: *Daubert*, Innocence, and the Future of Forensic Science" (2007) 43 Tulsa L. Rev. 229, referencing Jane Campbell Moriarty, "Misconvictions, Science, and the Ministers of Justice" (2007) 86 Neb. L. Rev. 1 (discussing the unwillingness of courts to exclude faulty forensic science when challenged by defendants). See also Michael J. Saks, "Protecting Factfinders from Being Overly Misled, While Still Admitting Weakly Supported Forensic Science into Evidence" (2007) 43 Tulsa L. Rev. 609 at 622.

16 Déirdre Dwyer, "(Why) Are Civil and Criminal Expert Evidence Different?" (2007) 43 Tulsa L. Rev. 381 at 383.

17 Saks, "Protecting Factfinders," above note 15 at 620.

18 Susan D. Rozelle, "*Daubert*, Schmaubert: Do Criminal Defendants Get the Short End of the Science Stick?" (2007) 43 Tulsa L. Rev. 597.

19 Brian J. Foley, "Until We Fix the Labs and Fund Criminal Defendants: Fighting Bad Science with Storytelling" (2007) 43 Tulsa L. Rev. 397 at 397–98, referencing Peter J. Neufeld, "The (Near) Irrelevance of *Daubert* to Criminal Justice and Some Suggestions for Reform" (2005) 95 Am. J. Pub. Health S107 at S109.

On the criminal side, the picture is quite different. Risinger found that, post-*Daubert*, in federal district courts defense challenges to government evidence succeeded less than 10% of the time. Government challenges to defense evidence succeeded two thirds of the time. On appeal, defense-proffered expertise was found to have been properly excluded 83% of the time. Prosecution-proffered expertise that had been admitted at trial was excluded only once on appeal. Defendants did somewhat better in state courts than in federal courts winning a quarter of their challenges. Prosecution challenges to defense expertise succeeded about three quarters of the time.

. . .

[W]hile *Daubert* ostensibly applies in the same way in criminal and civil cases, social scientists have increasingly raised the issue whether courts, in fact, employ *Daubert* more lackadaisically in criminal trials — especially in regard to prosecution evidence . . . . Early research lends some credence to this belief.[20]

The frustration with *Daubert*'s unfulfilled promise is succinctly captured in the following: "The judiciary admits the lousy science of the classically prosecution-friendly fingerprint evidence, while suppressing the sound science of the classically defense-friendly evidence about eyewitness identifications."[21] This view appears to reflect an inability to break through some innate judicial difficulties in appreciating the issues, perhaps the general scientific illiteracy suffered by people in general. In the aftermath of *Daubert*,[22] two commentators wrote:

Whatever its ambiguities, *Daubert* does make one thing clear. For judges, the scientific method must become the intellectual equivalent of pornography: They must be able to know it when they see it. *Daubert* does not require, however, that judges be familiar with the substance of any particular branch of science. On the contrary, at least at the gatekeeping stage, *Daubert* all but forbids comparing an expert's results to the accepted wisdom in the field. Thus, *Daubert*'s mandate is not to learn a little bit about many areas of scientific investigation, but rather to learn a fair amount about science itself.

The authors have between them many years of experience teaching science to judges. We can state with a conviction borne of that experience that judges, notwithstanding their general enthusiasm and diligence, tend to be highly resistant to the sort of learning that *Daubert* demands. Time and time again, we

20   David L. Faigman, "Admissibility Regimes: The 'Opinion Rule' and Other Oddities and Exceptions to Scientific Evidence, the Scientific Revolution, and Common Sense" (2008) Sw. U.L. Rev. 699 at 717 and 716 respectively.

21   Rozelle, "*Daubert*, Schmaubert," above note 18 at 597.

22   Above note 1.

have been told that studying methodology is too abstract, mere theory; judges are practical people who want to get down to concrete examples and talk about whether particular "studies" should be admitted into evidence. On our more sanguine days, we try to believe that the judges are telling us that they are willing to learn methodology, but want to do so in an inductive way. But they are not: Our nearly uniform experience with hundreds of judges at every level is that they think methodology is something for academics to worry about.

This zeal for getting to the evidentiary bottom line ... works in tandem with other problems to make judges a uniquely difficult audience for science education. First, because science aptitude plays no part in judicial selection, judges range from closet Einsteins to proud Luddites. Moreover, judges are rarely told that their ways of doing things are wrong (except, occasionally, by their appellate supervisors). Instead, lawyers and witnesses feel compelled to adapt to the judges' idiosyncrasies; what the judge is not interested in becomes unimportant. This state of affairs makes it extremely difficult to persuade judges to put aside the problems from new and sometimes forbidding perspectives. And finally, we teachers lack any effective "stick": No judge has ever been impeached for failing a statistics course.

The result of all this, in our experience, is that judicial education is often counterproductive. Instead of a few principles of general applicability, what judges take away from courses, seminars, and handbooks are fragments of information about particular kinds of cases. Having mastered a few details of, say, a toxic tort case, a judge will be tempted to transfer that learning to every case involving epidemiological proof. But unless the judge understands the principles that underlie the details, the result can be the misapplication of rules that had no bearing on the situation in the first place.[23]

Research has confirmed those fears:

A recent study of four hundred judges demonstrates that the vast majority of state court judges cannot comprehend or implement even the most basic scientific concepts.... The Gatowski study concluded that *Daubert* is neither accurately nor consistently applied.... The overwhelming majority of judges have no real understanding of two of the four *Daubert* criteria.... Specifically, while 88% of the judges reported that "falsifiability" ... is a useful guideline for assessing scientific evidence, 96% of these same judges lacked even a basic understanding of this core scientific concept.... Similarly, 91% of the judges

---

23 John M. Conley & David W. Peterson, "The Science of Gatekeeping: The Federal Judicial Center's New Reference Manual on Scientific Evidence" (1996) 74 N.C.L. Rev. 1183 at 1205–6.

reported that they found "error rates" . . . helpful, although when questioned, they had no real understanding of this basic scientific precept.[24]

These findings lead the researchers to conclude that "judges have difficulty operationalizing the *Daubert* criteria and applying them, especially with respect to falsifiability and error rate."[25]

The solution has been identified by other commentators as follows:

A perusal of all the reported opinions in criminal cases since the decision in *Kumho Tire* reveals a predominance of inappropriately global examination, especially in regard to experience-based claims of expertise. The Supreme Court has only itself to blame for this state of affairs. First, while it is clear in context that references to "discretion" and "flexibility" were meant only to allow the intelligent selection of the most rationally appropriate criteria of reliability for a particular kind of expertise and its claims in relation to the particular facts of the case, they have been seized upon by the lower courts as a warrant to avoid hard tasks of framing and evaluation, at least in regard to prosecution proffers. . . . No matter how clear this may appear to the scholarly observer, however, it is not likely to change until the Supreme Court once again returns to this area to inform the lower courts that it actually meant what it said.[26]

THE CANADIAN PARALLEL

IN THE AFTERMATH of *Daubert*, in Canada the test for admissibility of expert opinion evidence was less explicitly linked with the demands of good science, but the linkage was obviously there. A contrary view appears in an article by David E. Bernstein[27] who pessimistically concludes that in fact, Canadian law regarding the admissibility of expert testimony is in an unsatisfactory state, that really we have no rule at all, with admissibility simply being in the discretion of the trial judge.

The problematic nature of Canadian case law is exemplified by Bernstein:

The law of British Columbia with regard to scientific evidence is another example of this chaos. In *R. v. Dieffenbaugh*, 80 C.C.C.3d 97 (B.C. Ct. App.

---

24 Joëlle Anne Moreno, "Eyes Wide Shut: Hidden Problems and Future Consequences of the Fact-Based Validity Standard" (2003) 34 Seton Hall L. Rev. 89 at 96.

25 *Ibid.* at 97–98.

26 Mark P. Denbeaux & D. Michael Risinger, "*Kumho Tire* and Expert Reliability: How the Question You Ask Gives the Answer You Get" (2003) 34 Seton Hall L. Rev. 15 at 74–75.

27 "Junk Science in the United States and the Commonwealth" (1996) 21 Yale J. Int'l L. 123.

1993), the court considered various possible tests including "relevancy and help-fulness," "trustworthiness," Charles McCormick's "relevancy test," a "hybrid" test turning on the type of evidence and the context of its use, the Federal Rules of Evidence, and the "beyond the ken of the jury" test. Ultimately, the court, while not explicitly adopting a particular test, rejected the relevancy test alone "because the law has long recognized that there will often be cases where relevant evidence will not be admitted in a criminal prosecution where its pro-bative value is outweighed by its prejudicial effect." 80 C.C.C.3d at 108; *accord R. v. Baptiste*, 88 C.C.C.3d 211 (B.C. App. 1994); see also *R. v. Singh*, 23 W.C.B. 2d 558 (B.C. S.C. 1993) (holding that test for admissibility of novel scientific evidence is relevancy, reliability, and helpfulness).[28]

What Bernstein is alluding to can be understood as follows. Tests for admissibility of expert testimony can be grouped under three rubrics: the conservative Frye "general acceptance in the scientific community" test (named after the 1923 U.S. case excluding a version of the lie detector); a liberal "relevancy" test focusing mainly on the qualifications of the expert; or a flexible reliability test focusing on whether the expert's testimony is based on proper scientific methodology and reasoning. *Daubert* opted for the last test, while Canadian case law as described by Bernstein has generally opted for the second "relevancy" approach with a flavouring of "reliability." There is no doubt that the Canadian test has always to some extent considered reliability because, as stated above, "relevancy" is ultimately founded on reliability: junk science is logically relevant to nothing. The only issue is the speed of the increased hybridization that will undoubtedly occur in Canadian law. "General acceptance," like accuracy, is a factor within the reliability element.

After an excellent review of the Canadian case law, Bernstein concludes:

> The continued uncertainty in Canadian law regarding scientific evidence sug-gests that Canadian jurisprudence would benefit significantly from a *Daubert*-like decision that would suggest generally applicable criteria for courts to use when confronted with a challenge to expert scientific testimony. The Canadian Supreme Court should in fact improve on *Daubert* by giving lower courts more guidance regarding how to apply such criteria in actual cases. Unfortunately, the Canadian Supreme Court appears to favor deciding the admissibility of scientific evidence on a case-by-case basis depending on what it sees as the equi-ties of the situation.

This is now completely overtaken by *R. v. J-L.J.*[29] as will be seen below.

28 *Ibid.* at note 141.
29 [2000] 2 S.C.R. 600.

Although it is right that *R. v. Mohan*[30] did not quite constitute a revolutionary change along the lines of *Daubert*, this first major post-*Daubert* Canadian precedent on expert opinion evidence clearly restated and updated the test for admissibility of expert opinion evidence in at least the spirit of *Daubert*. One leading authority on the Canadian law of evidence in consequence wrote that "the court in *Mohan*, with no citations to . . . the United States cases [i.e. *Daubert* and its progeny], or to the longstanding controversy [about the appropriate standard for admissibility of expert testimony], has implicitly adopted the current United States position."[31] In *R. v. B.(R.H.)*,[32] the Supreme Court specifically referred to "scientific information" in the context of expert evidence.[33]

Subsequently, the matter was put beyond any doubt in *R. v. J-L.J.*[34] where the Supreme Court expressly referenced *Daubert* as a relevant authority[35] and referred to many of the same factors for analysis referenced by the *Daubert* court. The Canadian law has now been made clear by the Supreme Court.

Other appellate and trial courts in Canada have similarly embraced *Daubert* and the demands of science as an applicable precedent and standard.[36] The requirement for compliance with "good science" has also been made express in cases involving new or novel scientific evidence.[37]

THE U.K. STATUS QUO

ON THE OTHER hand, the U.K. law of expert opinion evidence has demonstrated little movement towards modernization. The British precedents regarding expert evidence may now be of little relevance because U.K. courts seem ill-disposed to

---

30 [1994] 2 S.C.R. 9. See also the detailed analysis in *R. v. A.K. and N.K.* (1999), 27 C.R. (5th) 226 at paras. 71–89 (Ont. C.A.).

31 R.J. Delisle, "The Admissibility of Expert Evidence: A New Caution Based on General Principles" (1994) 29 C.R. (4th) 267 at 269.

32 [1994] 1 S.C.R. 656.

33 *Ibid.* at para. 24.

34 Above note 29.

35 *Ibid.* at para. 33.

36 *R. v. Moore*, [2002] S.J. No. 124 (C.A.); *R. v. M.(B.)* (1998), 21 C.R. (5th) 324 (Ont. C.A.); *Wolfin v. Shaw*, [1998] B.C.J. No. 5 (S.C.), Dillon J.; *R. v. F.(D.S.)* (1999), 23 C.R. (5th) 37 (Ont. C.A.); *R. v. J.E.T.*, [1994] O.J. No. 3067 (Gen. Div.), Hill J.; *R. v. Hughes (Ruling No. 2)*, [1998] B.C.J. No. 1699 (S.C.), Romilly J.; *R. v. Murrin*, [1999] B.C.J. No. 2715 (S.C.), Henderson J.; *R. v. C.J.S.*, [1995] A.J. No. 634 (Prov. Ct. (Youth Div.)), Landerkin Prov. Ct. J.; *R. v. Sood*, [1997] O.J. No. 5580 (Gen. Div.), Donnelly J.; *R. v. Sood*, [1997] O.J. No. 5417 (Gen. Div.), Donnelly J.; *R. v. Campbell*, [1998] O.J. No. 6299 (Gen. Div.), Chilcott J.

37 *R. v. J-L.J.*, above note 29; *R. v. Terceira* (1998), 15 C.R. (5th) 359 (Ont. C.A.), aff'd [1999] 3 S.C.R. 866 (re DNA evidence).

reassess their traditional wide-open receptiveness to expert opinion. Unlike in the United States and Canada, it appears that gatekeeping with regard to reliability is not an aspect of the British judicial role with regard to expert evidence.

In a highly relevant U.K. example — the murder case of *R. v. Dallagher*[38] — the admissibility of earprint evidence had gone into evidence without objection at trial and was challenged on appeal. The Court of Appeal dismissed any concern about admissibility by stating:

> As is said in the current ninth edition of Cross and Tapper on Evidence at 523 after a reference to [U.S. law]
>
>> The better, and now more widely accepted, view is that so long as the field is sufficiently well-established to pass the ordinary tests of relevance and reliability, then no enhanced test of admissibility should be applied, but the weight of the evidence should be established by the same adversarial forensic techniques applicable elsewhere.

The appeal court in *Dallagher* was quite unconcerned with issues of science, seeming to be satisfied simply with the fact that the earprint proponents were "experts" because they had "training" and "skill."

The appeal court relied, surprisingly unabashedly, upon an earlier U.K. decision[39] that admitted voiceprint evidence without any concern about its scientific reliability. That case, in turn, had relied on a nineteenth-century precedent that put the British test for admissibility as whether "study and experience will give a witness's opinion an authority which the opinion of one not so qualified will lack, and [if so] whether the witness in question is skilled and has adequate knowledge."

The court in *Dallagher* even acknowledged in its judgment that the supposedly scientific technique (voiceprints) involved in the earlier precedent had subsequently been discredited and would not currently be admissible. But, surprisingly, it did so without any apparent concern that maybe it should ensure the earprint evidence at issue was reliable enough to avoid a similar fate.[40]

The British judicial philosophy, therefore, as reflected in the lax rule of admissibility, is to admit the evidence and allow any weaknesses in it, or even its completely bogus nature apparently, to be exposed before the trier of fact through

---

38 [2002] EWCA Crim 1903 [*Dallagher*]. See also chapter 1, the text at note 35. Ultimately, the court set aside the accused's convictions because the "expert" evidence of match in light of the fresh evidence of unreliability made the convictions unsafe. See also *R. v. Luttrell*, [2004] EWCA Crim 1344 where lip-reader evidence was admitted from a witness subsequently discredited: see chapter 3, the text at note 126.

39 *R. v. Robb* (1991), 93 Crim. App. R. 161 (U.K.C.A. (Crim. Div.)) [*Robb*].

40 Earprint evidence was also considered in *R. v. Kempster*, [2003] EWCA Crim 3555 and the conviction was upheld based upon the other evidence.

cross-examination and opposing evidence; in other words, the usual "~~adversarial~~ ~~forensic techniques~~" in Cross and Tapper's words.[41] In view of recent miscarriages of justice in the U.K. country that approach has come under fierce scrutiny.

> The adoption in English criminal proceedings of a liberal approach to the admissibility of expert evidence has already resulted in miscarriages of justice.[42]
>
> The principal weakness in the English law concerning the reception of expert evidence is that its development has been based on pragmatism rather than principle.[43]

Unsurprisingly, that commentator proceeds to mount an argument that the English law should follow the lead of the American jurisprudence, notes that the Supreme Court of Canada has already done so,[44] and argues that the English courts should elevate reliability to preeminent status, noting:

> The approach to the issue of reliability as a condition of the reception of expert evidence in English law might be considered, at best, vague, and at worst incoherent and inconsistent.[45]

The author concludes that "[t]he ~~law relating to the admissibility of expert evidence in English proceedings is in need of an overhaul~~."[46]

THE EXPERT'S DUTY

TWO RECENT ENGLISH cases discussed in detail the duties and obligations of expert witnesses. In *R. v. Harris and Ors*[47] the court said:

> It may be helpful for judges, practitioners and experts to be reminded of the

---

41 Yet other pronouncements from U.K. courts are more consistent with a modernized law of expert evidence. In *R. v. Kavanagh*, [2001] EWCA Crim 140 at para. 11, the court described the role of an expert witness as follows: "In criminal as well as civil trials expert witnesses should regard themselves as giving independent evidence to assist the court. The facts should be examined in a thorough and scientific manner. Reasons should be given for conclusions and whenever the conclusion is likely to be highly controversial the reasons should be full." This concern for a "scientific manner" is strangely absent in *Dallagher* and *Robb*.

42 Andrew Roberts, "Drawing on Expertise: Legal Decision-Making and the Reception of Expert Evidence" [2008] Crim. L. Rev. 443 at 443.

43 *Ibid.*

44 *Ibid.* at 446.

45 *Ibid.* at 448. The author notes the "anomolous" case of *R. v. Gilfoyle (No. 2)*, [2001] 2 Cr. App. R. 5, which appears to adopt a stricter standard of reliability.

46 Roberts, "Drawing on Expertise," above note 42 at 461.

47 [2005] EWCA Crim 1980, online: www.bailii.org/ew/cases/EWCA/Crim/2005/1980.html.

obligations of an expert witness summarised by Cresswell J in the *Ikerian Reefer* [1993] 2 Lloyds Rep. 68 at p 81. Cresswell J pointed out amongst other factors the following, which we summarise as follows:

(1) Expert evidence presented to the court should be and seen to be the independent product of the expert uninfluenced as to form or content by the exigencies of litigation.

(2) An expert witness should provide independent assistance to the court by way of objective unbiased opinion in relation to matters within his expertise. An expert witness in the High Court should never assume the role of advocate.

(3) An expert witness should state the facts or assumptions on which his opinion is based. He should not omit to consider material facts which detract from his concluded opinions.

(4) An expert should make it clear when a particular question or issue falls outside his expertise.

(5) If an expert's opinion is not properly researched because he considers that insufficient data is available then this must be stated with an indication that the opinion is no more than a provisional one.

(6) If after exchange of reports, an expert witness changes his view on material matters, such change of view should be communicated to the other side without delay and when appropriate to the court.

Wall J, as he then was, sitting in the Family Division also gave helpful guidance for experts giving evidence involving children (see *Re AB (Child Abuse: Expert Witnesses)* [1995] 1 FLR 181). Wall J pointed out that there will be cases in which there is a genuine disagreement on a scientific or medical issue, or where it is necessary for a party to advance a particular hypothesis to explain a given set of facts. He added (see page 192):

> Where that occurs, the *jury* will have to resolve the issue which is raised. Two points must be made. In my view, the expert who advances such a hypothesis owes a very heavy duty to explain to the court that what he is advancing is a hypothesis, that it is controversial (if it is) and placed [*sic*] before the court all material which contradicts the hypothesis. Secondly, he must make all his material available to the other experts in the case. It is the common experience of the courts that the better the experts the more limited their areas of disagreement, and in the forensic context of a contested case relating to children, the objective of the lawyers and the experts should always be to limit the ambit of disagreement on medical issues to the minimum.[48]

---

48 *Ibid.* at paras. 271–72.

In *R. v. Bowman*[49] the English appeal court provided further guidance:

In *R v. Harris and Others* [2006] 1 Cr App. R.5 this court gave guidance in respect of expert evidence given in criminal trials (see page 55). The way that the expert reports have been prepared and presented for this appeal leads us to believe that it would be helpful to give some further guidance in order to underline the necessity for expert reports to be prepared with the greatest care.

. . .

We desire to emphasise the duties of an expert witness in a criminal trial, whether instructed by the prosecution or defence, are those set out in *Harris*. We emphasise that these duties are owed to the court and override any obligation to the person from whom the expert has received instructions or by whom the expert is paid. It is hardly necessary to say that experts should maintain professional objectivity and impartiality at all times.

In addition to the specific factors referred to by Cresswell J in the *Ikarian Reefer* [1993] 2 Lloyds Rep 68 set out in *Harris* we add the following as necessary inclusions in an expert report:

1. Details of the expert's academic and professional qualifications, experience and accreditation relevant to the opinions expressed in the report and the range and extent of the expertise and any limitations upon the expertise.
2. A statement setting out the substance of all the instructions received (with written or oral), questions upon which an opinion is sought, the materials provided and considered, and the documents, statements, evidence, information or assumptions which are material to the opinions expressed or upon which those opinions are based.
3. Information relating to who has carried out measurements, examinations, tests etc and the methodology used, and whether or not such measurements etc were carried out under the expert's supervision.
4. Where there is a range of opinion in the matters dealt with in the report a summary of the range of opinion and the reasons for the opinion given. In this connection any material facts or matters which detract from the expert's opinions and any points which should fairly be made against any opinions expressed should be set out.
5. Relevant extracts of literature or any other material which might assist the court.
6. A statement to the effect that the expert has complied with his/her duty to the court to provide independent assistance by way of objective unbiased opinion in relation to matters within his or her expertise and an acknowl-

---

49   [2006] EWCA Crim 417.

edgment that the expert will inform all parties and where appropriate the court in the event that his/her opinion changes on any material issues.

7.   Where on an exchange of experts' reports matters arise which require a further or supplemental report the above guidelines should, of course, be complied with.

In this case, at times, some of the experts expressed to the court for the first time opinions which had not featured in their reports. . . . Failure to adhere to the guidelines can cause considerable difficulties and some delay in the conduct of the proceedings. These remarks are designed to help build up a culture of good practice rather than to be seen as critical of the experts in this case.[50]

The message from these cases could not be clearer. Experts are to be independent, not partisan. Their opinions are to be objective and unbiased. The underlying factual data utilized and assumptions applied are to be expressed and clear and demonstrable. One word describes the courts' requirements for acceptable expert opinion: scientific.

---

50   *Ibid.* at paras. 174 and 176–78.

CHAPTER 3

The Admissibility of Expert Opinion Evidence

NO OPINIONS EXCEPT . . .

IN THE ORDINARY course of things in our courtrooms, witnesses may not give opinion evidence. They can only testify about facts within their knowledge through observation and personal sensory experience. This is a basic tenet of our law of evidence.[1]

Witnesses may testify as to what they saw or heard, assuming that what they saw or heard is relevant to an issue in the case and otherwise admissible. But witnesses may not give evidence as to what they concluded, inferred, or came to believe as a result of what they saw or heard. It is for the trier of fact to draw inferences and other opinions or conclusions, not for any witness.

This limitation applies when the evidence is adduced as substantive evidence of the opinion, inference, and belief for the truth of its content. If the witness's state of mind is a relevant issue, then such evidence from the witness becomes admissible to prove the state of mind, but not its substantive content.

Expert opinion evidence is admissible as the main exception to the rule against opinion evidence. The courts describe this admission as "exceptional" and based upon necessity:

---

1   *R. v. A.K. and N.K.* (1999), 27 C.R. (5th) 226 at para. 71 (Ont. C.A.).

[Expert evidence and its associated dangers] ... are tolerated in those exceptional cases where the jury would be unable to reach their own conclusions in the absence of assistance from experts with special knowledge.[2]

The other major exception for opinion evidence is the lay opinion exception in respect of certain judgmental issues such as a vehicle's speed, a person's apparent age, the identification of persons or things, and ordinary, everyday mental or emotional states such as intoxication, anger, and the like.[3] The theory is that in such cases "it is virtually impossible to separate the witness' inference from the facts on which the inference is based [and] ... the admission of opinion evidence ... is merely a compendious way of ascertaining the result of the witness' observations."[4]

Evidence from an expert witness need not necessarily be opinion evidence. Sometimes an expert may be giving what is simply factual evidence devoid of any opinion. An example of this was *R. v. Collins*[5] where the witness testified regarding a simple experiment he conducted to determine the path of a bullet fired from a certain location.[6]

A useful fourfold division of the possible species of expert evidence has been suggested as follows:[7]

The traditional role of the expert witness is to express an opinion predicated upon facts in evidence.

In some cases, that opinion is predicated upon facts personally observed by the expert. Having testified to those facts, the expert then states his opinion based upon those facts. Normally, such experts as fingerprint examiners, ballistics specialists, and the physician who has actually treated the person who is

---

2   *R. v. D.D.*, [2000] 2 S.C.R. 275 at para. 51.
3   For statements of this principle and examples, see *R. v. Graat*, [1982] 2 S.C.R. 819, regarding lay opinion by police officers as to the accused's state of intoxication, and *R. v. Hill* (1986), 32 C.C.C. (3d) 314 (Ont. C.A.), regarding lay opinion as to the similarity of shoe treads.
4   *R. v. Graat, ibid.* at 823.
5   (2001), 160 C.C.C. (3d) 85 (Ont. C.A.).
6   See also *R. v. A.K. and N.K.*, above note 1 at para. 72. The distinction is discussed at length in Robert B. White, *The Art of Using Expert Evidence* (Aurora, ON: Canada Law Book, 1997) at 18–26. In *United States v. Norris*, 217 F.3d 262 (5th Cir. 2000), evidence related to "experimental" burning of $500,000 cash to refute accused's explanation for missing money.
7   Melvin B. Lewis, "The Expert Witness in Criminal Cases: General Considerations" (undated, unpublished paper) at 3–5, reproduced with permission in Mark J. Mahoney, "Materials on Examination of the Expert Witness" (Ontario Criminal Lawyers' Association for the Program "Experts and Junk Science," Toronto, 5 April 1997).

the subject of his testimony, offer expert opinions based upon their personal observations.

In other cases, the expert has no personal knowledge of the facts. The facts are placed in evidence by those who observe them. The expert then takes the stand and is confronted with a hypothetical question in which he is asked to assume the truth of the facts submitted by others and to offer an expert opinion, based upon the hypothesis that those facts are true. For example, the opinion of most pathologists testifying for criminal defendants will be based entirely upon facts observed by others. The corpse is usually no longer available for examination at the time the defense pathologist is consulted. Accordingly, he is not asked to make his own examination; instead, he is asked to make an independent evaluation of the facts reported by the prosecution's pathologist (and possibly other sources). If those facts lead him to a different conclusion from that expressed by the prosecution's expert, he may then testify hypothetically to that conclusion. Thus a defense pathologist, operating on the assumption that the prosecution expert who performed the autopsy properly observed and recorded the condition of the corpse, may express a conclusion concerning time or cause of death which is completely different from the conclusion reached by the prosecution pathologist.

Admixtures are, of course, readily conceivable. It is quite possible that an expert may testify to certain facts personally observed by him and then in response to a hypothetical question which postulates additional facts, render an opinion which is based upon the sum of all of those facts.

A third area of the proper employment of expert witnesses does not require that the witness be furnished any facts whatever. Instead, the witness, as an expert, testifies to the validity of certain principles commonly accepted by practitioners within his discipline. Thus, a criminal defendant may call an expert pathologist to testify that certain types of examinations are not only routine in autopsy procedures, but indispensable if cause of death is to be determined accurately. The significance of his testimony will probably lie in the fact that those examinations were not made by the prosecution's pathologist. But the "pure" expert, who testifies to abstract principles and ignores the facts of the case, is not concerned with what the examining experts actually did. He draws no conclusions concerning the facts of the case. He merely states, as an abstract proposition, that unless certain principles are observed or certain procedures followed, valid results will not be obtained.

There is yet a fourth role which an expert may play in some cases: that of the expert observer. This witness offers no opinions of any kind, except to the extent that every factual assertion may philosophically be regarded as a matter of opinion. The hallmark of this expert is that his observation is one which a layman is unqualified to make. If the observation is one which can be made without special training, the witness, although an expert in the field, is simply not giving expert testimony. Thus a physician who states that he observed a discoloration or a laceration is not testifying as an expert. Less obviously, he is still not testifying as an expert if, in a rape case, he states that he observed mucous [*sic*] in and around the vagina of the victim. But if he states that he examined the mucous [*sic*] under a microscope and found spermatozoa, he is testifying as an expert. He has made an observation that a non-expert is not qualified to make. The statement, "I saw spermatozoa," is a statement of fact and not of opinion, as those terms are commonly used — although a philosopher might well equate the two. But in reciting this fact, the witness is relying upon an observation accomplished through specialized knowledge and technique. He must therefore be regarded and judged as an expert.

The boundary of this fourth area of expert testimony is sometimes fuzzy. The physician who says that he observed a "discoloration" is not testifying as an expert; the physician who says that he found a "bruise" on a living body is not testifying as an expert; but a physician who claims that he observed a "bruise" on a corpse becomes subject to expert standards because he is offering an opinion as opposed to a fact. A bruise superficially resembles, but is medically very different from, postmortem lividity. Thus, in characterizing that discoloration as a bruise, the physician is offering an expert opinion as opposed to an objective fact. The same distinction must be drawn between the physician who saw a laceration and the physician who saw a knife wound: the former recites a fact; the latter offers an expert opinion in the nature of a conclusion.

The lawyer must note that regardless of his discipline, any expert witness may be called upon during his testimony, on direct or cross, to assume any one or more, or even all of the four available roles. Those roles, as above described, are:

1. To render an opinion based upon his own firsthand knowledge;
2. To render an opinion based upon facts supplied by others;
3. To render an opinion on a matter of abstract scientific principle relevant to the case, but without considering the facts of the case;
4. To testify to a fact — as opposed to an opinion — which he observed through the employment of specialized knowledge and techniques.

If a witness is not testifying within one of those four areas, then regardless of his training, he is not testifying as an expert. In that circumstance, his qualifications as an expert are completely irrelevant.

An example of the fourth category — testimony as to "fact observed through employment of specialized knowledge" — is found in *R. v. Maynard*,[8] where convictions in a murder case were set aside because police evidence regarding the accused's confession, which was crucial to the case, had doubt cast upon it by new expert evidence showing that the police, if their notebook was to be believed, would have had to be writing at an impossible speed.

> Dr Hardcastle is vastly experienced and in recent years has made a particular study of writing speeds. The CCRC invited Dr Hardcastle to examine the records of all the interviews of all the original defendants with a view to forming an opinion to whether each interview could have been contemporaneously recorded in the time stated.... On the Crown's evidence this was recorded contemporaneously in a hardbacked book on 23rd January 1976 between 4:28 p.m. and 5:18 p.m., that is to say over a period of between 49 and 51 minutes depending on how many seconds were rounded up or down when recording the first and last minutes. Dr Hardcastle considered that to be a physical impossibility. As the record contains 11,325 properly formed characters, it would mean that the writer would have had to achieve a speed of between 222 characters per minute in 49 minutes and 231 characters per minute in 51. The fastest speed recorded by Dr Hardcastle in controlled experiments has been 158 characters per minute. The fastest speed he has ever encountered has been below 170 characters per minute; and the fastest speed which he regards as possible of achievement by anyone, allowing a considerable margin, is 190 characters per minute. 222–231 characters per minute is far in excess of the possible.

The appeal court referred to this as expert opinion evidence, and it was in the sense that the witness effectively opined that the police notes could not have been written within the times noted. But this opinion was virtually a given once his experimental data were accepted.

The key component of Dr. Hardcastle's evidence was in fact the factual data: namely, the fastest recorded human writing times as personally observed by him in his controlled experiments. But this essentially factual evidence still required admission as expert evidence because it required demonstration of Dr. Hardcastle's expertise in obtaining the factual observations. An eccentric layperson who randomly happened to watch people write with a stopwatch in hand would not have been able to tell a court of the speeds he found because without experimental controls, his unsystematic observations would be irrelevant for not having any weight. It was Dr. Hardcastle's expertise, utilized in setting up and running the controlled experiments, which made the factual

---

8   [2002] EWCA Crim 1942.

results obtained probative and thus relevant. Once the data were gathered and explained in court, the conclusion followed without difficulty. In fact, a trier of fact given the data regarding maximum human writing speeds could have reached the same conclusion most easily. It was the factual evidence regarding maximum human writing speeds systematically and hence expertly gathered that was significant.

As has already been noted, sometimes the demarcation between fact and opinion is not clear-cut, nor the line between technical and nontechnical matters. A witness's observation through a microscope of a specific virus in one sense is a simple factual observation. But the proper operation of the microscope may involve technical training and thus be beyond the capability of the ordinary person. Therefore, the propriety of the witness's operation of the instrument could be an issue. "Seeing" the specific virus similarly in one sense is a simple observation, but the recognition will involve training in the virus's appearance and possibly other matters that allow the recognition to take place. Thus the "recognition," to the extent that it requires a previously educated observer, may seem a simple matter of fact to the observer, but to a layperson and in a court of law will involve issues of expertise. The correctness of the observation could well be an issue. It is important to keep in mind that simple "observations" by an expert may well involve implicit expertise regarding instruments, other devices used, or tests conducted. It may also involve opinions based upon education, and hence expertise, regarding what is being observed. In all such cases, the law regarding the admissibility of expert opinion evidence is implicated.

EXPERT OPINION EVIDENCE

THE ADMISSION OF expert evidence in Canada, according to the now leading case of *R. v. Mohan*,[9] as elaborated by *R. v. J-L.J.*,[10] requires a consideration of four elements: relevance, necessity (in assisting the trier of fact), absence of any exclusionary rule, and a properly qualified expert.

As the Supreme Court cautioned, "[t]he admissibility requirements of expert evidence do not eliminate the dangers traditionally associated with it. Nevertheless, they are tolerated in those exceptional cases where the jury would be unable to reach its own conclusions in the absence of assistance from experts

---

9   [1994] 2 S.C.R. 9 [*Mohan*]. See also the detailed analysis in *R. v. A.K. and N.K.*, above note 1 at paras. 71–89.

10 [2000] 2 S.C.R. 600.

with special knowledge."[11] Thus, expert opinion evidence is not routinely admissible, but only exceptionally admissible if it meets the test made up of these elements.

Each of these elements will be discussed below, but the essential point is that expert evidence is necessary where the judge or jury would otherwise not be aware of the information to be provided as a result of their own knowledge or experience. In other words, in the particular circumstances of the case, a "true verdict" requires the trier of fact to be educated about some matter, and such "educating" cannot be achieved through some other nontestimonial forensic mechanism, such as a focused jury instruction or the taking of judicial notice.

Although the absence of any exclusionary rule is a self-evident legal requirement, the other factors are concerned with insuring that the "education" offered is a sound and cogent one. The requirement of a *bona fide* qualified expert is an obvious one. The "relevance" inquiry requires a finding first and foremost of logical relevance to the case, thereby demanding, as will be seen below, reliability and validity from the testimony offered, which in turn necessitates adherence to the demands of science to obtain such assurances. It also implicates "legal relevance," a cost-benefit analysis that considers whether the benefits of the evidence (in terms of materiality, weight, and reliability) outweigh its costs (in terms of the dangers associated with expert opinion evidence, including the risk that it may be accepted uncritically by the trier of fact, its potential prejudicial effect, and the practical costs associated with its presentation).

Because of this balancing test that must be carried out, the admissibility of expert evidence is highly case-specific: "Each case turns on its facts. The conclusion of the *Garfinkle* trial judge, affirmed by the Quebec Court of Appeal, that in the circumstances there presented the evidence of Dr. Beltrami was probative and its benefit outweighed the cost, did not bind the trial judge on the facts of this case, who reached a contrary conclusion on the evidence presented in the *voir dire*."[12] Just because similar or even identical expert opinion evidence has been admitted in previous cases does not automatically mandate admission again. Admission depends upon a balancing that is highly dependent upon the particular issues and evidence in each individual case.

In *R. v. A.K. and N.K.*,[13] the court said, approving *R. v. C.(G.)*,[14] as follows:

> The probative value of the proposed evidence and its potential prejudicial effect can only be assessed in the context of a particular trial. It is therefore import-

---

11   *R. v. D.D.*, above note 2 at para. 51.

12   *R. v. J-L.J.*, above note 10 at para. 45.

13   Above note 1 at para. 76.

14   Indexed as *R. v. Chisholm* (1997), 8 C.R. (5th) 21 (Ont. Ct. Gen. Div.).

ant to keep in mind that the admissibility of expert opinion evidence is not a question of precedent. Both general and case-specific appellate pronouncements respecting the admissibility of expert opinion evidence in similar cases must always be considered in context. For example, expert opinion evidence on the phenomenon of delayed disclosure by victims of sexual abuse is by no means admissible in all cases simply because it has been admitted in some cases that have withstood appellate review. I agree with the approach taken by Hill J. in *R. v. C.(G.)* (1997), 8 C.R. (5th) 21 at 45 (Ont. Gen. Div.) on the proper use of precedents in the determination of this issue:

> To the extent that the record in the *voir dire* before me provides opinion evidence upon matters identical, or nearly identical, to expert evidence generically recognized by appellate authorities to be the proper subject of expert opinion this recommends itself as a factor worthy of consideration in the legal determination of admissibility.
>
> Nevertheless, I must bear in mind that the state of scientific knowledge is fluid. Differing challenges may be mounted case-to-case and the evidentiary record of each prosecution constitutes a case-specific context for the relevant inquiries and balancing of factors which the court is obliged to undertake.

This raises significant issues in the context of previously accepted types of expert evidence, especially when the standard for admission evolves to require adherence to scientific standards, a requirement that was not expressly in place previously. Courts have emphasized the case-specific nature of the expert evidence admissibility inquiry, but usually in the context of novel scientific evidence.[15] Logically, however, that admonition applies equally to a reconsideration of previously accepted types of expert evidence. Nevertheless, it would be unrealistic to deny that traditionally recognized areas of expert evidence enjoy the advantage of precedent in fact if not in law, no matter how illogical such advantage might be.[16] This reality must be confronted when, and as, traditional areas of expert evidence come to be challenged for their lack of scientific basis.[17]

---

15 *R. v. J-L.J.*, above note 10.

16 Denying any restriction to novel scientific evidence, the Court in *Daubert* specifically noted: "Of course, well-established propositions are less likely to be challenged than those that are novel, and they are more handily defended": *Daubert v. Merrell Dow Pharmaceuticals*, 509 U.S. 579 at 592, n.11 (1993) [*Daubert*].

17 For an example, see *Williamson v. Reynolds*, 904 F. Supp. 1529 at 1558 (E.D. Okla. 1995) (quoting *Daubert, ibid.*):

> The state of the art of hair analysis has not reached a level of certainty to permit such testimony. Although the hair expert may have followed procedures accepted in the

Like a persistent door-to-door salesman, expert evidence that has previously gotten its foot in the door may be harder to eject, but nothing in principle or logic supports any such advantage. Folly should not be grandfathered.

RELEVANCE

LOGICAL RELEVANCE

RELEVANCE REQUIRES THAT the evidence affect the probability whether a fact in issue is true or not. With nonexpert observational evidence, this simply depends on an application of the rules of logic to the content of the witness's evidence. For logical relevance, the requirement is simply that the evidence is so related to a fact in issue that it tends to establish or disestablish it. This is a matter of logic and the rules of proper reasoning.[18] Credibility issues arising from the witnesses's use of their senses are in general not part of the relevance analysis.

Regarding expert evidence, the situation is different because more than observational information acquired by the ordinary use of one's senses is involved. It is the *admissibility* of the expert opinion that is in issue, not the *content* of that opinion. Relevance of an expert opinion requires not just relevance of the content, since more than information simply obtained through the use of the human senses is involved. The method or procedure by which the opinion was formed must be examined. An opinion formed by subjective guess, consulting an astrology chart, or gazing into a crystal ball would be "irrelevant" because the methodology is unacceptable, being demonstrably unreliable.[19] Such meth-

---

community of hair experts, the human hair comparison results in this case were, nonetheless, scientifically unreliable. This court recognizes the long history of admissibility of such evidence, but as the *Daubert* Court stated, "Hypotheses ... that are incorrect will eventually be shown to be so."

See also chapter 5, note 17.

18 *R. v. Cloutier* (1979), 48 C.C.C. (2d) 1 (S.C.C.); *R. v. Corbett*, [1988] 1 S.C.R. 670; *R. v. Ferris* (1994), 27 C.R. (4th) 141 (Alta. C.A.), aff'd [1994] 3 S.C.R. 756.

19 "There is also a right, which probably rises to constitutional stature, to be convicted only on the basis of competent evidence. For example, if a state decided to start sending people to jail on the basis of testimony from the Psychic Friends Network, one would hope such efforts would fail on constitutional grounds." James V. DeLong, "The New 'Criminal' Classes: Legal Sanctions and Business Managers," originally published in 1997 and reprinted as part of Gene Healy, ed., *Go Directly to Jail: The Criminalization of Almost Everything* (Washington, DC: Cato Institute, 2004). Lest anyone think the example is farfetched, here is another example. In a respected American legal magazine published by the American Bar Association, the full-page advertisement for well-known criminal jus-

ods have not been demonstrated to provide accurate information. Relevance in respect of an expert opinion is a function not of the substance of the opinion, but rather its reliability, which is essentially a function of the methodology utilized to reach it.[20]

If a witness says: "My opinion is that the shoe print or fingerprint matches the accused's," the relevance test is to be applied to the fact that ~~that is the witness's opinion, not the alleged fact that the print matches.~~ In other words, the law recognizes that the senses — ~~seeing and hearing~~ — ~~are acceptable ways of obtaining information that can then be put forth testimonially in a courtroom.~~ However, with opinions, the development of a belief is not functionally the same thing,[21] and the methodology by which the opinion comes to be formed must necessarily be examined. It will occasionally be the case that the content of the opinion, if valid and reliable, can be characterized as irrelevant. For example, in the homicide case of *R. v. Haynes*,[22] expert evidence about the accused's "dependent personality disorder" (even if such expert opinion evidence was completely accurate) was held not to be relevant to a material issue since it was not directed at either his intention or to a mental disorder defence. Why he joined in the killing was not relevant, the court said. Thus, how the expert witness came to his opinion did not need to be explored.

However, what will generally be contentious is whether the opinion is valid and reliable having regard to its supporting data and logic, for an improperly founded opinion is not logically relevant. It does not really provide valid information to help decide the probabilities of the contentious fact in issue. There must be valid "science" being testified to, not mere impressionistic or anecdotal beliefs of the witness. The essence of "scientific information," as will be discussed in detail below, is its objective reality and provability (or more correctly,

---

tice publisher Charles C. Thomas of Springfield, Illinois, attracted my attention because of one book shown there. The title was "Psychic Criminology: A Guide for Using Psychics in Investigations," by Whitney S. Hibbard, Raymond W. Worring, & Richard Brennan. It was published in 2002 and was a *second edition*. The description began as follows: "Practical and authoritative, this book is a comprehensive manual of operations for using psychics in criminal investigations."

20 Regrettably, there is no general right to "reliable" evidence in the sense that, aside from expert evidence, reliability issues go to weight and not admissibility: *R. v. Buric* (1996), 28 O.R. (3d) 737 (C.A.), aff'd [1997] 1 S.C.R. 535. See also *R. v. Brooks*, [2000] 1 S.C.R. 237 dealing with jailhouse informants. However, in *R. v. Trochym*, [2007] S.C.J. No. 6, the Supreme Court, in imposing a complete ban on hypnotically refreshed testimony, relied strongly on a rationale of unreliability. It is to be hoped that the Court's concern with reliability will diffuse from the novel scientific evidence context to that of prosecution evidence generally.

21 In other words, "believing is not seeing."

22 (1997), 121 C.C.C. (3d) 1 at 23 (B.C.C.A.).

its falsifiability or testability). It is derived not from subjective beliefs or opinions, no matter how educated, but from knowledge gathered pursuant to the experimental paradigm in accordance with the scientific method. If the alleged information is not real "science," then it is not in fact logically relevant and will not assist the trier of fact.

Expert evidence that does not convey reliable or valid information is by its nature irrelevant. It is thus in the concept of relevance grounded on reliability that Canadian law links the admissibility of expert opinion evidence with the demands of good science and seeks to exclude from the courtroom pseudo- or junk science, or simply bad science or scientists.[23] As recommended by the Goudge Report,

> A concern about the reliability of evidence is a fundamental component of the law of evidence. Threshold reliability plays an important role in determining whether proposed expert evidence is admissible under the *Mohan* test. Reliability can be an important consideration in determining whether the proposed expert evidence is relevant and necessary; whether it is excluded under any exclusionary rule, including the rule that requires evidence to be excluded if its prejudicial effect exceeds its probative value; and whether the expert is properly qualified. Trial judges should be vigilant in exercising their gatekeeping role with respect to the admissibility of such evidence. In particular, they should ensure that expert scientific evidence that does not satisfy standards of threshold reliability be excluded, whether or not the science is classified as novel.[24]

---

23 *R. v. F.(D.S.)* (1999), 23 C.R. (5th) 37 at para. 45 (Ont. C.A.):

> In rejecting this evidence the trial judge noted that Ms. Sinclair's opinion was based almost entirely on her own experience. The trial judge held that the absence of evidence of an objective test of the reliability of such an opinion and of an objective means of evaluating the reliability of the opinion disqualified the evidence. The trial judge's reasoning in this respect turned on Ms. Sinclair's evidence that there was no existing profile or comprehensive statement of the impacts on or behaviour patterns of an abused person that would support a conclusion that one person had been abused and another had not.

> In *R. v. Dieffenbaugh* (1993), 80 C.C.C. (3d) 97 (B.C.C.A.), a physician who was an expert in the forensic examination of genitalia of children who were alleged to be the victims of sexual abuse testified about a phenomenon described as "anal gaping response," which the witness testified was abnormal and was not seen in children who had not been sexually abused.

> On cross-examination, however, the witness acknowledged that there was no scientific information concerning what percentage of the general population would exhibit such a response even though there has been no assault and that there never had been any proper control study done on this subject. The evidence was ruled improper expert evidence.

24 Commissioner Stephen T. Goudge, *Report of the Inquiry into Pediatric Forensic Pathology in Ontario* (Toronto: Ministry of the Attorney General, 2008) Recommendation 130 at 487 [Goudge Report].

Recent examples of cases where proposed expert evidence was disallowed based upon reliability concerns include "threat analysis,"[25] self-infliction of wounds,[26] and human foot impressions.[27]

In a case concerning barefoot insole impression evidence,[28] the court stated:

> The central thesis of "barefoot insole impression" evidence is that the primary wearer of footwear, over time, begins to leave an impression of the wearer's foot in the footwear's insole. Inked impressions of the suspected wearer's feet, photos of the suspected wearer's known insoles, and a standing cast of the suspected wearer's foot are compared to the impressions in the boots, both visually and by using calipers to compare distances between toes and other features among the various exhibits. A Canadian researcher (Kennedy), who testified for the State at trial, is currently conducting a study following R.C.M.P.... troopers and their new boots throughout the training process. Kennedy has compared the insole impressions made in some 200 Canadian army boots with the feet of the wearers. He began research in the area in 1989 after earlier work done by Dr. Louise Robbins was discredited.... Kennedy testified that different researchers use different methods in making these type comparisons, but

---

25 *R. v. LePore*, [1998] O.J. No. 5824 (Gen. Div.).
26 *R. v. Taylor*, [2001] B.C.J. No. 1630 (S.C.):

> Dr. Currie said, "In my opinion, all the wounds were inflicted from behind." He did not confine himself to saying the wounds he observed — and I may say he observed them in photographs and by reading reports and evidence, not by looking at the body itself "were consistent with an attack from behind." He was definitive. He said all the wounds were inflicted from behind, and he repeated that many times.
>
> In my view, the opinion expressed that way fails to achieve that threshold level of reliability which *Mohan* requires. Dr. Boone disagreed with the proposition that one can be definitive on the question of where the assailant was standing. I found Dr. Boone to be a well-qualified expert whose demeanour was in accord with what is expected of an objective or neutral expert in the courts. The textbooks upon which Dr. Currie relied (or purported to rely) for his opinion did not support the degree of certainty that he chose to ascribe to his view.
>
> On the other hand, the High Court of Australia recently held: "Whether wounds may have been suicidally self-inflicted is capable, in our opinion, of being the subject of expert evidence, if a suitable foundation as to the witnesses' training, study or experience has been laid": *Velevski v. The Queen*, [2002] HCA 4. The Court did go on: "We ... offer ... a caution, which ... we think appropriate, regarding the occasional imprecision of such evidence and the need to scrutinize it with great care."

> The transcript of argument in *Velevski* is available online: www.austlii.edu.au/cgi-bin/disp.pl/au/other/hca/transcripts/2000/S197/2.html ?query=%7e+velevski.
> See also *R. v. Anderson*, [2000] 1 V.R. 1 (C.A.).

27 *R. v. Sood*, [1997] O.J. No. 5417 (Gen. Div.).
28 *State (South Carolina) v. Jones*, 541 S.E.2d 813 at 818–19 (S.C. 2001).

that he felt his method (the one used by Agent Derrick) was the best. He also testified that he has revised some of his statements, but none of his methods, based on comments received after publication of his peer-reviewed articles.

In conducting the tests here, Agent Derrick relied upon a talk he heard several years earlier, three books, two of which were published before 1989, and a phone conversation with Kennedy.

We agree with appellant that the "scientific" evidence admitted at his trial does not meet the requirements for admissibility, and therefore need not address his contentions that Agent Derrick was not a qualified expert, and that the prejudicial impact of this evidence outweighed whatever probative value it may have had. . . . The Jones reliability factors take into consideration:

(1) the publications and peer reviews of the technique; (2) prior application of the method to the type of evidence involved in the case; (3) the quality control procedures used to ensure reliability; and (4) the consistency of the method with recognized scientific laws and procedures.

. . .

The State relies most heavily on Kennedy to establish that there is a science underlying "barefoot insole impressions." While Kennedy testified that he had published several peer-reviewed articles, he also testified that he was still in the process of collecting data in order to determine which standards were appropriate for comparison purposes. Further, he candidly acknowledged that earlier work in this area had been discredited.

We find the evidence presented here insufficient to meet the Jones' requirements that: (1) the technique be published and peer-reviewed; (2) the method has been applied to this type evidence; and (3) the method be consistent with recognized scientific laws and proceedings. In our opinion, it is premature to accept that there exists a science of "barefoot insole impressions."

An additional issue arises here as the result of the Jones requirement that the quality control procedures used ensure reliability. Neither Agent Derrick nor anyone connected with SLED had ever done this type of test before. Further, Agent Derrick admittedly had not conducted the testing in conformity with SLED's quality control precautions. The director of the SLED laboratories testified that SLED requires a written protocol on all laboratory procedures, which must be "thoroughly tested to prove their scientific validity, accuracy and repeatability." Here, there was no written protocol in existence . . . when Agent Derrick conducted his testing, much less one which had been subjected to SLED's quality control policies.

We find, therefore, that the trial judge erred in permitting expert testimony purporting to demonstrate that "barefoot insole impression" testing revealed appellant's foot to be consistent with the impression made by the primary wearer of the "steel toe" boot. The admission of this evidence mandates reversal of appellant's convictions.

In *Ramirez v. State (Florida)*,[29] a case about knife-mark identification evidence, the court held as follows:

> Ramirez asserts that the trial court erred in allowing the State's experts to testify that the knife found in Ramirez's car was the murder weapon to the exclusion of every other knife in the world. He contends that Hart's identification method is novel and untested and the State has failed to present sufficient proof of its reliability.
>
> . . .
>
> Traditional "knife mark" evidence is a subgroup of the broad category of evidence commonly referred to as "tool mark" evidence. The theory underlying tool mark evidence, which is explained below, is generally accepted in the scientific community and has long been upheld by courts. Many of the analytical methods that were developed for use with tool marks in general have been applied to knife marks in particular and have similarly been accepted by courts. Hart's theory of knife mark identification, however, departs from traditional knife mark identification theory in significant ways, and the State has cited no appellate decision upholding his theory.
>
> . . .
>
> According to Hart, a technician's ability to identify microscopic similarities in casts is developed by training and is passed on from one technician to another in the workplace. A "match" under his method is declared if there is "sufficient similarity" in the striated marks on the casts to eliminate the possibility of coincidence. This determination is entirely subjective and is based on the technician's training and experience; there is no minimum number of matching striations or percentage of agreement or other objective criteria that are used in this method. No photographs are made of the casts, Hart explained, because lay persons and those not trained in this procedure would be unable to understand the comparison process; similarly, no notes are made describing the basis for identification. Once a match is declared under his theory, no other knives are examined because an identification under this method purportedly eliminates all other knives in the world as possible sources of the wound. Under Hart's method of identification, a team of expert technicians trained by him would be virtually impossible to challenge notwithstanding the fact that his procedure is untested and yet to be accepted by the relevant scientific

---

29   810 So. 2d 836 (Fla. Sup. Ct. 2001) at 842, 845, and 847 [footnotes omitted].

community. There is no objective criteria that must be met, there are no photographs, no comparisons of methodology to review, and the final deduction is in the eyes of the beholder, i.e., the identification is a match because the witness says it is a match.

...

First, the record does not show that Hart's methodology — and particularly his claim of infallibility — has ever been formally tested or otherwise verified. At the Frye hearing below, the State submitted no substantive proof of scientific acceptance of such testing and its reliability. . . . Second, the record does not show that Hart's test has ever been subjected to meaningful peer review or publication as a prerequisite to scientific acceptance. . . .

The State's experts testified that the examining technician generally takes no photomicrographs of the casts because lay persons would be unable to understand the identification process. . . . This testimony, however, is belied by the published articles in the present record. Each article — including Hart's own article — contains photos of the matching striae, and the photos are instrumental in confirming — for the reader — the validity of the "match." . . . The State's experts further testified that they do not prepare notes or written reports delineating the basis for identification because to do so would not be helpful. . . . Again, this testimony is belied by the record. The German articles, for instance, describe at length the matching points of identification and then relate those points to specific features of the corresponding knife blade . . . and these descriptions, too, are helpful in confirming the validity of the "match."

Fourth, the record does not show that the error rate for Hart's method has ever been quantified. On the contrary, the State's experts testified that the method is infallible, that it is impossible to make a false positive identification. . . . Fifth, the record does not show that this method is governed by objective scientific standards. The State's experts repeatedly testified that the method is entirely subjective and that objective standards would be impractical. . . . This testimony, however, is contrary to language in Hart's own published article wherein he refers to the existence of objective scientific standards used in assessing the degree of match in striation marks. . . . And finally, the record contains no written authority — including Hart's own published article — that upholds his current methodology.

Other cases where "expert" evidence was disallowed as unreliable concerned a "psychological autopsy" where the issue was homicide or suicide,[30] hypnotic-

---

30 *R. v. Gilfoyle*, [2000] EWCA Crim 81.

ally refreshed testimony,[31] "statement validity analysis,"[32] the meaning of teardrop tattoos worn by street gang members,[33] the amount of marijuana that an individual dependent on the drug can ingest on a daily basis, or the shelf life of marijuana as testified to by a veteran police officer.[34]

One particular type of purported expert opinion evidence that is invariably rejected[35] on unreliability grounds as evidence is "profile" evidence.[36] Profiles that have been considered include drug-courier profile,[37] sex-offender profile,[38] smuggler's profile,[39] battering parent,[40] power rapist,[41] and even fleeing-driver

---

31 R. v. Trochym, above note 20.

32 R. v. Jmieff (1994), 94 C.C.C. (3d) 157 (B.C.C.A.): The court rejected the so-called statement validity analysis as a scientifically valid way to determine the reliability of a child's complaint. See Stephen J. Ceci & Helene Hembrooke, eds., *Expert Witnesses in Child Abuse Cases: What Can and Should Be Said in Court* (Washington, DC: American Psychological Association, 1998) at 176ff. regarding content-based analysis that wishfully thinks it can discriminate truthful from untruthful statements.

    See also D.A. Anson *et al.*, "Child Sexual Abuse Allegations: Reliability of Criteria-Based Content Analysis" (1993) 17 Law & Hum. Behav. 331; Lucy S. McGough, "Commentary: Assessing the Credibility of Witnesses' Statements" in John Doris, ed., *The Suggestibility of Children's Recollections* (Washington, DC: American Psychological Association, 1991) at 165; Gary L. Wells & Elizabeth F. Loftus, "Commentary: Is This Child Fabricating? Reactions to a New Assessment Technique" in *The Suggestibility of Children's Recollections, ibid.* at 168.

33 R. v. Abbey, [2007] O.J. No. 277 (S.C.J.).

34 R. v. Klassen, [2003] M.J. No. 417 (Q.B.).

35 Courts may allow "profiles" as an investigatory tool for search and seizure, arrest, or other investigatory purposes. But even there criticism has been made: *United States v. Hooper*, 935 F.2d 484 at 499 (2d Cir. 1991), Pratt J. dissenting, regarding the drug courier profile.

36 *People (California) v. Hernandez*, 63 Cal. Rptr. 2d 769 (Ct. App. 4 Dist., 1 Div. 1997): "We believe the crime analyst's testimony is also somewhat analogous to the inherently prejudicial 'profile' evidence which was held to be inadmissible for purposes of determining guilt or innocence in *People (California) v. Martinez* (1992) 10 Cal. App. 4th 1001." Profile evidence about an accused is inadmissible to suggest guilt of the crime charged: *Roy Dale Ryan v. State (Wyoming)*, 988 P.2d 46 (Wyo. 1999). See generally David C. Ormerod, "The Evidential Implications of Psychological Profiling" [1996] Crim. L. Rev. 863; Jane Campbell Moriarty, "Wonders of the Invisible World: Prosecutorial Syndrome and Profile Evidence in the Salem Witchcraft Trials" (2001) 26 Vermont L. Rev. 43.

37 *State (Arizona) v. Lee*, [1998] WL 268851 (Ariz. Sup. Ct. 28 May 1998); *State (Colorado) v. Salcedo*, 999 P.2d 833 (Colo. 2000); Mark J. Kadish, "The Drug Courier Profile: In Planes, Trains, and Automobiles; And Now in the Jury Box" (1997) 46 Am. U. L. Rev. 747.

38 *State (Idaho) v. Parkinson*, 909 P.2d 647 (Idaho Ct. App. 1996); *Flanagan v. State (Florida)*, 625 So. 2d 827 (Fla. 1993).

39 R. v. Cox (1999), 170 D.L.R. (4th) 101 (N.B.C.A.).

40 *People (California) v. Walkey*, 177 Cal. App. 3d 268 (Ct. App. 4 Dist. 1986).

41 *Reichard v. State (Indiana)*, 510 N.E.2d 163 (Ind. 1987).

profile.[42] Profile evidence as evidence of guilt is excluded because "the use of profile evidence to indicate guilt creates too high a risk that a defendant will be convicted not for what he did but for what others are doing. . . . [The profile fallaciously assumes that] . . . because someone shares characteristics — many of them innocent and commonplace — with a certain type of offender, that individual must also possess the same criminal culpability."[43]

The "flexibility" of profile evidence as a yardstick for guilt was emphasized in humorous fashion in *Harper's Magazine*[44] as follows:

THE LONG ARM OF THE LAW

From a list of characteristics included in the "drug-courier profiles" that are used by U.S. law-enforcement officials to identify which air travelers to stop and question. The profiles generally are kept secret; this list was compiled with the aid of court cases in which officers have used traits from their agency's profile to justify making allegedly unconstitutional stops. The list appears in *No Equal Justice*, by David Cole, to be published in January by The New Press. Cole is a professor at Georgetown University Law Center and an attorney with the Center for Constitutional Rights.

Arrived late at night
Arrived early in the morning
Arrived in afternoon
One of first to deplane
One of last to deplane
Deplaned in the middle
Purchased ticket at airport
Made reservation on short notice
Bought coach ticket

---

42 *State (Washington) v. Farr-Lenzini*, [1999] WL 5297 (Wash. Ct. App. 8 January 1999).

43 *State (Arizona) v. Lee*, above note 37, regarding drug-courier profile. The quotation expresses elegantly in this particular context the fallacy of concluding that if a person is a drug trafficker, fleeing driver, smuggler, or sex offender, he or she has the following characteristics. Reversing the reasoning is equally fallacious: if a person has the following characteristics, then he or she is a drug trafficker, fleeing driver, smuggler, or sex offender. See also Laurence Alison, Craig Bennell, Andreas Mokros, & David Ormerod, "The Personality Paradox in Offender Profiling: A Theoretical Review of the Processes Involved in Deriving Background Characteristics from Crime Scene Actions" (2002) 8 Psychol., Pub. Pol'y & L. 115; and D. Michael Risinger & Jeffrey L. Loop, "Three Card Monte, Monty Hall, Modus Operandi and 'Offender Profiling': Some Lessons of Modern Cognitive Science for the Law of Evidence" (2002) 24 Cardozo L. Rev. 193.

44 (October 1998), Readings at 26, available online: www.harpers.org.

Bought first-class ticket
Used one-way ticket
Used round-trip ticket
Paid for ticket with cash
Paid for ticket with small-denomination currency
Paid for ticket with large-denomination currency
Made local telephone call after deplaning
Made long-distance call after deplaning
Pretended to make telephone call
Traveled from New York to Los Angeles
Traveled to Houston
No luggage
Brand-new luggage
Carried a small bag
Carried a medium-sized bag
Carried two bulky garment bags
Carried two heavy suitcases
Carried four pieces of luggage
Overly protective of luggage
Disassociated self from luggage
Traveled alone
Traveled with a companion
Acted too nervous
Acted too calm
Made eye contact with officer
Avoided making eye contact with officer
Wore expensive clothing and gold jewelry
Dressed casually
Went to rest room after deplaning
Walked quickly through airport
Walked slowly through airport
Walked aimlessly through airport
Left airport by taxi
Left airport by limousine
Left airport by private car
Left airport by hotel courtesy van
Suspect was Hispanic
Suspect was black female

"Profile" evidence is considered further from a scientific point of view later in this book.[45]

LEGAL RELEVANCE

THIS FOREGOING REQUIREMENT of logical relevance is not the end of the admissibility inquiry even as far as the requirement of relevance is concerned. Admissibility is generally said to require "legal relevance,"[46] which involves additional requirements over and above logical relevance. These requirements reflect the dangers that expert evidence poses, as described above, and attempt to minimize those dangers in the particular case. Legal relevance requires logically relevant evidence of any kind (whether expert opinion or otherwise) to pass muster regarding these three additional matters that act as further hurdles to admissibility:

- whether its probative value is outweighed by its prejudicial effect;
- whether the time and effort involved in receiving the evidence is not commensurate with its value; or
- whether its influence on the trier of fact because of the prestige of the witness, the complexity and potential for confusion of the evidence, or any other cause will be out of proportion to its reliability.

It is at this stage of the calculations that an expert's ability to seduce the jury's mind is considered. The reality of that concern as it is assessed in the circumstances of the particular case is a highly significant factor in deciding admissibility. The particular expert witness, with her particular status and credentials, will be most important. The concern is whether "the triers would be disproportionately influenced, if not misled, by the aura of the scientific opinion and the prestigious credentials of the expert, into an indiscriminatory acceptance of the opinion evidence."[47] Albert Einstein put forth as an expert

---

45   Chapter 7, note 96.
46   *R. v. B.M.* (1998), 21 C.R. (5th) 324 (Ont. C.A.); *R. v. A.K. and N.K.*, above note 1 at paras. 4 and 79.
47   *R. v. Chisholm*, above note 14 at para. 57. In *R. v. B.M.*, *ibid.*, the purpose of expert testimony was not to diagnose the accused as a homosexual pedophile in a case where the physical contact forming the sexual offence charges was not unequivocally sexual in nature, but to show his intent. In *R. v. Pascoe* (1997), 5 C.R. (5th) 341 at para. 56 (Ont. C.A.), Justice Rosenberg said:

> In this case the jury were presented with the fact that the appellant was a homosexual paedophile and that in the opinion of the experts, both of whom had impressive credentials, his purpose was a sexual one notwithstanding the ambiguous nature of the conduct. In my view, there was an overwhelming danger that the jury would give

witness on virtually any topic would arguably have to be excluded because, as the "world's smartest man" his very utterances would determine the case. Any juror would consider it utter sacrilege not to accept his every word. Similarly, at the other end of the spectrum, the fact of an only marginally qualified expert might also speak against admissibility by being a negative factor as to the probative value of the evidence.

Another relevant factor is the nature of the evidence: Is it highly technical and intricate or easily comprehensible? The former raises a greater risk of confusion, usurpation, and attornment. Confusion is especially a risk when the evidence is directed to one purpose, such as credibility, but also has a potential to be misused as evidence of guilt. How susceptible will the evidence be to cross-examination is another relevant factor. This is a function not only of the degree of technical and conceptual difficulty of the evidence, but also its degree of transparency. Is the expert relying on arcane and highly technical rules and sources, or are all the underlying data and references easily available to opposing counsel? How easily will opposing counsel be able to demonstrate weaknesses or limitations in the data or references?

An important feature of this cost-benefit analysis is the nature of the opinion evidence to be given in relation to the issues to be decided by the trier of fact. At one time it was thought to be a rule of evidence that an expert witness could not give any opinion evidence that trenched on any specific issue that the trier of fact was charged with deciding. This was referred to as the "ultimate issue" rule.[48] It is now clear law that the fact that the expert testimony will opine even on the very issue the jury must decide does not automatically bar the evidence.[49]

However, as noted by the Supreme Court of Canada,[50] while there is no "ultimate issue" exclusionary rule that prohibits *per se* expert opinion on any ultimate issue that the trier of fact must decide, the fact remains that the greater the congruence between expert testimony and such an issue in the case, the greater the risk of usurpation. Thus, in such cases the proposed expert evidence is subjected to more intense scrutiny before it is admitted.

In a similar vein, expert evidence that involves credibility judgments raises dangers. A credibility opinion by an expert witness regarding the accused or

---

the expert evidence more weight than it deserves and, in any event, simply defer to the expert opinion.

48 See generally Earl J. Levy, *Examination of Witnesses in Criminal Cases*, 4th ed. (Toronto: Carswell, 1999) c. 14, "The Expert Witness" at 290.

49 *R. v. B.(R.H.)*, [1994] 1 S.C.R. 656.

50 *R. v. J-L.J.*, above note 10 at para. 37; *R. v. Pascoe*, above note 47 at 357.

a witness she has interviewed can also be admitted for the legitimate purpose of establishing, in part, the basis for the expert's opinion, but not as evidence of the truth thereof that the witness was truthful.[51] Such should be an important factor in the cost-benefit analysis regarding admissibility, especially in the case of prosecution witnesses because essentially an exclusionary rule is being implicated.

Issues of time and expense also enter the discussion here. Days of court time and expensive witnesses flown in from overseas will require greater justification, especially if the charges being tried are less than the most serious. Trial judges have been cautioned by appellate courts to "pay particular attention to whether ... the evidence would involve an inordinate amount of time that is not commensurate with its value."[52]

Sometimes prejudice can arise from the mere calling of an expert witness. An expensive and laborious expert evidence exercise on behalf of the prosecution will convey to a trier of fact the subtext that the accused is a worthwhile target for prosecution because no expense is being spared in that exercise. The communicative significance — and potential prejudicial effect — of the very fact of calling expert evidence should not be overlooked.

Another relevant consideration is the hearsay component that will be involved. As already noted, one of the dangers that accompanies expert evidence is the inevitable introduction before the trier of fact of hearsay evidence, albeit accompanied by appropriate jury instructions to attempt to prevent misuse. But, depending upon the circumstances of a particular case, the proffered expert evidence may necessarily involve substantial amounts of prejudicial hearsay evidence, or even a small amount of devastating hearsay. In such cases, jury instructions may provide at best a weak or even ineffective antidote, and exclusion of the evidence may be mandated.

A related issue is other foundational material for the opinion and the prejudice, if any, arising therefrom. For example, in *R. v. Pascoe*,[53] the opinions about the accused's sexual preference were based on his past criminal misconduct. To avoid prejudice from those other matters, the evidence was led without the addition of these foundational matters, but this deprived the jury of the means to evaluate the evidence. It also created the problem that, had the defence sought

---

51   *R. v. Marquard*, [1993] 4 S.C.R. 223; *R. v. Sullivan* (1995), 37 C.R. (4th) 333 (B.C.C.A.); *R. v. J-L.J.*, above note 10; and *R. v. Perlett*, below note 56.

52   *R. v. B.M.*, above note 46 at 390. In *R. v. Chisholm*, above note 14 at para. 57, an otherwise routine sexual assault prosecution, the Crown agreed that the presentation of expert evidence would take up to three days of court time. The trial judge noted that this might be followed by a defence expert, which would further extend the matter.

53   Above note 47.

to attack the foundation for the opinion, it would be prejudicing its own case by showing prior acts of bad character. The appellate court stated:

> The trial judge recognized that if all the information that formed the foundation for the opinion were disclosed to the jury then the prejudicial effect of the evidence would outweigh its probative value. Having made that determination, with which I agree, the trial judge should have recognized that this posed a serious impediment to admitting the opinions themselves.[54]

In a particular type of case or dealing with a particular expert witness, previous transcripts may be useful to support arguments about these factors. Examples of the witness's language, examples of difficulties in cross-examination, and even examples of problems in locating supporting reference materials can be highlighted from previous cases. Comments on the evidence from other judges or a demonstration that the evidence did not figure in the outcome in previous cases would also be useful in arguing legal relevance.

This cost-benefit analysis is generally described as being a matter of the trial judge's discretion, with appellate courts reluctant to intervene and reassess such decisions on appeal. Trial judges are thus given wide latitude in the acceptance or rejection of expert evidence applying these requirements for legal relevance.[55] However, it should be noted that this exclusionary analysis is applied less rigorously in favour of the defence. As was said in *R. v. B.M.*, "a trial judge should be particularly cautious when excluding expert defence evidence on the basis of a cost benefit analysis. . . . [T]he exclusionary rule only operates to exclude defence evidence where the prejudice effect of the evidence *substantially* outweighs its probative value."[56]

NECESSITY

TO BE ADMISSIBLE, expert testimony must be more than merely relevant or even helpful or useful; it must be necessary, in the sense that a correct result could not be reached without it. As reiterated in *R. v. D.D.*,[57] necessity exists

---

54   *Ibid.* at para. 55.

55   *R. v. K.(A.)* (1999), 27 C.R. (5th) 226 (Ont. C.A.), especially at para. 89; *R. v. M.(W.)* (1997), 115 C.C.C. (3d) 233 (B.C.C.A.).

56   Above note 46 at para. 88 [emphasis added]. See also *R. v. Perlett* (1999), 26 C.R. (5th) 343 (Ont. Ct. Gen. Div.), Platana J.; *R. v. Bell* (1997), 115 C.C.C. (3d) 107 (N.W.T.C.A.); R.J. Delisle, "The Admissibility of Expert Evidence: A New Caution Based on General Principles" (1994) 29 C.R. (4th) 267 at 273.

57   Above note 2 at para. 51.

"in those exceptional cases where the jury would be unable to reach their own [correct] conclusions in the absence of assistance from experts."[58]

Necessity has two aspects. The first and best-known aspect is that expert opinion is characterized as necessary when its substance is likely outside the experience and knowledge of the trier of fact, and the expert witness will assist the trier of fact in reaching the correct conclusion on the matter. The expert, it has been said, provides the trier of fact with ready-made inferences otherwise beyond its ability to know due to the technical or scientific subject matter. Conversely, where the trier of fact can form its own opinion on the matter without any help, the proposed expert evidence is unnecessary.

This is far from a bright-line rule. As was said in *R. v. F.(D.S.)*,

> [t]here is no exact way to draw the line between what is within the normal experience of a judge or a jury and what is not. The normal experiences of different triers of fact may differ. Over time the subject matters that come within the normal experiences of judges and juries may change. The normal experiences of those in one community may differ from those in other communities. In the end, the court in each case will be required to exercise its best judgement in deciding whether a particular subject matter is or is not within the normal experience of the trier of fact.[59]

In *R. v. D.D.*,[60] a sex case where the ten-year-old complainant "delayed" two and a half years before "complaining," proposed expert testimony on behalf of the Crown by a child psychologist that the length of time before disclosure was not indicative of lack of truth of an allegation because many factors and circumstances may affect the timing of a complaint was held inadmissible, with the necessity requirement especially being singled out. Since the "content of the expert evidence . . . was not unique or scientifically puzzling but was rather the proper subject for a simple jury instruction," its admission was not necessary, the Supreme Court of Canada majority held.

In *R. v. McIntosh*,[61] defence-tendered expert evidence regarding the dangers of identification evidence was held properly excluded:

> Very briefly, this testimony involved an analysis of the identification evidence as disclosed in the transcripts from the preliminary hearing. Dr. Yarmey commented on the factors that impair the witnesses' ability to make an accurate

---

58 See also *R. v. C.G.* (1996), 110 C.C.C. (3d) 233 (Nfld. C.A.).

59 Above note 23 at para. 65.

60 Above note 2.

61 (1997), 117 C.C.C. (3d) 385 (Ont. C.A.), leave to appeal to S.C.C. refused (1998), 121 C.C.C. (3d) vi (*sub nom. R. v. McCarthy*), 227 N.R. 279 (note) (S.C.C.) [*McIntosh*].

identification, the problem of cross-racial identification, the quality of memory recall for perceived events over different time spans, the influence of "post event information" on memory, the validity of the photographic lineup, the misconceptions of jurors with respect to photographic lineups, the difficulties with "in dock" identifications and police procedures relating to the identification of the two accused persons.[62]

. . .

In the case in appeal, I think that I can deal with relevance and necessity together because they appear to overlap. . . . This opinion evidence is directed to instructing the jury that all witnesses have problems in perception and recall with respect to what occurred during any given circumstance that is brief and stressful. Accordingly, Dr. Yarmey is not testifying to matters that are outside the normal experience of the trier of fact: he is reminding the jury of the normal experience.[63]

Finlayson J.A. stated that he

[h]owever, [did] not intend to leave the subject without raising some warning flags. In my respectful opinion, the courts are overly eager to abdicate their fact finding responsibilities to "experts" in the field of the behavioral sciences. We are too quick to say that a particular witness possesses special knowledge and experience going beyond that of the trier of fact without engaging in an analysis of the subject matter of that expertise. . . . Where is the evidence in this case that there is a recognized body of scientific knowledge that defines rules of human behaviour affecting memory patterns such that any expert in that field can evaluate the reliability of the identification made by a particular witness in a given case?[64]

---

62 *Ibid.* at para. 11.

63 *Ibid.* at para. 20. For a recent case, *contra*, see *People (New York) v. Lee (Anthony)*, 96 N.Y. 2d 157 (2001).

64 *McIntosh*, above note 61 at para. 14. See *R. v. Audy (No. 2)* (1977), 34 C.C.C. (2d) 231 (Ont. C.A.) for an earlier decision regarding the "unnecessary" nature of expert evidence regarding eyewitness identification issues. The missing evidence that Finlayson J.A. was seeking can be found in David L. Faigman *et al.*, *Modern Scientific Evidence*, 2 vols. (St. Paul, MN: West, 1997) c. 11, "Eyewitness Identification," 436–79, as well as in Elizabeth Loftus & James M. Doyle, *Eyewitness Testimony: Civil and Criminal*, 3d ed. (Charlottesville, VA: Lexis Law, 1997); A. Daniel Yarmey, "Probative v. Prejudicial Value of Eyewitness Memory Research" (1997) 5:3 Expert Evidence 89; Thomas Dillickrath, "Expert Testimony on Eyewitness Identification: Admissibility and Alternatives" (2001) 55 U. Miami L. Rev. 1059; "Special Theme: The Other-Race Effect and Contemporary Criminal Justice: Eyewitness Identification and Jury Decision Making" (2001) 7 Psychol., Pub. Pol'y & L. contains a number of articles on that subject. For an "aftermath" discussion of *McIntosh*, see Martin Peters, "Forensic Psychological Testimony: Is the Courtroom Door Now Locked and Barred?" (May 2001) 42 Can. Psychol. (Part 2) 101. The law is incor-

The very real "necessity" for expert defence evidence in this area will be demonstrated later in this book.[65]

The second, sometimes overlooked, aspect of necessity deals with necessity for the particular form of providing the information, by way of expert opinion testimony. "Necessity" is assessed not solely by the proposed subject matter of the opinion, *per se*, but also in light of all the circumstances of the case. If the information to be furnished by the expert will be revealed adequately by the particular evidence in the case, the expert evidence will be unnecessary.

Similarly, if the points to be made by the expert can be established through the submissions of counsel or by jury instructions, then the expert evidence will be unnecessary. In other words, the required "necessity" is necessity that the trier of fact receive the information expressly by way of expert evidence, and not simply necessity that it receive the information at all. If the trier of fact can receive the required information in some other fashion than expert opinion, the expert evidence is unnecessary.

Both *R. v. D.D.*[66] and *R. v. McIntosh*[67] referred to proposed jury instructions as sufficient substitutes for the excluded testimony. By way of other example, expert evidence relating to delayed disclosure in sex cases may be rendered "unnecessary" where the complainant herself gives evidence explaining the delay.[68] Judicial notice is another potential, albeit limited, mechanism whereby a court may acquire information to render proposed expert opinion evidence unnecessary.[69]

Psychiatric and psychological evidence regarding abnormal mental conditions that have an impact on an accused's criminal responsibility by negating it in whole or in part by denying a requisite mental element is a common form of expert opinion evidence, generally viewed to satisfy the "necessity" require-

---

porating science's lessons regarding identification procedures in demanding double-blind and sequential identification procedures: "Eyewitness Evidence Major Developments" (11 June 2001), ADGN/2001-765 (on Quicklaw in Commentary). See also A.M. Levi, "Some Facts Lawyers Need to Know about the Police Lineup" (2002) 46 Crim. L.Q. 176; Jill Copeland, "Helping Jurors Recognize the Frailties of Eyewitness Identification Evidence" (2002) 46 Crim. L.Q. 188. Lisa J. Steele, "Public Knowledge, Popular Wisdom, and Urban Legend: Educating the Jury about Memory on Closing Argument" (2000) 36 Crim. L. Bull. 316 contains an excellent summary of U.S. case law on what memory issues can be subject of expert evidence and what issues can be argued to jury by defence counsel without expert evidence.

65 See chapter 6.
66 Above note 2.
67 Above note 61.
68 *R. v. A.K. and N.K.*, above note 1 at para. 99; *R. v. Perlett*, above note 56 at para. 33.
69 For a discussion of judicial notice as a way for courts to receive "expert" evidence — especially regarding social science matters — on their own without an expert, see chapter 9.

ment. However, expert psychiatric or psychological evidence regarding the workings or state of mind of a "normal" or "reasonable" person is not generally admissible because of the "necessity" requirement here under discussion.[70] A trier of fact, be it judge or jury, is considered sufficiently capable of knowing the workings of a "normal" or "reasonable" person's mind.[71] Thus, expert evidence regarding trauma-related memories and their frequent inconsistencies was excluded in *R. v. Perlett*.[72] However, in *R. v. D.R.*,[73] the Supreme Court of Canada approved the defence calling a child psychologist to testify about the workings of children's memories.[74]

In *R. v. L.S.*,[75] it was held that a "highly qualified forensic psychologist ... with considerable experience in the sexual assault area" should have been allowed to give expert evidence on the "methods of assessment of the reliability of the child complainant's evidence" both on an application to admit hearsay evidence under the principled exception[76] and at trial. In *R. v. Tayebi*,[77] expert evidence on the effects of sexual abuse of children, including symptoms of sexual abuse, the significance of delayed or incomplete disclosures, and on human memory generally was allowed without objection by the defence. The appeal court seemed to approve.

In *R. v. R.A.C.*,[78] the expert purported to explain "how it could possibly be that the memory of the complainants had improved between the date of the preliminary hearing and the trial." The conviction was upheld. Unfortunately, no expert evidence was called by the defence to discuss the validity of the notion that memory improves with time and explain that, in fact, as time passes,

---

70 *R. v. McMillan* (1975), 23 C.C.C. (2d) 160 (Ont. C.A.), aff'd [1977] 2 S.C.R. 824; *R. v. Gowland* (1978), 45 C.C.C. (2d) 303 (Ont. C.A.); *R. v. Weightman* (1990), 92 Crim. App. R. 291 (U.K.C.A. (Crim. Div.)); *R. v. Turner* (1974), 60 Crim. App. R. 80 (U.K.C.A. (Crim. Div.)). *R. v. B.M.*, above note 46, considered the permissible limits on expert evidence of the workings of human "memory," especially in a therapeutic context.

71 It says the obvious to point out the difficulty of drawing this line between "normal" and "abnormal." A physically abused, immature, prelingually deaf emotionally disturbed accused was held "normal" in *Roberts v. The Queen*, [1990] Crim. L.R. 122 (U.K.C.A. (Crim. Div.)).

72 Above note 56.

73 [1996] 2 S.C.R. 291.

74 Evidence on the same topic was excluded in *R. v. M.(W.)* (1997), 115 C.C.C. (3d) 233 (B.C.C.A.). See also *R. v. J.C.W.S.*, [2006] EWCA Crim 1404 dealing with expert evidence regarding children's memories and *R. v. X*, [2005] All E.R. (D.) 06 (Jul) (U.K.C.A. (Crim. Div.)) dealing with the phenomenon known as "childhood amnesia."

75 (1999), 133 C.C.C. (3d) 493 (Ont. C.A.).

76 See *Khan v. College of Physicians & Surgeons* (1992), 76 C.C.C. (3d) 10 (Ont. C.A.).

77 (2001), 48 C.R. (5th) 354 (B.C.C.A.).

78 (1990), 57 C.C.C. (3d) 522 at 530 (B.C.C.A.).

people tend to fill in false details that seem reasonable and "round out the story" to substitute for those matters that have been forgotten.

In *R. v. Parrott*,[79] medical evidence regarding a complainant's "childlike mental condition" or "poor ability to sustain questioning" was held unnecessary as these were matters the trial judge was quite capable of assessing.

Psychiatric evidence of disposition may be admissible where the particular disposition or tendency in issue is characteristic of a distinctive group, the characteristics of which fall within the expertise of the psychiatrist.[80] The exception is based on the notion that psychical as well as physical characteristics may be relevant to identify the perpetrator of the crime and involves the psychiatrist in expressing his conclusion that the accused did or did not have the capacity to commit the crime with which he is charged.

In one of the few cases allowing such evidence, *R. v. Malboeuf*,[81] the "necrophilia-lust type of murder" was considered sufficiently distinctive that the Crown was allowed to lead expert evidence that the accused "demonstrated distinctive characteristics that would place him in the category of persons who would commit this type of crime." In *R. v. J-L.J.*, the Supreme Court noted:

> A high level of distinctiveness, of course, is in addition to the other limitations on the Crown's ability to lead such expert evidence, including the requirements that it be relevant to an issue other than "mere propensity," and that its probative value outweighs its prejudicial effect.[82]

The related concept of "profile" evidence involves the idea of proving a generic or group identity for the perpetrator of the offence, with the accused then being shown to be within (by the prosecution) or without (by the defence) that group by evidence of congruence or lack of congruence with that profile or group identity.

The now-leading precedent[83] describes the matter this way in the related context of an unsuccessful attempt by the defence to adduce exculpatory profile evidence:

> [It must be] . . . shown that the crime is such that it could only, or in all probability would only, be committed by a person having identifiable peculiarities

---

79 [2001] 1 S.C.R. 178.

80 *R. v. J-L.J.*, above note 10; *R. v. McMillan*, above note 70; *R. v. Lupien*, [1970] S.C.R. 263; *R. v. Robertson* (1975), 21 C.C.C. (2d) 385 (S.C.C.).

81 [1997] O.J. No. 1398 (C.A.), leave to appeal to S.C.C. refused, [1998] 3 S.C.R. vii.

82 Above note 10 at para. 42.

83 *Ibid.*

... or "the offence is of a kind that is committed only by members of an abnormal group".

. . .

[T]his precondition being established on a balance of probabilities, the personality profile of the perpetrator group must be sufficiently complete to identify distinctive psychological elements that were in all probability present and operating in the perpetrator at the time of the offence.

. . .

The trial judge should consider the opinion of the expert and whether the expert is merely expressing a personal opinion or whether the behavioural profile which the expert is putting forward is in common use as a reliable indicator of membership in a distinctive group.

The level of detail required in the "standard profile" may vary with the conclusiveness of individual elements. For example, if commission of an offence most likely requires so "distinctive" a psychological trait as necrophilia ... it may be sufficient for exclusion to show that an accused has no such tendency without requiring the rest of the perpetrator's psychological portrait to be completed.

. . .

More common personality disorders are perhaps less distinctive than necrophilia. They are less likely to serve as "badges" to distinguish the perpetrator class from the rest of the population.

. . .

Between these two extremes, the range and distinctiveness of personality traits attributed to perpetrators of different offences will vary greatly. The requirement of the "standard profile" is to ensure that the profile of distinctive features is not put together on an ad hoc basis for the purpose of a particular case. Beyond that, the issue is whether the "profile" is sufficient for the purpose to be served, whether the expert can identify and describe with workable precision what exactly distinguishes the distinctive or deviant perpetrator from other people.[84]

---

84 *Ibid.* at paras. 38–44. A related concept is the concept of "guilt-by-trait-association" such as "80 to 85 percent of child sexual abuse is committed by a close relative," which can be thought of as a one-dimensional profile. Courts have rejected such statistical proof: *Stephens v. State (Wyoming)*, 774 P.2d 60 (Wyo. 1989); *State (Washington) v. Maule*, 667 P.2d 96 (Wash. Ct. App. 1983); *State (Washington) v. Claflin*, 690 P.2d 1186 (Wash. Ct. App. 1984); *State (Washington) v. Steward*, 660 P.2d 278 (Wash. Ct. App. 1983); *State (Washington) v. Petrich*, 683 P.2d 173 (Wash. 1984); *Hall v. State (Arkansas)*, 692 S.W.2d 769 (Ark. Ct. App. 1985).

In *R. v. J-L.J.*, which involved sex offences against children, the Court held that the expert's evidence showed a lack of any real standard profile for the offences at issue. As well, the accused's exclusion was based upon two tests with significant error rates and doubtful validity for forensic, as opposed to clinical, purposes. The trial judge's refusal to admit the defence expert evidence was upheld.[85]

Expert evidence is generally unnecessary and therefore inadmissible regarding the credibility of witnesses,[86] except in exceptional cases where there is a hidden or latent defect that will be revealed by the expert evidence, so that the expert evidence is only thus rendered necessary.[87] The trier of fact is generally charged with the responsibility to determine issues of credibility, and expert evidence with regard thereto — assuming the evidence is actually reliable enough to be legally relevant — is excluded as unnecessary. This reason (as well as reliability concerns) is why polygraph-test-result evidence is inadmissible as substantive evidence of guilt or innocence.[88]

But latent defects, such as the complainant's suffering from delusions and borderline personality disorder, disabilities affecting her ability to give reliable testimony, can be the subject of expert evidence by the defence.[89] An accused's mental condition or psychopathic personality, relevant to the reliability of a confession to police because it involves a propensity to lie, can be the subject of expert defence evidence.[90]

---

85 *R. v. J-L.J.*, above note 10. To the same effect, see *R. v. Perlett*, above note 56.

86 *R. v. P.G.*, [2009] O.J. No. 121 (C.A.).

87 *R. v. Marquard*, above note 51; *R. v. French* (1977), 37 C.C.C. (2d) 201 (Ont. C.A.), aff'd [1980] 1 S.C.R. 158; *R. v. Kostuck* (1986), 29 C.C.C. (3d) 190 (Man. C.A.); *R. v. J-L.J.*, above note 10; *R. v. Warren* (1995), 35 C.R. (4th) 347 (N.W.T.S.C.).

88 *R. v. Béland*, [1987] 2 S.C.R. 398; *R. v. McIntosh* (1999), 30 C.R. (5th) 161 (Ont. C.A.); *R. v. Walrath*, [2001] B.C.J. No. 1319 (S.C.).

89 *R. v. Kliman* (1996), 47 C.R. (4th) 333 (B.C.C.A.); *R. v. Julien* (1980), 57 C.C.C. (2d) 462 (Que. C.A.). In *Farrell v. The Queen* (1998), 194 C.L.R. 286 (H.C.A.), psychiatric evidence regarding the impact of the complainant's personality disorder was ruled admissible.

90 *R. v. Dietrich* (1970), 11 C.R.N.S. 22 (Ont. C.A.), leave to appeal to S.C.C. refused (1970), 1 C.C.C. (2d) 68n (S.C.C.). *R. v. Leland*, [1998] B.C.J. No. 1584 (S.C.): forensic psychologist and psychiatrist in the accused's murder trial could testify that the accused had a personality disorder that might classify him as a pathological liar, to undermine the inculpatory effect of the accused's admissions to undercover police officers. "Scientific evidence which tends to establish the accused's mental condition and may reflect upon his admissions was admissible in the circumstances," the court held. *R. v. O'Brien* (25 January 2000), 98/6926/27/28/S1 (U.K.C.A. (Crim. Div.)): "[E]xpert evidence is admissible if it demonstrates some form of abnormality relevant to the reliability of a defendant's [or witness's] confession or evidence." Compare *R. v. Warren*, above note 87.

A credibility opinion by an expert witness regarding the accused or a witness he has interviewed can also be admitted for the legitimate purpose of establishing, in part, the basis for the expert's opinion, but not as evidence of the truth thereof that the witness was truthful.[91] Such should be an important factor in the cost-benefit analysis regarding admissibility and also provide an argument in the context of proposed prosecution evidence that an exclusionary rule is being implicated.

One area where the necessity requirement has been debated is the area of witness questioning, especially in the context of interviews of children in child abuse cases. In *R. v. D.R.*,[92] the Supreme Court of Canada reversed convictions where the trial judge had improperly prevented the defence from exploring the issue of suggestive child questioning. In two cases arising out of the infamous Martensville sex abuse hysteria, the Saskatchewan Court of Appeal clearly approved without question expert testimony regarding child questioning, and proper and improper techniques that may affect the evidence.[93]

In *R. v. D. and Others*,[94] it was held that in a sex abuse case, expert evidence is admissible about the child interviews and the propriety or lack thereof of the interviewing procedures and their compliance or lack thereof with applicable judicial or other guidelines. In *State (Wisconsin) v. St. George*,[95] it was held that that "exclusion of the testimony of the expert witness about recantation and interview techniques [utilized with the complainant] denied the defendant his constitutional right to present a defense." The same result was reached in *State (Arizona) v. Speers*.[96]

Pretrial handling of five children in a federal sexual abuse case presented a picture of possibly tainted testimony, making it a reversible error to exclude a defence expert's testimony about suggestibility in children's testimony, an appeal court ruled in *United States v. Rouse*.[97] More generally expert evidence re-

---

91 *R. v. Marquard*, above note 51; *R. v. Sullivan*, above note 51; *R. v. J-L.J.*, above note 10; and *R. v. Perlett*, above note 56.

92 Above note 73.

93 *R. v. Sterling* (1995), 102 C.C.C. (3d) 481 (Sask. C.A.); *R. v. S.(T.)* (1995), 40 C.R. (4th) 1 (Sask. C.A.). See also *David v. State (Alaska)*, 28 P.3d 309 (Alaska Ct. App. 2001).

94 (3 November 1995) (U.K.C.A. (Crim. Div.). See also *G. v. D.P.P.*, [1997] 2 All E.R. 755.

95 643 N.W.2d 777 (2002).

96 2004 Ariz. App. LEXIS 139.

97 100 F.3d 560 (8th Cir. 1996). See generally the authoritative reference Stephen J. Ceci & Maggie Bruck, *Jeopardy in the Courtroom: A Scientific Analysis of Children's Testimony* (Washington, DC: American Psychological Association, 1995) and *State (New Jersey) v. Michaels*, 642 A.2d 1372 (N.J. 1994) where it was held that for admission of testimony from children, the court will require "clear and convincing" evidence that children's testimony was untainted by any suggestive influences.

garding the investigative techniques and interview techniques utilized in the case was held proper in *R. v. Hamelin*.[98] U.S. courts are severely divided on whether a criminal defendant can present expert testimony from a psychologist that police interrogation techniques may have caused him to falsely confess.[99]

ABSENCE OF EXCLUSIONARY RULE

THE OPINION OF an expert must not only pass those standards applicable to expert evidence but must also comply with other rules of evidence. Exclusionary rules apply to expert evidence as to any evidence and may occasionally render inadmissible expert opinion evidence that otherwise complies with the requirements of admissibility.

For example, in *R. v. Pascoe*,[100] the exclusionary rule regarding propensity evidence was implicated. Expert evidence about the accused's psychosexual character was excluded because of the danger that it would be used (or rather, misused) by the jury solely as forbidden propensity evidence: to show that the accused was, because of his character, the kind of person likely to commit the crime alleged.[101]

A major exclusionary rule in the context of expert opinion evidence is the rule against oath-helping.[102] A witness cannot testify to the effect that another witness (usually the complainant or the accused) is telling the truth. Expert evidence that amounts to nothing more than that is thus prohibited. This is simply a restatement of the rule that credibility judgments regarding "normal" persons

---

98 (1999), 135 C.C.C. (3d) 228 (Que. C.A.).

99 Cases saying no: *State (New Jersey) v. Free*, 798 A.2d 83 (N.J. Super. Ct. App. Div. 2002); *People (California) v. Son*, 93 Cal. Rptr. 2d 871 (Ct. App. 4 Dist. 2000); *State (Kansas) v. Cobb*, 43 P.3d 855 (Kan. Ct. App. 2002); *State (Maine) v. Tellier*, 526 A.2d 941 (Me. 1987); *Commonwealth (Massachusetts) v. Nerette*, 935 N.E.2d 1242 (Mass. 2000); *State (Minnesota) v. Ritt*, 599 N.W.2d 802 (Minn. 1999); *State (Missouri) v. Davis*, 32 S.W.3d 603 (Mo. Ct. App. E.D. 2000); *People (New York) v. Philips*, 692 N.Y.S.2d 915 (1999); *State (New York) v. Green*, 683 N.Y.S.2d 597 (App. Div. 1998); *Kolb v. State (Wyoming)*, 930 P.2d 1238 (Wyo. 1996).

Cases saying yes: *People (California) v. Page*, 2 Cal. Rptr. 2d 898 (Ct. App. 1 Dist. 1991); *People (Colorado) v. Lopez*, 946 P.2d 478 (Colo. Ct. App. 1997); *Boyer v. State (Florida)*, No. 1D00-3714 (Fla. Ct. App. 2002); *United States v. Hall*, 974 F. Supp. 1198 (C.D. Ill. 1997); *Callis v. State (Indiana)*, 684 N.E.2d 233 (Ind. Ct. App. 1997); *Lenormand v. State (Texas)*, No. 09-97-150-CR (Texas Ct. App. 1998).

100 Above note 47.

101 See also *R. v. K.(A.)*, above note 55.

102 See *R. v. Marquard*, above note 51; *R. v. Sullivan*, above note 51; and *R. v. J-L.J.*, above note 10 at para. 60. Defence "oathhelping" was rejected in *R. v. Perlett*, above note 56.

are the province of the trier of fact and expert evidence is "unnecessary" for the performance of that task.

Even expert evidence that incidentally involves credibility judgments raises dangers. A credibility opinion by an expert witness regarding the accused or a witness she has interviewed can be admitted for the legitimate purpose of establishing, in part, the basis for the expert's opinion, but not as evidence of the truth thereof that the witness was truthful.[103] Obviously, such a factor is important in the cost-benefit analysis regarding admissibility, especially in the case of prosecution witnesses because essentially an exclusionary rule is in fact being implicated.

The similar fact evidence exclusionary rule is another example that may operate to exclude expert opinion evidence.[104]

A QUALIFIED EXPERT

"EXPERTISE" AS IT has been described by the courts has certainly had a relatively modest status. The test has often been described in vague terms as follows:

> From this it is clear that so long as a witness satisfies the Court that he is skilled, the way in which he acquired his skill is immaterial. The test of expertness, so far as the law of evidence is concerned, is skill, and skill alone, in the field in which it is sought to have the witness's opinion. If the Court is satisfied that the witness is sufficiently skilled in this respect for his opinion to be received, then his opinion is admissible.[105]

In *Mohan* the test for a "properly qualified expert" was described as follows: "[T]he evidence must be given by a witness who is shown to have acquired special or peculiar knowledge through study or experience in respect of the matters on which he or she undertakes to testify."[106]

Sometimes the test is stated in virtually tautological terms that expert status is achieved when the expert possesses special knowledge and experience going

---

103 *R. v. Marquard, ibid.*; *R. v. Sullivan, ibid.*

104 *R. v. A.K. and N.K.*, above note 1 at para. 103.

105 *R. v. Bunniss*, [1965] 3 C.C.C. 236 at 239 (B.C. Co. Ct.) [*Bunniss*], Tyrwhitt-Drake J., stating the effect of the oft-quoted definition of an expert witness given by Lord Russell of Killowen C.J. in *R. v. Silverlock*, [1894] 2 Q.B. 766.

106 *Mohan*, above note 9 at para. 27.

beyond that of the trier of fact,[107] though this appears to be a misunderstanding of precedent:[108]

> Defence counsel in resisting a Primary Objective attack will, no doubt, urge the Court to adopt a test which is very easy for almost any expert to pass. Reference will likely be made to the statement of McLachlin J. in *R. v. Marquard*, which is found at p. 224:
>
>> The only requirement for the admissibility of expert opinion is that the "expert witness possesses special knowledge and experience going beyond that of the trier of fact." *R. v. Beland* (1987), 36 C.C.C. (3d) 481 at p. 494: Deficiencies in the expertise go to weight, not admissibility.
>
> I will for the purpose of this paper refer to this as the *Marquard* test.
>
> What do these words mean? Defence counsel will likely submit it means that if the proposed expert witness possesses special knowledge which is greater than that of the trier of fact, then his or her opinion is admissible and any deficiencies in the expertise go to weight, not admissibility.
>
> . . .
>
> It is important to note that McLachlin J. attributes the wording of the test, or at least the operative words of the test, to McIntyre J. in *Beland, supra*. In that case, the Court was dealing with the admissibility of a polygraph test. It was conceded that the polygraph operator had substantial expertise in the workings of the polygraph machine and knowledge of the scientific basis on which the machine operated. The majority of the Supreme Court of Canada ruled the polygraph results to be inadmissible because, amongst other things, it felt that the jury could determine the credibility of the accused without the need of the polygraph results. The words which McLachlin J. incorporates into the *Marquard* Test come from the following portion of McIntyre J.'s reasons in *Beland* at 493–94:
>
>> The function of the expert witness is to provide for the jury or other trier of fact an expert's opinion as to the significance of, or the inference which may be drawn from, proved facts in a field in which the expert witness possesses special knowledge and experience going beyond that of the trier of fact. The expert witness is permitted to give such opinions for the assistance of the jury. Where the question is one which

---

107 *R. v. Terceira* (1998), 15 C.R. (5th) 359 (Ont. C.A.), aff'd [1999] 3 S.C.R. 866, regarding DNA evidence; *R. v. Kinnie* (1989), 52 C.C.C. (3d) 112 (B.C.C.A.); *R. v. Russell* (1994), [1995] 95 C.C.C. (3d) 190 (Ont. C.A.).

108 Harvey Spiegel, "Attacking the Defence Expert's Qualifications" (The Ontario Trial Lawyers Association's 1997 Fall Conference, 7–8 November 1997).

falls within the knowledge and experience of the trier of fact, there is no need for expert evidence and an opinion will not be received. Here the sole issue upon which the polygraph evidence is adduced is the credibility of the accused, an issue well within the experience of judges and juries and one in which no expert evidence is required.

McIntyre J. was not using these words in reference to the qualifications of the expert but rather in relation to the type of subject matter with respect to which an expert witness is entitled to give opinion evidence. In *Beland*, the determination of the credibility of the accused was the subject matter of the proposed opinion evidence, and that was not something going beyond the knowledge and experience of the trier of fact. Therefore no expert evidence was required. Nowhere in *Beland* did Justice McIntyre state that the requirement for the admission of expert opinion is that the expert witness possess special knowledge and experience going beyond that of the trier of fact. Indeed I have not been able to find any case prior to *Marquard* where such a test was utilized.

The qualification must be proved on a balance of probabilities.[109]

Various aspects of a witness's background are relevant to expertise. These include academic qualifications, additional training, practical experience, publications, books and articles authored, papers and presentations given at conferences and meetings, and professional memberships in societies and organizations (especially those involving membership on merit rather than merely upon payment of a fee[110]). Honours and awards received in a professional capacity are also relevant. The witness's prior court and tribunal experience as an expert witness, both positive and negative, will be considered. Previous occasions in which the witness was or was not declared an expert witness in the specific area in issue and about which he proposes to testify will be of great interest.[111]

Expert witnesses must not only be qualified, but also qualified with respect to the areas or subjects upon which they are to testify. This is an important point often overlooked. Expertise in the abstract is irrelevant to the court. What must be shown is expertise and qualification "in an area" of relevance in the case.

---

109 *R. v. Terceira*, above note 107.

110 The American College of Forensic Examiners (ACFE) offers diplomate status for forensic examination, forensic medicine, forensic dentistry, and psychological specialties. Five years old, it has 11,500 members and membership is easy to achieve, with a one-year membership and board membership presently costing $450. Qualification may be satisfied by education alone and in fact, a J.D. (LL.B.) suffices for certification by the American Board of Forensic Medicine. The membership directory is online: www.acfei.com/main.php and any prospective expert witness can be looked up in it.

111 See generally Levy, above note 48 at 286–87 and 310.

Relevant expertise is determined during a *voir dire*. The precise area of expertise of the witness is defined for the court at that time. Counsel will advise the court that the witness is to be presented to give opinion evidence on a particular subject or particular area. Witnesses are not permitted to offer opinion evidence on matters beyond their established expertise.

Two similar breathalyzer cases that reached opposite conclusions provide an object lesson in the qualification of an expert witness. *R. v. Edson*[112] and *R. v. Bunniss*[113] both deal with the admissibility of testimony by a breathalyzer technician regarding the relationship of blood-alcohol reading to impairment.

In *Edson*, it was held that the technician, whose expertise was primarily with regard to the operation of the breathalyzer, was not qualified to give an opinion on that topic and his general statement that a person with a reading of 0.15 percent is impaired was held to be valueless. However, in *Bunniss*, a police officer in similar circumstances was held to be qualified. The court there was impressed with the fact that the officer had read scientific literature on the physiological effects of alcohol in the human bloodstream and had performed his own experiments on the machine itself.

Examples where experts arguably strayed outside their proper areas of expertise include *R. v. Nielsen and Stolar*,[114] *R. v. Warren*,[115] and *R. v. Marquard*.[116] In *R. v. Woods*,[117] it was held that a pharmacologist can opine on drug effects but not whether an accused formed the required specific intent, as that required a qualified psychiatrist. In *R. v. Kinnie*,[118] it was held by the majority that a pharmacologist with a doctorate degree in biology was not qualified to testify as to the effect of taking prescription drugs and alcohol where the witness had no particular experience with the drug ingested by the accused.

It is always important to examine credentials carefully and not simply accept them at face value as having worth. Bogus or vacuous credentials do not come so designated on a witness's curriculum vitae or résumé, and they are not unheard of. Careful investigation is necessary to expose credentials of convenience. In a surprising number of cases, experts have lied about their credentials.[119]

---

112 (1976), 30 C.C.C. (2d) 470 (B.C. Co. Ct.) [*Edson*].
113 Above note 105.
114 (1984), [1985] 16 C.C.C. (3d) 39 at 69–70 (Man. C.A.).
115 Above note 87.
116 Above note 51.
117 (1982), 65 C.C.C. (2d) 554 (Ont. C.A.).
118 Above note 107.
119 Paul C. Giannelli, "Forensic Science Expert Qualifications: Traps for the Unwary" (2000) 36 Crim. L. Bull. 249 at 254.

In *Kline v. State (Florida)*,[120] a forensic hypnotist testifying for the defence in the Ted Bundy case falsely claimed he had a doctoral degree in clinical psychology. Affirming the expert's perjury conviction, the court said that "[m]isrepresentations which tend to bolster the credibility of a witness, whether successful or not, are regarded as material for purposes of supporting a perjury conviction."[121] In *Correll v. State (Florida)*,[122] the prosecutor in a capital murder case had called as an expert on blood splatters a woman who falsely claimed she had a high-school diploma and claimed she had been an assistant and technical specialist at the medical examiner's office for twelve years when actually she was a secretary for four of those years and a specialist for only five months. Other cases of false credentials have involved serologists,[123] arson experts,[124] and laboratory technicians.[125] A British "forensic lip-reader" who was accepted in several significant cases was discredited and dropped as an acceptable expert witness when a claimed credential was exposed as false.[126]

Furthermore, even technically accurate credentials may be worthless. An extreme example is described by Steve K. Dubrow Eichel in "Credentialing: It May Not Be the Cat's Meow."[127] Dr. Eichel tells how his cat became "Dr. Zoe D. Katze, Ph.D., C.Ht., DAP." Dr. Katze possesses certificates proving she is a Diplomate of the American Psychotherapy Association, a Registered Hypnotherapist of the American Board of Hypnotherapy, a Certified Hypnotherapist of the National Guild of Hypnotists, and a Certified Hypnotherapist from the International Medical and Dental Hypnotherapy Association.

Another example was given in Paul Giannelli's article:

> [A]n article in *The Wall Street Journal*, entitled "The Making of an Expert Witness: It's in the Credentials" discusses the American College of Forensic Examiners (ACFE), which makes $2.2 million a year certifying experts. The roots of this organization, according to its founder, can be traced to the *Daubert* decision, which (paradoxically) was intended to tighten the standards for ex-

---

120 444 So. 2d 1102 (Fla. Ct. App. 1 Dist. 1984).

121 *Ibid.* at 1104–5.

122 698 So. 2d 522 (Fla. 1997).

123 *Maddox v. Lord*, 818 F.2d 1058 at 1062 (2d Cir. 1987) (serologist); *Doepel v. United States*, 434 A.2d 449 at 460 (D.C. 1981) (FBI serologist).

124 *People (Illinois) v. Alfano*, 95 Ill. App. 3d 1026 at 1028–29 (Ill. Ct. App. 2 Dist. 1981) (arson expert).

125 *State (Kansas) v. Elder*, 433 P.2d 462 (Kan. 1967) (laboratory technician); *Commonwealth (Pennsylvania) v. Mount*, 257 A.2d 578 at 579 (Pa. 1969) (laboratory technician).

126 *R. v. Croitoru*, [2005] O.J. No. 6404 at paras. 90 to 102 (S.C.J.), referencing the lip-reader who appeared in *R. v. Luttrell*, [2004] EWCA Crim 1344.

127 Dr. Katze's story is online: www.dreichel.com/Articles/Dr_Zoe.htm.

pert testimony. This organization appears to be a "certification" mill. It cost $350 to get certified — just dial 1-800-4A-Expert. Professor Carol Henderson applied the term "checkbook credentials" to this type of certification procedure. Nevertheless, the "ACFE is the biggest credentialing body in forensic science and the only one that credentials experts in many specialties. It has 13,000 members and nearly 17,000 board-certified diplomates."[128]

NOVEL EXPERT EVIDENCE

ALL THE ABOVE requirements are said to be applied most strictly in the case of new forms of expert evidence regarding novel scientific measures. "Novel science is . . . subject to 'special scrutiny.'"[129]

With respect to reliability, the trial judge must be satisfied that the evidence "reflects a scientific theory or technique that has either gained acceptance in the scientific community, or if not accepted, is considered otherwise reliable in accordance with the methodology validating it."[130] The judge is to decide whether the novel technique is sufficiently reliable to put to the jury for its review, given the dangers that the evidence presents. The higher scrutiny is warranted for novel science because it involves both the usual risk that triers of fact may accept it uncritically, as well as the added risk that the opinions offered may be based on science that is wrong or overstated.[131] For excellent examples of the comprehensive consideration of novel science, see *R. v. Warren*[132] and *R. v. Johnston*.[133]

CHECKLIST

THE LEGAL PRINCIPLES regarding expert opinion evidence detailed above can be summarized in a checklist to ensure that no relevant consideration is overlooked. This checklist follows the scheme of the legal rule but elaborates it into the practical particulars relevant to each part of the rule, thus ensuring that

---

128 Above note 119 at 253.

129 *R. v. J-L.J.*, above note 10 at para. 35; *R. v. Mohan*, above note 9 at 25; *R. v. Pascoe*, above note 47; *R. v. A.K. and N.K.*, above note 1.

130 *R. v. Terceira*, above note 107 at 384 [cited to C.R.], dealing with the admissibility of DNA evidence.

131 *R. v. A.K. and N.K.*, above note 1 at paras. 85–86.

132 Above note 87.

133 (1992), 69 C.C.C. (3d) 395 (Ont. Ct. Gen. Div.).

nothing is overlooked by counsel in preparing to deal with the expert evidence on the admissibility hearing.

PROPERLY QUALIFIED EXPERT

- Has the proposed expert by virtue of education, training, or experience acquired special or peculiar knowledge in respect of the matters to be testified about?
- Even if the witness is an expert generally, is the subject matter of her testimony within her area of expertise?
- Even if the subject matter of her testimony is within her area of expertise are there any important tests or aspects of the evidence that are novel or outside the witness's experience?
- Have all the references on the witness's CV been verified and examined?
- Are any items stated or cast in a misleading and exaggerated positive fashion?

NECESSITY

- Is the evidence necessary — not merely relevant or even helpful or useful — in the sense that first, its substance is outside the experience and knowledge of the trier of fact, and second, there is no satisfactory alternative such as judicial notice or a jury instruction to otherwise provide the same "education?"

ABSENCE OF ANY EXCLUSIONARY RULE

- Does the evidence involve presentation of otherwise inadmissible hearsay or bad act evidence or evidence carrying the danger of propensity reasoning?
- Does the evidence involve express or implicit credibility judgments in favour of any witness and thus violate the rule against oath helping?

LOGICAL RELEVANCE

- Have all the facts and materials upon which the expert has relied in any way in forming his opinion been available (and examined)?
- Does the expert have an accurate understanding of *all* the relevant or material facts or data?

- Have any relevant or material facts or data been overlooked by the expert wittingly or unwittingly?
- What is the error rate of any test utilized?
- What is the witness's error rate in any test performed?
- Have any scientific principles or other rules or assumptions upon which the expert has relied in any way in forming his opinion been examined and evaluated for accuracy and acceptability?
- Have all the references been checked? Do they say what it is claimed they say?
- Is the opinion one of identity or merely sameness?
- Has the expert formulated his general conclusions based on an unsystematic collection of data (anecdotes) or a biased sample? Or without doing a comparison with a "control group"?
- Is the expert's opinion based on conclusions drawn in accordance with the rules of logic and proper reasoning? Are there any logical reasoning errors?
- Has the expert overlooked the issue of base rate?
- Is the opinion one of certainty or merely probability? If probability, are the probabilities accurately and fairly expressed?

LEGAL RELEVANCE

- Due to status or ostensible credentials does the witness pose the danger of unduly influencing the trier of fact?
- Is the evidence highly technical or complex?
- Will it consume inordinate time or trial resources, either directly or because of the responding evidence that will be necessary?
- How close is the evidence to the very issues to be decided?
- Does the evidence involve presentation of otherwise inadmissible hearsay or bad act evidence or evidence carrying the danger of propensity reasoning?
- Does the evidence involve express or implicit credibility judgments in favour of any Crown witness or against the accused?
- In a particular type of case or dealing with a particular expert witness, previous transcripts may be useful to support arguments about the factors involved here.
- Examples of the witness's language, examples of difficulties in cross-examination, and even examples of problems in locating supporting reference materials can be highlighted from previous cases. Comments on

the evidence from other judges or a demonstration that the evidence did not figure in the outcome in previous cases would also be useful in arguing legal relevance.

CHAPTER 4

Science: Some Basic Concepts

GIVEN THAT THE rules of admission and valuation of expert evidence need to be based on the scientific method to save the justice system from beguiling but worthless, fallacious, or misleading "expertise," the time has come to focus on the unrivalled achievement called science and to understand why it is so informative.[1]

THE SCIENTIFIC METHOD

THE SCIENTIFIC METHOD is simply a set of procedures — logically and demonstrably effective — for testing the validity of empirical claims. "Science" is

---

1   Some references I have found useful include Robyn M. Dawes, *Rational Choice in an Uncertain World* (New York: Harcourt Brace Jovanovich, 1988); Julian Meltzoff, *Critical Thinking about Research — Psychology and Related Fields* (Washington, DC: American Psychological Association, 1998); Jeffrey Katzer, Kenneth H. Cook, & Wayne W. Crouch, *Evaluating Information: A Guide for Users of Social Science Research*, 2d ed. (New York: Random House, 1982): "Much information reported by scientists, published in reputable journals, and used by students, practicing professionals, and the general public is misleading. Some of it is just plain wrong. The purpose of this book is to help you detect such misinformation"; Kenneth R. Foster & Peter W. Huber, *Judging Science: Scientific Knowledge and the Federal Courts* (Cambridge, MA: MIT Press, 1999) at 148–50: "The mere fact that research reports are published, even in the most prestigious journals, is no guarantee of their quality." Fred Wilson, *The Logic and Methodology of Science and Pseudoscience* (Toronto: Canadian Scholars' Press, 2000); Stephen S. Carey, *A Beginner's Guide to Scientific Method*, 2d ed. (Belmont, CA: Wadsworth, 1997); and Arthur Strahler, *Understanding Science: An Introduction to Concepts and Issues* (Buffalo, NY: Prometheus Books, 1992).

a process, not a product, that makes phenomena recognizable and predicts outcomes. It and it alone has put planes in the air, bridged giant valleys, prolonged life expectancy (and is still doing so), and allowed us to understand phenomena from the closest point at hand to the farthest reaches of the universe. Its fundamental activities comprise:

- observing and describing phenomena and developing general conclusions about them;
- integrating new data with organized observations that have been confirmed;
- formulating testable hypotheses based on the results of such integration;
- testing such hypotheses under controlled, repeatable conditions;
- observing the results of such testing, recording them unambiguously, and interpreting them logically and clearly; and
- seeking criticism from fellow participants in the endeavour called "science."

In a leading work on scientific evidence,[2] its authors state:

Science is neither mechanical nor magical. It is a process of drawing inferences from evidence. The evidence for those inferences is generated by research which necessarily employs a selection of research methods. A finding is only as good as the methods used to find it. There is no one best way to study a phenomenon of interest. Each methodological choice involves tradeoffs. The issue, always, is whether the methodology of the research is appropriate for the questions posed by the study, and whether the conclusions drawn are justifiable in light of the data collected and everything about the methods by which those data were generated. The choices of methods require careful thought, both by researchers and consumers of the research.[3]

If the tests or experiments bear out the hypothesis, it may come to be regarded as a theory or law of nature. If the experiments do not bear out the hypothesis, it must be rejected or modified. The physicist Richard Feynman put it so well: science is what we have learned about how to keep from fooling ourselves.[4]

---

2   David L. Faigman *et al.*, *Modern Scientific Evidence*, 2 vols. (St. Paul, MN: West, 1997).
3   *Ibid.*, vol. 1, c. 2 at 80. The entire section from 47 to 82 "constitutes a primer on scientific method."
4   This reference cannot be sourced although the quote is ubiquitous on the Internet. It may be a corruption of what Feynman actually said on the following occasion: "Science is a way of trying not to fool yourself. The first principle is that you must not fool yourself, and you are the easiest person to fool." From "What Is and What Should Be the Role of Scientific Culture in Modern Society," presented at the Galileo Symposium in Italy, 1964.

A classic example of the scientific method's defeat of authoritative wrong-headedness is the "childbed fever" chapter in nineteenth-century medicine.[5] Ignaz Semmelweis, a young Hungarian doctor working in the obstetrical ward of Vienna General Hospital in the late 1840s, was dismayed at the high death rate among his patients. He had noticed that nearly 20 percent of the women under his and his colleagues' care in Division I of the ward (i.e., the division attended by physicians and male medical students) died shortly after childbirth. This phenomenon had come to be known as "childbed fever." Alarmingly, Semmelweis noted that this death rate was four to five times greater than that in Division II of the ward (i.e., the division attended by female midwifery students).

On one particular occasion, Semmelweis and some of his colleagues were in the autopsy room performing autopsies as they often did between deliveries. They were discussing their concerns about death rates from childbed fever. One of Semmelweis's friends was distracted by the conversation, and he punctured his finger with the scalpel. Days later, Semmelweis's friend became quite sick, showing symptoms not unlike those of childbed fever.

This observation, however tragic, suggested a link between the performing of autopsies and the childbed fever being suffered by women being seen by medical staff immediately after the autopsies. The next step was to "test" this hypothesis, however vague and apparently ill formed. Semmelweis instituted a strict hand-washing policy among his male medical students and physician colleagues in Division I of the ward. Everyone was required to wash his hands with chlorinated lime water before attending patients. Mortality rates immediately dropped from 18.3 percent to 1.3 percent and, in fact, not a single woman died from childbirth between March and August of 1848 in Semmelweis's division.

Thus, even before medical science had reached the stage where a theory or explanation was possible, because the discovery of germs and other invisible disease carriers still lay in the future, observation leading to hypothesis leading to systematic testing achieved remarkable results. This obvious lesson from the childbed fever example is important; but even more important is a second lesson that demonstrates both the importance of science and also the hurdles it must overcome.

Despite the dramatic reduction in the mortality rate in Semmelweis's ward, his colleagues and the greater medical community greeted his findings with hostility. To the "experts" of the day, the idea that disease might be carried by invisible entities from person to person was preposterous. Even after presenting

---

5   Described in various sources. See, for example, Christa Colyer, "Childbed Fever: A Nineteenth-Century Mystery," online: www.sciencecases.org/childbed_fever/childbed_fever.asp.

his work on childbed fever (more technically referred to as puerperal sepsis) to the Viennese Medical Society, Semmelweis was not able to secure the teaching post he desired, and so he returned to Hungary. There, he repeated his successful hand-washing attack on childbed fever at the St. Rochus Hospital in Pest. In 1860, Semmelweis finally published his principal work on the subject of puerperal sepsis but this, too, it is said, was dismissed by the contemporary medical community. Semmelweis died in 1865 apparently without receiving the recognition that he deserved.

As this classic example demonstrates, this methodology known as science does not come naturally or intuitively.[6] It had to be discovered as a curative for human beings' innate *inability* to form valid and reliable beliefs. Our brains are designed for our physical and emotional survival, not our wisdom. They are designed to believe; they have to be trained how to know. Left to their own devices, our brains take in information from the outside world that is heavily laced with our preconceptions, biases, cultural perspectives, and the like. External reality becomes congruent with our internal beliefs, and not the other way around. Evidence to support pre-existing pet theories is astonishingly easily found, though surprisingly it disappears when sought by nonbelieving investigators. Our brains have an Olympian ability to jump to conclusions, and they will, for example, decide that A caused B simply because A occurred before B. They will also commit reasoning errors and fallacies so routine and mundane they were catalogued by the ancients three thousand years ago, but so ingrained and persistent that three thousand years of warnings against them have done nothing to abate their prevalence.

One author, comparing science to religion, has made a compelling argument that the former is much more difficult for the human animal than the latter and thus explains the constant never-ending human struggle against foolishness, bad reasoning, and false beliefs:

> Science showed not only that some stories about the formation of planets were decidedly below par but also that there was something dramatically flawed in principle about religion as a way of knowing things and that there was a better way of gathering reliable information about the world.
>
> Religious concepts ... invariably recruit the resources of mental systems that would be there, religion or no. This is why religion is a *likely* thing. That is, our minds' evolved dispositions, the way we live in groups, the way we communicate with other people and the way we produce inferences, it is very likely

---

6   See generally Lewis Wolpert, *The Unnatural Nature of Science* (London: Faber & Faber, 1992).

that we will find in any human group some religious representations of the form described in this book.

...

In contrast ... scientific activity is quite "unnatural" given our cognitive dispositions.... This is why acquiring some part of the scientific database is usually more difficult than acquiring religious representations.

What makes scientific knowledge-gathering special is not just its departure from our spontaneous intuitions but also the special kind of communication it requires, not just the way one mind works but also how other minds react to the information communicated. Scientific progress is brought about by a very odd form of social interaction, in which some of our motivational systems (a desire to reduce uncertainty, to impress other people, to gain status, as well as the aesthetic appeal of ingenuity) are recruited for purposes quite different from their evolutionary background. In other words, scientific activity is both cognitively and socially very *unlikely*, which is why it has only been developed by a very small number of people, in a small number of places, for what is only a minuscule part of our evolutionary history.

... [Science] is every bit as "unnatural" to the human mind as religion is "natural."[7]

History also provides an interesting intellectual justification for scientific literacy: the scientific method and the recognition of basic human rights are related fundamental insights that historically arose from the same intellectual struggle.

The two progeny of the Enlightenment, democracy and the scientific method ... are indeed siblings. Both democracy and the scientific method — empirical experimentation designed to approach objective truth — are closely related in their preference for intellectual authority over institutional authority, their insistence on universalism and objectivity, and their intellectual skepticism. In science as in democracy, what matters is not who says it but whether it is right. We are all free to reject another's beliefs, and no dogma is too sacred to challenge.[8]

More generally, the age-old dichotomy between Platonic rationalism and Aristotelian empiricism was resolved when Newton showed the immense intellectual power that resulted from combining reason and observation, just as

7   Pascal Boyer, *Religion Explained: The Evolutionary Origins of Religious Thought* (New York: Basic Books, 2001) at 321–22.

8   Daniel A. Farber & Suzanna Sherry, *Beyond All Reason: The Radical Assault on Truth in American Law* (New York: Oxford University Press, 1997) at 106–8.

Bacon had predicted. As obvious as this may seem to us now, it had generally been denied up until then because it undercut the basic religious principle that knowledge of God comes from intuition. Religion must deny the importance of empiricism because none of its doctrines can be validated empirically. But once empiricism is accepted as the equal partner of reason, the whole world — and everything one has ever been told about it — becomes open to inquiry.

. . .

Thus it was that revolutionary thinking in science stimulated revolutionary thinking in social and political philosophy.[9]

Not all the childbed fever examples are in the past. The contemporary example of "facilitated communication" (FC) is another demonstration of how sheltered pet theories and wishful "expert" thinking (like those of Semmelweis's opponents) continue unabated.[10] Facilitated communication is a supposed way for autistic children to communicate via a facilitator and a computer terminal. It was originally developed for use with subjects whose cognitive abilities were normal, but whose communicative ability was impaired. FC then started to be used with subjects whose cognitive abilities were unproved. This difference and its implications were ignored. FC was developed in Australia in the 1970s and imported to the United States in the late 1980s by Dr. Douglas Biklen, who eventually became associated with Syracuse University in New York. There, Dr. Biklen established a following, with the result that New York is currently the state where FC is most widely practised. FC believers produced case reports, established associations, published a journal, established standards for practice, and began training programs, adopting all the paraphernalia of a "science." However, simple controlled experiments have shown that where the child and the facilitator do not have the same knowledge, it is virtually always the facilitator's knowledge that is reported. FC seems incapable of producing communication that is unknown to the facilitator. One authoritative examination of the subject concluded:

Facilitated communication (FC) is a method of assisting people with severe developmental disabilities to communicate. Before its adoption as a teaching-

---

9   Alan Cromer, *Connected Knowledge: Science, Philosophy, and Education* (New York: Oxford University Press, 1997) at 110.

10 Brian J. Gorman, "Facilitated Communication in America: Eight Years and Counting" (1998) 6:3 Skeptic 64; Gina Green, "Facilitated Communication: Mental Miracle or Slight of Hand?" (1994) 2:3 Skeptic 68; Raymond G. Romanczyk *et al.*, "The Myriad of Controversial Treatments for Autism — A Critical Evaluation of Efficacy" in Scott O. Lilienfeld *et al.*, eds., *Science and Pseudoscience in Clinical Psychology* (New York & London: Guilford Press, 2003) c. 13 at 365–69.

treatment technique, the only research evidence in support of its validity consisted of a small number of descriptive reports in the professional literature and anecdotal reports in the popular press and disability media. In use, this technique, which involves providing physical support to people with disabilities as they type out messages on a keyboard or letterboard, appears to result in unexpected literacy and to disclose normative or superior intellectual skills among people with lifelong histories of severe developmental delay. Controlled research using single and double blind procedures in laboratory and natural settings with a range of clinical populations with which FC is used have determined that, not only are the people with disabilities unable to respond accurately to label or describe stimuli unseen by their assistants, but that the responses are controlled by the assistants.[11]

The proponents of FC can wish and hope and believe all they want, but that does not prove their claims the way the data from a well-designed empirical study would. If tests consistently show that FC cannot accurately communicate information from the subjects, but only the facilitators, its continued existence and support is a testament to the power of junk science and the ability to believe despite, not because of, evidence.

For the time being, FC, unlike Cold Fusion, lives on with the blessing of one of the nation's largest universities. Syracuse continues to sponsor revenue raising seminars and offer FC related products through the FCI and its internet homepage. Thus, FC remains a tool for raising money at Syracuse despite its rejection by the scientific community, and thus stands as a classic example of pseudoscience in the service of emotion.[12]

It is a sad commentary that FC was not relegated to history's dustbin. The regret is not just theoretical. Soon allegations of abuse started to arise, supposedly from the autistic children. According to a press report in 1996,[13] through FC a couple's autistic son allegedly accused them both of repeated sexual assault. They were both arrested and spent a considerable amount of money defending

---

11 John W. Jacobson, James A. Mulick, & Allen A. Schwartz, "A History of Facilitated Communication: Science, Pseudoscience, and Antiscience — Science Working Group on Facilitated Communication" (1995) 50:9 Am. Psychol. 750–65. It is not unfair to call FC a forensic Ouija board because it is the same small muscle movements involved that account for the channeller's movements on the Ouija board.

12 Gorman, above note 10 at 71.

13 "Autism 'Miracle' a Nightmare for Family" *The Toronto Star* (21 January 1996) 1. See also *Children's Aid Society Belleville (City) v. M.(S.),* [1993] O.J. No. 2963 (Prov. Div.); *Auton (Guardian ad litem of) v. British Columbia (Minister of Health),* [2000] B.C.J. No. 1547 (S.C.).

themselves. The charges were dropped the day before the scheduled trial when tests at Toronto's Clark Institute of Psychiatry revealed that the boy could not count beyond three, despite supposedly claiming to have been assaulted nine times, and was unaware of his own or others' sex. Tests showed that he could not describe objects that he had seen but which had not been seen by his "facilitators." The couple have filed an $8.5 million suit against York Region police, the York Region Catholic Separate School Board, and Christian Horizons, Inc., operator of the group home where their son lived.

It is important to understand that the perceptual and logical failings demonstrated in the foregoing passages are not malevolent. The errors and biases are not inexplicable, random, thinking errors. Through science, they are quite understandable and explicable. The clearest finding about human reasoning error is that we err in systematic ways. Such errors reflect the operations of mental mechanisms and strategies that generally serve the human organism well in many circumstances, though not in the particular context. They are "domain specific" failings.[14] And because they are systematic they are knowable, understandable, and therefore avoidable. Simply put, that is what scientific literacy is all about. Scientific reasoning is controlled thinking,[15] the disciplined version of what human beings do constantly, but the version that seeks to eliminate false beliefs and reasoning errors by knowing how to know, having learned how to learn.

Scientists aim to minimize potential errors in their investigation of the external world by using standard procedures and criteria that are demonstrably effective. The essence of the experimental method is the manipulation and control of the events to be studied so that findings are generated from which valid, logical conclusions can be drawn. And the entire process is recorded so that examination and repetition can occur. What must be emphasized is that the validity and reliability of opinions lie in their underlying methodology. Reliance on the personal authority of any expert, however pre-eminent, is the fallacy of appeal to authority. It is an acceptance of faith, not based on objective assessment.

Methodology — the logic of research design, measures, and procedures — is the engine that generates knowledge that is scientific and real. Observation (or

14 See Thomas Gilovich, *How We Know What Isn't So: The Fallibility of Human Reason in Everyday Life* (New York: The Free Press, 1991): "It ain't the things we don't know that get us into trouble. It's the things we know that just ain't so." How we "know" so much that is not so, why we persist to believe in the face of evidence to the contrary, why more people believe in ESP than evolution, how our perceptual and cognitive mechanisms doom us to mistaken beliefs, is the subject matter of this book.

15 Robyn M. Dawes, *Rational Choice in an Uncertain World*, above note 1 at 4–5.

hunch or guess) is a starting point for science in suggesting areas of inquiry, but the whole point of real science is to test observation (or hunch or guess) systematically. As Carl Sagan allegedly put it, credibility is the product of methodology.[16] And as an American judge put it after *Daubert*,[17] "[o]ur task, then, is to analyze not what the experts say, but what basis they have for saying it."

Recent research on the use of insects to determine time of death provides a graphic illustration.

An investigation of the way insects colonise corpses left decomposing in the open has cast doubt on one of the key techniques used to estimate when a murder victim died.

Along with assessments of the body's state of decomposition, insect analysis is the most common means for estimating time of death. Many species of flies and beetles may live on a human body as it decomposes. By identifying their stage of development, and comparing them to those on a pig or human body deliberately left to rot in a similar environment, forensic entomologists can work out how long a corpse has been lying dead. These estimates are often claimed to be accurate to within months or weeks — or even days if the body has been dead for less than a month. In an experiment to test the accuracy of insect analysis, Melanie Archer of the Victorian Institute of Forensic Medicine in Melbourne, Australia, placed five piglet carcasses in scavenger-proof wire cages in bush land. At least once a week for four months she identified the insects living on the carcasses and on the ground underneath them. She repeated the experiment each season for two years. Blowfly maggots: Archer found unexpected variations. For example, blowfly maggots left the carcasses after nine weeks in the first winter, but after only four weeks in the second winter. A beetle species, *Creophilus erythrocephalus*, arrived after four weeks in the first winter, but after only two in the second

The differences could be due to several factors, such as varying weather or changes in insect numbers. But until now, Archer says, none of the published studies on reference corpses has been repeated over successive years, so no one takes the variations into account. Another potential source of error lies in the

---

16 Carl Sagan, a twentieth-century astronomer whose work with NASA is well-known, also produced award-winning science books and television programs, aimed at educating and exciting the general public. Books such as *Broca's Brain: Reflections on the Romance of Science*, *The Dragons of Eden: Speculation on the Evolution of Human Intelligence*, and *Cosmos* made science popular without ever sacrificing rigorous standards of truth.

17 *Daubert v. Merrell Dow Pharmaceuticals*, 43 F.3d 1311 at 1316 (1995), on remand from *Daubert v. Merrell Dow Pharmaceuticals*, 509 U.S. 579 (1993) [*Daubert*]. See chapter 2, section titled "U.S. Developments" for details on the *Daubert* case.

way temperatures are estimated, Archer found. Insect infestation of a corpse is strongly affected by temperature.[18]

SCIENTIFIC LITERACY

SCIENTIFIC LITERACY — a knowledge of the scientific method and the ways and means of science — is necessary no matter how the legal rule regarding the admissibility of expert evidence is formulated. If the legal rule is grounded in the requirements of science, as in the United States and arguably Canada, then that knowledge is needed to debate admissibility. Scientific literacy is also needed to properly assess expert testimony, its limitations and weaknesses. If, as in England, the legal rule admits opinions more loosely, including those that fail to meet the standards of science, then scientific literacy is required to expose these weaknesses.

In short, expert opinion evidence must be subjected to vigorous scrutiny, either by the judge of law or the trier of fact. That scrutiny of everything from the data, references, and assumptions to the logic and conclusions of the opinion is only effective if it is ultimately grounded in a knowledge of science. Requiring that expert opinion evidence meets the demands of good science involves the following basic matters of principle.

ACCURATE RECORDING OF MEANINGFUL DATA

FIRST AND FOREMOST, science is based upon evidence. History is replete with beautiful explanations that sprang full blown from the human mind, only to turn out to be completely wrong. This is what Thomas H. Huxley was alluding to as the "great tragedy of Science — the slaying of a beautiful hypothesis by an ugly fact."[19]

It is useful to recall Galileo's debate with Church officials concerning whether it was the Sun or the Earth that revolved around the other. Galileo kept urging: "Just look through the telescope, just look through the telescope." The Church's intricate, rationalized doctrine, along with the Sun's daily observable east to west travel, made it irrefutable that the Sun travelled around the Earth; it was "obvious" there was no need to examine the evidence. Needless to say,

---

18   Rachel Nowak, "Murder Detectives Must Rethink Maggot Theory," *New Scientist* (April 2004), online: www.newscientist.com/article/dn4836.

19   The *Quotations Page* online: http://quotationspage.com/subjects/science/21.html.

such "knowledge" was the stuff of religion, not science. Many expert witnesses, especially of the treatment-oriented clinical sort, such as clinical psychologists and social workers, have been forced to their regret, in cross-examination, to metaphorically "look through the telescope."

The clear documentation of objective evidence is the most basic requirement of science. For the evidence to have substance, all concepts under discussion must be meaningful and capable of measurement. Measurement, even if it only consists of noting the presence or absence of the characteristic of interest, requires objective standards, a counting or measurement of something capable of being counted or measured. Otherwise, all that is obtained is unreliable, subjective pronouncements. Subjective measurements are meaningless as support for any conclusions.

Thus, declaring that sex abuse destroys the victim's self-esteem requires, if it is to be anything other than a subjective impression, a clear standard for the measurement of self-esteem. Many psychological concepts are fuzzy, and conclusions about them need to examine how they were measured. Ziskin appropriately refers to them as "literary definitions" involving ambiguity or uncertainty.[20]

Phrases such as "often," "most commonly," "not unusual," and "are likely" imply some quantification and some data. However, if there is no quantification but only reliance on personal experience and observations, the analysis is more personal speculation than science. More than forty years of research have demonstrated that clinical observations and experience are unreliable and are best used as a source for hypotheses that then must be carefully examined by a quantified approach.[21]

The accurate recording and documentation of the evidence for later re-examination is the next basic requirement.[22] Relying on memory as a record of observations or other data, as clinicians claim to do, is simply a recipe for scien-

---

20 Jay Ziskin, *Coping with Psychiatric and Psychological Testimony*, 3d ed., 2 vols. (Venice, CA: Law and Psychology Press, 1981) vol. 1 at 71–75.

21 H.J. Einhorn & R.M. Hogarth, "Confidence in Judgment: Persistence of the Illusion of Validity" (1978) 85:5 Psychol. Rev. 395; B. Brehmer, "In One Word: Not from Experience" (1980) 45 Acta Psychologica 223; R.M. Dawes, "Experience and Validity of Clinical Judgment: The Illusory Correlation" (1989) 7:4 Behav. Sci. & L. 457; R.M. Dawes, D. Faust, & P.E. Meehl, "Clinical versus Actuarial Judgment" (1989) 243 Science 1668–74; K.E. Stanovich, *How to Think Straight about Psychology*, 3d ed. (New York: HarperCollins, 1992).

22 In *R. v. J-L.J.*, [2000] 2 S.C.R. 600 at para. 57, the Court specifically criticized the expert witness because he "offered a packaged opinion but was not prepared to share with the trial judge the data which he relied on."

tific disaster.[23] There is great truth in the classic Chinese proverb: "The palest ink is better than the best memory."

If the data are to be found in other people's references, then this principle of transparency applies to those sources. Summaries of data or someone's interpretation of data is not science because of the real possibility of error made immune from detection by the lack of transparency. The records of all measurements and results must be accurately preserved, available for re-examination to verify the data and results claimed. This aspect of publicness is an important feature of science — the transparency that allows third parties to revisit and assess all aspects of the claimed foundation for a scientific conclusion. Accurate and complete records of all contacts, communications, and work done in connection with testing or research is a foundational requirement of good science.[24]

In *R. v. F.(D.S.)*,[25] "expert evidence" that was not completely "transparent" was held not to warrant setting aside the accused's conviction for the following reasons:

Although it would have been preferable if these studies had been produced and evidence had been led with respect to the methodology employed and the specific conclusions reached, I am satisfied that there was a sufficient basis to find that the subject matter of the admitted evidence met the test for reliability discussed in *McIntosh*. That, it seems to me, was the fundamental difference between the evidence that was admitted and the excluded evidence. I find no inconsistency in the trial judge's reasoning in this respect.

Next, the appellant argues that the trial judge erred in admitting the evidence because the studies referred to by Ms. Sinclair had not been produced. Although, as I said above, it would have been preferable if those studies had been made available, that is a matter that went to the weight not the admissibility of Ms. Sinclair's evidence. At trial, it was open to the defence to challenge Ms. Sinclair's general statements about the empirical or scientific support for her opinions. It did not do so. I do not think the trial judge erred in this respect.

23 Robyn Dawes, "Experience and Validity of Clinical Judgment: The Illusory Correlation" (1989) 7 Behav. Sci. & L. 457; Robyn Dawes, "Biases of Retrospection" (1991) 3:1 Issues in Child Abuse Accusations 25.
24 See The Honourable Fred Kaufman, Commissioner, *Report of the Kaufman Commission on Proceedings Involving Guy Paul Morin* (Toronto: Ministry of the Attorney General, 1998) at 351–54 [Kaufman Commission Report], online: www.attorneygeneral.jus.gov. on.ca/english/about/pubs/morin.
25 (1999), 23 C.R. (5th) 37 (Ont. C.A.).

In a properly prepared expert's report, the requisite contents should allow a reader to completely understand and personally observe what was done with what, why it was done, and what the outcomes were.[26] It is useful to recall that the second item in *Daubert's* list of factors relevant to scientific admissibility of expert evidence was peer review and publication of the theory, and the fourth was general acceptance of the methodology underlying the theory in the scientific community.[27] Both of these presuppose the publicness and transparency that are important elements of science.

Another point flowing from the publicness and publication requirements should be highlighted: replication and its consequences. The point of the publicness and transparency is to eliminate error through repetition. Science does not rely on once-only events or experiments because of the possibility of error in the best-designed situation. Science expects that important and significant results will be tested by repetition of the experiment, or better-designed ones, or variously designed ones that systematically test the conclusions being put forth.

The important consequence of these repeated tests is that real science experiences a "thickening of the evidence." Real phenomena and valid hypotheses soon come to be demonstrated in a variety of experiments and a multiplicity of theoretical settings. Sometimes an experimental result remains unfathomable until it is suddenly realized that the results in fact support some hypothesis whose relevance is only then recognized. Such serendipitous confirmations are often the hallmark of real scientific results.

On the other hand, junk science invariably fails to demonstrate this phenomenon. Instead, over time junk science is defended by "data dredging": literally, the marshalling of every shred of disparate and often obscure isolated results, comments, and references that can in some fashion be interpreted as confirmatory of the pet theory.[28] It is a useful rough guide in distinguishing real science from the bogus to do a quick examination of the supporting materials from this perspective.

---

26 Kaufman Commission Report, above note 24 at 331–33.

27 Above note 17 and see chapter 2 of this book for list of factors.

28 A classic example of this is "recovered memories." Based upon the theory its proponents offer, and given the realities of our relatively "cruel world," this should be a robust phenomenon supported by thickening evidence. Instead, as exemplified by a website dedicated to cataloguing every "corroborated case" of recovered memories, proponents are reduced to data-dredging and a relative handful of cases — at last count 101 — as all that can be offered. See online: www.brown.edu/Departments/Taubman_Center/Recovmem/archive.html, listing 101 Corroborated Cases of Recovered Memory shown as "43 Cases from Legal Proceedings, 25 Clinical Cases and other Academic/Scientific Case Studies, and 33 Other Corroborated Cases of Recovered Memory."

As well, negative results have much more significance than results that appear positive for a theory. This is especially true if there are numerous negative results, notwithstanding some positive results. If a phenomenon is real, those studying it should reach the point where they can reliably demonstrate it and where they can teach others to do so as well. Disparate results — some positive, many negative — indicate at least a foreshadowing of the theory's death knell, rather than a thickening of the evidence.

A related point can be made about the publication of data. Not surprisingly, just as "bank robbed today" is likely to make the newspaper whereas no one would think of publishing an article declaring "bank not robbed today," experiments announcing a positive result are more likely to be published, or perhaps even submitted for publication, than research reaching a negative result.[29] As a result, a review of the literature may reveal three positive studies and three studies reaching negative conclusions. It is important to bear in mind the greater significance of the latter. An overall assessment of all the studies against that background reality should be carried out in reaching a conclusion.

BIAS AND SUGGESTION

THE VERY ACTION of collecting data has built-in errors of bias and suggestibility that must be guarded against.[30] Experimenter bias, confirmation bias, or bias of observation reflects the reality that observing is not a neutral, mechanical exercise like electronic recording; whether running the test or being tested, knowledge and beliefs about a situation will influence responses, observations, and other data. The bias of interpretation occurs when people, including experimenters or other scientists, see what they want to see or what they expect to see[31] and jump to favoured conclusions.

---

29   Referred to as the "file drawer effect": what is "news" gets published, what is not stays in the file drawer. See, for example, Scott O. Lilienfeld, James M. Wood, & Howard N. Garb, "The Scientific Status of Projective Techniques" (November 2000) 1:2 Psychological Science in the Public Interest 27: "Abstract — . . . This meta-analysis also provides the first clear evidence of substantial file drawer effects in the projectives literature as the effect sizes from published studies markedly exceeded those from unpublished studies."

30   See generally Raymond S. Nickerson, "Confirmation Bias: A Ubiquitous Phenomenon in Many Guises" (1998) 2:2 Rev. Gen. Psych. 175.

31   This issue is admirably discussed in the context of forensic identification tests in D. Michael Risinger et al., "The Daubert/Kumho Implications of Observer Effects in Forensic Science: Hidden Problems of Expectation and Suggestion" (2002) 90 Cal. L. Rev. 1. See also Lisa J. Steele, "'All We Want You to Do Is Confirm What We Already Know': A

An elementary principle of modern psychology is that the desires and expectations people possess influence their perceptions and interpretations of what
they observe. In other words, the results of observation depend upon the state
of the observer as well as the thing observed. This insight is not new; long
before cognitive scientists began formally studying the psychological foundations of such effects, the phenomenon was noticed and commented upon.
Julius Caesar, for instance, noted that "men generally believe quite freely that
which they want to be true."[32]

Another commentator writes:

If the examiner has a prior belief or expectation that two toolmarks will, or
will not, match, then two potential psychological biases arise. "Cognitive confirmation bias" is a tendency to seek out and interpret evidence in ways that fit
existing beliefs. "Behavioral confirmation bias," commonly referred to as the
self-fulfilling prophecy, is a tendency for people to unwittingly procure support for their beliefs through their own behavior.[49] The danger of confirmation bias affecting an examiner's subjective opinion is rarely discussed in the
firearms examination literature or in the court cases upholding admissibility
of the technique.

Confirmation bias has caused famous scientists to fail to report easily visible phenomena that do not conform to their expectations[50] and to "observe"
non-existent phenomena.[51] Expectations have caused laboratory workers un-
consciously to conform test results to an expected norm.[52][33]

Daubert Challenge to Firearms Identifications" (2002) 38 Crim. L. Bull. 466 at 474–75
and 477–78, and accompanying footnotes.

The influence of bias on experts was expressly recognized in *R. v. Howard*, [1989] 1
S.C.R. 1337 at 1348, where it was stated: "An expert cannot take into account facts that
are not subject to his professional expert assessment as they are irrelevant to his expert
assessment. *A fortiori*, the expert should not be told of and asked to take into account a
fact that is corroborative of one of the alternatives he is asked to scientifically determine as
that could inject bias into the application of his expertise." This precedent could be used
to build an argument against allowing suggestive identification procedures.

32 Risinger *et al., ibid.*

33 Steele, above note 31 at 474–75. Footnotes in Steele are summarized as follows:

[49] R.S. Nickerson, "Confirmation Bias: A Ubiquitous Phenomenon in Many
Guises" (1998) 2 Rev. Gen. Psych. 175–220; M. Snyder, "Motivational Foundations of
Behavioral Confirmation" (1992) 25 Advances in Experimental Soc. Psych. 67–114;
M. Zuckerman *et al.*, "Hypothesis Confirmation: The Joint Effect of Positive Test
Strategy and Acquiescence Response Set" (1995) 68 J. Personality & Soc. Psych.
52–60.

[50] Edwin G. Boring, "Newton and the Spectral Lines" (1962) 136 Science 600 at
600–1 (Sir Isaac Newton's failure to note absorption lines visible in his apparatus that

The same author gives the following highly relevant example:

One illustration of this problem occurred in a 1987 experiment involving hair samples. Students who were given hair samples from a crime scene and a single suspect in a suggestive manner had a 30.8 percent error rate. In contrast, students who were given hair samples from a crime scene and from five possible suspects had a 3.8 percent error rate. Similar errors should be expected from firearms examiners given suggestive information.[34]

Another study showed an even more dramatic effect:

Expert latent fingerprint examiners were presented with fingerprints taken from real criminal cases. Half of the prints had been previously judged as individualizations and the other half as exclusions. We're presented the same prints to the same experts who had judged them previously, but provided biasing contextual information in both the individualizations and exclusions. A control set of individualizations and exclusions was also re-presented as part of the study. The control set had no biasing contextual information associated with it. Each expert examined a total of eight past decisions. Two-thirds of the experts made inconsistent decisions.[35]

In another case, an individual whose fingerprint was *not* declared a match had his fingerprints subsequently declared a match after he became the police's main suspect in the murder.[36]

Risinger and colleagues observe that the cognitive biases they discuss can introduce errors at every stage of analysis. Thus, they conclude, cognitive biases may create:

---

did not conform to his theory). See generally Risinger *et al.*, "The *Daubert/Kumho* Implications of Observer Effects in Forensic Science: Hidden Problems of Expectation and Suggestion" (2002) 90:1 Cal. L. Rev. 1.

[51] See generally Risinger *et al.*, *ibid.*

[52] Berkson, "The Error of Estimate of the Blood Cell Count as Made with the Hemocytometer" (1940) 128 Am. J. Physiology 309 at 322; Johnson, "Seeing's Believing" (1953) 15 New Biology 60 at 79; Cordaro & Ison, "The Psychology of the Scientist: X. Observer Bias in Classical Conditioning of the Planarian" (1963) 13 Psychol. Rep. 787. See generally Risinger *et al.*, *ibid.*

34 Steele, *ibid.* at 478.
35 Itiel E. Dror *et al.*, "Why Experts Make Errors" (2006) 56 J. Forensic Identification 600. Dr. Dror is a leading researcher into bias in the area of expert evidence. See his website: http://users.ecs.soton.ac.uk/id/biometrics.html.
36 Elizabeth F. Loftus & Simon A. Cole, "Contaminated Evidence" (2004) 304 Science, Issue 5673 at 959.

- Errors of Apprehending (errors that occur at the stage of initial perception);
- Errors of Recording (errors that creep in at the stage where what is observed is recorded, assuming a record beyond memory is even made);
- Errors of Memory (errors that are induced by both desires and the need for schematic consistency, and that escalate over time when memory is relied on);
- Errors of Computation (errors that occur when correct observations accurately recorded or remembered are transformed into incorrect results when calculations are performed on them); and
- Errors of Interpretation (errors that occur when examiners draw incorrect conclusions from the data).[37]

These perceptual and intellectual biases are most likely to operate in certain conditions: where the data or processes are ambiguous, where the wrong conclusion is already available, and where bias is a motivating factor. Forensic evidence provides a fertile environment: "match" tests such as fingerprints, toolmarks, and handwriting comparisons generally involve ambiguous data where one can "see" what one "wants" to see. Further, the tests are done by a one-to-one matching process so the conclusion that the unknown matches the suspect can be readily reached (as opposed to selecting the match from a "lineup" where the suspect's evidence is not readily known). Finally, forensic evidence involves the criminal justice context: the conviction of generally undesirable individuals often charged with despicable crimes. Communications between investigators and examiners of evidence may involve expressions of the enormous significance of determining a match so that an innocent victim may secure justice by the conviction and imprisonment of a despicable accused who, if not convicted, may go on to rape or murder again. Criminal forensic evidence currently is practised in a hothouse environment where the high motives of those involved in crime detection and solution provide a setting for the perceptual and intellectual biases to flourish. These issues are particularly significant where the expert witnesses are in fact police officers or related persons.[38]

"Anecdotal evidence" is simply a disparaging term for deficient observational evidence (assuming the teller is speaking first-hand). The inherent problems involving a bias in reporting, a bias in observing, and a bias in interpreting explain science's difficulties with professions such as the clinical ones that refuse to understand the problematic nature of their "case studies."

37 Risinger *et al.*, above note 31 at 25–26.
38 *R. v. Klassen*, [2003] M.J. No. 417 (Q.B.).

Clinical experience is only a prestigious synonym for anecdotal evidence when the anecdotes are told by someone with a professional degree and a license to practice a healing art.

. . .

It is the same old error of "men mark where they hit, and not where they miss." . . . This is not a complicated problem in epistemology or higher mathematics; it is simply the ineradicable tendency of the human mind to select instances for generalizations that it favours. It is the chief source of superstitions.

. . .

All policymakers should know that a practitioner who claims not to need any statistical or experimental studies but relies solely on clinical experience as adequate justification, by that very claim is shown to be a nonscientifically minded person whose professional judgments are not to be trusted.[39]

Data collection must be structured so as to be immune from contamination by subjective expectations of the experimenters, but a similar danger arises from expectations or beliefs on the part of the subjects being tested or examined. Their responses can be affected by their subjective beliefs. Expectation bias, or subjects telling the examiner what they believe the examiner wants to hear, or behaving in a way that they believe is expected, can affect any research involving human subjects. This is why verbal reports are not acceptable for measurement or recording of a phenomenon, aside from the fact that verbal reports are also, of course, prone to all the errors that result from the inevitable deficiencies of human memory.[40]

---

39 William M. Grove & Paul Meehl, "Comparative Efficiency of Informal (Subjective, Impressionistic) and Formal (Mechanical, Algorithmic) Prediction Procedures: The Clinical-Statistical Controversy" (June 1996) 2:2 Psychol., Pub. Pol'y & L. 293 at 302, 308, and 320.

40 For example, see Carol Tavris, *The Mismeasure of Woman* (New York: Simon & Shuster, 1992) at 145: The evidence for the existence of premenstrual syndrome depends on retrospective questionnaires wherein female subjects will often recount depression, weepiness, and other *indicia* at the relevant time of the month. However, when the same subjects have recorded their actual daily emotional states in contemporaneous diary entries, any evidence for PMS disappears.

In one study (*ibid.* at 18), the evidence was so contrary the researcher wryly concluded she had found evidence for a "premenstrual elation syndrome."

"When clients try to understand why they have behaved maladaptively or why they are distressed, their memories may be affected by their implicit theories about the causes of behaviors and feelings . . . . For example, if an individual believes that stress can cause maladaptive behavior or distress, and if the person behaves maladaptively or experiences distress, then the person's memories may become distorted and the person may be inclined

Suggestive influences can arise from the very questions asked. Ask someone: "How often do you get a headache?" and the mean answer may be 1 per week. Ask instead: "Do you get headaches frequently, and if so, how often?" and the mean answer will rise to 2.2 per week. Ask instead: "Do you get headaches occasionally, and if so, how often?" and the mean answer will drop to 0.5 per week. Ask: "How many car trips do you take a month: 10, 30, 50, 100?" and the mean answer may be 60. Ask: "How many car trips do you take a month: 10, 20, 30, 40?" and the mean answer may be 20. Asking "How long was the movie?" will produce a mean of 130 minutes, while asking "How short was the movie?" will produce a mean answer of 100 minutes.[41]

Asking people if they would "allow" something (e.g., speeches against democracy) will produce a different response than if the question were phrased in terms of whether they would "forbid" something. Generally, people are instinctively in favour of "allowing" and against "forbidding," no matter what is being spoken of. Thus, for any valid scientific research, the effects of suggestion as described above must be guarded against. Human beings are notoriously suggestible.[42] Any conclusions depending on human behaviour or reporting must be based upon an experimental design that is insulated against the effects of suggestion.[43]

In the scientific world such bias originating with the experimenters or the subjects is sought to be eliminated by the mechanism of "blind" and "double-blind" experimental design. In other words, the subjects (in the blind situation) and both the subjects and the experimenters (in the double-blind situation) are kept unknowing or "blinded" with respect to the design of the test, what is being done, and what is being sought after. If a medicine is being tested, some of the pills are placebos and neither the experimenters nor the test subjects know which they are receiving.

There is one particular category of data that deserves special mention in the forensic context: data about "sameness." Much expert evidence in the criminal

---

to recall that stressful events occurred": Howard N. Garb, *Studying the Clinician: Judgment Research and Psychological Assessment* (Washington, DC: American Psychological Association, 1998) at 86.

41 See Scott Plous, *The Psychology of Judgment and Decision Making* (New York: McGraw-Hill, 1993) c. 6, "The Effects of Question Wording and Framing" at 64–76.

42 See, for example, Plous, *ibid.*, c. 3, "Memory and Hindsight Bias" at 31–37, and c. 6, "The Effects of Question Wording and Framing" at 64–76; Jeffrey Katzer, Kenneth H. Cook, & Wayne W. Crouch, *Evaluating Information: A Guide for Users of Social Science Research*, 3d ed. (Boston: McGraw-Hill, 1991) c. 3, "Observation: Seeing Is Not Believing" at 27–38, and c. 6, "Bias: A Systematic Error" at 59–67.

43 This subject will be discussed in "Experimental Design and Research Quality," below in this chapter.

justice system is concerned with the opinion that two items are the same in the sense of having no distinguishable features. The scientific method requires that "sameness" be documented so that it can be independently verified. Photographic or other permanent records of the disparate items must be maintained so that their sameness can be observed by any other person who wishes to do so.[44]

Sometimes, however, sameness is a little more complicated. Sometimes the items do have dissimilarities, but the expert observer as a matter of expertise finds the dissimilarities explicable and insignificant, and so an opinion of identity is nevertheless offered.[45] In this situation, an observer looking at the same two items might not see the sameness that the expert has decided is present. In these cases, the expert's ability to determine sameness is in issue because the expert's opinion is not necessarily one that every observer would form. In such cases, science demands that the expert's opinion of identity be tested by proper experimental methods (as will be described in the next section), methods that avoid bias and the effects of suggestion and truly test whether the expert really can identify the items as being identical. In such cases, blind and double-blind testing of the expert's ability to identify is required before the opinion can be relied on.

> With respect to issues of sameness or identity, the lineup to test the recognition of persons is an example of a blind test procedure: the witness or test subject does not know who the suspect is, or even if a suspect is present when asked to observe the lineup to see if he or she can identify anyone. The procedure is improved even more to eliminate any suggestive influences if the lineup procedure is made double-blind by having the police personnel conducting the lineup equally ignorant of the identity of any suspects being presented.
>
> A similar logic applies to any test of identity where the result involves judgment or alleged expertise and is not simply a matter of naked perception. Science would respect such a conclusion only if established by a test involving blindness on the part of the examiner. A simple one-to-one comparison in-

---

44 In the context of firearms examinations, this point is well made in Steele, above note 31 at 482, n.86, as follows: "If the examiner has not taken pictomicrographs or will not make them available to the defense, defense counsel should be skeptical of the alleged identification . . . [W]ithout good photographs evidence of identification must consist merely of statements of opinion, when its value is not very great."

45 The phraseology used is that the examiner looks for "unaccountable differences," which is essentially undefined if not undefinable, and gives the examiner considerable subjective licence: see, for example, Clive A. Stafford Smith & Patrick D. Goodman, "Forensic Hair Comparison Analysis: Nineteenth Century Science or Twentieth Century Snake Oil?" (1996) 27 Colum. Hum. Rts. L. Rev. 227 at 243.

volves such obvious suggestive influences and dangers of confirmation bias as to be completely unscientific.[46]

Sound methodology for testing recognition, identification, and effects requires "blinding" the tester and the tested as much as possible to secure uninfluenced and effectively impartial results. These principles apply even to that epitome of scientific evidence — DNA evidence. A detailed example of this effect in the DNA context is found in William C. Thompson, "Examiner Bias in Forensic RFLP Analysis."[47] Thompson concludes:

> The danger of examiner bias has led scientists in many fields to insist that procedures for interpretation of potentially ambiguous data be either blind or objective. Both reports of the National Research Council call for the use of blind or objective "scoring" procedures by forensic DNA laboratories. But forensic laboratories have not followed the NRC's recommendations in this area. Their failure to do so cannot be explained on scientific grounds. If there is a scientific justification for the continued use of subjective interpretive procedures in forensic DNA testing, in the face of contrary recommendations from the broader scientific community, it has yet to be articulated in the forensic science literature.

Thompson also provides an informative primer on the subject for criminal defence counsel,[48] cautioning them not to be overawed by such evidence and advises them as follows regarding the DNA judgment of "match":

- Check the actual test results. Do they in fact "match" as claimed? Are there differences that the laboratory is ignoring? If the testing is not "blind" is extraneous knowledge influencing the examiner's judgment?
- Mixtures are difficult to interpret. The number of contributors can be problematic. Laboratories assume that taller peaks are associated with primary contributor and shorter peaks with a "secondary contributor." This is simply assumption and may not even be consistently applied (e.g., shorter peak is primary contributor when it matches the suspect).
- Degradation of samples causes problems by affecting peak heights and causing "noise" and fuzziness, turning interpretation into guesswork.

---

46 Risinger *et al.*, above note 31.
47 Online: www.scientific.org/case-in-point/articles/thompson/thompson.html.
48 Summarized from William C. Thompson *et al.*, "Part 1: Evaluating Forensic DNA Evidence: Essential Elements of a Competent Defense Review" *The Champion* (April 2003) at 17, online: www.bioforensics.com/articles/champion1/champion1.html. See also note 9 in chapter 1 of this book.

- Spurious peaks or technical artifacts are produced by unavoidable imperfections of the DNA analysis process. There are other problems making "match" a subjective judgment.

As a result, protection against the effects of bias and suggestibility has been suggested even for DNA sample examinations, in the form of sequential unmasking to prevent the examiner from being influenced by knowledge of the target's DNA profile.[49]

ERROR RATES

THOMPSON INTRODUCES THE important point regarding error rates as follows: "As a result, no matter how reliable DNA testing is, the examiner's error rate and the limits imposed by the above make DNA a less than perfect evidence." The concept of error rate regarding a test or conclusion is simply another way of recognizing chance (based upon mistake), and not actuality, as the explanation for the conclusion drawn. Errors may be explicable, by, for example, contamination,[50] or remain a mystery. Science recognizes there is a difference between a match and the reporting of a match. Logically, as previously stated, a judgment of "sameness", or other test result can never be given a greater weight than the prevailing error rate. The theoretical accuracy of a test assumes it is done correctly. Error rates on the part of the examiner or otherwise in carrying out the test represent an accuracy boundary in the real world generally far more limiting than the test's theoretical limitations.

> Statistical methods are used to calculate the probability that chance is so likely to be the explanation that we cannot accept the reliability of astrology. Perhaps to their dismay, judges in federal courts, and those of the twenty-one states that have accepted *Daubert* . . . must be conversant with the details of scientific testing and inferential statistical analysis. The United States Supreme Court held that "in the case of a particular scientific technique, the court ordinarily should consider the known or potential rate of error . . . and the existence and maintenance of standards controlling the technique's operation." . . . Understanding the role of the error rate in reliability has three aspects: (1) appreciat-

---

49 D. Krane *et al.*, "Sequential Unmasking: A Means of Minimizing Observer Effects in Forensic DNA Interpretation" (2008) 53:4 J. Forensic Sci. 1006–7, online: www.bioforensics. com/articles/sequential_unmasking.html.

50 Kristen Edwards, "Ten Things about DNA Contamination That Lawyers Should Know" (2005) 29 Crim. L.J. 71.

ing the practical significance of a quantified statement regarding the likelihood of error; (2) interpreting the statistical significance of that measured error rate; and (3) evaluating the quality of the scientific method underlying the measurement.

. . .

1. Error Rates: Practical Significance

There are two relevant aspects to error rate. The first is a summary measure of how consistent and strong the theory is in correctly predicting outcomes. Testing of fingerprint identification methods may show that technicians correctly match the print to the individual sixty percent of the time. This success rate is often described as one measure of the practical significance . . . of the test. Whether this success rate is high enough for the evidence to be admissible and ultimately for the fact-finder is a question in the first instance for the court.

The second aspect of error rate is a measure of whether the test is designed to distinguish between the reliability of the technique and other reasons for success. If crime lab technicians are only given prints from people about whom there is other strong evidence of guilt, it may be the investigators' other evidence, rather than the reliability of the technique, that accounts for successes. . . . Scientific studies are typically designed to produce both the first and second measures of error.[51]

Even the very high probability of a verdict of guilt arising in DNA cases from matching test results depends on an accurate result. The impressive substantive DNA test result probability, such as 1 in 25 million or 1 in 100 million, or whatever other impressive ratio is announced to show the accused must be guilty based upon the DNA test result, presumes that a DNA test result is an accurate one without error. In other words, it is presumed that the error rate for DNA testing is zero. Otherwise, the much greater chance of an incorrect DNA result undermines the value of the impressive probability of guilt.[52]

Error rates are always highly relevant. Error rates for examiners and laboratories are not logically irrelevant on the basis that errors in other cases have nothing to do with the issue "whether there was error in our case." This is simply another example of ignoring the logical relevance of the general presence of a phenomenon, something discussed below in the topic of base rates. Base rates

---

51 Lee Smolin, *The Trouble With Physics: The Rise of String Theory, the Fall of a Science, and What Comes Next* (Boston: Houghton Mifflin, 2006) at 319.

52 Thompson *et al.*, above note 48. See also note 9 in chapter 1 and text at chapter 5, note 9, of this book.

and error rates do not "prove" error in a particular case, but they are highly relevant to "*inform* estimates about the chance of an error in the focal case."[53]

EXPERIMENTAL DESIGN AND RESEARCH QUALITY

WITH RESPECT TO issues of sameness or identity, the lineup to test the recognition of persons is an example of a blind-test procedure: the witness or test subject does not know who the suspect is, or even if a suspect is present when asked to observe the lineup to see if she can identify anyone. The procedure is improved even more to eliminate any suggestive influences if the lineup procedure is made double-blind by having the police personnel conducting the lineup equally ignorant of the identity of any suspects being presented.

A similar logic applies to any test of identity where the result involves judgment or alleged expertise and is not simply a matter of naked perception. Science would respect such a conclusion only if established by a test involving blindness on the part of the examiner. A simple one-to-one comparison involves such obvious suggestive influences and dangers of confirmation bias as to be completely unscientific.[54] Sound methodology for testing recognition, identification, and effects requires blinding the tester and the tested as much as possible to secure uninfluenced and effectively impartial results. Tests of identification (e.g., fingerprints) and all identification procedures require the double-blind lineup protocol, not the show-up. These issues in the context of forensic tests are discussed in greater detail in chapter 5.

Just as bias must be eliminated from the acts of measuring and gathering data, it must also be eliminated from the very structure of the research. Drawing conclusions about a group or population based on only a sample of that group requires that the sample be representative. This is usually done by random selection. Anything else will only provide a biased, nonrepresentative sample that will make any findings of problematic application to the entire target group.

No one would think of purporting to gather data about the eating habits of the entire population by surveying only persons standing in line at the local McDonald's. But much research commits essentially that same fundamental error. History has recorded the most famous example:

---

53 Jonathan J. Koehler, "When Do Courts Think Base Rate Statistics Are Relevant?" (2002) 42 Jurimetrics 373 at 395, n.123 [emphasis in original].
54 See above note 31.

Hardly anyone writes about the folly of nonrepresentative sampling in surveys without mentioning the *Literary Digest* poll of 1936 . . . which occupies a unique niche in the history of sampling. In excess of 2.5 million people were asked their preference during the Franklin Roosevelt-Alf Landon presidential campaign. The poll predicted a rousing victory for Landon. For this the pollsters selected respondents from automobile registration and telephone listings. Because the country was in the midst of the Great Depression, however, people who owned cars and telephones were hardly representative of the entire population, nor were they in the Roosevelt camp. President Roosevelt was reelected in a landslide. The *Literary Digest* magazine became a metaphor, lost its social authority, and never recovered.[55]

Faigman and colleagues report how "doctors learned about the nature of the disease histoplasmosis by studying patients who came to their hospitals with the disease, and concluded that it was a rare disease which was almost always fatal."[56] By contrast, when the same disease was investigated among the general population, it was found to be more common and rarely dangerous. The doctors overlooked the implicit bias in their research methodology: the most serious cases would go to hospital while the more prevalent, less serious cases would stay home. Precisely the same mistake is made by child-abuse researchers who confine their studies to clients in therapy or clients who self-select for support or counselling groups. They are studying in effect a subgroup of the relevant population that is not representative. The group being studied is biased in its composition so that the results are useless for any generalization. Similarly, clinicians who purport to know that child abusers "never stop on their own" fail to appreciate the flaw in basing such conclusions upon the child abusers referred to them for treatment. The ones that stopped on their own would never be referred to come to their attention.

Furthermore, just as valid conclusions about a group being studied by means of a sample require a representative sample, so valid conclusions about a group require the study of nongroup members as well — the control group. Valid scientific knowledge can only come from comparison. The comparison group must be like the control group in all aspects except for the one being studied. For example, conclusions derived from the fact that 70 percent of arrested male sex offenders have some form of pornography in their residences are invalid without knowing whether or not 70 percent of males generally in that area would have such material. Studying a target group can only provide suggestions that lead to possible further exploration and testing.

55   Julian Meltzoff, *Critical Thinking about Research*, above note 1 at 50.
56   Above note 2, vol. 1 at 61.

As well, logic demands that a conclusion about a group or the probative value of evidence regarding a group characteristic or behaviour depends inevitably on knowledge about the nongroup or comparison sample. It may seem surprising that the concept of a control group needs defending, but this notion is not obvious to everyone. For example, a newspaper report cautioned airline travellers to note aircraft exits before takeoff because a survey of passengers who survived aircraft accidents found that 95 percent of them had done this. However, the reporter failed to note that those who had not survived could not be surveyed. Perhaps 95 percent of them had likewise noted the exits. Perhaps 97 percent of them would have reported so noting, in which case, would the conclusion be that noting the exits was actually detrimental to survival?

A problem of this type was a tragic reality in sex abuse prosecutions. For the longest time, prosecution experts were prepared to state that any physical finding they considered abnormal was the product of supposed sex abuse. But what is abnormal cannot be known without an examination of what is normal,[57] and only in recent years has such basic research been done.[58] *Bona fide* researchers were shocked to find that what they had been considering abnormal was in fact statistically normal in the general population.[59] Base rate studies of nonabused children indicate that many of the findings often used to support a diagnosis of

---

57 For example, "Experts have identified . . . age-inappropriate sexual behavior . . . as a primary predictor of sexual abuse . . . . One of the drawbacks to making this link is defining 'abnormal' sexual activities or knowledge. For example, masturbation is common in children; thus, the issue arises as to when masturbation is so excessive as to indicate sexual abuse. Moreover, a child's heightened sexual activity may result from stimulus other than sexual abuse, such as clandestinely observing parents or others engaging in sexual activity. 'In addition, highly sexualized behavior is sometimes seen in children who are not thought to have been abused'": Susan J. Becker, "Child Sexual Abuse Allegations against a Lesbian or Gay Parent in a Custody or Visitation Dispute: Battling the Overt and Insidious Bias of Experts and Judges" (1996) 74 Denv. U.L. Rev. 75, text accompanying notes 158–65, citing Howard Dubowitz *et al.*, "The Diagnosis of Child Sexual Abuse" (1992) 146 Am. J. Diseases Children 688 at 688.

58 J. McCann *et al.*, "Genital Findings in Prepubertal Girls Selected for Nonabuse: A Descriptive Study" (1990) 86:3 Pediatrics 428–39; J. McCann *et al.*, "Perianal Findings in Prepubertal Children Selected for Nonabuse: A Descriptive Study" (1989) 13 Child Abuse & Neglect 179; S.J. Emans *et al.*, "Genital Findings in Sexually Abused, Symptomatic and Asymptomatic Girls" (1987) 79 Pediatrics 778.

59 Debbie Nathan & Michael Snedeker, *Satan's Silence: Ritual Abuse and the Making of a Modern American Witch Hunt* (New York: Basic Books, 1995) c. 9, "The Medical Evidence" at 178–91. *R. v. O'Connor* (1995), 100 C.C.C. (3d) 285 (Ont. C.A.) is an example of a case where suspect gynecological evidence was admitted without objection at trial and upheld on appeal. *R. v. Dieffenbaugh* (1993), 80 C.C.C. (3d) 97 (B.C.C.A.) is an example of similar bad science in this area; "anal gaping" was properly rejected as expert evidence for lack of any established validity.

abuse are found with a high enough frequency in normals that they do not support an opinion that abuse occurred.[60] It is alleged that as a result, the leading researcher sardonically quipped, "It took us three years to find a 'normal.'"

The same point — the necessity for comparisons — has been made regarding nonphysical characteristics of allegedly abused children:

> Unhappily, many experts who testify about the characteristics of abused children claim to do so on the basis of their "experience," but claim to have little or no experience with children who weren't abused but who at one point claimed to have been. Hence, such experience is — not just "strictly speaking" but profoundly — irrelevant to "the determination of an action." Ironically, such pseudo-experts often try to support their alleged expertise by claiming that almost all the children they see claiming abuse have in fact been abused. If taken seriously, such a claim should automatically disqualify them as having any experience-based expertise in the matter of most urgent interest to the court, *which is the rational determination whether or not the child has been abused as claimed.*[61]

---

60 *Lillie v. Newcastle City Council*, [2002] EWHC 1600(Q.B.), Eady J. at para. 399: "It is important for me also to bear in mind that much attention has been given over the last 15 years or so to the scope and extent of 'normal' genital anatomy. As Dr. Watkeys explained, in girls there is recognised nowadays a wide range of attributes within the definition of 'normal' including the presence of nodules, notches, hymenal bands and adhesions."

   See generally J. McCann, J. Voris, & M. Simon, "Genital Injuries Resulting from Sexual Abuse: A Longitudinal Study" (1992) 89 Pediatrics 307; McCann *et al.*, "Comparison of Genital Examination Techniques in Prepubertal Girls" (1990) 85:2 Pediatrics 182–87; McCann *et al.*, "Genital Findings in Prepubertal Girls . . . ," above note 58; McCann *et al.*, "Perianal Findings in Prepubertal Children . . . ," above note 58.

61 Quoted in Debra A. Poole & D. Stephen Lindsay, "Assessing the Accuracy of Young Children's Reports: Lessons from the Investigation of Child Sexual Abuse" (1998) 7 Applied & Preventive Psychology 1 at 21 [emphasis in original]. The same author has elsewhere labelled this phenomenon "pseudodiagnosticity" as follows:

   > "Pseudodiagnosticity" refers to making an inference about the validity of a hypothesis *h* on the basis of evidence *e* without considering alternative hypotheses, in particular without considering the hypothesis *-h* . . . . People do that when they state that a bit of evidence is "consistent with" or "typical of" some hypothesis without concerning themselves about alternative hypotheses, or in particular the negation of the hypothesis. For example, after the William Kennedy Smith rape trial, a number of "experts" on a talk show expressed the opinion that they wish they could have testified in order to inform judge and jury of "what a rape victim was like." These experts who work in such places as women's shelters in fact had a great deal of experience with rape victims. What none had, however, was experience with women who claimed they were raped when they were not. But the whole point of the trial was to make a judgment about whether the person claiming was actually raped or not. Thus, all the experiences in the world with actual rape victims simply can yield some estimate of the probability of particular types of evidence given that person was a rape victim.

Another important requirement is the composition of the comparison or control group. For valid conclusions, the two groups must be the same in all respects except for the one element or variable being studied. Otherwise, any observations or results are attributable, at least in theory, to the other differences between the groups and not to the item being studied.

Thus, if an effect or outcome is being tested for (e.g., a fever is reduced, subliminal tapes through the night improve grades), membership as between the two groups must be assigned by random chance. Any other intentional or structured assignment opens the possibility of some other factor being responsible for any outcome. The concept of a random control group, simple as it sounds now, was one of science's most important insights. Remarkably, much so-called social science or clinical research remains abysmally ignorant:

> An investigator who is studying the benefits of group therapy for anxiety in wives of service personnel selects three groups of Marine wives at Camp Pendleton, California, and three groups at Camp Lejeune, North Carolina. Wives at both installations are pretested for anxiety on a valid and reliable test and are found to be equivalent on mean scores and standard deviations. Comparison on demographic characteristics such as age, length of marriage, children, living arrangements, show no differences. The Camp Pendleton wives attend twice a week group therapy sessions for 12 weeks. The Camp Lejeune groups meet a comparable number of times for social interaction but receive no psychotherapy. Posttest shows reduction in anxiety for the groups treated at Camp Pendleton but an increase in anxiety for the Camp Lejeune groups. The results are interpreted as showing clear benefits of group psychotherapy. *A sentence in the discussion section acknowledges that many of the husbands of the Camp Lejeune contingent were shipped overseas to a troubled hot spot during the period of the investigation.*[62]

Sometimes it takes some reflection to realize the impropriety of an alleged proper comparison group. Harvard University takes great pride in its academic record and the post-university success of its graduates. Statistics demonstrating that Harvard graduates earn significantly more and occupy significantly more successful government and corporate positions than non-Harvard graduates is used to justify a very substantial tuition structure.

But using that probability alone yields a "pseudodiagnostic" inference, because no comparison is made: Robyn M. Dawes, "Behavioral Decision Making and Judgment" in *The Handbook of Social Psychology* (Danile Gilbert, Susan Fiske, & Gardner Lindzey, eds., McGraw-Hill, 1996).

62 Meltzoff, above note 1 at 95 [emphasis added].

But is the comparison between Harvard graduates and non-Harvard graduates valid? Before giving credit for success to the Harvard education, should not the other possible "causes" of success, such as superior intelligence and qualities of character, be accounted for? Yet the two comparison groups are not necessarily equal in those respects. Persons who have not gone to Harvard include some comparable persons, surely, but also include all other persons who lack the qualities and abilities to succeed. In short, the comparison is not a fair one.

How should a comparison be done that controls for the qualities and characteristics of the individual students and allows measurement of any "Harvard effect"? One useful surrogate measure for such innate qualities would be admission to Harvard. It would be reasonable to assume that everyone granted admission into Harvard is roughly equal with regard to success factors. Thus, an appropriate comparison might be between Harvard graduates and other nongraduates who did not attend Harvard but who were in fact accepted to Harvard. This then allows the creation of two groups that differ only in the target feature: a Harvard education. When this comparison is made, the differences in future life success might substantially disappear. In other words, it is not that a Harvard education brings about success for Harvard graduates. It is that the same pre-existing qualities and characteristics that ultimately lead to success in fact enable such persons to get into Harvard and attend there if they wish to do so.

DRAWING CONCLUSIONS OR WHAT IT MEANS

ACCURATELY RECORDED MEANINGFUL data from a well-designed research enterprise is only part of the scientific method. The final significant component involves the procedures governing the interpretation of results. Good science requires a knowledge of the rules of logic and how valid conclusions are drawn. A proper logical understanding of research results does not necessarily require sophisticated analysis, but just a willingness to carefully reason through a situation before jumping to desired conclusions. The rules of logic are the antidote for the bias of interpretation that can confound any subsequent interpretation of observations and other research data. It is important to recognize the pre-eminence of logic, rather than overvalued "common sense," in deciding issues of reliability and hence relevance: "Logic is the lifeblood of American law. . . . It is no exaggeration to say that the syllogism lies at the heart of legal writing."[63]

---

63 Ruggero J. Aldisert & Stephen Clowney, "Logic for Law Students: How to Think Like a Lawyer" (2007) 69 U. Pitt. L. Rev. 1.

Conclusions about correlation and causation are especially prone to error. Illusory correlation is a common fallacy, endemic in the clinical professions, generally resulting from a reliance on subjective, impressionistic anecdotal evidence rather than a controlled, accurate recording of data.[64] Ziskin gives several examples of beliefs that continue to be widely held notwithstanding their disproof by experiments, such as the belief that large eyes drawn in the Draw-A-Person test correlates with paranoia. A recent relevant reference states:[65]

Abstract — Although projective techniques continue to be widely used in clinical and forensic settings, their scientific status remains highly controversial. In this monograph, we review the current state of the literature concerning the psychometric properties (norms, reliability, validity, incremental validity, treatment utility) of three major projective instruments: Rorschach Inkblot Test, Thematic Apperception Test (TAT), and human figure drawings. We conclude that there is empirical support for the validity of a small number of indexes derived from the Rorschach and TAT. However, the substantial majority of Rorschach and TAT indexes are not empirically supported. The validity evidence for human figure drawings is even more limited. With a few exceptions, projective indexes have not consistently demonstrated incremental validity above and beyond other psychometric data. In addition, we summarize the results of a new meta-analysis intended to examine the capacity of these three instruments to detect child sexual abuse. Although some projective instruments were better than chance at detecting child sexual abuse, there were virtually no replicated findings across independent investigative teams. This meta-analysis also provides the first clear evidence of substantial file drawer effects in the projectives literature as the effect sizes from published studies markedly exceeded those from unpublished studies. We conclude with recommendations regarding the (a) construction of projective techniques with adequate validity, (b) forensic and clinical use of projective techniques, and (c) education and training of future psychologists regarding projective techniques.

---

64 Ziskin, above note 20, vol. 1 at 91–94.
65 Lilienfeld *et al.*, above note 29 at 27. See also Barry Ritzler, Robert Erard, & Gary Pettigrew, "Protecting the Integrity of Rorschach Expert Witnesses: A Reply to 'Grove and Barden (1999) Re: The Admissibility of Testimony under *Daubert/Kumho* Analyses'" (2002) 8 Psychol., Pub. Pol'y & L. 201; William M. Grove *et al.*, "Failure of Rorschach-Comprehensive-System-Based Testimony to Be Admissible under the *Daubert-Joiner-Kumho* Standard" (2002) 8 Psychol., Pub. Pol'y & L. 216; Barry Ritzler, Robert Erard, & Gary Pettigrew, "A Final Reply to Grove and Barden: The Relevance of the Rorschach Comprehensive System for Expert Testimony" (2002) 8 Psychol., Pub. Pol'y & L. 235. See generally John Hunsley *et al.*, "Controversial and Questionable Assessment Techniques" in Lilienfeld *et al.*, above note 10, c. 3 at 39–76.

Further, correlation, even if it in fact exists, is not causation. The fact that things appear to be related does not in any way prove a causal relationship between them even if there is in fact a valid correlation.[66] As well, temporal sequence is not causation. For centuries, human beings have committed the fallacy of *post hoc ergo propter hoc (after which, therefore because of which)*. It continues to be a common fallacy. The fact that a sex abuse victim's life is visited with inadequacies and miseries does not in any way justify the conclusion of causal responsibility that clinicians are prone to make.

In a sociological investigation, D.P. Phillips (1983) studied all homicides in the United States between 1973 and 1978. During this period, 18 heavyweight championship prize fights were held. Any homicide that occurred within 3 weeks after a match was counted as a consequence. He concluded that fatal, aggressive behavior was stimulated by heavyweight prize fights. Although the prize fights were antecedents, there is no evidence that they were necessary antecedents of the homicides that followed. It is not even known whether the assailants knew about the fights or had anything more than a casual interest in them.

In another study, D.P. Phillips (1978) reported that a significant increase in small-plane crashes followed highly publicized murder-suicides. This led him to speculate that at least some of the crashes were intentional and were stimulated by the murder-suicides. No evidence other than *post hoc ergo propter hoc* was offered.[67]

Two common logical fallacies have been known to the human race since the time of the ancient Greeks: *affirming the consequent* and *denying the antecedent*. In a situation where a complete logical relationship between two matters is established (i.e., if A, then B) — for example, that in every case a child that was abused would become a bedwetter (if abused, then bedwets) — it would be fallacious therefrom to deduce: if there was no abuse, the child would not bedwet (i.e., if no A, then no B). This is the fallacy of *denying the antecedent*:

---

66 Cromer, above note 9 at 194, n.9:

> Between 1973 and 1982 the snowfall in Amherst, Massachusetts and the U.S. unemployment rate had a correlation of 0.98 .... This shows an almost perfect correlation can't prove a relationship if there's no underlying theoretical justification for the relationship .... [I]f one looks hard enough one will find ten years of something that is highly correlated with ten years of something else. This is known as the indefinite endpoint, and is used very successfully by magicians and con artists, and is constantly confounding the unwary empiricist.

See also Plous, above note 41, c. 15, "Correlation, Causation and Control," 162–73.

67 Meltzoff, above note 1 at 24–25.

the proposition may be true but it requires separate proof and does not follow logically from the first proposition.

A more common and invidious error made constantly by clinicians is *affirming the consequent*: if the child bedwets, she was abused (i.e., if B, then A). This backwards (in more ways than one) reasoning is completely fallacious. A clinician sees a number of children who allege abuse and who bedwet. In his own mind, he develops the syllogism: "If a child is abused, the child bedwets." When retained by the Crown to opine whether a child has been abused, on finding out the child bedwets, the clinician wrongly suggests: "The child bedwets, so the child has been abused." The description of bedwetting is now a diagnosis — the fallacy of *affirming the consequent* in action.

Sometimes the reverse proposition can be proved and is therefore true. For example, if it were demonstrated that only abused children bedwet and non-abused children never did so. Then the proposition "if a child bedwets, the child is abused" would be true. But this requires a separate demonstration. It does not follow logically from the proposition simply that "if a child is abused, then the child bedwets." It is the difference between that latter proposition and the proposition "*only* a child who is abused bedwets."

In fact, all examples of indicators, syndromes, and profiles[68] can be viewed from the same logical perspective. Descriptive elements of allegedly abused children or battered wives or terrorists or arsonists or sexual predators are fallaciously used diagnostically to determine identity.[69] This fallacy, combined with the base rate fallacy to be described shortly, explains the practical problems with such theoretical constructs and why they simple "do not work" without creating great injustice: fathered by fallacies these indicators and syndromes and profiles are simply wrong too much of the time.

A most important point is that just because the evidence seems to support a desired result or theory or explanation, it is not necessarily proved. Chance explains all phenomena, and only data obtained with an experimental design that renders chance an unlikely explanation allow another explanation to be put forth. A knowledge of the importance of chance as a confounding explanation means knowing about probabilities and phenomena such as base rates[70] and regression to the mean (and why they are important).

---

68 See chapter 3, note 36 and chapter 7.
69 Discussed in greater detail in chapter 7.
70 Ziskin, above note 20, vol. 1 at 83.

A recent news story titled "June babies have higher risk of anorexia"[71] that was picked up widely across the media illustrates one of the more common statistical fallacies, and, unfortunately, the medical profession's ignorance:

> Anorexic women are most likely to have been born in the spring or early summer, reports a researcher in Scotland. The finding raises the possibility that a common winter infection, such as flu, may predispose an unborn baby to the condition.
>
> "It's not the whole answer," says John Eagles of the Royal Cornhill Hospital in Aberdeen. "But it could be an unrecognised cause of anorexia nervosa, which affects around one per cent of girls in the US."

In fact, the team reportedly studied 446 women who had been diagnosed as anorexic and observed that 30 percent more than average were born in June. As the average monthly births are about 37, the June number must be 48. At first sight, this looks like a significant result (at least by epidemiological standards). Applying simple probability mathematics to a random selection from a population of 446 with a probability of 1/12 indicates that the probability of getting 48 or more in a random month is about 3 percent.

But that is not what the researchers were doing! They were effectively making twelve such selections by checking each month's results and then picking the biggest, which happened to be June. Statistics tells us that the probability of the largest of twelve such selections being 48 or greater is in fact 30 percent, a much less amazing figure.

In short, the largest value of 48 observed for June is totally unremarkable if one understands the question to ask is *not* what are the odds June will have such a result but rather what are the odds *any* one month will show such a result. Chance as the explanation for the results was improperly ignored by these researchers.

"Regression to the mean" is another phenomenon that represents the effects of chance on test results that is often the true explanation for obtained results, and not the preferred conclusion that the experimenters jump to. A well-known example of this phenomenon is found in "The Connecticut Crackdown on Speeding":[72]

---

71   This example and analysis was taken from the excellent website Numberwatch, online: www.numberwatch.co.uk/, which is replete with similar unfortunate examples.

72   As described in Michael D. Maltz, "Which Homicides Decreased? Why?" (1998) 88 J. Crim. L. & Criminology 1489 at 1491–93. There the phenomenon is raised as a possible explanation of declining homicide rates.

In 1956, following a year in which Connecticut experienced a very high rate of traffic fatalities, then-Governor Abraham Ribicoff instituted a new policy for the State Police: zero tolerance of speeding. The next year there were 40 fewer traffic fatalities (a 12.3% decrease) . . . which the governor attributed to this policy.

But it's not always that simple; a before-after comparison can often be very misleading. When Campbell and Ross added to the picture prior and subsequent years . . . the attribution of the decrease to the policy seemed much more debatable: . . . the fatalities in the first two years after the treatment were higher than five of the six years prior to the treatment.

It appears that two conditions made the policy makers mistakenly conclude that the new policy had caused the reduction. First, there was a great deal of volatility, or year-to-year variation, in the traffic fatality rate. . . . This means that it would be difficult to determine the extent to which any change (up or down) is due to the policy and the extent to which it is due to the inherent variation in the data.

Second, the policy was implemented in a year following one that had a rather extreme number of traffic fatalities. One would expect that, regardless of any change in policy, the next year's rate would be more moderate (i.e., closer to the historical mean rate): it is harder to go up from an all-time high than it is to go down. In fact, a better name for the phenomenon might be "selection of the extreme," because it was the selection of an extremely high rate as the "before" year that foreordained a more moderate rate — a decrease — in the "after" year.

But base rates and their implication for logical and accurate thinking about evidence claims are probably the single most important feature of scientific reality for the assessment of expert opinions. The following example shows the importance of considering base rates for the target phenomenon.

If a drug test is 95 percent accurate, what is the appropriate evidentiary value of a positive result? For example, what does it mean for an accused who denies taking any drug in the face of a positive test result? Does the test mean it is 95 percent certain the accused in fact took the drug, contrary to his protestations? Answering these questions requires a modicum of scientific literacy, but it is easily achievable.

The first thing that scientific literacy would convey is the recognition that answering the questions requires consideration of the alternative hypothesis to guilt, namely, that the test is in error. That can happen 5 percent of the time. The next point is the realization that what must be considered is the base rate of the phenomenon being looked for, namely, drug use. If no one used the drug, the test with 95 percent accuracy (and 5 percent inaccuracy) would still (wrongly) identify 5 percent of the persons tested as drug users. So deciding the probabilities in the accused's case requires some knowledge of drug use within the population in general, or the "base rate" as it is known.

Assume the incidence of drug use in the population is 5 percent. To return to our question, given that base rate: the accused has been tested at random with positive results. Then what are the chances that the accused was in fact a user of the drug? Was it 95 percent? Absolutely not. In fact the probabilities are merely 50 percent (or "fifty-fifty").

Consider a population of 10,000 people. With a 5 percent rate of incidence, 9,500 are nonusers and 500 are users. For the 9,500 nonusers, 95 percent accurate means the test will identify 9,025 negatives but it will also be wrong 5 percent of the time and thus identify 475 false positives. For the 500 users, 95 percent accurate equals 475 true positives and 25 false negatives. Thus, among 10,000 people this test will show 950 positive test results, consisting of 475 true users and 475 false positives (nonusers falsely shown as users). The accused in our hypothetical could be one of the 475 true results or one of the 475 false results, thus the "fifty-fifty" chance description.

A positive test's meaning is not knowable without knowing not just the test's error rate but also the base rate: the rate at which the phenomenon to be tested for occurs in the general population. Ninety-five percent represents the probability that, if given the test and subject in fact has what is being tested for, the test will be correctly positive. It is not the probability: given a positive test result, what are the chances the test subject in fact has what is being tested for? The latter is a different probability, but it is extremely common to confuse the two.[73] Let this be repeated to ensure understanding. If everyone had the disease or used the drug, then the test's accuracy of 95 percent would be the correct assessment. But in such a case there would be no need for any test as we already know 100 percent of the subjects are ill/using drugs. Once the target phenomenon's prevalence is less than 100 percent then it will be absent in some percentage of subjects. And if the test is less than 100 percent accurate, then it will be wrong some percentage of the time. It will be wrong not only about subjects that have the illness/use the drugs, but also wrong about the innocent subjects who do not have the illness or use the drug. Being wrong about those people means the test will incorrectly label some healthy people as ill and some innocent nonusers as drug users. This is reality. There is no way to avoid this inevitability.

---

73   This is why screening or preliminary tests for drugs or other substances should never be
     viewed as evidence: they simply generate too many false positives. See Kaufman Commis-
     sion Report, above note 24 at 326–28.

Another excellent example relates to police evidence of drug detection:[74]

What do you do when an officer says that he "can tell you are on some type of drug just by looking at you," and to prove he can do so displays his Drug Recognition Evaluation certificate? This new type of certificate allows officers to arrest and prosecute for drugs, particularly in Driving While Intoxicated (DWI) cases.... [F]irst hand observations by officers are admissible in court and are being used as "proof" in lieu of blood testing.

The basic steps are to establish the following on direct examination of the officer:

1. Get the officer to agree that he is 98% accurate in evaluating whether a driver is on some type of drug "just by looking at him."
2. Get the officer to agree that only about H% of all drivers are "on" some type of drug — marijuana, cocaine or amphetamines, to the extent that they display outward signs of intoxication.

Use the blackboard to perform the following mathematics for the jury to calculate the probability of accuracy:

Start by assuming the officer evaluates 10,000 drivers. The officer must admit — if he has had the proper training — that only about H% of these drivers, i.e., 50 drivers per 10,000 — are actually "on" some type of drug to the extent that they show observable signs of drug intoxication.

Since 98% of the 50 will test positive, by the officer's own admitted error rate, when he looks at them he will miss one and detect 49 positives. Of the 9,950 non-drug drivers, 2% of them will test positive too due to the officer's 98% accuracy rate (2 per 100 are wrong, e.g., 9,950 × .02 = 199 are wrong). So the officer can generate a total of 248 positive police reports (199 + 49) for every 10,000 drivers he evaluates.

The inescapable conclusion is that most — 199 — of the officer's drug "positives" for drugs are false positives.

This is the heart of a scientific flaw that lets the officer get away with spouting non-science junk to the jury.

The jury sits in the dark about how many people are actual drug drivers, e.g., how many are "on" some drug. Therefore, when the officer brags that he's 98% accurate, he makes himself sound highly trained and capable. The jurors just don't think they themselves could do better than his 98% accuracy rate.

---

74 James Woodford, Ph.D., Chemist, "What Do You Do When an Officer Says That He 'Can Tell You Are on Some Type of Drug Just by Looking at You,'" online: www.crime-lynx.com/probab.html.

Remember that we established earlier that for every 9,950 drivers not using drugs, 199 of them can get falsely accused of being on drugs by this officer. This turns out to be quite significant when you realize that if he should test all 80 million drivers in America today, he could arrest, put in jail and help convict 1,592,000 people. And he could do the same thing tomorrow, and the day after, and the day after that, and so on.

. . .

Remember, when you begin your cross-examination of the officer, get him to admit that he's 98% accurate (e.g., 2% wrong). This lets you calculate "199" which is the number of false-positives the officer creates on the 9,950 non-drug drivers when he's 98% accurate ($0.02 \times 9,950$ non-drug drivers = 199 false positives).

You've gotten the officer to admit that H% of the 10,000 total number of all drivers are observably drug drivers. That's where the number 50 comes in ($.005 \times 10,000 = 50$). However, since he's 98% accurate, he will miss one of these too ($.02 \times 50 = 1$) and will report 49 positives ($50 - 1 = 49$).[75]

Davis and Follette give an example[76] where the same type of analysis is applied to evidence in a criminal case involving the probative value of evidence that a husband charged with the murder of his wife was unfaithful. It would be natural for a court to intuitively feel that unfaithful husbands are more likely to kill their wives than faithful husbands, and therefore rule the evidence of unfaithfulness admissible as relevant.

	FAITHFUL	UNFAITHFUL	TOTAL
KILLED WIFE:	0	1,000	1,000
DID NOT KILL WIFE:	750,000	249,000	999,000
TOTALS:	750,000	250,000	1,000,000

In other words, 1,000 out of 250,000 unfaithful husbands killed their wives, but 249,000 or 249 times as many did not. The probability of murder if unfaithful is 1000/250,000 or .4 percent. In other words, 99.6 percent of the unfaithful men did not kill their wives. Thus, the fact of unfaithfulness makes it less than 1 percent more likely a husband is the killer even if every husband killer is unfaithful. If nothing else, the admission of such evidence should be ac-

75 See *R. v. Wood*, [2007] A.J. No. 895 (Q.B.).
76 Deborah Davis & William C. Follette, "Rethinking the Probative Value of Evidence: Base Rates, Intuitive Profiling, and the 'Postdiction' of Behavior" (2002) 26 Law & Hum. Behav. 133.

companied by analysis along the lines above so the trier of fact gets an accurate understanding of how much or how little the evidence is actually worth.

Assume 90 percent of abused children bedwet and only 20 percent of non-abused children bedwet. If a child bedwets, is it indicative of anything? Consider 100 abused children and 100 not abused children:

	BEDWETTING	
	YES	NO
ABUSED	90	10
NOT ABUSED	20	80

The incidence seems significantly different. Does this mean that if a child bedwets, we can infer abuse? The answer is no. The base rate must be considered to determine properly the different probability: if a child bedwets, then the child was abused.

Assume a base rate of 10 percent; that is, 10 percent of children selected at random would be abused. Now consider a population of 100 children where we do not know whether any particular individual child is abused or not. Ten percent on average will be abused, which equals 10 children; 90 will not be abused. Of the 10 abused, 90 percent or 9 will bedwet; of the 90 not abused, 20 percent or 18 will bedwet. So of the 100 children, 27 (9 + 18 = 27) will bedwet, but only 9 out of these 27 will be abused, and 18 of 27 will not be abused. So with respect to a given child who bedwets, we do not know whether the child is one of the 9 abused or the 18 not abused, so the odds are 2:1 that the child is not abused. In short, there is all the difference in the world between the probabilities: "Given the child was abused it will bedwet," which is 90 percent, and "Given the child bedwets it was abused," which is 33 percent. Note that in our hypothetical example, the fact that the child bedwets does change the probabilities. The probability the child is abused went from 1 in 10 to 1 in 3 because of the additional fact of bedwetting. This is a reflection of the difference in the proportion of abused, versus nonabused children who bedwet. But the fact of bedwetting does not make it more probable than not that the child is abused.

In real life the evidence should be inadmissible because we lack the data necessary to make a similar proper evidentiary assessment:

- we do not know the base rate for abused children;
- we do not know the proportion of abused children who bedwet; and
- we do not know the proportion of nonabused children who bedwet.

The significance of any evidence depending upon the presence or finding of a characteristic (or anything of alleged significance for that matter) first and foremost cannot ever be assessed without knowledge of that characteristic, or thing's, base rate. Whether reference is being made to a characteristic such as bedwetting or an item such as scales found in an alleged drug dealer's home, the evidence logically has no significance unless the base rate is very low: few children bedwet; almost no one has scales in her home. Otherwise, the phenomenon is simply being observed by chance, or there is a real risk of that. Considering base rate is simply another way of considering expressly the nonsignificance of the finding for the proposition sought to be proved.[77] Whether express reference is made to the term base rate or not, clear thinking requires consideration of the comparison or standard necessary to assess significance, and that requires knowing the frequency with which the phenomenon occurs generally. As a forensic tactic, proponents of a proposition will often assume a low base rate ("How many people have expensive scales in their home?") and try to convince their audience to share that assumption. Because chance is not an intuitive, favoured explanation, and because base-rate data regarding common phenomena such as having scales in one's home are nonexistent, opponents will often produce another explanation ("the scales were left by a visitor") rather than rely on pure chance as an explanation. Without realizing it, however, the parties are really having a debate whose logic is captured by the concept of base rate.

The second important point is that when evidence of a characteristic or item of interest is alleged to be diagnostic or discriminatory — that is, it allegedly will identify the particular subject as a member of a target group — logic demands that the nongroup has been studied and the prevalence of the characteristic or item of interest can be shown to be *absent* in the nongroup. This is simply the application of the control group concept and the necessity for comparisons. Furthermore, anything less than 100 percent accuracy in discrimination will inherently involve false negatives and, most importantly, false positives. Any "test," including simply the presence or absence of a characteristic, unless perfect in its application with 100 percent accuracy, will falsely misidentify target group members as not in the target group and, most importantly, falsely identify innocent subjects as members of the target group. False positives are inherent in any identification task based on a less than perfect test. There is no way to avoid them. The absolute number of false positives has less to do with the accuracy of the test and more to do with the base rate of the characteristic. False positives are the product of the test's inaccuracy applied to the control group or nontarget group. If that is a large absolute number, the number of false positives will be substantial no matter how accurate the test is (unless it is perfect of course).

---

77 See Koehler, above note 53 at 373: "Courts are likely to view base rates as relevant when base rates . . . (b) are offered to rebut an it-happened-by-chance theory."

These two important points apply to much of the evidence adduced in courts of law, but they take on particular importance when, in sex cases, a phenomenon — everything from behavioural indicators to physical observations of the genitalia — was claimed to be significant in a diagnostic or discriminating sense by "experts" completely ignorant of these basic principles.

One author has pointed out that because of the relatively low base rate of child abuse in the general population, even the presence of emotional or behavioural reactions, which occur in a high percentage of abused children and a very small percentage of nonabused children, indicates that in absolute numbers, many more nonabused children have the symptoms. Thus, testimony about psychological consequences is implicitly misleading because triers of fact are unlikely to understand the significance of base rates in weighing such testimony.[78]

Judges have certainly fallen victim to such errors in reasoning. In *R. v. N.(R.A.)*,[79] the court, in defending the absence of expert evidence regarding behavioural symptoms, said:

> In this case, common sense and common experience of human behaviour suggest that the multiple behavioural changes observed were indicative of some emotional trauma in the life of the complainant. It was not necessary for an expert to opine that a 10- or 11-year-old girl does not begin bedwetting and to display behavioural problems without some provocation. That simple truth does not require special knowledge nor is it outside the realm of understanding of an ordinary person.[80]

The court failed to appreciate the meaninglessness of the evidence without knowledge of base rates of the phenomenon, or the reasoning fallacy taking place. A highly relevant question not addressed would be to consider whether some other source resulting in the bedwetting might also not be related to the making of a false allegation. Of course, this assumes causation in the context of bedwetting is a valid question, which raises a whole separate issue regarding the state of our real knowledge about such matters.[81]

---

78 As referenced in Stephen J. Ceci & Helene Hembrooke, eds., *Expert Witnesses in Child Abuse Cases: What Can and Should Be Said in Court* (Washington, DC: American Psychological Association, 1998) at 16.

79 (2001), 152 C.C.C. (3d) 464 (Alta. C.A.).

80 *Ibid.* at para. 29.

81 An Internet search turned up voluminous material on the subject of bedwetting that had two clear, common themes: 1) bedwetting is very common; and 2) no one knows what causes it. Such facts make pronouncements linking sex abuse to bedwetting quite demanding of the greatest forensic scrutiny.

Even more troubling, there is evidence that the error rate with regard to important tests frequently used in the criminal justice system is unacceptably high.

> For example, if this factor [error rate] is considered by judges and applied in a rational manner, much of the testimony based on a medical examination for evaluation of a child sexual abuse allegation will be inadmissible. The best scientific evidence that gives an indication of the potential error rate for medical examinations concludes that the error rate when a physician claims a medical examination supports penile penetration is 63%, for digital penetration 73%, and for a general conclusion of abuse over 70%. . . . Such a high error rate, always in the direction of false positives, can only confuse the entire process.[82]

Such high error rates combined with the low base rate of sex abuse foreshadows many false positive judgments. The same is true of syndromes and indicators. Their application can be viewed as a "test" whose accuracy must be determined by asking and answering two questions: what percentage of persons with that constellation of factors is a battered wife, terrorist, or in the case of fires, an arsonist, and what percentage is not; and second, what is the base rate of such phenomenon in the general population of similar persons or fires? Without knowledge of these figures their reliability is an unscientific claim. Further, the hypothesis can be offered reasonably that the actual figures will be such as to result in a significant number of false positives. No matter how much a person may fit the stereotype for a particular category or designation, one cannot accurately judge the likelihood the person actually falls into that category without knowing the base rate of members of that category in the population. And further there is no way around the reality that because of the base rate concept, even a high success rate in the context of a small subpopulation will give a smaller absolute number than the smaller failure rate for the large balance of the population, making the detection of the target group in a particular instance problematic.[83]

---

82 Ralph Underwager & Hollida Wakefield, "A Paradigm Shift for Expert Witnesses" in J.J. Krivacska & J. Money, eds., *Handbook of Forensic Sexology* (Amherst, NY: Prometheus Books, 1994) 541.

83 For a good discussion see Foster & Huber, "*Judging Science*," above note 1, c. 3 at 49, 51, & 52 and c. 6 at 148–50. Also see *George v. R.*, [2007] EWCA Crim 2722, online: www. bailii.org/ew/cases/EWCA/Crim/2007/2722.html.

FALSIFIABILITY

IT PROBABLY HAS not escaped the reader's notice that the very first *Daubert* requirement has yet to be mentioned in this chapter: falsifiability of the theory.[84] This is the basic requirement of science, and in fact it implicitly underlies all that has been covered above. Without falsifiability, none of the above matters. There is no point designing research and carrying it out, no point fussing about comparison groups or trying to reason logically, if none of it matters because whatever the results the proffered theory or "explanation" will still be standing. If anything and everything is consistent with a theory, it is not science. If the theory is self-sealing against any result like a religion that accounts for everything as "God's will," it is not science.[85]

Confirmation bias means that we instinctively search for and interpret data and evidence in conformity with our expectations and wishes. This powerful, robust effect has been demonstrated over and over again. Unfalsifiability is confirmation bias carried to the ultimate extreme. With enough theoretical gerrymandering and imaginative rationalizations, anything and everything can be interpreted as consistent with a favoured hypothesis. No real knowledge lies down that road. Consider the following test:[86] Four cards are laid out on a table, showing an E, K, 4, and 7, respectively. The question to be answered is: "Which cards — if only two can be turned over — should be turned over to prove the following hypothesis: "If a card has a vowel on one side, then it has an even number on the other side." The vast majority, including in one study four out of five "highly regarded" mathematical psychologists, answer "E and 4."

This answer demonstrates confirmation bias: the tendency to seek confirmatory evidence. The proposition can be written as "If vowel, then even number" or "If X, then Y." The only way to falsify such a statement is to find "X and not-Y" or "vowel and odd number." Turning over a vowel will disconfirm if there is an odd number on the other side, so "E" is correct. But turning over even numbers tells you nothing. The proposition was not that even numbers are only paired with vowels; just that vowels are paired with even numbers. It does not matter whether a vowel or a consonant is on the other side of "4." In short, even numbers and consonants are simply irrelevant to the truth of the hypothesis. What matters is what is on the other side of "7," the odd number, because if it is a vowel, then the hypothesis has been disproved. That gives the correct answer: "E and 7."

---

84 Above note 27.
85 Lilienfeld *et al.*, above note 10 at 6.
86 Plous, above note 41 at 231–32.

It is only down the other road of disconfirmation that real knowledge lies. That is why science is referred to as a search for disconfirmation.[87] Scientists try to disprove, by experiment or the use of the rules of logic, the desired hypothesis. Only when logic can show no other explanation is the desired result accepted. In short, to a scientist the hypothesis that is wanted is the last resort for the outcome of the experiment, not the first choice gladly jumped to. Good science requires an exercise in devil's advocacy as other possible explanations are considered and properly eliminated. Immediately jumping to the desired explanatory conclusion is a hallmark of pseudo-science.[88]

Therefore, to be science, the most important, fundamental requirement is that the hypothesis, opinion, or conclusion being put forth must be testable in accordance with the above principles and theoretically falsifiable. In other words, there must be a way, a procedure, a test that can be devised that will determine whether the claim is true or false.

To understand the concept of falsifiability one must recognize the difference between two different meanings of the word "falsifiable." . . . In the first meaning, falsifiable is a logical-technical term related to the criterion of falsifiability. This means that the theory or concept in question must be capable of being falsified — that is, be precise and specific enough to have something count against it. In the second meaning, falsifiable is used in the sense that the theory or concept in question can be "definitively or conclusively or demonstrably falsified (demonstrably falsifiable)."

The first sense refers only to the potential logical possibility of a theory or concept being falsified in principle. The second sense includes a persuasive practical demonstration using scientific procedures to produce a proof of falsity. That is, do credible research studies produce results that mean the theory cannot be maintained? There has been some discussion suggesting that final empirical proofs of falsity cannot be obtained but Popper maintains the potential uncertainty of falsity should not be taken too seriously. . . . Thus the principle of falsification provides two basic ways in which a judge may determine that proffered expert testimony does not meet the criterion of falsifiability. The first is whether or not it is, in principle, falsifiable and the second is whether or not it has been falsified.

The practice of blood letting provides an example from which an understanding of the different meanings of these two uses of "falsifiable" can be promoted. For about two hundred years, physicians believed that drawing off

---

87 This was the essential feature emphasized in the Kaufman Commission Report, above note 24 at 345–48.

88 Lilienfeld *et al.*, above note 10 at 7.

blood cured disease. The standard treatment was to open a vein and draw a basin of blood. George Washington died from this treatment. For centuries physicians reasoned that a person who was bled and lived was saved by the procedure. Conversely, a person who died was considered to have been so sick that nothing would have helped anyway. With this line of reasoning, it is impossible to falsify bleeding as a specific treatment for disease. This represents the first meaning of the term "falsifiable." Subsequent research predicated on germ theory and other medical advances eventually proved blood letting to be a false cure, thus showing the theory was demonstrably falsifiable — the second meaning of the term.[89]

A prime example of such bogus science is psychiatry, certainly in its psychoanalytic sphere. The theories and concepts used by psychiatrists postulate all manner of internal processes and hidden events that cannot be falsified because they are not testable.

Sir Karl Popper, who advanced the concept of falsifiability, and is specifically quoted in the *Daubert* decision, demonstrates at great length in his two volumes, *The Open Society and Its Enemies*, that Freudian theory, like Marxism, is unfalsifiable. . . . Popper's critique of Freud draws heavily on the first meaning of the criterion of falsifiability. Freudian theory uses a convoluted conceptual structure that explains all human behavior after the fact. Adherents to Freudian psychoanalytic theory offer authoritative sounding explanations for all human behaviors, from individual quirks and slips of the tongue to large-scale social phenomena such as religion. It is unscientific because nothing can count against it. There is no point at which it is subject to falsification. This type of theory attempts to provide a posthoc explanation for every possible event, however, it is incapable of predicting any particular event. A successful scientific theory, by contrast, predicts outcomes from a discrete set of events with an ascertainable degree of reliability.[90]

It is also the case that to the limited extent that it has been possible to squeeze a prediction out of Freudian theory and subject it to empirical tests, it has failed dramatically.

Freud was a borrower and generated few original ideas. But given our inability to identify the true originator, we must credit Freud with one singularly objectionable rhetorical discovery that continues as a mainstay of junk science to this day: the idea that something and its opposite could both serve as evidence for the same hypothesis.

---

89 Underwager & Wakefield, above note 82.
90 *Ibid.*

Unfalsifiable claims are not science and their acceptance is a matter of taste, and not valid knowledge. If a belief is immune from disconfirmation, then it is in the nature of an arbitrary or religious belief. It is not science and not a matter of expertise. This is why the Supreme Court in *Daubert* put this requirement first. It is the essence of science, the fundamental requirement.

CHAPTER 5

Science and the Forensic Sciences

THE FORENSIC IDENTIFICATION sciences[1] have come under renewed critical scrutiny in light of evidence law's newfound emphasis on science.[2] Critics say there is too much of the forensic and too little of the scientific.[3] Most expert evidence is given by employees of government-owned and police-related laboratory facilities, which are seen to owe their survival more to precedent than to merit. They have been described as "Science Constructed in the Image of the Criminal Law."[4] A reassessment of some of these facilities is needed to see if they can meet the standards for admissibility grounded upon "good science."

It remains too early to discern how courts will respond to the wide range of techniques that fall within the forensic science category. The principal difficulty, it appears, is that many of these techniques have been relied upon for so

---

1   For a traditional review, see generally G.M. Chayko, E.D. Gulliver, & D.V. Macdougall, *Forensic Evidence in Canada* (Toronto: Canada Law Book, 1991).

2   For example, a leading article by Michael J. Saks, "Merlin and Solomon: Lessons from Law's Formative Encounters with Forensic Identification Science" (1998) 49 Hastings L.J. 1069, begins one section with the introduction: "This Part reviews the task of forensic identification science, the field's origins, the evidence on which its claims rest, and possible reasons for its arrested development as a science."

3   Andre A. Moenssens, "Novel Scientific Evidence in Criminal Cases: Some Words of Caution" (1993) 84 Crim. L. & Criminology 1 at 6, asserting that most crime lab personnel are "technicians," not trained scientists, and are prone to pro-police bias and averse to rigorous scientific investigation.

4   Saks, above note 2 at 1090.

long that courts might be reluctant to rethink their role in the trial process. Topics like handwriting identification analysis, ballistics, bite marks, fiber analysis and so on are the staples of expert testimony. Yet, even from a distance, it is immediately apparent that many forensic techniques could not pass the most minimal *Daubert* scrutiny. At the very least, *Daubert* requires judges to ask where are the data. In many forensic areas, effectively no research exists to support the practice.[5]

The types of evidence to be reviewed here run the gamut from fingerprint, firearm, and toolmark identification to handwriting analysis and hair and fibre comparison. The history of these categories and the explanation why forensic sciences have not proceeded along the rigorous lines of "real science" are well described by one commentator:

> Forensic science plainly has something of value to offer criminal investigators and the courts. Why, then, does so much of it cling, instead, to an untenable absolution and committed subjectivity? By contrast, conventional science would have proceeded along a different course, one guided by the necessity of collecting and analyzing data to test assumptions. In court, conventional scientists might be expected to share with the fact finder the analytic basis of their opinions, their data, and their data-based assessments of the risk of error. In short, conventional scientists would collect better data and offer them to the courts without overselling them. Why doesn't forensic science proceed along that more recognizably scientific path?
>
> The answer likely is that forensic science grew up in the criminal law. The exigencies imposed on it by police and prosecutors molded it into its contemporary shape. A particularly dramatic demonstration of this is the lengths to which some forensic scientists have been willing to go to provide courts with the testimony prosecutors wanted courts to hear, regardless of the truth.
>
> ...
>
> The institutional setting of forensic science promotes habits or thought that more closely resemble the thinking of litigators than of scientists. While science pursues knowledge through disconfirmation, prosecutions are won by confirmatory proofs. This confirmatory bias dominates the thinking of most forensic scientists. Where science advances by open discussion and debate forensic science has been infected by the litigator's preference of secrecy. Tests of the proficiency of crime laboratories are conducted anonymously, kept secret, and are not routinely published. It is ironic that while studies of the effective-

---

5   David L. Faigman *et al.*, *Modern Scientific Evidence*, 2 vols. (St. Paul, MN: West, 1997) vol. 1 at 33.

ness and accuracy of so many professional enterprises are available in published literature, the same is not true of a field whose sole purpose is to do some of the public's most public business.[6]

The issue is not a new one.[7] The weaknesses in forensic science's theoretical underpinnings that must be recognized in the aftermath of *Daubert* have been described succinctly:

> Forensic identification science has selected for itself — or had thrust upon it — a project that is unknown to other fields: the unique identification or, more properly, *individualization* of various objects including persons, distinct from all others in the world. "Criminalistics is the science of individualization."
>
> The question posed is whether a bullet can be traced back to the one and only one barrel through which it was fired, a signature to the hand that wrote it, a bite mark to the mouth of the biter, cut bolts to the instrument that cut them and so on. Affirmative answers are offered daily in courtrooms across the country as firearms examiners, document examiners, forensic odontologists, tool mark experts, and numerous other forensic identification scientists purport to identify the gun, hand, mouth, tool, and so on, that left its traces at the crime scene. DNA typing is merely the latest addition to the family of forensic identification sciences. Each member of this family subscribes to the same assumptions and draws its inferences from the same basic logic. Typically, testimony based on such identifications is offered to place a defendant at the scene of a crime.
>
> The capacity to make such identifications depends on the validity of a series of premises: That many kinds of biological and physical entities exist in unique, one-of-a-kind form: that they leave correspondingly unique traces of themselves: and that the techniques of observation, measurement, and inference employed by forensic science are adequate to link these traces back to the object that produced them. The claim usually has been presented in essentially this strong form: Individualization is "absolute specificity and absolute identification."
>
> . . .
>
> Asked for hard evidence — even today — each of the subfields of forensic identification science rests its claims of infinite variation and unique identifiability on . . . [the concept] that if objects vary on a number of independent (i.e.,

---

6   Saks, above note 2 at 1090–94 [footnotes omitted].
7   James W. Osterburg, "The Evaluation of Physical Evidence in Criminalistics: Subjective or Objective Process?" (1969) 60 J. Crim. L. & Criminology 97.

uncorrelated) dimensions, the probability of occurrence of any one combination of characteristics is found by multiplying together the probabilities associated with each dimension. Such calculations typically produce probabilities that are vanishingly small. Having made this general point, the next step in the argument ... is to appeal to the audience's intuition to make the leap into concluding that no two handwritings, tool marks, fingerprints, gun barrels, or whatever, could be alike.[8]

Saks goes on to point out the problems with the "leap from notions of probability to belief in a doctrine of unique individuality":

Even if unique individuality did rule the universe, establishing the validity of a forensic technique would require testing the system of measurement and classification as well, even (or especially) if its principal tool is human perception and judgment.

Second, many of the rule's applications to forensic science may violate the independence assumption, so that the probabilities are not so small as the usual illustration imagine them to be.

Third, with the exception of recent work involving biological markers, such as DNA typing, the various forensic identification sciences have not taken the trouble to collect data on populations of forensically relevant objects so that the probability of erroneous matches can be calculated. Instead, examiners implicitly assume the odds are one-to-infinity.

Fourth, the steps from observation of similarity to the conclusions that are offered to courts must traverse a minefield of potential errors of probabilistic inference that few forensic scientists, and even fewer lawyers or judges are equipped to navigate.

. . .

Additional reasons exist for preferring forensic identification techniques to be constructed on a foundation of real data and formal probability models. One is that it is the main road from subjective impressions to science. Another is that for several identification techniques, the assumption of no-two-alike has already been empirically disconfirmed. As a result, the need to make more accurate estimations of the reduction in uncertainty afforded by these techniques has become patent.

. . .

For every other identification technique, the only way to find false matches would be to conduct special studies to look for them. . . . [One] document exa-

8   See generally Michael J. Saks & Jonathan J. Koehler, "The Individualization Fallacy in Forensic Science Evidence" (2008) 61 Vand. L. Rev. 199.

miner ... went looking for signatures from different people that were indistinguishably alike. He found them in abundance. [FN: See John Harris, "How
Much Do People Write Alike: A Study of Signatures" (1958) 48 J. Crim. L. &
Criminology & Pol. Sci. 647 (noting the indistinguishable similarity of many
signatures).] In so doing, he fatally falsified the core claim of handwriting identification.

. . .

In addition, proficiency studies, undertaken only in the past 20 years, revealed varying rates of error. For example, for DNA typing, the error rate has
been about 1–2%; for tool marks as much as 35%; for handwriting identification
about 36%. While these proficiency values are open to alternative calculations
and interpretations, what is most significant is that these error rates exist at all.[9]

Again, the relevance of precedent should be noted. The highly case-specific
nature of the decision regarding the admissibility of expert evidence has already been pointed out.[10] Just because similar or even identical expert opinion
evidence has been admitted in previous cases does not automatically mandate
admission again. Admission depends on a balancing of the issues and evidence
in each individual case. Although traditional areas of expert evidence enjoy the
advantage of precedent, the dictates of good science now make some of these
highly suspect.

FINGERPRINT IDENTIFICATION

FINGERPRINTS ARE OFTEN considered to be the classic example of incontrovertible expert evidence.[11] Yet it has been noted:

> [i]ndeed, fingerprint evidence may present courts applying *Daubert* with their
> most extreme dilemma. As this chapter explains, by conventional scientific
> standards, any serious search for evidence of the validity of fingerprint identifi-
> cation is likely to be disappointing. Yet the intuitions that underlie fingerprint

---

9   Saks, above note 2 at 1080–90 [most footnotes omitted]. See also Michael J. Sales, "Ban-
     ishing *Ipse Dixit*: The Impact of *Kumho Tire* on Forensic Identification Science" (2000) 57
     Wash. & Lee L. Rev. 879; Faigman *et al.*, above note 5, vol. 2, c. 20, "The General Assump-
     tions and Rationale of Forensic Identification" at 1–49.
10 *R. v. J-L.J.*, [2000] 2 S.C.R. 600; *R. v. A.K. and N.K.* (1999), 27 C.R. (5th) 226 at para. 76
     (Ont. C.A.); *R. v. Chisholm* (1997), 8 C.R. (5th) 21 at para. 57 (Ont. Ct. Gen. Div.).
11 Though fabrication of such evidence is quite possible: Pat A. Wertheim, "Latent Fingerprint
     Evidence: Fabrication, Not Error" *The Champion* (November–December 2008) at 16.

examination, and the subjective probability judgments on which specific case opinions are based, are powerful and persuasive.[12]

...

The criteria for absolute identification in fingerprint work are subjective and ill-defined. They are the product of probabilistic intuitions widely shared among fingerprint examiners, not of scientific research. This generally is unappreciated.[13]

One way to look at the fingerprint problem is to understand that a fingerprint comparison, being a test of comparison and recognition, is not in substance much different than eyewitness identification, which involves a comparison and recognition test between a subject and an internal mental image. The claim that "no two fingerprints are alike," even if true, does not address the important issue or answer the crucial question whether two fingerprints are so similar that one might be mistaken for the other. No two persons are exactly alike, yet daily it is a fact that two different persons are perceived as similar enough to be mistaken one for the other. The assumption that no two of something are alike is quite logically distinguishable from the logically quite distinct proposition: no two of something are sufficiently similar so as to be mistaken one for the other. Assuming the former is questionable but fingerprint examiners are really assuming the quite different and even less defensible latter.

The eyewitness identification analogy raises an important point regarding the methodology as well: Why do we tolerate what are in effect show-up identification tests with fingerprints, while realizing that the same *modus operandi*

---

12   Faigman *et al.*, above note 5, vol. 2 at 55. See also Saks, above note 2 at 1100–6. At 1106 the author concluded: "A vote to admit fingerprints is a rejection of conventional science as the criterion for admission."

13   Faigman *et al.*, *ibid.*, vol. 2 at 70–72. See also Ian Freckelton & Hugh Selby, *Expert Evidence*, 5 vols., looseleaf (Sydney: Law Book Company, 1993 plus updates to May 2002) c. 15, "Fingerprint Evidence." Ian W. Evett *et al.*, "DNA Profiling: A Discussion of Issues Relating to the Reporting of Very Small Match Probabilities" [2000] Crim. L. Rev. 341 is not only a good article on DNA evidence but also has some insightful comments on the scientific inadequacies of fingerprint evidence (at 344 and 349). Michael Specter, "Do Fingerprints Lie?" *The New Yorker* (27 May 2002) at 96 reports how "[t]he gold standard of forensic evidence is now being challenged" and tells of a British case that may involve an impossible fingerprint match. *R. v. Buisson*, [1990] 2 N.Z.L.R. 542 at 549 (C.A.) and *R. v. Lawless*, [1974] V.R. 398 at 423 (C.A.) reference the "expertise" required in fingerprint examinations. In *United States v. Llera Plaza*, [2002] WL 27305 (E.D. Pa. 7 January 2002), rev'd [2002] WL 389163 (E.D. Pa. 13 March 2002), the trial judge first excluded fingerprint analysis testimony proffered by the government on the ground that it failed to meet *Daubert*'s standard of reliability and then, upon reconsideration, reversed that decision. These cases are known as the *Llera Plaza I* and *Llera Plaza II* cases.

in the context of eyewitness identification is highly suggestive and unreliable? Why are fingerprint examiners allowed to compare a single known and unknown? If real recognition is taking place, why are the examiners not being asked to select the match from a fingerprint "lineup" of similar distracters?[14] With computerization of fingerprint collections, it would be very easy to generate a number of similar fingerprints to see whether the examiner can select the accused's as the match.

As presently constituted, fingerprint evidence, like its other forensic brethren that involve evidence "'matching,'" fails to accept the simple scientific principle that tests of comparison or recognition must be done blind, with the test subject not knowing the "right" answer, to avoid ubiquitous confirmation bias.[15] Only in that way is there proof of actual recognition and match (subject to the possibilities of chance, of course).[16]

Furthermore, there are real issues around the notions of "sameness" employed by fingerprint examiners — it is a "sameness" that sometimes only they can see.

> The first thing that must be understood is what the fingerprint examiner means by the term "points of identification." He does not mean the general slant or curvature of the print lines; such a gross similarity proves nothing. Instead, he relies on "minutiae" — ridge endings, bifurcations, "short ridges" and "dots."
>
> . . .
>
> The fundamental article of faith of the fingerprint examiner is that no two fingers will leave the same print. As a corollary, one "unexplained dissimilarity" renders "the conclusion . . . inescapable that the prints were not made by the same finger."
>
> . . .

---

14 Lisa J. Steele, "Physical Evidence Lineups: An Argument Which Deserves Exploration" (1998) 34 Crim. L. Bull. 348: suggestibility of witnesses applies equally whether viewing person, car, gun, or fingerprint. So why should only person identifications require lineups? Other than inertia, there is of course no good reason, the author concludes.

15 Discussed in chapter 4, "Falsifiability." See generally D. Michael Risinger *et al.*, "The *Daubert/Kumho* Implications of Observer Effects in Forensic Science: Hidden Problems of Expectation and Suggestion" (2002) 90 Cal. L. Rev. 1, cogently making the case for blind testing and evidence lineups. Confirmation bias was implicated in one of the most famous wrong fingerprint identification cases: Robert B. Stacey, "A Report on the Erroneous Fingerprint Individualization in the Madrid Train Bombing Case" (2004) 54 J. Forensic Identification 706; see also Boaz Sangero & Mordechai Halpert, "Why a Conviction Should Not Be Based on a Single Piece of Evidence: A Proposal for Reform" (2007) 48 Jurimetrics J. 43 at 66–68; Paul C. Giannelli, "Scientific Evidence: Confirmation Bias" (2007) 22:3 Criminal Justice 60.

16 See chapter 4, note 31.

Catch 22 is the word "unexplained." . . . The defense lawyer can no more afford to accept the fingerprint examiner's decision that a dissimilarity is "explained" than he can afford to be guided in his sex life by a lobster's evaluation of the attractiveness of a crustacean of the opposite sex. In both cases, the opinion may reflect total sincerity, but the information is helpful only to the informant.

Suppose, for example, that the fingerprint left on a murder weapon displays a ridge ending at a given point. Your client's fingerprint contains no such ridge ending but does show a bifurcation at a slightly different point. This is a dissimilarity, to be sure; but the fingerprint examiner has an explanation. He will solemnly explain that variations in pressure and other circumstances can frequently cause a bifurcation to appear as a ridge ending, and vice versa. . . . The variance in geometric position is likewise explainable; two prints of the same finger "may show considerable variation" in that aspect. . . . The two prints may not look the same; but reliance on the "judgment of the technician" can be more important than the "physical data."

. . .

Well then, suppose that the print on the gun shows a break in a ridge line and that your client's prints shows no such break. Again, the variance is explained: the "nature of latent prints" and the "means of development," although virtually infallible when they prove guilt, have certain deficiencies when they establish innocence. . . . And the print lifted from the gun can always be "enhanced" to show that the ridge didn't really end or that the line didn't really split.

. . .

Is there a dot or short ridge on the latent print that does not appear on your client's print? That's explainable; it was a speck of dust, or a skin flap, or an irregularity in the impression surface, or a poltergeist. Does the dot or short ridge appear on your client's print, but not on the print lifted from the gun? . . . [He] can explain that as an inherent problem with latent prints, and anyway, he can always "enhance" the missing characteristic into existence.

It is small wonder indeed that such gifted technicians, whose talents transcend mere "physical data," have been able to explain every last dissimilarity that ever has been observed in two prints that have twelve common points of identification — e.g., twelve ridge endings on one of them and twelve bifurcations on the other.[17]

---

17 Melvin B. Lewis, "The Expert Witness in Criminal Cases: General Considerations" (undated, unpublished paper) at 22–24, reproduced with permission in Mark J. Mahoney,

In the context of identification evidence, the Supreme Court of Canada had no trouble enunciating this incontrovertible point: "Regardless of the number of similar characteristics, if there is one dissimilar feature there is no identification."[18]

Paul C. Giannelli in a recent article[19] provides an excellent overview of the current American debate over fingerprints:

> *Llera Plaza II* is far from a ringing endorsement of fingerprint analysis. Judge Pollak recognized that the basic science (i.e., empirical testing) is missing. He admitted fingerprint testimony only as non-scientific expertise. Indeed, he encouraged the National Institute of Justice (NIJ) to proceed with its research. It will be interesting to see if the only agency that has the money to underwrite research in forensic science will undertake it. To date, the FBI's own proficiency testing appears to be inadequate. Recall the British expert's comment, "they'd fall about laughing."
>
> In the long term, decisions such as the two *Llera Plaza* opinions will hopefully lead to systematic research that will not only give us a better appreciation of the limits of contemporary forensic techniques but, more importantly, yield improved, more reliable techniques. The contrast between *Llera Plaza I* and *Llera Plaza II* poses the essential question about the admissibility of forensic science in the short term. In the current state of the art, fingerprint analysis seems to share many characteristics with other forensic techniques such as questioned document examination and microscopic hair analysis: Although the extant data does not qualify them as "scientific . . . knowledge" . . . it is clear that controlled scientific experiments could be conducted to validate or falsify the basic premises of these forensic techniques.
>
> . . .
>
> In *Daubert,* Justice Blackmun sharply distinguished admissibility analysis from both legal sufficiency and weight. . . . *Llera Plaza I* and *Llera Plaza II* press the issue: How "shaky" can non-scientific expertise be and yet successfully run the *Daubert-Kumho* gauntlet?

The first appellate consideration of fingerprints in light of *Daubert*'s principles has now taken place and the issue has been vigorously joined. In *United States v. Crisp,*[20] the admissibility of fingerprint evidence was upheld but only by a 2:1 majority and with an exhaustive and perceptive dissent. The majority

---

"Materials on Examination of the Expert Witness" (Ontario Criminal Lawyers' Association for the Program "Experts and Junk Science," Toronto, 5 April 1997).

18 *Chartier v. Quebec (Attorney General),* [1979] 2 S.C.R. 474.
19 "Forensic Science: Fingerprints" (2002) 38 Crim. L. Bull. 642 at 650.
20 324 F.3d 261 (4th Cir. 2003).

decision saving fingerprint evidence was based substantially on a respect for precedent and the decades of undoubted admission. The dissent examined all the relevant scientific principles and found the evidence wanting. The following are the points made by Judge Michaels in dissent:

- Just because fingerprint examination is generally accepted under Frye does not mean it's admissible under *Daubert* standards.
- Adversarial testing is not just cross-examination; it also involves independent review and analysis of the fingerprint evidence in the case. However, many defendants are indigent, and there is often a lack of funds to hire an independent examiner. Further, there is a lack of independent crime laboratories to complete the work.
- The government failed to satisfy the *Daubert* factor of testing and validation. It did not offer a record of reliability testing, and it appears there have not been sufficient validation tests to prove that a latent print will match only one known print in the world. Proficiency tests are inadequate when they involve "superior" latent prints that do not reflect "real-world conditions." "The government did not introduce evidence of studies or testing that would show that fingerprint identification is based on reliable principles and methods."
- The government failed to satisfy the *Daubert* factor of peer review and publication. Fingerprint publications do not prompt critique or reanalysis by other scientists, and therefore fingerprint-related identification analysis techniques and methodologies have not changed much over the years.
- The government ignored the *Daubert* factor of error rate in this case. The examiner testified that "[a]s far as statistics, off the top of my head at this point, I cannot give you any. I do know that ... errors have been made in the field of fingerprints." Error rate must be demonstrated by reliable scientific studies, not by assumption. Further, proficiency tests containing non-real world latent prints are not sufficient to test the error rate of individual examiners. The 1995 CTS proficiency data and a similar 1998 test reveal that about half of the examiners were able to make correct identifications and eliminations on all the prints. "An error rate that runs remarkably close to chance can hardly be viewed as acceptable under *Daubert*."[21]

---

21 Also see Tara Marie La Morte, "Sleeping Gatekeepers: *United States v. Llera Plaza* and the Unreliability of Forensic Fingerprinting Evidence under *Daubert*" (2003) 14 Alb. L.J. Sci. & Tech. 171:

> The 156 examiners who agreed to participate in the study were asked to compare seven latent crime scene prints with four suspect inked ten-print cards. The IAI designed

- The government failed to establish the *Daubert* factor as to whether there are standards that govern the application of the technique. Testimony by the examiner that the degree of similarity required to find that prints are matching "is left up to each individual examiner." One forensic expert (Stoney) contends that there are no standards; there are no minimum point requirements. The movement away from point requirements "is not based on scientific study. (Epstein)" and there is disparity in the field regarding the use of level 3 detail for identification (because of distortion). "One dissimilarity" in two impressions is thought to be a universal standard, but if an examiner believes the prints match she explains away the difference rather than discounting the match. Verification is considered to be essential, but cases exist where no verification took place; and even verification that does take place is not independent and objective. All of this leads (Stoney and Cole) to the belief that "[t]he criteria for absolute identification in fingerprint work are subjective and ill-defined."

- The government failed to establish the *Daubert* factor of general acceptance by the scientific community. General acceptance by fingerprint examiners, the public, or the legal system does not sufficiently establish that fingerprint evidence has valid, general acceptance in the scientific community.

- "Even if the proponent of scientific expert evidence does not satisfy the *Daubert* factors, the evidence may be admissible if it is otherwise shown to be reliable. The government also failed to provide other reasons to establish that its fingerprint evidence in this case is reliable."

- "To put it bluntly, the precedent of prior admission, rather than exacting scientific scrutiny" has led to the general acceptance of fingerprint evidence.

- Fingerprinting arose because it offered a "quick, cheap, supposedly less scientific way of identifying those whose crimes did not justify the expense of anthropometry" under the Bertillon system, even though fingerprinting was "believed to be considerably less reliable." Demonstrating

---

and reviewed the test, and both the manufacturer and test referees agreed that the test was challenging, fair, and a satisfactory representation of 'real' conditions. Despite empirical data confirming 'that non-blind proficiency testing leads to more accurate results than when the samples are treated as regular laboratory work,' only forty-four percent of tested examiners provided perfect answers. Fifty-six percent of experts provided answers that differed in some respect from the manufacturer. Overall, fifty-eight identifications were found to be incorrect, which amounted to twenty-two percent of the total. Perhaps the most disturbing result was the presence of false positive misidentifications. If this occurred in actual casework, one in five participants would have provided extremely damaging evidence against the wrong person.

this is an FBI survey involving two crime scene impressions sent along with the defendant's exemplars to all fifty state crime laboratories. The results suggest that the profession of absolute certainty in fingerprint identification is "a false comfort." "The history of fingerprint identification and the dogged certainty of its examiners are insufficient to show that the technique is reliable.

- "I conclude that the district court's decision to admit the fingerprint evidence was an abuse of discretion."
- "A judge who takes *Daubert*'s commands seriously would be hard pressed to write a coherent opinion justifying a decision to admit the expert [fingerprinting] opinion."

Crisp will undoubtedly furnish the blueprint for future forensic consideration of the issue.[22]

HANDWRITING IDENTIFICATION

TO TURN TO another area of police-produced evidence, specifically handwriting identification evidence, objective assessment of this purported area of expertise demonstrates a "lack of sufficient proof of special ability on the part of these experts."[23]

> The . . . most generous reading of all the data from all the tests would give the experts a score of 57% correct. That percentage would seem damning enough, but the authors would discount the easy tests and count as a correct answer only a correct response to the submitted material, then count the non-responding examiners as false or inconclusive, thereby reducing the grade to eighteen percent.[24]

As a result, "[n]umerous courts have now limited the scope of expert testimony in the area of handwriting analysis; although the expert may still describe points of comparison between two samples of handwriting, courts have

22 Paul C. Giannelli, "Forensic Science: Under the Microscope" (2008) 34 Ohio N.U.L. Rev. 315 at 321.

23 D. Michael Risinger *et al.*, "Exorcism of Ignorance as a Proxy for Rational Knowledge: The Lessons of Handwriting Identification Expertise" (1989) 137 U. Pa. L. Rev. 731.

24 Jon P. Thames, "It's Not Bad Law — It's Bad Science: Problems with Expert Testimony in Trial Proceedings" (1995) 18 Am. J. Trial Advoc. 545 at 552–54. See generally Faigman *et al.*, above note 5, vol. 2, c. 22, "Handwriting Identification," 79–123; Saks, above note 2 at 1094–1100; see *United States v. Hines*, 55 F. Supp. 2d 62 (D. Mass. 1999) for a better than usual examination of handwriting analysis.

refused to allow the expert to testify as to the ultimate authorship of the handwriting sample in question."[25]

The critical literature is both voluminous and compelling.[26] At least part of the problem may be the fact that different individuals may well have similar handwriting:[27] "After standing unquestioned for most of this century, a re-evaluation of handwriting identification expertise has resulted from the Supreme Court's decision in *Daubert*."[28]

In *United States v. Hines*,[29] the trial judge excluded the testimony of an FBI document examiner as to the authorship of a "stick-up" note found at the scene of a crime. The Court found that the expert's testimony met virtually none of *Daubert*'s standards for reliability. "There are no meaningful and accepted validity studies in the field. . . . This is a 'field' that has little efficacy outside of a courtroom. There are no peer reviews of it." The Court noted that it had been presented with no information regarding the examiner's error rate, nor was there a standard protocol that could be tested and that could be used to evaluate the witness's methodology. There was no standard regarding how many similarities are required for a "match" or how many dissimilarities require the contrary conclusion.

---

25 Griffin & LaMagna, below note 45 at 21.

26 D. Michael Risinger & Michael J. Saks, "Science and Nonscience in the Courts: *Daubert* Meets Handwriting Identification Expertise" (1996) 82 Iowa L. Rev. 21; Roger C. Park, "Signature Identification in the Light of Science and Experience" (2008) 59 Hastings L.J. 1101. See generally Sandy L. Zabell, "Fingerprint Evidence" (2005) 13:1 J. Law & Pol'y 143, online: www.brooklaw.edu/students/journals/bjlp/jlp13i_zabell.pdf; Edward J. Imwinkelried & Michael Cherry, "The Myth of Fingerprints" *The Champion* (September–October 2003) at 36.

27 John J. Harris, "How Much Do People Write Alike: A Study of Signatures" (1958) 48 J. Crim. L. & Criminology 647; Jodi Sita *et al.*, "Forensic Handwriting Examiners' Expertise for Signature Comparison" (2002) 47 J. Forensic Sci. 1117; Michael J. Saks, "Commentary, Individuality of Handwriting" (2003) 48 J. Forensic Sci. 916. Handwriting examiners have also argued that differences in writing between identical twins support the conclusion that handwriting is unique. See for example, *United States v. Hidalgo*, 229 F. Supp. 2d 96 at 963 (D. Ariz. 2002) (referencing several such studies). The court found that the studies presented did not support that conclusion. As has been noted, "[o]n the other hand, it is hard to understand why one should expect that having the same genotype would cause twins to write indistinguishably alike, and why a finding that they did not write indistinguishably alike would lead to the inference that no writings on earth are indistinguishably alike": Michael J. Saks & Jonathan J. Koehler, "The Individualization Fallacy in Forensic Science Evidence" (2008) 61 Vand. L. Rev. 199 at n.71.

28 Michael J. Saks, "Merlin and Solomon: Lessons from the Law's Formative Encounters with Forensic Identification Science" (1998) 49 Hastings L.J. 1069 at 1097.

29 Above note 24.

The Court understood the logic of nonblind identification procedures and correctly compared the proffered testimony to "one-on-one show-ups," a highly suggestive method of eyewitness identification. The Court noted that there was no evidence that the handwriting expert could have selected the defendant's handwriting as most similar to the robbery note out of a lineup of similar handwriting exemplars. The Court concluded the testimony was inherently unreliable.

District courts in Nebraska and New Jersey have similarly rejected handwriting and text analysis testimony, respectively, for failure to meet *Daubert*'s validity and reliability requirements.[30] However, three recent cases came to the conclusion that the offered expert testimony on handwriting identification, including the ultimate opinion of a "match," was fully admissible as meeting both the *Daubert* and the *Kumho Tire* requirements.[31] In *United States v. Crisp*,[32] handwriting evidence was held admissible by a 2:1 majority over a vigorous and scientifically literate dissent.[33]

HAIR AND FIBRE IDENTIFICATION

REGARDING FORENSIC HAIR comparison, it has been written:

> By and large, however, forensic hair analysis has been generally accepted by our courts for many years, with little fuss or skepticism. It is time for a reevaluation. If the purveyors of this dubious science cannot do a better job of validating hair analysis than they have done so far, forensic hair comparison analysis should be excluded altogether from criminal trials.
>
> . . .
>
> Has the empirical evidence on the subject of forensic hair comparison analysis evolved and gained such acceptance that the courts may say with confi-

---

30 See *United States v. Rutherford*, 104 F. Supp. 2d 1190 (D. Neb. 2000) (holding that handwriting analysis testimony on unique identification lacks both the validity and reliability of other forensic evidence); *United States v. Van Wyk*, 83 F. Supp. 2d 515 at 523 (D.N.J. 2000) (holding that, like handwriting analysis, text analysis is questionable because there is no known rate of error, no recognized standard, no meaningful peer review, and no system of accrediting an individual as an expert in the field). See also *United States v. Santillan*, [1999] WL 1201765 (N.D. Cal. 3 December 1999).

31 *United States v. Prime*, 220 F. Supp. 2d 1203 (W.D. Wash. 2002); *United States v. Thornton*, Case No. 02-M-9150-01, decided by the United States District Court for the District of Kansas on 24 January 2003; and *Williams v. State (Wyoming)*, 60 P.3d 151 (Wyo. Sup. Ct. 2002). See generally Lynn C. Hartfield, "*Daubert/Kumho* Challenges to Handwriting Analysis" *The Champion* (November 2002) at 24.

32 Above note 20.

33 See generally Giannelli, "Forensic Science," above note 22 at 318.

dence that a so-called "match" between hairs is actually probative enough to overcome the confusion it may induce? It is here that we must focus the debate. The major effort made to quantify hair analysis, by Barry Gaudette, was a valiant foray into the field, but it was made over twenty years ago. No effort has yet been made by others attempting to replicate Gaudette's pubic hair comparison probabilities, and but one scalp hair comparison effort has been made. There is no empirical evidence that would support the admission of evidence concerning non-Caucasian hair. Therefore, with respect to scalp and pubic hair, the evidence is insufficient to justify its admission in the courtroom. The same is true of body hair from any individual, Caucasian or not, since no empirical studies have been published on the subject of body hair.

No effort has been made in the United States to empirically prove anything in the field, at any time, yet men and women lose life and liberty on the basis of this untested evidence. If the state wants to use the evidence, the state needs to make convincing efforts to show its scientific validity. Furthermore, even if hair analysis evidence is admitted, we must exclude evidence concerning any multiplier effect where more than one hair "matches," or any other pseudo-statistical evidence which the hair technician puts before the jury as empirical fact unless empirical study establishes the true significance of such factors. Until and unless empirical evidence that supports the use of hair analysis is considerably improved, forensic hair comparison analysis results must be kept from the jury.[34]

This reality about hair-comparison evidence (as well as fibre comparison) was highlighted by the Kaufman Commission Report in the case of Guy Paul Morin.[35] Many of the critical comments could apply equally to other similar kinds of identification evidence.

At Mr. Morin's second trial, the Crown led evidence of two forensic analysts as to hair and fibre comparisons. The prosecution relied upon the hair and fibre findings made by these scientists to demonstrate that there was physical contact

34 Clive A. Stafford Smith & Patrick D. Goodman, "Forensic Hair Comparison Analysis: Nineteenth Century Science or Twentieth Century Snake Oil?" (1996) 27 Colum. Hum. Rts. L. Rev. 227 at 231 and 290–91 [footnotes omitted]. See also Paul C. Giannelli & Emmie West, "Hair Comparison Evidence" (2001) 37 Crim. L. Bull. 514.

35 The Honourable Fred Kaufman, Commissioner, *Report of the Kaufman Commission on Proceedings Involving Guy Paul Morin* (Toronto: Ministry of the Attorney General, 1998) [Kaufman Commission Report], online: www.attorneygeneral.jus.gov.on.ca/english/about/pubs/morin at 311–24 regarding hair comparisons and 324–26 regarding fibre comparisons. See also Griffin & LaMagna, below note 45 at 22–23, referencing a case where the hair "expert" testified that the crime scene hair sample was "unlikely to match anyone other than the defendant," but DNA evidence subsequently exonerated the defendant.

between the victim and the accused, and that the victim had been transported in the Morin vehicle to her death by the accused. The evidence was said to refute Morin's denial that he had had any physical contact with the victim and his specific assertion that the victim, his next-door neighbour, had never even been in the Honda.

The following summarizes the relevant portions of the Commission's Report:[36]

The Hair Comparisons

When Christine Jessop's body was discovered, a single dark hair was found embedded in skin tissue adhering to her necklace ("the necklace hair"). This hair was not Christine's and was presumed to originate with her killer. This hair was said to be microscopically similar to Guy Paul Morin's hair and could have originated from him. After Mr. Morin's first trial and before his second, an analysis of hairs belonging to Christine Jessop's classmates revealed that two classmates had hairs which were also microscopically similar.

Three hairs found in Mr. Morin's car ("the car hairs") were said to be dissimilar to Mr. Morin's hairs. It was said that these were similar to Christine Jessop's hairs and could have come from her.

The Commissioner's findings included:

- The necklace hair comparison, properly interpreted, yielded nothing more than a conclusion that Guy Paul Morin, together with countless others, could not be excluded as the donor of the necklace hair. The car hairs comparison, properly interpreted, yielded nothing more than a conclusion that Christine Jessop, together with countless others, could not be excluded as the donor of these hairs. Properly understood, the hair comparison evidence had little or no probative value in proving Mr. Morin's guilt.
- Ms. Nyznyk did not adequately or accurately communicate the limitations upon her hair comparison findings to police and prosecutors prior to the second trial.
- Prior to Guy Paul Morin's arrest, Ms. Nyznyk conducted a hasty, preliminary comparison of the necklace hair and Guy Paul Morin's hairs in the investigators' presence. She communicated a preliminary opinion to the officers. That opinion was overstated and, to her knowledge, left the officers with the understanding that the comparison yielded important evidence implicating Mr. Morin.

---

36 What follows is from Mark J. Sandler, "Lessons for Appellate Courts from the Morin Inquiry" (2001, unpublished paper). Mr. Sandler was counsel to the Kaufman Commission.

- Had the limitations on Ms. Nyznyk's early findings been adequately communicated by her, Mr. Morin may not have been arrested when he was — if, indeed, ever.

. . .

The hair comparison evidence was misused by the prosecution in its closing address at the second trial (though this was not done malevolently).

The Fibre Comparisons

Fibres were collected from the taping of Christine Jessop's clothing and recorder bag found at the body site, from the taping and vacuuming of the Morin Honda and from tapings of the Morin residence. Many thousands of fibres (perhaps hundreds of thousands) were examined. Several became significant. Ms. Nyznyk and Mr. Erickson testified at the Morin criminal proceedings that several of the fibres from the Morin-related locations were similar and could have come from the same source as several fibres found at the body site.

The Commissioner found that the similarities, even if they all existed, proved nothing.

. . .

The contribution of the CFS [Centre of Forensic Sciences] to Mr. Morin's wrongful arrest, prosecution and conviction was substantial. Hair and fibre evidence formed the justification, in large measure, for his arrest, and for the searches of his car and home; was cited by the prosecution to support his detention pending trial; was cited by the Court of Appeal and Supreme Court of Canada as evidence relevant to whether his acquittal should be reversed; formed a substantial part of the case against him and undoubtedly, given its prominence at the second trial, was relied upon by the jury at the second trial to convict him. The failings identified at the Inquiry were found to be rooted in systemic problems, many of which transcend even the CFS and have been noted in cases worldwide where science has been misused.

. . .

The Morin case provides an illustration of virtually everything that can go wrong when science is injected into a criminal case.

. . .

The introduction of evidence that hairs "could have come from" Guy Paul Morin or Christine Jessop raises an important systemic issue: does the probative value of such evidence, even if viewed as a piece of circumstantial evidence to be evaluated cumulatively, truly outweigh its prejudicial effect and justify its reception in support of guilt? Although our subsequently acquired knowledge that these hairs did not originate from Guy Paul Morin or Christine Jessop cannot dictate the answer to this question, the dangers associated with this evidence are surely highlighted by that known fact. The introduction of evidence that fibres "could have come from" Guy Paul Morin or Christine Jessop ... raise[s] similar issues.

[The Commentary concluded:]

I do not think it appropriate to articulate any hard and fast rules as to when such evidence should be admitted in a criminal trial. As — [was] pointed out, the potential uses of the evidence will vary case by case, and advances in technology may alter the value of a particular analysis. In my respectful view, however, it is appropriate for trial judges to undertake a far more critical analysis of the admissibility of this kind of evidence. My own view is that hair comparison evidence of the kind introduced in the Morin case should rarely be admitted for inclusionary purposes.

Courts generally have recognized the unscientific and misleading nature of such evidence.[37]

FIREARM IDENTIFICATION

FIREARMS EXAMINATION RAISES precisely similar issues.[38] First, it also assumes that there are individual characteristics that are unique to one specific firearm. If a firearm is suspected, the examiner compares microscopic marks on the cartridge or bullet recovered from the crime scene with test bullets and cartridges fired from the suspect weapon to see if the markings are consistent. In other cases, the examiner may compare bullets to each other, or cartridges to each other, to see if the markings are consistent.

The examiner is looking for a certain quality and quantity of agreement. Some differences always exist between a recovered bullet and a test bullet, even if they come from the same weapon. Similarly, one would expect some differences between cartridges that come from the same weapon. The examiner's judgment determines "consistency."

---

37   Erica Beecher-Monas, "Blinded by Science: How Judges Avoid the Science in Scientific Evidence" (1998) 71 Temp. L. Rev. 55 at 86–87 describing trial court's rejection of hair evidence for failure to meet standards of validation, despite recognition of "long history of admissibility."

38   What follows is also covered in the excellent article by Lisa J. Steele, "'All We Want You to Do Is Confirm What We Already Know': A *Daubert* Challenge to Firearms Identifications" (2002) 38 Crim. L. Bull. 466 [footnotes omitted].

Second, again "sameness" may be only in the eye of the forensic laboratory beholder: "The examiner's conclusion, based on his observations, is a subjective judgment. There are no objective criteria established in this field. . . . Each examiner develops for himself 'his own intuitive criteria of identity gained through practical experience.'"[39]

After explaining the theory of firearms identification, one author tested the methodology to see if it passed the *Daubert* standards (reviewed earlier in this book) and found it wanting. Error rates were found to be substantial:

> The only apparently blind study done yielded an error rate of 9.1%. A 1995 study of fingerprint examiners yielded an error rate of 22%. In all but one of the tests described in the AFTE [Association of Firearms and Toolmark Examiners] Journal, the examiner apparently knew the sources of the bullets he or she was comparing. This strongly suggests that the theory has not been adequately tested by proper scientific methods.[40]

Most important, the dangers of the nonblind-testing procedure for identity are well highlighted in words applicable to all forms of forensic identification evidence:

> [Regarding subjectivity of identifications] . . . fingerprint comparisons, like firearms identifications, are based on the examiner's subjective opinion about the quantity and quality of microscopic markings that may show a high degree of correspondence without matching, or a small degree of correspondence while matching.
>
> . . .
>
> [C]onsider the fundamental problem in any subjective comparison[:]. . . the psychological phenomena known as "confirmation bias." If the examiner has a prior belief or expectation that two toolmarks will, or will not, match, then two potential psychological biases arise. "Cognitive confirmation bias" is a tendency to seek out and interpret evidence in ways that fit existing beliefs. "Behavioral confirmation bias," commonly referred to as the self-fulfilling prophecy, is a tendency for people to unwittingly procure support for their beliefs through their own behavior. The danger of confirmation bias affecting an examiner's subjective opinion is rarely discussed in the firearms examination literature or in the court cases upholding admissibility of the technique.

Confirmation bias has caused famous scientists to fail to report easily visible phenomena that do not conform to their expectations and to "observe" non-existent phenomena. Expectations have caused laboratory workers un-

---

39 Steele, *ibid.*
40 *Ibid.*

consciously to conform test results to an expected norm. Logically, that same confirmation bias can cause firearms examiners to overestimate the quality or quantity of striae when they have external reasons to expect a match and to underestimate the quality and quantity of striae when they have external reasons to expect a non-match.

...

The basic flaws in the theory underlying individual characteristics are that (1) the bulk of the research has not been done in a blind or double-blind fashion and (2) the standards in the area are entirely subjective, depending solely on the examiners' own training and experience. It is difficult to conclude that the current state of firearms identification theory passes the first *Daubert* criterion.[41]

Steele concludes by allowing that "[f]irearms identification may be valid and probative evidence in criminal trials. However, adherents of this technique simply have not proven their theory with sufficient rigor to pass a *Daubert* challenge if one is made in the trial courts." She urges that the problems resulting from confirmation bias and suggestive information be addressed before firearms identification evidence is presented at trial. "Courts should disallow firearms identification testimony that is not supported by appropriate proof that the theory and methodology pass scientific scrutiny. Defence counsel must be alert to the potential problems in firearms identification evidence and challenge that evidence in appropriate cases."[42]

Another critic concludes:

Adequate statistical empirical foundations and proficiency testing do not exist for firearms and toolmark identification. Examiners themselves admit and results on CTS proficiency tests show that misidentifications as well as missed identifications occur. Far from solving the fundamental scientific problems, the development of computerized firearms identification has shown that the possibility of missed identifications and misidentifications by firearms and toolmark examiners is even greater than previously believed. . . . [C]ourts that have admitted toolmark and firearms identifications have [not] recognized the systemic scientific problems with the field. Judicial reluctance to rock the prosecutorial boat may partially explain why, despite widespread concern among firearms and toolmark examiners, courts have failed to recognize the inadequacy of the field's scientific foundations.[43]

---

41 *Ibid.*
42 See e.g., *Sexton v. State (Texas)*, 93 S.W.3d 96 (Tex. Ct. Crim. App. 2002).
43 Adina Schwartz, "A Systematic Challenge to the Reliability and Admissibility of Firearms and Toolmark Identification" (2005) 6 Colum. Sci. & Tech. L. Rev. 2 at 41, online: www.stlr.org/html/volume6/schwartz.pdf.

Steele offers a useful "Checklist for Defence Attorneys"[44] with regard to firearms evidence. This list can easily be generalized to any type of forensic identification evidence, and what follows is a modified version of her checklist:

Questions to ask the expert or points to consider:

- What are your credentials (training, experience, teaching experience, and professional affiliations)?
- What books, journals, and magazines do you consider authoritative? Have you published any articles?
- What is your methodology: protocols, quality control reviews, safeguards, laboratory accreditation?
- Did you properly calibrate the microscope at the time of the identification?
- What are the data on sources of error: false positives, rate of error, and controls? (Ask to see preliminary reports, notes, pictomicrographs, photos, and other materials.)
- How many test bullets or cartridges were compared? [or fibres, teeth marks, and so on]
- Did you compare the test bullets and cartridges to each other before examining the suspect bullets and cartridges? Did you have any trouble doing so?
- Explain the difference between class marks, marks from the manufacturing process, and individual marks from that specific weapon.
- Did a single expert compare the bullets and cartridges or was it reviewed by a second expert?
- What are your standards of agreement for concluding that a specified tool made a specific evidence toolmark? How does this standard compare to others in your agency and with any professional organizations to which you belong?
- Have you ever deliberately compared known nonmatch bullets?
- Would you expect to find agreements (matching striae) on marks known to have been made from different firearms? How does this match differ from those known nonmatches?
- Has your work ever been subjected to a blind test or review? If so, what was the error rate?
- What information did you know at the time you examined the marks and suspect firearm?
- Are you familiar with various confirmation biases? If so, what precautions do you take to minimize their effects?

---

44 This checklist has been modified in style, but not content. For original see Steele, above note 38 at 481–84.

- Consider whether the examiner
  - » felt pressured to complete the exam, or
  - » tried to be "helpful" to the investigation, or
  - » intentionally fabricated or falsified the test results.
- Make certain that any ammunition used for creating comparison bullets is of the same type as the ammunition recovered from the crime scene.
- If the recovered firearm appears to be newly manufactured, ask about the differences between manufacturing characteristics and those that occur over time through normal wear.
- If the recovered ammunition was lead bullets, not jacketed ammunition, ask about the effects of lead deposits on firearms comparisons.

Other authors have also outlined explicit steps to follow in "mounting a *Daubert* challenge to ballistics evidence."[45]

OTHER EXAMPLES

THE EXAMPLES OF forensic matching evidence build an ever-expanding list. "Barefoot insole impressions,"[46] lip-prints,[47] "earprints,"[48] "bite-marks,"[49] "facial

---

45 Joan Griffin & David J. LaMagna, "*Daubert* Challenges to Forensic Evidence: Ballistics Next on the Firing Line" *The Champion* (September–October 2002) 20 at 24 and 58–62; Schwartz, "A Systematic Challenge to the Reliability and Admissibility of Firearms and Toolmark Identification," above note 43; Adina Schwartz, "Challenging Firearms and Toolmark Identification — Part I" *The Champion* (October 2008) at 44; Adina Schwartz, "Challenging Firearms and Toolmark Identification — Part II" *The Champion* (November–December 2008) at 44. See generally Giannelli, "Forensic Science," above note 22 at 323.

46 See chapter 3, "Logical Relevance."

47 The first appellate (and perhaps the only) case in the United States admitting lip-print evidence to identify the perpetrator of a crime was *People (Illinois) v. Davis*, 710 N.E.2d 1251 (Ill. App. 2 Dist. 1999), appeal denied 720 N.E.2d 1097 (Ill. 1999). The decision assimilates lip-prints to fingerprints.

48 See chapter 1, note 33.

49 "[D]ental experts seldom agree with one another at trial," citing controlled studies finding erroneous identifications or exclusions of between 24% and 91%, "63.5% false positives," and "false positive identifications of 11.9–22.0% for various groups of forensic odontologists": C. Michael Bowers, "Problem-Based Analysis of Bitemark Misidentifications: The Role of DNA" (2006) 159 Forensic Sci. Int'l S104 at S106–7 (Supp. 2006). Bowers further cited seven cases in recent years where DNA typing contradicted the conclusions of forensic dentists that the defendant was the source of a crime scene bite-mark. See chapter 1, note 19. See also Paul C. Giannelli, "Bite Mark Analysis" (2007) 43 Crim. L. Bull. 930. See *Howard v. State (Mississippi)*, 701 So. 2d 274 (Miss. 1997) regarding inadmissible evidence. See also Faigman *et al.*, above note 5, vol. 2, c. 24, "Identification from Bite Marks," 156–87; Saks, above note 2 at 1119–27.

mapping,"[50] lip-reading,[51] toolmark, including knife-mark identifications,[52] and voiceprints,[53] are some examples. Some areas of evidence turn out to be better

---

50 *R. v. Gray*, [2003] EWCA Crim 1001. In that case the court was alive to the reliability concerns regarding such evidence.

> We do not however wish to pass from this appeal without making general observations about the use of facial imaging and mapping expert evidence of a reliable kind. Mr Harrow, like some other facial imaging and mapping experts, said that comparison of the facial characteristics provided "strong support for the identification of the robber as the appellant." No evidence was led of the number of occasions on which any of the six facial characteristics identified by him as "the more unusual and thus individual" were present in the general population, nor as to the frequency of the occurrence in the general population, of combinations of these or any other facial characteristics. Mr Harrow did not suggest that there was any national database of facial characteristics or any accepted mathematical formula, as in the case of fingerprint comparison, from which conclusions as to the probability of occurrence of particular facial characteristics or combinations of facial characteristics could safely be drawn. This court is not aware of the existence of any such database or agreed formula. In their absence any estimate of probabilities and any expression of the degree of support provided by particular facial characteristics or combinations of facial characteristics must be only the subjective opinion of the facial imaging or mapping witness. There is no means of determining objectively whether or not such an opinion is justified. Consequently, unless and until a national database or agreed formula or some other such objective measure is established, this court doubts whether such opinions should ever be expressed by facial imaging or mapping witnesses. The evidence of such witnesses, including opinion evidence, is of course both admissible and frequently of value to demonstrate to a jury with, if necessary, enhancement techniques afforded by specialist equipment, particular facial characteristics or combinations of such characteristics so as to permit the jury to reach its own conclusion — see *Attorney General's Reference No. 2 of 2002* [2002] EWCA Crim 2373; but on the state of the evidence in this case, and if this court's understanding of the current position is correct in other cases too, such evidence should stop there. (*Ibid.* at para. 16.)

51 See chapter 3, "A Qualified Expert."
52 See chapter 3, note 29 regarding *Ramirez v. State (Florida)*; Schwartz, "A Systematic Challenge to the Reliability and Admissibility of Firearms and Toolmark Identification," above note 43; Faigman *et al.*, above note 5; Saks, above note 2.

> In ruling knife-mark identification evidence inadmissible for lack of reliability, the court in *Ramirez* had occasion to consider "traditional" knife-mark evidence, "a subgroup of the broad category of evidence commonly referred to as 'tool mark' evidence .... The theory underlying tool mark evidence ... is generally accepted in the scientific community and has long been upheld by courts. Many of the analytical methods that were developed for use with tool marks in general have been applied to knife marks in particular and have similarly been accepted by courts."

53 Erica Beecher-Monas, "Blinded by Science," above note 37 at 97: "Voice identification also has failed the scientifically valid prong of *Daubert*"; *United States v. Bahena*, 223 F.3d 797 (8th Cir. 2000); *People (California) v. Kelly*, 549 P.2d 1240 (Cal. 1976); *R. v. O'Doherty*, [2002] Crim. L.R. 761 (Irish C.A.); *R. v. Medvedew* (1978), 43 C.C.C. (2d) 434 at 448

than others, such as DNA evidence, but even that is not "perfect."[54]

Comparative bullet analysis is another example but one where science has triumphed, in the sense that the evidence has been successfully debunked and is no longer attempted. Composition bullet lead analysis (CBLA) evidence confirms that the lead in the fragments recovered from the decedent and the lead in bullets the defendant possessed were analytically indistinguishable, that both the lead fragments recovered from the decedent's body and the defendant's bullets came from the same source of lead, and both the fragments recovered from the decedent's body and the defendant's bullets came from the same box or boxes and were packaged on the same date by the manufacturer.[55] After much credible criticism,[56] the FBI halted any use of the evidence.[57]

SUMMARY

ON A GENERAL level then, applying the requirements in *Daubert* and the general elements of the scientific method described above, the types of evidence here being considered share certain features in common and also share certain deficiencies when measured against the dictates of good science:

- The evidence is generally evidence of identity or at least lack of dissimilarity, which requires either an assumption of uniqueness (no two fingerprints are alike, and so on) or data regarding that issue. No such data exist.
- There are usually transparency issues because the actual comparison data are not preserved for later independent viewing.

(Man. C.A.), O'Sullivan J.A., dissenting; *People (New York) v. Collins*, 405 N.Y.S.2d 369 (1978); and *D'Arc v. D'Arc*, 385 A.2d 278 (N.J. Super. Ct., Ch. Div. 1978). Unfortunately, the battle continues: *State (Alaska) v. Coon*, 974 P.2d 386 (Alaska 1999). See generally *On the Theory and Practice of Voice Identification* (Washington, DC: National Research Council, Committee on Evaluation of Sound Spectrograms, 1979). See Saks, above note 2 at 1112–19; Faigman *et al.*, above note 5, vol. 2, c. 25, "Talker Identification," 188–226.

54 See chapter 4, note 47.

55 *State v. Behn*, 2005 N.J. Super. LEXIS 73; *Clemons v. State*, 2006 Md. LEXIS 192.

56 William A. Tobin, "Comparative Bullet Lead Analysis (CBLA) Evidence: Valid Inference or *Ipse Dixit*?" (2004) 40 Crim. L. Bull. 163; Edward J. Imwinkelried & William A. Tobin, "Comparative Bullet Lead Analysis (CBLA) Evidence: Valid Inference or *Ipse Dixit*?" (2003) 28 Okla. City U.L. Rev. 43.

57 FBI, News Release, "FBI Laboratory Announces Discontinuation of Bullet Lead Examinations" (1 September 2005), online: www.fbi.gov/pressrel/pressrel05/bullet_lead_analysis.htm.

- The definition of sameness, or lack of "unaccountable differences," is a subjective "rubber yardstick." A "match" or "sameness" is declared notwithstanding actual differences if the differences are not "unaccountable."
- The evidence is usually obtained by a highly suggestive, potentially biased, one-on-one comparison with no elements of "blindness."[58] Confirmation bias is a ubiquitous possibility. The problem exists whether or not it is actual police officers giving the evidence, but the permissibility of such witnesses is most dubious.[59] In any event, it borders on the tragic and should signal the inadmissibility of forensic evidence where "forensic scientists remain stubbornly unwilling to confront and control the problem of bias, insisting that it can be overcome through sheer force of will and good intentions."[60]
- There is either no real testing of examiners to evaluate their actual error rates or if such is in fact done, the error rates are substantial and unacceptable, especially under field conditions.
- There are no reliable data on false positive rates or, if there are, the rates are substantial and unacceptable, especially under field conditions.

---

58 See note 31 in chapter 4 of this book.
59 See the too-little-noticed comments in *R. v. Klassen*, [2003] M.J. No. 417 (Q.B.).
60 Elizabeth F. Loftus & Simon A. Cole, "Contaminated Evidence" *Science* (14 May 2004) at 959.

CHAPTER 6

Science and Psychiatric and Psychological Evidence

PSYCHIATRIC AND PSYCHOLOGICAL evidence is often given by an expert witness regarding abnormal mental conditions that have an impact on an accused's criminal responsibility — either by negating it entirely or in part by denying a requisite mental state. Such evidence is viewed as "necessary" for the trier of fact within the requirements of the *Mohan* rule for the admissibility of expert evidence, and, as set out in chapter 3, its legal relevance (i.e., its reliability and probative value) is often not disputed.

Critics say that this area of expert evidence is a prime example of "survival by precedent" because psychiatry's claimed ability to understand human psychic difficulties is not based in science.[1] Even before *Daubert* and recent concerns

---

1   See, for example, Peter Shea, *Psychiatry in Court: The Use(fulness) of Psychiatric Reports and Psychiatric Evidence in Court Proceedings*, 2d ed., The Institute of Criminology Monograph Series (Annandale, NSW: Hawkins Press, Division of the Federation Press, 1996). This psychiatrist/author has described accurately and honestly the limitations of psychiatric evidence in court. The section "The Language of Psychiatry" includes subsections on Psychopathy ("decided advantage to both psychiatry and the law if the clinical concept could be put to one side and excluded from legal debate until a great deal more research is done"); Post-traumatic Stress Disorder (reflects the American "penchant for elevating human problems into psychiatric disorders," quoting a journalist), as well as Schizophrenia and the Depressive Disorders. The Major Schools of Psychiatry are outlined, as well as a succinct discussion of the two main classification schemes (nosology) of psychiatric disorders, the ICD-10 (International Statistical Classification of Diseases and Related Health Problems, World Health Organization) and the DSM-IV (*Diagnostic and Statistical Manual of Mental Disorders*). "Dangerousness" includes subsections entitled

about the quality of expert evidence, an excellent reference text by Jay Ziskin[2] on psychiatric and psychological testimony began with the following: "It is the aim of this book to demonstrate that despite the ever increasing utilization of psychiatric and psychological evidence in the legal process, such evidence frequently does not meet reasonable criteria of admissibility and, if admitted, should be given little or no weight."[3] The Ziskin text contains exhaustive and scientifically literate chapters whose titles point to scientific difficulties with psychiatry and psychology:

- The Bases of Expert Testimony: The Dubious Status of Psychiatrists and Psychologists
- Science and the Scientific Method
- Base Rates, "Barnum" Effect, Illusory Correlation and Double Standards of Evidence
- Challenging Theories and Principles
- Challenging Principles of Diagnosis (DSM-III)
- Challenging the Clinical Examination
- Challenging Psychological Tests[4]

"The Concept of Dangerousness," "The Relationship between Mental Disorder and Dangerousness," and "The Prediction of Dangerousness" and reminds (at 141) that "psychiatrists are often called upon to make judgments on . . . future dangerousness . . . and yet . . . their track record in predicting dangerousness is generally rather poor."

Julio Arboleda-Florez & Christine J. Deynaka, *Forensic Psychiatric Evidence* (Toronto: Butterworths, 1999) is an excellent attempt to consider psychiatric evidence from a scientific perspective. But ultimately it claims psychiatry to be a science as well as an "art."

Even a passing familiarity with David Rosenhan's famous study "Being Sane in Insane Places" must inevitably raise serious questions about the real validity of psychiatric diagnoses: see Neil Vidmar, "Evaluating Expert Scientific Evidence" (5 November 1999), ADGN/RP-093 at paras. 46–52 (on Quicklaw in Commentary) for an excellent summary.

2 Jay Ziskin, *Coping with Psychiatric and Psychological Testimony*, 3d ed., 2 vols. (Venice, CA: Law and Psychology Press, 1981).

3 Ziskin, *ibid.*, vol. 1 at vii. This two-volume work then goes on to provide excellent information and ammunition to demolish virtually any psychiatric or psychological claim.

4 A relevant reference is Scott O. Lilienfeld, James M. Wood, & Howard N. Garb, "The Scientific Status of Projective Techniques" (November 2000) 1:2 Psychological Science in the Public Interest 27. For an abstract of this article, see text at note 29 in chapter 4 of this book. See also John Hunsley *et al.*, "Controversial and Questionable Assessment Techniques" in Scott O. Lilienfeld *et al.*, eds., *Science and Pseudoscience in Clinical Psychology* (New York & London: Guilford Press, 2003) c. 3 at 39–76.

See also Dennis P. Saccuzzo, "Still Crazy after All These Years: California's Persistent Use of the MMPI as Character Evidence in Criminal Cases" (1999) 33 U.S.F. L. Rev. 379: argues the MMPI was intended for use as a psychological test to evaluate such conditions as schizophrenia or depression, and that it is misused in criminal court as profile evidence

- Challenging Reliability and Validity of Psychiatric and Psychological Evaluations
- Challenging the Expert's Experience
- Psychiatry: Not Science, Not Medicine

One of the foundations of modern psychiatry and psychology, the authoritative *Diagnostic and Statistical Manual of Mental Disorders* (DSM-IV) — an encyclopedic catalogue intended to be used to diagnose in a consistent fashion psychiatric diseases based on clinical symptoms — has been exposed as an arbitrary nosology rather than a scientific work.

The DSM mostly concerns itself with the description of behaviors while largely ignoring the issue of what causes those behaviors. You can be given the label of borderline personality disorder, for example, if you manifest five out of a list of nine rather vague behaviors, such as inappropriate intense anger, chronic feelings of emptiness, a persistently unstable self-image, or a pattern of unstable and intense interpersonal relationships. But there is no mention of what might cause such symptoms. Often avoiding the issue of cause, the DSM encourages psychiatrists and therapists alike to believe they have diagnosed the patient when they have only described the patient's symptoms.

. . .

"Reliability, and not validity, is the goal of the DSM," write psychiatrists Paul McHugh and Phillip Slavney. The DSM gives rules that make it likely that two different psychiatrists will give the same label to a given patient. This is little more than an extensive and complicated word game, for there is nothing in the DSM that would guide these two psychiatrists to come to the same conclusion about the source of this patient's problems. As McHugh points out, the questions the DSM does not address include: "How do these disorders come about? How are they to be avoided? What is necessary to correct them?" In short, the questions the DSM does not address are precisely the central questions a differential diagnosis seeks to answer.[5]

(by the prosecution) or character evidence (by the defence) and whose admissibility should be re-evaluated.

5   Ethan Watters & Richard Ofshe, *Therapy's Delusions: The Myth of the Unconscious and the Exploitation of Today's Walking Worried* (New York: Scribner, 1999) at 218. See also *Psychiatric Research Report* (Summer 2001) by Paul R. McHugh, M.D., Director and Psychiatrist-in-Chief, Department of Psychiatry and Behavioral Sciences, Johns Hopkins Medical Institutions, Baltimore, MD, online: www.hopkinsmedicine.org/press/2001/august/McHugh.htm.
     See also Allan V. Horwitz, *Creating Mental Illness* (Chicago: University of Chicago Press, 2002); Ziskin, above note 2, vol. 1, c. 5, "Challenging Principles of Diagnosis (DSM-III)" at 130; and Herb Kutchins & Stuart A. Kirk, *Making Us Crazy; DSM: The Psychiatric*

There are real circularity of reasoning problems with much psychiatric theorizing, including diagnoses. The diagnosis is based upon conduct or other alleged symptoms, which are then sought to be explained by the diagnosis. For that reason at least one psychiatrist has urged forensic psychiatrists to recognize: "[i]t is a waste of time pursuing the fine details of psychiatric diagnosis in court. . . . Instead of a diagnostic label what you need to know about (for forensic purposes) are the person's symptoms, the short and long term effects of those symptoms on the person's behavior and lifestyle, the degree of impairment the symptoms produce, both individually and in concert and whether or not anything can be done about any of these things."[6]

Concerns about the intellectual foundations of much psychic evidence have grown in response to the successful attempts by the psychiatric and psychological professions in the last two decades to expand their forensic market penetration. What was previously understood as the behaviour (and accompanying mental states) of normal, albeit troubled, distraught, victimized (in fact or in perception), enraged, or even cold-blooded, vicious people was recast in terms of syndromes and behavioural evaluations that, some argue, did nothing but echo the proponents' interpretation of events in pseudo-medical argot.[7] Concepts were fuzzy and ill-defined, capable of being applied or disavowed at the whim of the examiner (or because of the operation of one or more of the biases described in chapter 4). Conclusions about groups were reached without regard to issues of the representative nature or otherwise of the sample upon which the conclusions were based, or without proper study of relevant comparison groups. "Treatments" are offered without any scientific investigation or foundation.

Bible and the Creation of Mental Disorders (New York: Free Press, 1997). This latter book is a follow-up to the authors' *The Selling of DSM: The Rhetoric of Science in Psychiatry* (New York: Aldine de Gruyter, 1992) and continues the exposé of DSM as substantial pseudo-science.

Compare Christopher Slobogin, "Doubts about *Daubert*: Psychiatric Anecdata as a Case Study" (2000) 57 Wash. & Lee L. Rev. 919; Thomas G. Gutheil & Marshall D. Stein, "*Daubert*-Based Gatekeeping and Psychiatric/Psychological Testimony in Court: Review and Proposal" (2000) 28:2 J. Psychiatry & Law 235.

See also Vidmar, above note 1 at paras. 22–25.

6   Shea, above note 1 at 8. See also Horwitz, *ibid*.

7   Tana Dineen, *Manufacturing Victims: What the Psychology Industry Is Doing to People*, 2d ed. (Montreal: Robert Davies Multimedia, 1998). See Dr. Dineen's website at http://tanadineen.com/. In *United States v. Finley*, 301 F.3d 1000 (9th Cir. 2002), the accused attempted to negotiate transparently bogus financial instruments obtained from Montana Freemen. At trial on fraud charges, he defended on the ground that he honestly believed the instruments to be valid, offering testimony from psychologist Dr. John J. Wicks that accused suffered from "atypical belief system." The appellate court reversed the trial court's exclusion of the evidence, stating the defence psychologist relied on standard techniques of psychological testing, interviews, and gathering patient history, and his experience in evaluating thousands of persons "should not be undervalued."

It has been about 30 years since the first rumblings of discontent with the state of academic psychology began to be heard.... It is a remarkable feature of mainstream academic psychology that, alone among the sciences, it should be almost wholly immune to critical appraisal as an enterprise. Methods that have long been shown to be ineffective or worse are still used on a routine basis by hundreds, perhaps thousands of people. Conceptual muddles long exposed to view are evident in almost every issue of standard psychology journals.[8]

* * * * *

A 10-credit course in "Trauma, Terror, and Treatment," offered by an APA-approved vendor, psychceu.com, contains information on identifying the symptoms of acute stress and post-traumatic stress disorder. But it also suggests treating those conditions through Jungian sandplay therapy, "elemental therapy," and other New Age techniques. One passes the course by completing a short test that includes the following true-false items:

> "In trauma, first chakra (earth element) impact is the most severe, as it involves life or death issues."

> "Fire is the element of the second chakra, and it correlates to attachment."

Questions about chakras, a series of "energy fields," associated with kundalini yoga, "have no place on a continuing-education test for mental-health professionals," says Scott O. Lilienfeld, a professor of psychology at Emory University and an editor of the *Science and Pseudoscience* volume. "There is no scientific evidence whatsoever for the existence of such energy fields, let alone for the claim that manipulating them produces psychological benefits."[9]

In many cases, the problem is the lack of appropriate challenge by opposing counsel. This was true regarding the concept of "recovered memories," which took nearly a decade, and some wrongful convictions as well as numerous ill-founded prosecutions, to pass through the system.[10] A pro-science defence of recovered memories has been offered as follows:

---

8 R. Harre, "Acts of Living" *Science* (August 2000) at 1303.

9 David Glenn, "Sandplay Therapy and Yoga: Do They Belong in Continuing-Education Courses for Psychologists?" online: http://chronicle.com/free/v50/i09/09a01501.htm.

10 See Alan D. Gold, "Admissibility of Evidence of 'Repressed' or 'Recovered Memories'" (Presentation to National Judicial Institute Criminal Law Seminar, Montreal, 19 March 1998), ADGN/RP-059 (on Quicklaw in Commentary); Mike Redmayne, "A Corroboration Approach to Recovered Memories of Sexual Abuse: A Note of Caution" (2000) 116 Law Q. Rev. 147; Alan D. Gold, "False Memory Syndrome in Perspective" (1996) 6 Can. Insurance L. Rev. 155; Campbell Perry & Alan D. Gold, "Hypnosis and the Elicitation of True and False Memories of Childhood Sexual Abuse" (1995) 2 Psychiatry, Psychology &

Consider ... the so-called "false memory syndrome," wherein therapists are alleged to create false memories of childhood sexual abuse in patients, sometimes resulting in criminal charges against a parent or other adult. A substantial body of research shows how easily false memories can be easily implanted, and examination of the testimony of some experts who testify about the reality of sexual abuse and recovered memory reveals pseudo science that is akin to astrology. Nevertheless, there is a genuine scientific debate about whether memories, including childhood sexual abuse, can be repressed and then recovered. In a thought-provoking article Arrigo and Pezdek[FN13] point out that "psychogenic amnesia" — a technical phrase for repressed memory — has been documented, studied, and verified in other domains. Persons involved in disasters or other accidents, who are engaged in military combat, who attempt suicide, who witness criminal acts like homicide, who are raped, or who witness a violent death of a parent during their childhood often have loss of memory that is gradually recovered. Moreover, neurological research has indicated that traumatic memories are processed and stored differently in the brain than events with less emotional content.[FN14] Recovery of traumatic memories can occur, and this often proceeds in phases wherein fragments of the event invade consciousness over a period of time, sometimes resulting in complete recovery of the event. These findings have caused Nadel and Jacobs to conclude that "at least some memories 'recovered' during therapy should be taken seriously."[FN15]"

However, the references in this defence do not withstand critical examination; nor can they support the existence of repressed memories for sexual mis-

---

Law, ADGN/RP-061 (on Quicklaw in Commentary); FMS (False Memory Syndrome) Foundation (Legal Staff), "United States Judicial Response to Repressed Memory Claims" (11 November 1996) ADGN/RP-002 (on Quicklaw in Commentary).

See also *R. v. K.M.M.*, [1999] N.B.J. No. 137 (Q.B.); David L. Faigman *et al.*, *Modern Scientific Evidence*, 2 vols. (St. Paul, MN: West, 1997) vol. 1, c. 13, "Repressed Memories," 528–50; August Piper, Harrison G. Pope, & John J. Borowiecki, "Custer's Last Stand: Brown, Scheflin and Whitfield's Latest Attempt to Salvage 'Dissociative Amnesia'" (2000) 28 J. Psychiatry & Law 148; David L. Faigman *et al.*, *Science in the Law — Social and Behavioral Science Issues* (St. Paul, MN: West, 2002) c. 10, "Repressed Memories"; *Commonwealth (Massachusetts) v. Frangipane*, 744 N.E.2d 25 (Mass. Sup. Ct. 2001).

11   Vidmar, above note 1 at para. 12. Footnotes summarized as follows:

[13] Arrigo and Pezdek, "Lessons from the Study of Psychogenic Amnesia" (1997) 6 Current Directions in Psychological Science 148.

[14] Nadel and Jacobs, "Traumatic Memory Is Special" (1998) 7 Current Directions in Psychological Science 154.

[15] *Ibid.* at 156.

behaviour that does not involve physical force to the brain and head area. All the cases referenced are explicable without resort to a mechanism called "repression" and its aftermath "recovery."[12]

It is important from a scientific point of view to remember that the claimed recovery of repressed memories is not some inexplicable phenomenon where one is of necessity driven to speculative theorizing.[13] Rather, recovered memories can be explained as the confabulation of pseudo-memories through the influence of suggestion rather than the remarkable excavation of pristine, decades-old memories entombed through the Freudian mechanism of repression. Simple forgetting — with or without amplification as an artifact of human suggestibility — can comfortably be the accepted explanation, given the absence of scientific evidence to support the requisite concept of repressing or the corresponding mechanism of retrieving that which has been repressed (recovery of memory).

The most recent scientific examination of all the evidence on the topic of recovered memories is an admirable example of scientific inquiry, carefully examining the evidence, revealing distortions and faulty reasoning, and exposing biases. It flawlessly concluded:

> Are memories of distressing events commonly repressed? In a recent issue of *The Journal of Psychiatry & Law*, Brown, Scheflin, and Whitfield argued passionately in defense of the theory that individuals can repress recollections of a traumatic experience and later accurately recover them. We examine these arguments in detail, specifically elucidating their fundamental flaws in logic. We also direct attention to Brown, Scheflin, and Whitfield's unsupported assertions, misleading quotations of other authors, and inaccurate reporting of evidence. We conclude that on the basis of currently available evidence, neither science nor the courts can responsibly accept repression as a valid entity.
>
> . . .
>
> We hope this discussion will help to enforce a more rigorous and scientifically valid evaluation of the concept of dissociative amnesia. As we have noted,

---

12 Richard J. McNally, Ph.D., "Debunking Myths about Trauma and Memory" (2003) 50 Canadian Journal of Psychiatry 817: "Unfortunately, the evidence they adduce in support of the concept of traumatic dissociative amnesia fails to support their claims. The purpose of this review is to dispel confusions and debunk myths regarding trauma and memory."

13 See generally Cara Laney, M.A., & Elizabeth F. Loftus, Ph.D., "Traumatic Memories Are Not Necessarily Accurate Memories" (2003) 50 Canadian Journal of Psychiatry 823: "We discuss several research paradigms that have shown that various manipulations can be used to implant 'false memories' including false memories for traumatic events. These false memories can be quite compelling for those who develop them and can include details that make them seem credible to others."

it would not be technically difficult to employ properly designed, methodologically sound prospective studies to determine, once and for all, whether or not the concept is valid. We continue to eagerly await such studies. But for now neither science nor the courts can responsibly accept dissociative amnesia as a valid entity.[14]

Another authoritative work[15] on recovered memories explained how the researchers proceeded to analyze this subject:

First, rather than review the entire literature on all aspects of trauma and memory, we have focused on one specific operational question: can human beings develop amnesia for seemingly unforgettable traumatic events? This hypothesized process has been variously termed "repression," "dissociative amnesia," or "psychogenic amnesia,"—depending in part on the intrapsychic process believed to underlie it. For simplicity, we have used the term "repression" throughout this section, since our question remains the same regardless of the particular terminology used, or the particular mechanisms postulated to occur within the brain.

Second, we have surveyed general studies of victims of known trauma. Upon examining 73 studies of more than 11,000 victims of various traumas (table 1), together with a review of 45 additional studies of 3369 victims of childhood sexual abuse, we find that in general, human beings remember traumatic events clearly, barring such factors as loss of consciousness or early childhood amnesia. Therefore, we have concluded that, as a working hypothesis, we must begin with the assumption that people generally do remember traumatic events, and that the burden of proof therefore falls on investigators to demonstrate that some people can instead develop amnesia for such events.

This second assumption reflects a fundamental principle of science, namely that when a new hypothesis of causality is proposed, it remains unproven until other, already established causes have been excluded.

. . .

This burden of proof, furthermore, must not be shifted merely because a concept enjoys widespread cultural acceptance.... But the fact that repression is widely endorsed in our culture does not render it an established fact of science. Therefore, the burden of proof still rests on investigators to "reject the null hypothesis" — namely to prove that, although most people remember traumas, certain people, under certain circumstances, do not.

---

14 Piper *et al.*, above note 10 at 148 and 203. The entire article repays reading not only as a reference on its topic but as a classic debunking of junk science.
15 Faigman *et al.*, *Science in the Law*, above note 10 at 517–21.

Third, we have proposed minimum criteria . . . necessary for a study to reject the "null hypothesis." These include 1) documentation that a traumatic event actually occurred and 2) demonstration that a group of individuals developed amnesia for the event, not explainable by known processes such as early childhood amnesia, biological insults, ordinary forgetfulness, or deliberate allegation of amnesia for secondary gain. We have also noted that individual case reports, or even retrospective anecdotal case series, are insufficient to reject that null hypothesis.

Fourth, we have applied these methodologic criteria to available studies where groups of individuals were reported to have developed amnesia for traumatic events, including all of the studies known to us that have been cited as evidence for repression of memories of childhood sexual abuse. Upon analysis of these studies, we have been unable to find evidence of repression that satisfies our minimum criteria. We conclude that, at present, there is insufficient evidence to permit the conclusion that individuals can "repress" such memories.

The writers go on to deal with possible criticisms of their analysis such as "that absence of evidence is not evidence of absence. In other words, although none of the above studies presents clear evidence of repression, one is not justified in concluding that repression cannot occur." They believe that if there were actual cases of repression, there would be evidence found in laboratory studies:

[T]here are already many well-documented reasons why people may fail to report past life events, including biological amnesia, early childhood amnesia, ordinary forgetfulness, allegations of forgetfulness for secondary gain, and elective non-disclosure. In science, when simple explanations of a phenomenon are already available, it is inappropriate to postulate another, more complex explanation without adequate evidence.

Another criticism they suggested might be that their proposed criteria for scientific proof are impossible to meet. However, "simply because a hypothesis is difficult to prove does not require that we relax our standards for accepting it. Furthermore, if repression of childhood sexual abuse afflicts hundreds of thousands of individuals, as discussed above, one might reasonably expect rigorous demonstrations of this phenomenon, even if only a small fraction of the available cases fully met our methodologic criteria."

Another criticism might be that they had "selectively omitted relevant data that would contradict [their] reasoning." They respond by listing the papers and reports they included, both against and in favour of the repression hypothesis. They also acknowledge that "DSM-IV and its more recent text revision, DSM-IV-TR recognize the category of 'dissociative amnesia' as a diagnostic entity."

However, the controversy among psychiatrists about this diagnosis runs the gamut with some believing it has been underdiagnosed, while others think it has been "overdiagnosed in individuals who are highly suggestible."

They conclude by outlining how an investigation of repressed memory could be done, meeting rigorous scientific criteria: "Repression, in short, is a testable hypothesis, but has not yet been appropriately tested. Pending satisfactory studies, therefore, the most reasonable scientific position is to maintain skepticism."[16] Since this was written, the investigation of recovered memories has continued to the point that no reasonable and credible argument remains for the concept:[17] "The debate regarding the existence of repression has focused mainly on clarifying whether people remember or forget trauma. However, repression ... is a multidimensional concept. ... The overall findings from all five domains seriously challenge the classical psychoanalytic notion of repression. ... [T]he abandonment of repression seems inevitable in light of the comprehensive empirical evaluation presented in this article."[18]

As the above discussion suggests, in general, clinical witnesses are rarely trained in the scientific method and invariably overly trust the accuracy of their clients' narrative reports,[19] making them extremely problematic expert witnesses when challenged by the standards of scientific evidence.[20]

A body of accurately collected data, measuring solid and objective matters, may not at all prove what is claimed. Advocacy researchers, clinicians, and

16 See also the most recent objective examination of this topic in Richard J. McNally, *Remembering Trauma* (Cambridge, MA: The Belknap Press of Harvard University Press, 2003) at 171–85 and 190–209.

17 A. Piper, L. Lillevik, and R. Kritzer, "What's Wrong with Believing in Repression?" (2008) 14 Psychol., Pub. Pol'y & L. 223; Elizabeth F. Loftus & Deborah Davis, "Recovered Memories" (2006) 2 Annual Review of Clinical Psychology 469; Stephen Porter *et al.*, "'He Said, She Said': A Psychological Perspective on Historical Memory Evidence" (2003) 44:3 Can. Psychol. 190.

18 Y. Rofe, "Does Repression Exist? Memory, Pathogenic, Unconscious and Clinical Evidence" (2008) 12:1 Rev. Gen. Psych. 63.

19 Scott O. Lilienfeld, Steve J. Lynn, & Jeffrey M. Lohr, *Science and Pseudoscience in Clinical Psychology* (New York & London: Guilford Press, 2003), especially "Understanding Why Some Clinicians Use Pseudoscience Methods," c. 2 at 7–38.

20 See the glaring exemplars in *R. v. Olscamp* (1994), 95 C.C.C. (3d) 466 (Ont. Ct. Gen. Div.); *R. v. Kavanagh*, [2001] EWCA Crim 140. See also William M. Grove & Paul E. Meehl, "Comparative Efficiency of Informal (Subjective, Impressionistic) and Formal (Mechanical, Algorithmic) Prediction Procedures: The Clinical-Statistical Controversy" (June 1996) 2:2 Psychol., Pub. Pol'y & L. 293. To really see how bad clinical practitioners have become — be they Ph.D. psychologists or even medically trained psychiatrists — see Scott O. Lilienfeld, Steven Jay Lynn, & Jeffrey M. Lohr, eds., *Science and Pseudoscience in Clinical Psychology* (New York: Guilford Press, 2003).

others unschooled in, or uncaring about, the scientific method are especially prone to jump to their desired conclusions. *Lillie v. Newcastle City Council*[21] is illustrative of this point:

One of the recurring features of this case has been the willingness of psychologists, professional or amateur, to impose pre-conceived stereotypes or theories upon the facts of the case. I have had to remind myself that evidence must always come first and theory kept in its proper place. (para. 97)

. . .

It is interesting that Dr Friedrich has also prayed in aid the relationship of Joyce and Susan Eyeington (i.e. aunt and niece by marriage) as support for an increased "odds ratio" of the children being maltreated. This is what he describes as the "incestuous nature of the nursery staffing." This example of prejudice may be somewhat less "refined," and I am wary of an expert who is prepared to clutch at straws in this way on the basis of incomplete information. His expertise as a clinical psychologist does not assist me to take into account factors of that kind, in so far as they are relevant. (para. 429)

. . .

Unfortunately, when the court re-assembled . . . Professor Friedrich's cross-examination went into a downward spiral. He appeared to be out of his depth. It soon emerged that I could place no reliance on his evidence at all. He was very frank and apologetic about it but agreed with Miss Page that his report was of very poor quality. . . . It now became quite apparent why there had been such a divergence between his original report and his cautious approach in the witness box. (para. 443)

. . .

Professor Friedrich was also pressed on how he could possibly, on the limited information before him, make the claim . . . that the weight of the evidence pointed to abuse by Christopher Lillie and Dawn Reed. Miss Page put to Professor Friedrich that his evidence was flawed, unscientific and lacking in objectivity. He begged to differ, but she was clearly right. It might be thought offensive of Miss Page to suggest, as she did, that Professor Friedrich's reasoning represented no advance on the reading of tea-leaves. But it was a good deal less offensive than the accusations he was making against Christopher Lillie and Dawn Reed, for which he was claiming scientific and professional objectivity. He told me that he had his introduction to the two Claimants through the Review Team Report. That clearly coloured his whole approach. Everything he addressed was used as a pointer to child abuse. That is the opposite of scientific

---

21   [2002] EWHC 1600 (Q.B.).

objectivity. It is simply a case of the very phenomenon of cross-contamination he was being asked to analyse. (para. 464)

...

Miss Page asked several times for the validation of his evaluator scale methodology. She got nowhere. His supplemental report included a statement that it had been validated by the research of a postgraduate, but he was being supervised by Professor Friedrich himself. In any event, this research was not produced. As a checklist, there is nothing wrong with a catalogue of symptoms or behaviours, as Dr Cameron recognised, but just because he accords it the smart title of "Evaluator Rating Scale" it does not mean that Professor Friedrich's opinions need to be given particular weight. Fundamentally important for any scientist's opinions, in court or elsewhere, are the data on which they are based. Here the material was so partial, incomplete and misleading as to render any opinion worthless. Once flaws are pointed out, a scientist will go back to the drawing board or the laboratory bench and start afresh. Here what was so astonishing was that Professor Friedrich clung to his original opinions with whatever piece of rope he was thrown. In re-examination, for example, he was shown odd bits and pieces of material he had not seen at the time of his original report and adopted it as support for his conclusions without any testing or analysis at all.

...

At the conclusion of his evidence, I was glad that I had not encouraged greater brevity the day before ... because the longer he went on the more it became apparent just how feeble his pseudo-scientific claims were. (paras. 467 to 469)

...

It emerged early on in Professor Barker's testimony that he has a fundamentally different attitude towards the weighing and analysis of evidence from that of a lawyer. At several points, it became apparent that he is rather dismissive of what he called "a forensic approach." He resorted from time to time to impressionistic mode, referring to his "professional judgment" and to discussions in academic and other published work. His colleagues were similarly minded. Indeed, Ms Jones voluntarily espoused the word "impressionistic." Yet the issue of whether any given individual has raped or assaulted a small child, or for that matter upwards of 60 small children, is not a matter of impression, theory, opinion or speculation. It should be a question of fact.

The Professor is entitled to be disparaging about the criminal justice system, or "forensic analysis", or the testing of evidence in cross-examination. Many people are. Such criticism from the sidelines may or may not be made on an informed basis. But surely when such a critic steps forward to take on the responsibility of condemning a fellow citizen as being guilty of such wicked behaviour, a little humility may be thought appropriate. . . . (paras. 1136 to 1143)

In *R. v. T.H.O.*,[22] an appeal by the accused was dismissed and convictions for sex offences upheld. An important contribution to the conviction and its being upheld by the appellate court was "expert" evidence by a psychologist that was used to "explain" away what would otherwise appear to be obvious credibility and reliability deficiencies in the complainant's evidence.

There appears to have been no objection to this "expert" evidence at trial nor was its admissibility challenged on appeal either. In fact, on appeal, defence counsel appears from the judgment to have accepted the validity of the evidence by attempting to argue its interpretation in his favour.

This is a most disappointing situation because the opinions expressed at that trial regarding memory functioning and related issues are simply not supported in the scientific literature. The decision may well enter history as a classic case of junk science.

The evidence was summarized by the appeal court as follows:

> The Crown called Dr. Richard Berry to give expert evidence concerning the memory process in human beings and delayed recall. Dr. Berry testified that, generally, information is stored in an explicit memory system. The individual is consciously aware of it and it is available to him for recall. Memory is subject to change and decay with the passage of time. While the central theme of an incident or core memory tends to remain intact, peripheral memories may be modified by intervening events. So, for example, while one would retain the memory of going on a camping trip, the colour of the canoe or the kind of tent may be lost, or change in recounting over time.
>
> Dr. Berry further testified that information that overwhelms an individual may, however, result in dissociative amnesia with the information stored in an implicit memory system, where it is not readily available. Recovery of that memory may occur either as a result of a situation that parallels the original traumatic incident or the presence of cues, such as smells, that are similar to the original incident. The onset of memory may begin with a vague feeling that things are wrong. Memory generally returns over an extended period of time, often in a fragmented form that is usually out of sequence, so that memory recovery may never be complete.

Later in the judgment "[k]ey portions of Dr. Berry's evidence" are excerpted:

---

22 [2001] O.J. No. 4772 (C.A.).

In an implicit memory system ... [t]he information could be there, but they may not be aware of the events and not able to access that or retrieve it. ... Now, I guess, one of the points that you're raising here is the issue of rehearsal. That is, how often does a person think about an event, and that's part of this pattern of changing, information changing for an individual that is not immutable, it's not like this video recording. A person has an experience, they may store some information, but that information is subject to modification according to the point where the event occurs and the point of recall and it can be modified by intervening events. It is not as though everything changes dramatically, but it may be modified by, if you are a child, there is some kind of experience that you had with your family, perhaps it was a camping trip, and that camping trip is then talked about by yourself or with family members on later occasions. That tends to rehearse, tends to refresh the memory. And there may be bits and pieces that get modified in the re-telling that get incorporated into. So that aspects of the memory may change, but the central core tends to ... remain intact.

...

But there is definitely fairly convincing evidence to indicate individuals can have traumatic kinds of experiences for which they appear to have no awareness for a lengthy period of time and later can recount aspects of that. They may later recount the whole event.

...

Now the explicit memory system as I say will register the conscious available information. Implicit when you have traumatic amnesia — the theoretical model and the empirical data to support that indicates that there is bio-chemical change that occurs. And that information that goes into the implicit memory system appears to be relatively impervious to change while it's stored in this dissociated state.

The following propositions are express or implied in the foregoing evidence:

1. There are two different memory systems labelled "explicit memory" and "implicit memory."
2. Traumatic or "overwhelming" "information" is stored in the implicit memory system where it "is not readily available" but is "impervious to change."
3. "Memories" come back from the implicit memory system in fragments and may never be complete.
4. Such "recovered memories" from the implicit memory system are historically accurate.
5. The implicit memory system is the mechanism to explain recovered memories whereby a supposedly traumatic event that is completely unavailable to consciousness, and inaccessible to the ordinary memory system (explicit memory), is subsequently recovered (into the explicit memory system).

According to this evidence, the implicit memory system turns on and off automatically, its playback is incomplete, it is capricious in terms of what it reveals, but what it reveals is accurate.

In fact, the foregoing misrepresents the science involved and misuses the two labels of explicit and implicit memory. In the science of memory, implicit memory covers a variety of phenomena that include behavioural, emotional, and perceptual learning unaccompanied by a sense of conscious recollection when retrieved. Because the phenomena covered are somewhat diverse, the label "implicit memory" has been abandoned, with specific labels for each different phenomenon becoming the preferred conceptualization. One team of researchers wrote that

> implicit memory does not exist. Implicit memory phenomena are distinct from explicit memory phenomena at a neural and information processing level, but there is such variety among the implicit memory phenomena that nothing holds them together in a common category. Other researchers have distinguished among different types of implicit memory, but have retained the superordinate category. Extant data are evaluated in light of how classification systems should be developed, and it is concluded that there is currently not a reason to retain the construct "implicit memory."[23]

In its most general meaning, implicit memory refers to the fact that human subjects can be affected by stimuli that leave a memorial residual of which they are not "consciously" aware. For example, persons are faster to fill in the blanks of _SS_S_IN with "assassin" when they have seen that particular word recently. This is a far cry from the claim that people can store a stream of traumatic experiences in implicit memory that are then reliably recovered at a later date.

---

23 Daniel B. Willingham & Laura Preuss, "The Death of Implicit Memory" (October 1995) 2:15 Psyche. The authors are from the Department of Psychology, University of Virginia, Charlottesville, VA, and can be reached online: dbw8m@virginia.edu and lap2c@virginia.edu. This article is available online: http://journalpsyche.org/ojs-2.2/index.php/psyche/article/view/2419.
   See also Laurie T. Butler & Dianne C. Berry, "Implicit Memory: Intention and Awareness Revisited" (May 2001) 5:5 Trends in Cognitive Sciences 192.
   See also the website of John F. Kihlstrom, University of California at Berkeley, Member, Institute of Cognitive and Brain Sciences, Institute of Personality and Social Research, Center for Health Research, and an expert on the topic of "implicit memories" online: ist-socrates.berkeley.edu/~kihlstrm/special.htm. Available on the website is an excellent overview article putting the whole issue in perspective: Katharine Krause Shobe & John F. Kihlstrom, "Is Traumatic Memory Special?," an edited version of which appeared in (1997) 6 Current Directions in Psychological Science 70.

Experimental evidence regarding such implicit memory is not proof of the kinds of things for which the recovered memory proponents want to use the concept of implicit memory. The evidence simply does not support the recovered memory phenomenon and to offer it up as if it did is simply to either misunderstand or misrepresent the evidence. Furthermore, implicit memory is viewed by the researchers as similarly subject to error as explicit memory. "[I]mplicit memory is not immune to . . . interference."[24]

There is no empirical evidence to support the notion of an "implicit memory system" that stores historically accurate narrative memories, let alone ones that subsequently transmute (years later) into explicit memories. Any links that emerge in therapy or personal introspection between alleged implicit memories and explicit autobiographical memory must be recognized as possible, if not probable, constructions or creations of the mind.[25] There is ample evidence that suggestion and imagination can create "memories" of events that did not actually occur. Implicit memory is found in every person every day. It has no empirically established relationship with traumatic experiences, much less the catch-all construct "sex abuse."

Two other points bear mention. The trial judge's reasons in *R. v. T.H.O.* contain the following additional statement of evidence purportedly given by the witness: "Amnesia, he stated, is fairly prevalent for cases of trauma."

Such a statement is, as has been referenced above,[26] simply false as applied to nonphysical trauma. After several decades of debate and extremely contentious and intense scrutiny of all available evidence, there is a paucity of evidence for emotional, nonphysical trauma occasioning actual amnesia.[27]

---

24 Cindy Lustig & Lynn Hasher, "Implicit Memory Is Vulnerable to Proactive Interference" (September 2001) 127:5 Psychol. Bull. 408 at 417.

25 See McNally, above note 16 at 30–39 and 179–81.

26 See Piper *et al.*, above note 10; Faigman *et al.*, *Science in the Law*, above note 10 at 517–21.

27 See, for example, J. Laurence, D. Day, & L. Gaston, "From Memories of Abuse to the Abuse of Memories" (1998) in S.J. Lynn & K.M. McConkey, eds., *Truth in Memory* (New York: Guilford Press, 1998) at 323–46. Another excellent reference on this point is Piper *et al.*, *ibid.* at 149–213, where the studies that supposedly evidence nonphysical traumatic amnesia are examined and the misrepresentations exposed.

Just one example: a study we can label Dollinger 1986 is cited by the recovered memory proponents as evidence that "Two of 38 lightning victims [or 'over 5%'] suffered amnesia for the event." However, Piper *et al.* point out that these authors "fail to mention that the two amnestic boys were 'side-flash victims' who 'suffered medical complications.' Thus, these boys in effect received an electroconvulsive treatment from lightning and ECT has been known for more than a half-century to cause simple biological amnesia." More similar examples from Piper *et al.* are at "Recovered Memories, Dissociation and Junk Science," ADGN/2001-326 (on Quicklaw in Commentary).

As well, what the foregoing amounts to is simply a recasting of the "dissociation" concept in terms of implicit memory. Dissociation reflects the foundational notion of emotional trauma occasioning an amnesia reversed by the recovery of memories, and recovered-memory proponents often use the concept of dissociation as support. It is important to note that this concept — besides being without empirical support as referenced earlier[28] — occasions the support of only a minority of psychiatrists throughout North America.[29] More correctly, the dubious nature of historical memories allegedly being revived has been authoritatively recognized by major psychological and psychiatric institutions.

R. v. T.H.O. does not auger well for the justice system's determination to rely on real science and avoid junk science. However, in the end result, its impact on other cases should deservedly be nil. It is clear that issues surrounding the admissibility of expert evidence are highly case-specific.[30] Admission is not a matter of precedent. This allows the law, at least in the area of expert evidence, to avoid repeating its mistakes.

There will be plenty of such opportunities. To any profession, the administration of justice can be viewed as a potential market into which an expansion of services is desirable, and it is no wonder that competitive market forces make expert testimony an attractive potential source of income. Regarding alleged expertise about human beings and their behaviours, psychiatrists initially had a monopoly. That territory was soon invaded by psychologists, no slouches when it comes to aggressively seeking expansion of their intellectual territories.[31] A generally clinical, unscientific background and a banner of good, helping intentions does little to restrain proclamations of knowledge and wisdom far beyond anything objectively justified. Sociologists were not far behind, though less aggressive because they were more likely to be trained in scientific methodology and thus aware of their limitations in propounding conclusions. Even anthropologists are eager to assist courts with their knowledge of the human animal.[32]

---

28 See Piper *et al.*, above note 10; Faigman *et al.*, *Science in the Law*, above note 10.

29 Notwithstanding it is listed in the current volume of the DSM, two recent studies show its disapproval by psychiatrists in the United States: Harrison G. Pope *et al.*, "Attitudes toward DSM-IV Dissociative Disorders Diagnoses among Board-Certified American Psychiatrists" (February 1999) 156:2 Am. J. Psychiatry 321; and Justice K. Lalonde *et al.*, "Canadian and American Psychiatrists' Attitudes towards Dissociative Disorders Diagnoses" (June 2001) 46 Can. J. Psychiatry 407.

30 *R. v. D.D.*, [2000] 2 S.C.R. 275; *R. v. A.K. and N.K.* (1999), 27 C.R. (5th) 226 (Ont. C.A.).

31 Noam Chomsky: "One waits in vain for psychologists to state the limits of their knowledge," quoted in Dineen, above note 7 at 11.

32 Allen C. Turner, "Prolegomenon to a Forensic Cultural Anthropology" (1992) 16 Am. J. Trial Advoc. 391.

This is not to say, however, that in some areas psychology can credibly assist the law's tasks. Experimental psychology's properly conducted research can inform the law about issues such as improper questioning techniques that engage a child's inherent suggestibility, so that a seemingly credible accusatory statement can be accurately assessed by the trier of fact.[33] Well-documented phenomena of memory such as "childhood amnesia"[34] or problematic memory for conversations[35] or phenomena such as "change blindness"[36] can be of great assistance to the courts.[37]

An area that deserves special mention is expert evidence regarding eyewitness identification principles. Courts have been loath to admit this evidence. As it has been sardonically noted, "The judiciary admits the lousy science of the classically prosecution-friendly fingerprint evidence, while suppressing the sound science of the classically defense-friendly evidence about eyewitness identifications."[38]

A summary of the types of issues upon which such an expert witness can inform a trier of fact is found in an article by A. Daniel Yarmey:[39]

> Many problems inherent in eyewitness testimony are counterintuitive and contradict common beliefs. Assessments of knowledge about eyewitness memory, evidence from prediction studies, written or simulated videotaped trials, and cross-examination of eyewitnesses to staged crimes conducted in Canada, Australia, the United States, and the United Kingdom show that lay persons, police officers, defence attorneys and prosecutors hold several misconceptions about eyewitness memory.... For example, a common misconception is the belief that the more confident a witness is, the more accurate the testimony

---

33 See chapter 3, note 94.

34 See chapter 3, note 74.

35 Deborah Davis & Richard D. Friedman, "Memory for Conversation: The Orphan Child of Witness Memory Researchers" in M.P. Toglia *et al.*, eds., *The Handbook of Eyewitness Psychology*, vol. 1: *Memory for Events* (Mahwah, NJ: Lawrence Erlbaum, 2007).

36 Deborah Davis & William C. Follette, "Foibles of Witness Memory for Traumatic/High Profile Events" (2001) 66 J. Air L. & Com. 1421 at 1444. This entire article is a magnificent primer on the state of the knowledge regarding human memory. It is available online: www.sierratrialandopinion.com/papers/FOIBLESWITNESSMEMORY.doc.

37 See generally British Psychological Society, "Guidelines on Memory and the Law: A Report from the Research Board" (June 2008) online: http://www.bps.org.uk/downloadfile. cfm?file_uuid=07F99CF1-1143-DFD0-7EBD-70F5FDA6CE19&ext=pdf.

38 Susan D. Rozelle, "*Daubert*, Schmaubert: Criminal Defendants and the Short End of the Science Stick" (2007) 43 Tulsa L. Rev. 597 at 597.

39 "Expert Testimony: Does Eyewitness Memory Research Have Probative Value for Courts?" (2001) 42 Can. Psychol. 92.

is likely to be. Research shows that there may be little between-witness confidence-accuracy relationship, especially when observation conditions are poor and highly stressful (Penrod & Culter, 1995). Another misconception is the belief that police officers make better eyewitnesses than ordinary citizens. Research shows that the testimony of law enforcement personnel is generally not more accurate than that of an ordinary citizen, and in some circumstances may be inferior.

. . .

The effects of system or procedural variables, however, are much easier to justify in terms of relevancy and potential assistance to the courts because the testimony centres on the fairness of the process, that is, was there bias in the preparation and conduct of the lineup? Studies show that jurors are insensitive to proper lineup procedures (Lindsay, 1994). They assume that because the police are experienced in such matters that they are also highly knowledgeable and, therefore, experts in the proper conduct of identification techniques. Expert witnesses can inform the court that certain practices and procedures promote bias, suggestibility, and unfairness and that procedural errors are more or less likely to have occurred in any specific case. For example, [one study] found that people assume that when a lineup contains the actual culprit and a number of foils who are similar in appearance, that this will lead to a decrease in identification accuracy. It is believed that because the foils and culprit are similar in appearance that this would create a source of interference and make it difficult to pick out the suspect. Research shows that this is not the case. When the actual culprit is present in the lineup, accuracy of identification is not influenced by the similarity of foils to the target. On the other hand, when foils are used that are not similar to the accused, misidentifications are much more likely to occur. When a set of foils and a suspect are presented simultaneously, witnesses use a relative judgment procedure in making their decision. That is, they choose the person who most closely resembles the culprit relative to all other lineup members. This process is not a problem when the lineup or photo array included the culprit, but when the offender is not present, this procedure can lead to the false identification of an innocent person. And by chance alone, an innocent suspect may be the person who most closely resembles the actual offender.

It is not only ordinary citizens who fail to appreciate the subtleties of proper line up procedures. Both lawyers and trial judges improperly recognize some of the biases in lineup procedures . . . . Expert psychological knowledge on the fairness of lineup procedures is not a normal, everyday process, understood on the basis of common sense. Reliability and helpfulness are interrelated concepts. The better the proof as to scientific reliability, the greater the likelihood that the courts will find the expert's opinion helpful to the jury.[40]

As stated above, so long as fingerprints are automatically admitted and eyewitness identification experts are invariably excluded from evidence the law is not getting it right regarding expert psychological evidence.[41]

---

40 A comprehensive reference to the topic is found in Tanja Rapus Benton *et al.*, "On the Admissibility of Expert Testimony on Eyewitness Identification: A Legal and Scientific Evaluation" (2006) 2 Tenn. J.L. & Pol'y 392.

41 See Brian H. Bornstein, Sid O'Bryant, & Douglas J. Zickafoose, "Intuitions about Arousal and Eyewitness Memory: Effects on Mock Jurors' Judgments" (2008) 32 Law & Psychol. Rev. 109 showing that mock jurors' judgments of witness credibility, as well as their verdicts, were influenced by their prior, generally incorrect, beliefs about eyewitness testimony and what impacted upon its accuracy. However, expert testimony about the limitations of eyewitness testimony could correct the situation.

CHAPTER 7

Science and Syndromes, Profiles, and Indicators

THREE TYPES OF expert opinion evidence share a misleading logic and are unacceptable from a scientific point of view: syndromes, profiles, and indicators. Profiles have already been described in chapter 3[1] and their unscientific nature alluded to in chapter 4;[2] this chapter explores all three types of evidence in greater detail. What they have in common is their attempt to establish a diagnosis from a description. For example, if an examination of known child molesters establishes that most or all possess child pornography, the diagnosis is that a person found with child pornography is a child molester. Or if a person proven to be a drug courier is found to have paid for his plane ticket with cash, boarded the plane last, and looked around constantly when deplaning, that information is turned around to claim that a person who buys his ticket with cash, boards last, and looks around a lot is in fact a drug courier. This reasoning makes use of a well-known logical fallacy: affirming the consequent. Clearly, the view that if a person is a child molester then he will have child pornography cannot logically be reversed to claim that if a person has child pornography then he is a child molester.

Besides the basic problem of flawed logic, all three categories share an additional weakness. They are wrong more often than they are right. Because the characteristics that make up the syndrome, profile, or indicators are invariably present in other than the target group, these types of evidence invariably en-

---

1   At note 36.
2   At note 68.

gage the base rate fallacy described in chapter 4 and generate many more false positives than true positives. They simply lack sufficient reliability to qualify as admissible evidence.

Finally, in almost all cases even the characteristics on which the syndrome, profile, or group of indicators are based are unreliable. Often they are fuzzy and ambiguous, based on subjective interpretation. Or they may be tautological, where anything and everything is "consistent with" the syndrome or profile or condition indicated.

SYNDROMES

BATTERED WOMAN SYNDROME

AN IMPORTANT DECISION in the area of expert evidence, which highlights the questionable scientific nature of many psychological pronouncements, is the leading authority on battered woman syndrome. This became a recognized area of expert evidence when the concept was accepted by the Supreme Court of Canada in 1990 in *R. v. Lavallee*.[3] It was not the Court's finest hour, as far as expert evidence is concerned. Since then, some steps towards limiting the judicial acceptance of this material have taken place.[4] However, Canadian courts have yet to admit the intellectual error made in admitting this evidence. Elsewhere, one judge has described the concept as an "advocacy driven construct designed to 'medicalise' the evidence in a particular case to avoid the difficulties which might arise in the context of a criminal trial . . . [regarding] the accused's motivations."[5]

Faigman and Wright[6] have elsewhere said all that can and should be said on this topic. They begin with an appropriately scathing denunciation of Lenore Walker's book, *The Battered Woman*,[7] which was so uncritically accepted and figured so prominently in Justice Wilson's judgment in *Lavallee*:

> The battered woman syndrome illustrates all that is wrong with the law's use of science. The working hypothesis of the battered woman syndrome was first introduced in Lenore Walker's 1979 book, *The Battered Woman*. When

3 [1990] 1 S.C.R. 852 [*Lavallee*].
4 *R. v. Malott*, [1998] 1 S.C.R. 123; *R. v. F.(D.S.)* (1999), 23 C.R. (5th) 37 (Ont. C.A.); *R. v. Trombley* (1998), 126 C.C.C. (3d) 495 (Ont. C.A.), aff'd [1999] 1 S.C.R. 757.
5 *Osland v. The Queen* (1998), 159 A.L.R. 170 at para. 161 (H.C.A.).
6 David L. Faigman & Amy J. Wright, "The Battered Woman Syndrome in the Age of Science" (1997) 39 Ariz. L. Rev. 67 at 67.
7 (New York: HarperCollins, 1980).

it made its debut, this hypothesis had little more to support it beyond the clinical impressions of a single researcher. Five years later, Walker published a second book that promised a more thorough investigation of the hypothesis. However, this book contains little more than a patchwork of pseudo-scientific methods employed to confirm a hypothesis that its author and participating researchers never seriously doubted. Indeed, the 1984 book would provide an excellent case study for psychology graduate students on how not to conduct empirical research. Yet, largely based upon the same political ideology driving the researchers, judges have welcomed the battered woman syndrome into their courts. Because the law is driven by precedent, it quickly petrified around the original conception of the defense. Increasingly, observers are realizing that the evidence purportedly supporting the battered woman syndrome is without empirical foundation, and, perhaps more troubling, that the syndrome itself is inimical to the political ideology originally supporting it. In short, in the law's hasty effort to use science to further good policy, it is now obvious that the battered woman syndrome is not good science nor does it generate good policy.[8]

Another author put it more dispassionately:

[T]he largely unrestrained admissibility of BWS [battered woman syndrome] cannot be explained solely on the basis of evidentiary doctrine and scientific validity. Instead, it involves politics and reflects a normative judgment typically associated with changes in criminal liability rather than evidentiary admissibility.[9]

It is one thing to enunciate a new, normative, criminal law rule regarding self-defence, to the effect that a woman in an abusive relationship may kill a sleeping, despicable partner in self-defence, even absent the "immediacy of threat" requirement generally required by the law of self-defence.[10] But such change, for example, by a statutory amendment would be fully debated (and I hope easily defeated). However, it is quite another thing to justify such an amendment by judicial pronouncement as a "common law" change, based allegedly on "psychological science," especially when the science is bogus.

---

8   Faigman & Wright, above note 6 at 67.
9   Robert P. Mosteller, "Syndromes and Politics in Criminal Trials and Evidence Law" (1996) 46 Duke L.J. 461; see also Janet C. Hoeffel, "The Gender Gap: Revealing Inequities in Admission of Social Science Evidence in Criminal Cases (2001) 24 U. Ark. Little Rock L. Rev. 41.
10 Joshua Dressler, "Battered Women and Sleeping Abusers: Some Reflections" (2006) 3 Ohio St. J. Crim. L. 457, abstract online: http://papers.ssrn.com/sol3/papers.cfm?abstract_id=896789.

What the Court did in *Lavallee* was scientifically indefensible. It purported to recognize a descriptive rule (people with a certain condition behave a certain way because of the condition they have developed) that was claimed to be derived as a matter of psychological science. By labelling the situation of a battered woman as a syndrome, the accused's factual claim of victimization — but one within the sphere of "ordinary" or "normal" human life — was transmuted into a topic for expert testimony. There was, and is, simply no empirical data to support the claims accepted in *Lavallee* as factual and descriptively accurate. The Supreme Court recontoured the landscape of self-defence in an ideologically and politically popular manner in *Lavallee*. But its descriptive, factual, and supposedly scientific support for that exercise, which was claimed to lie in the psychological pathology of abused women who killed their supposedly despicable husbands, was scientifically bogus.[11]

Lavallee opened the door[12] to a new body of expert evidence characterized by the following logic: certain behaviours cannot be accurately translated by triers of fact but must be "interpreted" for them by an expert, usually a clinician. Such translation is permitted when the behaviours can be viewed as related to a "syndrome" being suffered by the actor. The problem is the completely unscientific characteristics of the entire situation.

BWS exemplifies all the faults of this category of evidence. The elements of the syndrome are but vaguely set out as follows:

> [T]here are three distinct phases associated in a recurring battering cycle: (1) tension building, (2) the acute battering incident, and (3) loving contrition. During the first phase, there is a gradual escalation of tension displayed by discrete acts causing increased friction such as name-calling, other mean intentional behaviors, and/or physical abuse. The batterer expresses dissatisfaction and hostility but not in an extreme or maximally explosive form. The woman attempts to placate the batterer, doing what she thinks might please him, calm him

---

11   David L. Faigman *et al.*, *Modern Scientific Evidence*, 2 vols. (St. Paul, MN: West, 1997) vol. 1, c. 8, "The Battered Woman Syndrome and Other Psychological Effects of Domestic Violence against Women," 319–79, especially at 351–79; Ian Freckelton & Hugh Selby, *Expert Evidence*, 5 vols., looseleaf (Sydney: Law Book Company, 1993 plus updates to May 2002) c. 13, "Novel Psychological Evidence."

12   As if to prove the adage "Give him an inch and he'll take a mile," proponents then tried to use BWS as affirmative evidence of guilt. In *Roy Dale Ryan v. State (Wyoming)*, 988 P.2d 46 (Wyo. 1999), the court rejected as inadmissible the submission that testimony on battered wife syndrome that goes beyond the victim to suggest that batterers kill when faced with separation from the victim and thus supports the prosecution's theory for the homicide charged.

down, or at least, what will not further aggravate him. She tries not to respond to his hostile actions and uses general anger reduction techniques. Often she succeeds for a little while which reinforces her unrealistic belief that she can control this man.

The tension continues to escalate and eventually she is unable to continue controlling his angry response pattern. "Exhausted from the constant stress, she usually withdraws from the batterer, fearing she will inadvertently set off an explosion. He begins to move more oppressively toward her as he observes her withdrawal .... Tension between the two becomes unbearable." ... The second phase, the acute battering incident, becomes inevitable without intervention. Sometimes, she precipitates the inevitable explosion so as to control where and when it occurs, allowing her to take better precautions to minimize her injuries and pain.

"Phase two is characterized by the uncontrollable discharge of the tensions that have built up during phase one." ... The batterer typically unleashes a barrage of verbal and physical aggression that can leave the woman severely shaken and injured. In fact, when injuries do occur it usually happens during this second phase. It is also the time police become involved, if they are called at all. The acute battering phase is concluded when the batterer stops, usually bringing with its cessation a sharp physiological reduction in tension. This in itself is naturally reinforcing. Violence often succeeds because it does work.

In phase three which follows, the batterer may apologize profusely, try to assist his victim, show kindness and ... remorse, and shower her with gifts and/or promises. The batterer himself may believe at this point that he will never allow himself to be violent again. The woman wants to believe the batterer and, early in the relationship at least, may renew her hope in his ability to change. This third phase provides the positive reinforcement for remaining in the relationship, for the woman. In fact, our results showed that phase three could also be characterized by an absence of tension or violence, and no observable loving-contrition behaviour, and still be reinforcing for the woman.

Dr. Walker defines a battered woman as a woman who has gone through the battering cycle at least twice.[13]

These are obviously matters of subjective judgment that can be determined to be present in virtually all cases if the accused wife chooses to claim their

---

13 *Lavallee*, above note 3 at paras. 45–46 [citations omitted].

presence in the unhappy marriage that culminated in the homicide. Further, no reliable data exist that show the prevalence of these or similar characteristics in the population of unhappy marriages generally. Nor is the base rate of "battered wives" known. And finally, of course, the fact that some if not all battered wives share these characteristics proves nothing absent proof that such characteristics cannot be located in unhappy but unbattered wives who choose to kill their spouses.

> Today, we have the following labels: "The Battered Wife Syndrome"; "The Battered Woman Syndrome"; "The Battered Child Syndrome"; "The Battered Husband Syndrome"; "The Battered Parent Syndrome"; "The Familial Child Sexual Abuse Syndrome"; "The Rape Trauma Syndrome"; "The Battle Fatigue Syndrome"; "The Viet Nam Post-Traumatic Stress Syndrome"; "The Policeman's Syndrome"; "The Post-Concussive Syndrome"; "The Whiplash Syndrome"; "The Low-Back Syndrome"; "The Lover's Syndrome"; "The Love Fear Syndrome"; "The Organic Delusional Syndrome"; "The Chronic Brain Syndrome"; and "The Holocaust Syndrome." Tomorrow, there will probably be additions to the list, such as "The Appellate Court Judge Syndrome." ... Another commentator has aptly coined the phrase "forensic abuse syndrome."
>
> . . .
>
> Syndrome evidence continues to be widely admitted ... yet it does not come close to satisfying either *Daubert* or *Kumho Tire* standards.[14]

Clinicians are the last group that the administration of justice can rely upon for valid and reliable "scientific evidence."[15] They are concerned with sympa-

---

14 Mark S. Brodin, "Behavioral Science Evidence in the Age of *Daubert*: Reflections of a Skeptic" (2005) 73 U. Cin. L. Rev. 867 at 881–82. Munchausen's Syndrome by Proxy, an invention of the infamous Dr. Meadow, was rejected in *R. v. L.M.*, [2004] QCA 192 (Queensland); Rod Liddle, "Mumbo-jumbo Syndrome" *Times Online* (26 June 2005): "Munchausen's syndrome by proxy is an ailment dreamt up by Professor Sir Roy Meadow back in 1977." Shaken baby syndrome as a reliable proof of homicide is now doubted: Genie Lyons, "Shaken Baby Syndrome: A Questionable Scientific Syndrome and a Dangerous Legal Concept" [2003] Utah L. Rev. 1109; Shaoni Bhattacharya, "'Diagnostic' Child Abuse Sign Can Be Misleading" *New Scientist* (26 March 2004), online: www.newscientist. com/article/dn4821-diagnostic-child-abuse-sign-can-be-misleading.html. The research is reported by P.E. Lantz *et al.*, "Perimacular Retinal Folds from Childhood Head Trauma" (2004) 328 Brit. Med. J. 754; compare *R. v. Harris*, [2005] EWCA Crim 1980.

15 William M. Grove & Paul E. Meehl, "Comparative Efficiency of Informal (Subjective, Impressionistic) and Formal (Mechanical, Algorithmic) Prediction Procedures: The Clinical-Statistical Controversy" (June 1996) 2:2 Psychol., Pub. Pol'y & L. 293 at 318 stated:

> In the majority of training programs in clinical psychology, and it is surely as bad or worse in psychiatry and social work, no great value is placed on the cultivation of skeptical, scientific habits of thought; the role models — even in the academy, but

thetically treating presumptively victimized patients, not with any skeptical analysis of historical claims.[16]

> The concept of psychological syndromes was originally developed by practitioners for therapeutic and not truth-detection, purposes. . . . Mental health professionals are trained to assist patients, not judge their credibility. "While it may be entirely proper for a clinician to accept a patient report of sex abuse at face value and proceed to render treatment on that basis, for forensic purposes, such an assumption is," as one court observed, "utterly inappropriate."
> . . . It is far from self-evident that methodologies useful in choosing a course of psychotherapy are reliable enough "to provide a sound basis for investigative conclusions and confident legal decision-making." . . . Indeed the American Psychiatric Association's own *Diagnostic and Statistical Manual of Mental Disorders* (DSM) warns against using these categories for forensic purposes.[17]

Furthermore, the context was highly emotional and replete with built-in biases. If syndrome evidence was an exculpatory curative prescription to be written by a kindly clinician, battered wives and rape victims were ideal candidates for generous dispensing.

A therapist does not get overly involved with what "really" happened. The patient's psychic reality is reality. In part, this is related to the fact that psychotherapy is a context laden with persuasion and suggestibility. Therapy has been described as "developing a storyline" with patients — where they have been, where they are, and where they want to go.

The law, on the other hand, is concerned with historical reality: who did what and when. It is supposed to be an investigation into the actual and real past. However, it is an unfortunate reality of human experience that not all persons tell all the truth all the time, especially those that have committed serious crimes or perpetrated other wrongs. Even two honest and well-intentioned

---

more so in the clinical settings — are often people who do not put a high value on scientific thinking, are not themselves engaged in scientific research, and take for granted that clinical experience is sufficient to prove whatever they want to believe.

See also Scott O. Lilienfeld, Steve J. Lynn, & Jeffrey M. Lohr, *Science and Pseudoscience in Clinical Psychology* (New York & London: Guilford Press, 2003), especially "Understanding Why Some Clinicians Use Pseudoscience Methods," c. 2 at 7–38.

16 See generally Harold I. Lief, "Psychiatry's Challenge: Defining an Appropriate Therapeutic Role When Child Abuse Is Suspected" *Psychiatric News* (21 August 1992). See *Messina v. Bonner*, 813 F. Supp. 346 (E.D. Pa. 1993) (daughters sue father for sexual abuse that occurred eighteen to twenty-four years previously); Carol Tavris, "Beware the Incest-Survivor Machine" *The New York Times* (3 January 1993) Book Review 1, and the debate engendered by her article in the *The New York Times* (14 February 1993) Book Review 3 and 27.

17 Brodin, "Behavioural Science Evidence," above note 14 at 882–83.

observers do not always agree on what was seen. As a result, the law's concern also has an added dimension of proof: truth is not just what was, but what was, which can be proved to have been. In other words, certainty that something was in fact so is irrelevant for the law without admissible proof thereof. In criminal cases, the proof must be beyond a reasonable doubt; in civil cases, a lesser burden of a balance of probabilities is accepted. But burden of proof is a mechanism the law must have to decide when proof is sufficient to become truth.

Comparing the concerns of therapy with those of law would show these contrasts: "In recent times, this fundamental difference between law and psychiatric therapy has been lost sight of in some quarters, to the detriment of both professions."[18]

Another author has made the distinction between "the concept of truth as it exists in the therapist's office and truth in the criminal justice process" as follows:

> Mental health professionals are not trained fact-finders. It is neither the function nor the goal of the clinician in the normal therapeutic setting to determine the factual reality of what the patient is saying; the purpose of the clinical experience is therapy and, by and large, the truth is whatever the patient says it is. The therapeutic relationship must be based on acceptance and trust, and a therapist is not going to enhance this relationship by challenging or questioning the patient's story when she describes what happened to her as a child. In many instances, the therapist will, instead, assure the patient ... that he believes her story. The factual truth is not the point in therapy; rather, the point is for the patient to make sense of the experience and to heal. Sometimes this principle is referred to in psychiatry as "the shared delusion." Other psychiatrists sum it up differently: "The patient never lies." Therapists are, by nature and training, healers, not truth-finders.[19]

Yet another writer made the same point eloquently:

> [T]he assumption [is] that therapy uncovers legally relevant "facts" connecting past trauma to current distress. A psychiatrist or other mental health profes-

---

18 Of course, the problem is compounded when 1) litigation is incorporated into therapy and "healing" by therapists and self-help books that (completely ignoring this gap between therapeutic and legal reality) take the position that a lawsuit or criminal charge against the perpetrator is a condition precedent to any therapeutic recovery; and 2) the law, in similar ignorance, imposes mandatory reporting obligations that treat the suspicion of sex abuse in therapy or counselling as if it had the clarity and reality of a bruised and broken limb in an emergency ward.

19 Harry N. MacLean, *Once upon a Time: A True Story of Memory, Murder and the Law* (New York: HarperCollins, 1993) at 356–57.

sional, however, is not a detective. In psychiatry, mental reality is more important than objective reality. Punctilious history taking is not vital to therapy,
and a patient does not — and need not — take an oath like a witness to tell
the truth, the whole truth, and nothing but the truth. What a patient tells a
therapist about his or her childhood is not necessarily related to what actually
happened. In the psychoanalytic dialogue, attention is focused on continuity
and coherence, not on historical truth. Psychoanalysis or other psychotherapy
is not an archeological dig but a search for a regenerative story.

Whether or not the patients' stories about the past are literally true may be
only tangentially related to improvement in therapy. The two ends — clinical
utility and historical accuracy — can work against each other, however. For example, clinicians are most concerned with clinical utility and will allow memories to be used in treatment if they are effective regardless of their accuracy, but
historical accuracy is essential in the courtroom and to scientific inquiry.[20]

The crucial element, the "syndrome" concept itself, was far from a rigorous,
bright-line definitive concept that would preclude inappropriate application. In
theory, the concept of a syndrome is related to that of "disease."[21] A syndrome
involves a cluster of symptoms occurring together and characterizing a specific
disease. A syndrome may be recognized and utilized even before its cause is
known, as in Down's syndrome. Description of a syndrome logically requires
systematic definition (define a "case" so that what is being examined is clear)
and systematic investigation: examine the cases and determine the occurrence
of various symptoms, and examine non-cases for comparison. The distinction
from a disease is that the latter's causation is substantially known and that
serves as the prime diagnostic variable:

> Both diseases and syndromes share the medically and forensically import-
> ant feature of diagnostic value. Both point, with varying degrees of certainty,
> to particular causes. However, whereas the relationship between symptoms
> and etiology is clear with many diseases, this relationship is often unclear or
> unknown with respect to syndromes. The certainty with which a syndrome
> points to a particular cause varies with the syndrome.[22]

20 Ralph Slovenko, "The Effect of Return of Memory in Sexual Abuse Cases on Statute of
    Limitations and the Justification for a Counter Attack" (Paper delivered at Conference on
    "Memory and Reality," Valley Forge, PA, 16 April 1993) at 11–12.
21 John E.B. Myers, "Expert Testimony Describing Psychological Syndromes" (1993) 24 Pac.
    L.J. 1449.
22 Ralph Underwager & Hollida Wakefield, "A Paradigm Shift for Expert Witnesses" in J.J.
    Krivacska & J. Money, eds., *Handbook of Forensic Sexology* (Amherst, NY: Prometheus
    Books, 1994) 541.

However, a syndrome, absent scientific rigour, can effortlessly be located any-where a sympathetic social advocate may desire.[23]

The door thus opened in *Lavallee* was a most unfortunate one, leading down an intellectually disappointing path. As will be seen, that path was sub-stantially taken, with even worse to come. The requirement of a "syndrome," minimal as it was, was overrun by sympathy for sex complainants so that "trans-lation" by experts came to be viewed as acceptable in any case where "the jury just wouldn't understand." In effect, the crime of sexual assault (a construct covering a range of behaviour from the slightest touching to the most brutal rape) was presumed to leave victims "not normal" so their behaviours could be translated by an expert. And completely illogically, this reasoning was found acceptable when the very issue was whether in fact the sexual assault had taken place and whether in fact the complainants were actually victims!

TRAUMA SYNDROMES: CREDIBILITY OPINIONS AND BEHAVIOURAL CHARACTERISTICS

AS PREVIOUSLY NOTED, expert evidence is generally inadmissible when dir-ectly targeted at the credibility of a witness. Societal concern regarding a newly perceived problem of underreporting and underprosecuting of sex abuse cases moved the topic of sex abuse to the top of the political agenda from the mid-1970s onwards. By the early 1980s, North America saw the dawning of the sex abuse prosecution era, which brought with it advocacy researchers and others who claimed to have new forms of "expert evidence" specifically designed to facilitate convictions in such cases.[24] Such witnesses and evidence implicitly challenged the rule prohibiting expert opinion evidence that directly targeted and supported the credibility of a witness, such as a rape complainant. At their foundation, these witnesses and the evidence they presented depended almost entirely upon the acceptance of the complainant's claims as to what had taken place. In other words, they begged the question of the complainant's credibility in favour of the complainant and the prosecution.[25]

In a New Zealand case *R. v. C.S.*,[26] Williamson J. found that the problem in allowing such expert opinion testimony is that "it may in reality be little

---

23 See Neil Vidmar, "Evaluating Expert Scientific Evidence" (5 November 1999), ADGN/RP-093 at paras. 28–34 (on Quicklaw in Commentary).

24 An invaluable text in this area is Stephen J. Ceci & Helene Hembrooke, eds., *Expert Wit-nesses in Child Abuse Cases: What Can and Should Be Said in Court* (Washington, DC: American Psychological Association, 1998).

25 *R. v. A.K. and N.K.* (1999), 27 C.R. (5th) 226 at para. 95 (Ont. C.A.).

26 (1993), 11 C.R.N.Z. 45 (C.A.).

more than a cleverly packaged endorsement of the complainant's truthfulness or that it may be perceived by the jury as such an endorsement."[27] In the earlier case of *R. v. B.*[28] where a father was accused of sexually assaulting his adopted daughter, a psychologist gave evidence of a number of tests and observations she had carried out while interviewing the girl. Some of these were formalized tests and others were simply observations of the matters the child talked about, for example, her dreams and her self-image. In discussing each observation, the psychologist made some comment such as: "[This] is typical of sexually abused girls/children/young persons," save for the dreams about which she said: "[D]reams of this kind are frequently experienced by sexually abused young people." The court regarded the psychologist's evidence as inadmissible for a number of reasons, one of which was: "[L]arge parts of the evidence clearly reflect the psychologist's view that she was examining a child who had been sexually abused by her father."[29]

Courts also have little trouble recognizing the logical error in other contexts. In *People (California) v. Pizarro*,[30] in the course of a complete discussion of all aspects of DNA evidence, the court held:

[T]he exceptionally compelling nature of DNA evidence requires us to demand a high degree of accuracy and accountability in its use.

In this case, we hold the following:

(1) The frequency of the perpetrator's genetic profile (the random match probability) calculated from the Hispanic database was admitted without adequate foundation because there was insufficient evidence that the perpetrator is Hispanic. . . . To make the ethnic database relevant, the prosecution was required to present sufficient foundational evidence to show that the perpetrator is

---

27 See also *R. v. Schmit* (1992), 8 C.R.N.Z. 376 (C.A.).
28 [1987] 1 N.Z.L.R. 362 (C.A.).
29 *Ibid.* at 372, Casey J. See also *Lillie v. Newcastle City Council*, [2002] EWHC 1600 at para. 438 (Q.B.):

> Miss Page was doing well, it seemed, because later the same afternoon she asked another question he characterised as "excellent." This time she wanted to know (with reference to paragraph 14 of his report) how he could have concluded that "the perpetrators shaped the child's view both of himself and of the abuse" unless he assumed that abuse had taken place. Similarly, one needs to know how he could have arrived at his conclusion in paragraph 13 (that the children had been threatened to ensure their silence) unless an assumption had been made. These "excellent" questions required a cogent answer. There was a long rambling response extending over two pages (164–66) of the transcript. It was, however, no more than incomprehensible verbiage. It would be a waste of space to include it in this judgment.

30 100 Cal. App. 4th 1304 at 1313–14 (2002).

within that database's ethnicity .... In the absence of sufficient proof that the perpetrator is Hispanic, the Hispanic database was irrelevant, and the Hispanic profile frequency was irrelevant and created substantial danger of confusing the issues and misleading the trier of fact.

. . .

This error was compounded when the prosecution and the FBI improperly relied on defendant's ethnicity to justify use of the ethnic database .... [Thus] the jury was directly informed that the FBI used the Hispanic database because defendant is Hispanic — and thus the jury was indirectly informed that defendant's ethnicity served as proof of the perpetrator's ethnicity and was relied upon to render the ethnic database relevant. In other words, this bootstrap logic allowed defendant's ethnicity to justify calculation of an ethnic frequency, which when presented to the jury effectively operated as proof of the perpetrator's ethnicity — which in turn served as evidence of defendant's guilt. Reliance on defendant's ethnicity was founded on the improper assumption that defendant is in fact the perpetrator, and that assumption was conveyed by implication to the jury.

. . .

(2) The perpetrator's genotype at one of the genetic loci was also admitted without adequate foundation because there was insufficient evidence of the perpetrator's genotype at that locus. The relevance of data from that genetic locus, including defendant's genotype and the conclusion that defendant matches the perpetrator at that locus, required that the prosecution present sufficient foundational proof of the perpetrator's genotype at that locus .... Without such proof, data from that locus were irrelevant and inadmissible.

In other words, the DNA evidence could not be based on an assumption of the accused's guilt by limiting the database to the accused's race.

Canadian courts simply did not appreciate that when they said things such as "[t]he behaviour of a person who has been systematically abused is one example of a matter on which experts may assist,"[31] they were not only stating something quite at odds with the presumption of innocence, but also something quite irrelevant and quite different from the correct question to ask. The correct question should be as follows: "Is the determination from a person's behaviour whether he or she has in fact been systematically abused a matter on which experts might assist?" The correct answer to that latter relevant question is "no," because of the vagueness, lack of specificity, and substantial base rates of the behaviours involved.

---

31   *R. v. B.(R.H.)* (1994), 89 C.C.C.(3d) 193 at 201 (S.C.C.).

The evidence initially entered the criminal courts as "syndrome" evidence, specifically, Rape Trauma Syndrome, which was derived as a conceptual off-shoot from Post Traumatic Stress Disorder. The dubious nature of both these concepts is well documented.[32]

The diagnosis of post-traumatic stress disorder (PTSD) reflects the generally accepted belief in the clinical community that traumatic stress can have serious negative consequences for individuals. Whatever the merits of this self-serving, market-expanding presumption for clinical purposes,[33] the first and fundamental requirement to make a diagnosis of PTSD is that there be a known stressor experience beyond the stress level often experienced in life. Given such a trauma, it is one thing for clinicians to claim to catalogue and thus more easily recognize anticipated sequelae for their treatment purposes. But it is quite another matter to improperly use this "diagnosis" to infer backwards in time from the present purported observations of "sequelae" to an unknown but hypothesized stressful event in an attempt to buttress with an aura of medical practice a claim that the alleged prior event was a real experience. This deduction is of course the previously described logical error: the fallacy of affirming the consequence. Clinicians untrained in, and often disparaging of, science quite naturally fell into this error and clients, thus assured of insurance payments or other funding for their psychiatric diagnosis, were understandably grateful.

Once rape was characterized as a traumatic event, the application and misuse of the PTSD diagnosis in the criminal forensic context was inevitable. Once rape was abolished in favour of sexual assault, the latter then became the traumatic event, notwithstanding that sexual assault is a generic label covering the widest possible spectrum of human activity, from violent and traumatic rape to the mildest, even pleasurable fondling.[34]

---

32 See Hoeffel, "The Gender Gap," above note 9, where the author reviews the background of two well-accepted theories, Battered Woman Syndrome and Rape Trauma Syndrome, and reaches several disturbing conclusions about these theories, including that neither of these theories is particularly reliable. See generally Paul C. Giannelli, "Forensic Science: Rape Trauma Syndrome" (1997) 33 Crim. L. Bull. 270; note "Checking the Allure of Increased Conviction Rates: The Admissibility of Expert Testimony on Rape Trauma Syndrome in Criminal Proceedings" (1984) 70 Va. L. Rev. 1657; Faigman *et al.*, above note 11, vol. 1, c. 10, "Rape Trauma Syndrome," 402–35, and "Post-traumatic Stress Disorder," 260–72; Freckelton & Selby, above note 11, c. 13A. See also *Lillie v. Newcastle City Council*, above note 29 at paras. 493–94 regarding PTSD.

33 See Richard J. McNally, *Remembering Trauma* (Cambridge, MA & London, UK: Belknap Press of Harvard University Press, 2003) c. 3, "What Is Psychological Trauma?" 78–104 and "Emerging Controversies," 276–84.

34 Hoeffel, "The Gender Gap," above note 9 at 41.

Then there appeared the Child Sexual Abuse Accommodation Syndrome. A grouping of supposed behavioural indicators, such as delayed reporting, was so collectively labelled by a clinician and child abuse syndrome advocate named Roland Summit, M.D.[35] Summit postulated the "syndrome" operates as a coping mechanism for a child who has been sexually abused by a family member. The syndrome is said to have been identified as a result of "clinical study" of "large numbers" of children and their parents in "proven cases" of sexual abuse.

According to one written account, the syndrome had the following components:

1. secrecy;
2. helplessness;
3. entrapment and accommodation;
4. delayed, conflicted, and unconvincing disclosure; and
5. retraction.

Secrecy refers to the child's failure to reveal the abuse, as a result of varying degrees of intimidation by the adult. Comments ranging from "This is our secret," "Nobody will believe you," "If you tell it will break up the family," to threats to inflict harm on the family pet or the child him/herself, are said to cause the child to remain silent about the abuse.

Helplessness refers to the intrinsic power imbalance between a child and an adult, particularly an adult caretaker. Dependent children are unable to resist, cry out for help, or attempt to escape from the adult. As the abuse continues, the child learns to accept the situation, because there is no other option.

The phenomenon of entrapment and accommodation leads the child to assume responsibility for the abuse and even to seek out contact with the abuser. She develops psychic survival skills such as dissociation from the body when the abuse occurs, or expresses feelings of rage through delinquent behaviour.

An eventual breakdown of the accommodation mechanisms can lead to disclosure. According to Summit, the disclosure usually is delayed rather than immediate, and often is disbelieved by adults.

Lastly, Summit identifies retraction (or recantation) as the fifth element of the syndrome. Unless the child receives support following her disclosure, she is likely to retract it, in the face of the chaos caused to the family by the allegation.

Summit concludes his delineation of the child sexual abuse accommodation syndrome by stating that it is a "maxim" among child abuse counsellors

---

35   Roland Summit, "The Child Sexual Abuse Accommodation Syndrome" (1983) 7 Child Abuse & Neglect 177 at 179.

that "children never fabricate the kinds of explicit sexual manipulations they divulge in complaints or interrogations."[36]

This "syndrome" was immediately seized upon as a diagnostic tool and subject for expert opinion evidence. Later, Summit tried to defend his overreaching pronouncement as "merely an aid to understanding," as a "consciousness raising experience" for mental health professionals to sensitize them to what Summit believed was a tendency to minimize the prevalence of sexual abuse. In various cross-examinations in court proceedings in the United States, Summit was forced to admit the obvious: his article was not "a scientific study"[37] and was certainly not validated by his own practice; in fact, he had no practice involving abused children. Summit's article is not a systematic review of a large number of cases; rather, it is simply an impressionistic collection of second-hand "observations," a purported summary of many discussions with other clinicians and adult abuse victims. Thus was second-hand hearsay turned by the misuse of the rubric "syndrome" into sex abuse expert evidence. Summit has since maintained he never intended the concept to be used to make any diagnosis or determination of fact. People who attempt to use it in that fashion were misusing his concept, Summit claimed in his published admission as to the nonscientific nature of what he labels a "clinical opinion," "a summary of diverse clinical consulting experience."[38]

---

36 Michelle K. Fuerst, "Syndrome Evidence" in Mr. Justice Kenneth Matthews *et al.*, eds., *The Expert: A Practitioner's Guide* (Scarborough, ON: Thomson Canada, 1995) vol. I, c. 9 at 9–10.

37 The following excerpt from one of Summit's cross-examinations is typical:

Q: Witnesses have testified in this proceeding that the Child Abuse Accommodation Syndrome is not really a scientific study or theory. Can you comment . . . ?

A: I'd say it's not a study in the technical sense, and it's certainly not a theory. It's an observation. It's a clinical observation, and in my case it's clinical observations at least the second level of removal. I am dealing with other clinicians who are treating the individuals who are reporting their behaviour to me . . . .

Q: Would you agree with me that your syndrome is an impressionistic collection of observations?

A: Yes I would.

Q: It is not properly used as a test whether or not abuses occurred?

A: That is correct.

38 Roland Summit, "Abuse of the Child Sexual Abuse Accommodation Syndrome" (1992) 1 J. Child Sexual Abuse 153. These deficiencies are discussed (in benign terms) in *R. v. A.K. and N.K.*, above note 25 at paras. 61–62. The implicit use of the "syndrome" to boost the complainants' credibility led to convictions being reversed in that case: *ibid.* at paras. 125*ff.*

There is no scientific basis for this "syndrome" concept at all.[39] There is simply no factual research data supporting it and much data contradicting it. It was only a speculative, subjective, and personal conceptualization with no scientific merit. Its reception in criminal prosecutions was completely unmerited, as some, though not all, appellate courts quickly held.[40]

---

39 Summit claimed he worked by analogy to the Battered Child Syndrome. Underwager & Wakefield, above note 22, noted:

> Myers . . . discusses the difference between two syndromes often offered in expert testimony in cases of alleged child abuse. The battered child syndrome has high certainty since a child with the symptoms of the syndrome is very likely to have suffered nonaccidental injury. In this syndrome, research evidence has accumulated which demonstrates that nonaccidental injuries can be successfully discriminated from accidental injuries by the nature of the injuries. The predictions from this theory, therefore, meet the criterion of falsifiability of the *Daubert* decision and consequently, evidence regarding this syndrome has high probative value and, in fact, has been approved by every appellate court to consider it.

It is in fact instructive to compare the Summit article with the earlier "Battered-Child Syndrome" article, which Summit completely erroneously used as a "model": Henry Kempe *et al.*, "The Battered-Child Syndrome" (1962) 181 J.A.M.A. 17; see Myers, above note 21.

40 See *R. v. A.K. and N.K.*, above note 25. One of the clearest decisions rejecting the "child abuse syndrome" and its variations is *Commonwealth (Pennsylvania) v. Dunkle*, 602 A.2d 830 at 834–35 (Pa. 1992), where the court wisely stated:

> [U]nlike battered child syndrome evidence which describes characteristics unique to physically abused children, evidence of the typical behaviors of sexually abused children is so general as to have no probative value: Clearly, drug and alcohol abuse, eating disorders, low self-esteem and not doing school work are common phenomena not solely related to child abuse. To permit the jury to speculate that they might be, however, violates every notion of what constitutes probative and relevant evidence. It is neither scientifically supportable nor legally supportable. Such a laundry list of possible behaviors does no more than invite speculation and will not be condoned.

See also *State (Tennessee) v. Bolin*, 922 S.W.2d 870 (Tenn. 1996); *Hadden v. State (Florida)*, 690 So. 2d 573 (Fla. 1997): (good review of literature and discussion of issue); *People (California) v. Leon*, 263 Cal. Rptr. 77 (Ct. App. 2 Dist. 1989): (a case in which Summit testified as a witness); *State (New Jersey) v. J.Q.*, 599 A.2d 172 (N.J. Super. Ct. App. Div. 1991), aff'd 617 A.2d 1196 (N.J. 1993); *R. v. Olscamp* (1994), 95 C.C.C. (3d) 466 (Ont. Ct. Gen. Div.); *R. v. Mathieu* (1994), 90 C.C.C. (3d) 415 (Que. C.A.), aff'd [1995] 4 S.C.R. 46; *R. v. Villamar*, [1996] O.J. No. 2742 (Gen. Div.); *People (New York) v. Singh*, 588 N.Y.S.2d 573 (App. Div. 2 Dept. 1992); *People (California) v. McAlpin*, 812 P.2d 563 (Cal. 1991); *People (California) v. Renfro*, 3 Cal. Rptr. 2d 909 (Ct. App. 3 Dist. 1992); *R. v. P.(H.)*, [1992] O.J. No. 1536 (Gen. Div.); *R. v. Field*, [1990] O.J. No. 2779 (C.A.) (court refused to judicially note such "facts"); *State (Tennessee) v. Ballard*, 855 S.W.2d 557 (Tenn. 1993); *State (New Hampshire) v. Cressey*, 628 A.2d 696 (N.H. 1993); *R. v. Meisner*, [1992] N.S.J. No. 112 (C.A.).

See also David McCord, "Syndromes, Profiles and Other Mental Exotica: A New Approach to the Admissibility of Nontraditional Psychological Evidence in Criminal Cases"

As Summit's "syndrome" was being discredited, its spurious content was still being purveyed with the suspect "syndrome" label being dropped. Various aspects of the complainant's conduct and behaviours[41] were simply recast in pseudo-scientific terms, to become "symptoms" or "sequelae" of the claimed sexual abuse. Everything and anything was characterized by prosecution witnesses as such a "symptom,"[42] including the very absence of any symptoms, in the sense that absence was not proof of the lack of abuse.[43]

(1986) 66 Or. L. Rev. 19. An early, but still insightful, criticism is found in R.J. Levy, "Using Scientific Testimony to Prove Child Abuse" (1989) 23 Fam. L.Q. 83. See also David McCord, "Expert Psychological Testimony about Child Complainants in Sexual Abuse Prosecutions: A Foray into the Admissibility of Novel Psychological Evidence" (1986) 77 J. Crim. L. & Criminology 1; Mary Ann Mason, "A Judicial Dilemma: Expert Witness Testimony in Child Sex Abuse Cases" (1991) J. Psych. & Law 185: an excellent article reviewing the 122 American court decisions dealing with such expert testimony, showing how contradictory the evidence was, the lack of real qualifications of the so-called expert witnesses, and discussing in an intelligent fashion the issues raised. A. Cohen, Note "The Unreliability of Expert Testimony on the Typical Characteristics of Sexual Abuse Victims" (1985) 74 Geo. L.J. 429 is an early article whose sage comments were unfortunately ignored by too many courts.

41   *Irving v. State (Florida)*, [1998] WL 44486 (Fla. Ct. App. 1 Dist. 1998): the admission of a prosecution's "expert" testimony expressing the opinion, based upon purported "diagnostic" standards, that the complainant's behaviour "is consistent with children who have been sexually abused" was held to be a reversible error even if the state's clinical psychologist witness did not expressly refer to specific syndromes or profiles.

See the summary of behavioural indicator lists and their logical flaws in Vidmar, above note 23 at paras. 58–60. An excellent article that reviews the current state of expert knowledge on the effects of sexual abuse is K.A. Kendall-Tackett, L.M. Williams, & D. Finkelhor, "Impact of Sexual Abuse on Children: A Review and Synthesis of Recent Empirical Studies" (1993) 113 Psychol. Bull. 164. See also Stephen J. Ceci & Maggie Bruck, *Jeopardy in the Courtroom: A Scientific Analysis of Children's Testimony* (Washington, DC: American Psychological Association, 1995) at 279.

42   In *R. v. Taylor* (1986), [1987] 31 C.C.C. (3d) 1 (Ont. C.A.) where the defence had adduced evidence that the complainants had told far-fetched stories of sexual assaults by other persons, it was held that the Crown could adduce expert evidence in reply to the effect that sexually abused children have a rich fantasy life, and that borderline personality disorders are consistent with having been sexually abused as a child. In other words, the evidence tended to explain that the stories related by the complainants were in fact symptomatic of sexual assaults upon them.

See Ceci & Hembrooke, above note 24, c. 10, for a comprehensive discussion of the various kinds of expert evidence in sex cases and how American appellate courts have dealt with such evidence.

43   See *Lillie v. Newcastle City Council*, above note 29 at paras. 1202–8 regarding such a cavalier approach to evidence interpretation:

It is necessary to be wary of this Humpty Dumpty approach to words, since it pervades the entire Report and the Review Team's evidence. It betokens a mindset which leads to the following examples of how to approach evidence:

Syndrome theory, however, defies such exactitude both because it operates at a level of meaningless generality and makes contradictory claims. By way of example, indicia of abuse include such commonplace behavior as biting lips, clenching fists, tapping fingers, biting nails ... stomachaches and nightmares ... and "fatigue, poor sleep and headaches, emotional changes including anxiety, irritability, depression and hopelessness, and behavioral manifestations including aggression, cynicism, and substance abuse, leading to poor job performance, [and] deterioration in interpersonal relationships."

If a child is calm during a genital examination, that may be taken as evidence that she is used to being handled in that way; but a child who resists during the exam may also be viewed as having experienced sexual trauma. ... A victim's relating of conflicting versions of the events is considered a sign of abuse ... but so is the consistency of the victim's story over time .... Even courts that admit rape trauma syndrome concede that "the behavior exhibited by a rape victim after the attack can vary. While some women will express their fear, anger and anxiety openly, an equal number of women will appear controlled, calm, and subdued." ... Behavioral response checklists include such opposites as increased or decreased eating or smoking ... and preoccupation with or aversion to sex.

This contradictory ... nature of syndrome evidence ... [makes it] look more like drug courier profiles, which have a "chameleon-like way of adapting to any particular set of observations."[44]

What is logically indefensible regarding these political tactics and what makes the entire matter a sorry example of junk science is the failure to recog-

---

If a child says that she has been raped, or had a knife stuck up her vagina, and yet she has an intact hymen and no signs of abnormality, one just resorts to the proposition (in general terms, of course, unassailable) that the absence of physical findings does not mean that abuse has not taken place;

If a child makes no allegations about anyone abusing him or her, then it is probably explicable on the basis of terrorisation by the supposed abuser;

If a child exonerates a person voluntarily, despite pressure and leading questions, then she is saying the opposite of what she means (i.e. that the person exonerated actually did abuse her);

If a child is peppered with leading questions over three hours of interviews, then one can include in one's report the cavalier and unsupported conclusion that there was no evidence of leading questions;

If a child says that she was taken out and abused at Christopher Lillie's house accompanied by another member of staff, and that is not borne out by that member of staff, then it probably means that the abuse took place in the nursery in the absence of that member of staff.

As an approach to weighing evidence, this is unscientific and irrational.

44 Brodin, "Behavioral Science Evidence," above note 14 at 912–15 [footnotes omitted].

nize the circular reasoning and question-begging taking place. No attempt was made to study similar phenomena in cases of false accusations because to the advocacy researchers there were no such cases. Yet, without a comparison of cases of false or untrue accusations, without a consideration of the alternative hypothesis that would reflect the presumption of innocence, no rational, logical consideration of the proposed evidence was possible.[45]

Other authors have summarized the problems with testimony in cases of alleged child sexual abuse as follows:

> [A]lmost any circumstance, behavior or observation can be rationalized as supporting the conclusion that sexual abuse occurred. What makes such testimony, and its underlying theory, not falsifiable is the fact that there is no circumstance, behavior, or observation which could be used to conclude that abuse did not occur. Consequently, there are no circumstances under which one could endeavor to prove the underlying theory false.
>
> The widely disseminated lists of behavioral indicators, many of which are contradictory, are frequently offered as evidence to support the accusation of abuse. In testimony, all manner of behaviors are declared to be typical of abused children, all absent scientific evidence to support the claims. Depression or mania, hyperactivity or hypoactivity, social aggression or social withdrawal, heightened modesty or no modesty, poor hygiene or excessive concern about cleanliness, overly compliant or oppositional all are offered as evidence of abuse. This is done in spite of the fact that reasoning backward in time from observed symptoms to some prior entity or event is to commit the logical error of affirming the consequence. There are no behavioral indicators, including the absence of any problem behaviors, that can falsify abuse.[46]

The basic rules of science were violated in the following ways:

1. The phenomena being studied were not carefully defined and objectively ascertained, but highly dependent on subjective impressions of

---

45 A few courts recognized this fact. An exceptional but unfortunately uninfluential decision noting the evidentiary uselessness of the Crown's expert's list of behaviourial symptoms was *R. v. LeBlanc* (1992), 71 C.C.C. (3d) 527 (N.B.C.A.). See also *State (New Hampshire) v. Cressey*, 628 A.2d 696 (N.H. 1993); *State (New Hampshire) v. Luce*, 628 A.2d 707 (N.H. 1993); *United States v. Velarde*, 214 F.3d 1204 (10th Cir. 2000). Cohen, Note "The Unreliability of Expert Testimony," above note 40; G.B. Melton & S. Limber, "Psychologist Involvement in Cases of Child Maltreatment: Limits of Role in Expertise" (1989) 44 Am. Psychol. 1225.

An excellent, if traditionally couched, summary and analysis of the case law can be found in David M. Paciocco, "Coping with Expert Evidence about Human Behaviour" (1999) 25 Queen's L.J. 305.

46 Above note 22.

sympathetic researchers, who talked in vague generalities like "not un-common," which precluded any real knowledge of accurate facts.

2. Claims were made about group characteristics when the group being studied was problematically ascertained (most of the research claimed to have been done on "victims of sex abuse" should accurately have been described as done on persons who "*claimed to be* victims of sex abuse").

3. Conclusions about the group were drawn in the complete absence of any control groups or comparison groups — which is required to draw valid conclusions about the significance of any observed characteristics — and without any concern for base rates or their significance.

4. In general terms, the conclusions being drawn constituted the fallacy of affirming the consequent in that they took characteristics, behavioural or otherwise, that might appear if a person was abused, and reasoned backwards from the existence of the characteristics to conclude there had been abuse previously.

The use of syndrome evidence or behavioural characteristics to indicate guilt creates too high a risk that an accused will be convicted not for what he did but for what others in other cases did or were found to have done. The syndrome reasoning fallaciously assumes that because someone shares characteristics — many of them innocent and commonplace — with a certain type of victim, that individual must also have suffered the same criminal victimization.[47]

Typical examples of such evidence follow:

Dr. Raylene DeLuca, an expert in child abuse and sexual abuse opined that children who are victims of sexual abuse often suffer from post-traumatic stress syndrome. She testified that typical behaviour associated with this disorder includes lying, acting out negatively, dizziness, headaches, nightmares, problems in school and with concentration. Commonly such victims do not disclose abuse within the family until it becomes unbearable. The child may often not openly resist the continuation of abuse as the abuser is doing other things the child enjoys. The symptoms, she said, usually occur in clusters. When they do there is a strong causal connection to the offence of sexual abuse. On cross-examination Dr. DeLuca confirmed that these typical clusters of behaviour are also consistent with causes which are not linked to sexual abuse. There are, in fact, various reasons why a child might manifest these symptoms or a combination of them. She acknowledged that allegations of the kind made in this case can be fabri-

---

47 The observant reader will recognize this as analogous to the judicial commentary on why profiles are illogical and inadmissible: see chapter 3, note 44.

cated, but in her experience if there is detail and a good, full description of the incident, the literature indicates that it is unlikely to be a fabrication.[48]

In fact, the first portions of Dr. DeLuca's statement are unsupported by any reliable data and, by ignoring base-rate issues, grossly overstate the proper conclusions. The last claim about what "the literature indicates" is difficult to discuss further in the absence of any specification of the literature in mind. It is not possible to locate any reliable scientific literature supporting that claim.

Another example[49] involved the sexual assault of a seven-year-old girl by three young offenders. The Crown called a clinical psychologist who "specialized" in the treatment of young victims of sexual offences. Dr. Wollert's evidence at trial was that there were several behavioural characteristics that are experienced by young victims of sexual offences. These include bedwetting, nightmares, and anxiety. He also testified that these problems may be caused by other occurrences in the child's life.

The trial judge appeared to give little weight to Dr. Wollert's testimony, and on the successful Crown appeal from acquittal, this opinion was described as erroneous in the following terms:

> I think it can now be taken that evidence of an expert, in the nature of that given by Dr. Wollert as to the psychological and physical conditions which frequently arise as a result of sexual abuse of a child, is admissible. It provides assistance to a trial judge in concluding whether an assault has occurred. This kind of testimony is helpful, because it provides a bench-mark which can hardly be doubted, as it is entirely unlikely that such things as bed wetting and nightmares are subject to be concocted or contrived by a youthful witness to support or buttress the reliability of any testimony that witness may later be called upon to give in court.

On the subsequent appeal to the Supreme Court of Canada, that Court agreed and has since repeated this acceptance in subsequent cases.[50] The fallacies apparent in the evidence should by now require no elucidation.

The time period between the alleged crime and its reporting, a commonsensically relevant credibility factor that would obviously increase in probative value as the delay increased without reasonable explanation, was converted into the symptom of "delayed disclosure."[51] Experts were ready to testify in pseudo-

---

48 *R. v. D.D.* (1998), 126 C.C.C. (3d) 435 at para. 8 (Man. C.A.).

49 *R. v. B.(G.)* (1990), 56 C.C.C. (3d) 200 at 204 (S.C.C.).

50 *R. v. Marquard*, [1993] 4 S.C.R. 223; *R. v. B.(R.H.)*, above note 31.

51 *R. v. C.(R.A.)* (1990), 57 C.C.C. (3d) 522 (B.C.C.A.): evidence of a counsellor as to the characteristics of children who have been sexually abused, and as well the "dynamics" of

medical jargon regarding the impact of threats by a perpetrator on children, as if that somehow needed special expertise to understand, as if jurors had never been children themselves.[52] A complainant's admission of falsehood in making the original complaint itself was turned into a symptom: recantation.[53]

Courts sailed a difficult course between the Scylla of sympathy for victims of sex offences and the Charybdis of the flawed logic that they uncomfortably recognized in varying degrees was underlying the evidence they were being given. Many did not make it.

The Supreme Court of Canada, especially early on, was unreservedly sympathetic to the admission of expert evidence regarding the behaviour "of a person who has been systematically abused."[54] The Court did not appreciate the lack of reliability or validity of such evidence, and the fact that, to the extent that such evidence contained any degree of truth, it was well within the knowledge of reasonable laypeople (especially after appropriate jury instructions disabused them of any unacceptable sexist stereotypical assumptions).

Other courts demonstrated varying degrees of acceptance towards the supposed behavioural characteristics of sex abuse victims.[55] In one case, the child's

---

sexual abuse was held admissible. This included an explanation as to why children delay in disclosing sexual abuse and maintain an association with the abuser.

The question-begging involved in the term "disclosure" has not escaped the more observant judiciary: see *Lillie v. Newcastle City Council*, above note 29 at para. 15 regarding "disclosures": "Those allegations have often been referred to as 'disclosures,' despite the fact that this term had been deprecated in the Report of the Inquiry into the Child Abuse in Cleveland (1987)." See also paras. 506–11.

52 *C. v. The Queen* (1993), 60 S.A.S.R. 467 (Austl. C.A.): excluding such evidence, stating "jurors were children once."

53 *R. v. J.(F.E.)* (1989), [1990] 53 C.C.C. (3d) 64 (Ont. C.A.): evidence that children who have been sexually abused commonly recant their allegations was held to come within the proper scope of expert evidence.

54 *R. v. Marquard*, above note 50; *R. v. B.(R.H.)*, above note 31.

55 See *R. v. W.(S.)* (1996), 47 C.R. (4th) 354 (Ont. Ct. Gen. Div.); *R. v. Lance* (1998), 130 C.C.C. (3d) 438 at para. 24 (Ont. C.A.); *R. v. Mathieu* (1994), 90 C.C.C. (3d) 415 (Que. C.A.); *R. v. E.A.L.*, [1998] O.J. No. 4160 (C.A.); *R. v. Jmieff* (1994), 94 C.C.C. (3d) 157 (B.C.C.A.); *R. v. Chisholm* (1997), 8 C.R. (5th) 21 (Ont. Ct. Gen. Div.); *Khan v. College of Physicians & Surgeons* (1992), 76 C.C.C. (3d) 10 (Ont. C.A.); *R. v. J.(F.E.)*, above note 53; Alan D. Gold, "Expert Evidence — Admissibility" (1994) 37 Crim. L.Q. 16 at 21–30.

A really bad decision is *R. v. N.(R.A.)* (2001), 152 C.C.C. (3d) 464 (Alta. C.A.), where the court dispensed with the necessity of expert evidence and simply "knew" the significance of behavioural symptoms on its own (at para. 29):

In this case, common sense and common experience of human behaviour suggest that the multiple behavioural changes observed were indicative of some emotional trauma in the life of the complainant. It was not necessary for an expert to opine that a 10- or 11-year-old girl does not begin bedwetting and to display behavioural problems with-

"passivity during medical examination" was offered as a "characteristic" of abused children, notwithstanding a complete absence of any data that would possibly support such an unqualified assertion, not to mention the problematic subjectivity of the concept of "passivity."[56] A more hopeful example was *R. v. G.G.*,[57] where the "expert" witness testified that certain observed behavioural characteristics were consistent with sexual abuse but, the witness admitted, they were also consistent with absence of sexual abuse. In reversing a conviction, Laskin J.A. for the court noted that "evidence equally consistent with either of two diametrically opposed possibilities cannot support either possibility." Regrettably, the very admissibility of the evidence appears not to have been contested.

Tragically, as late as 1994, the infamous "sexual abuse accommodation syndrome" of Roland Summit was still being referred to without appropriate denunciation.[58] One appeal court has described the matter as settled by precedent,[59] ignoring that the doctrine of precedent settles matters of law, not factual matters and scientific reality. Preferable is the approach described by Justice Hill in *R. v. Chisholm*[60] and adopted by the Ontario Court of Appeal in *R. v. A.K. and N.K.*[61] to the effect that prior instances of admission may be looked to as a relevant factor in deciding admissibility, but the matter is not one of precedent and must be considered on a case-by-case basis.

The New Zealand Court of Appeal was wiser in rejecting such evidence,[62] as

---

out some provocation. That simple truth does not require special knowledge nor is it outside the realm of understanding of an ordinary person.

The court failed to appreciate the meaninglessness of the evidence without knowledge of base rates of the phenomenon, or the *post hoc* fallacy being engaged in. A highly relevant question not addressed would be to consider whether some other cause resulting in the bedwetting might also not be causing a false allegation. Of course, this assumes causation in the context of bedwetting is a valid question, which raises a whole separate issue regarding the state of our real knowledge about such matters. See chapter 4, note 81.

56 *R. v. Marquard*, above note 50.
57 (1995), 97 C.C.C. (3d) 362 (Ont. C.A.).
58 *R. v. T.(D.B.)* (1994), 89 C.C.C.(3d) 466 (Ont. C.A.). Compare the same court in *R. v. A.K. and N.K.*, above note 25.
59 *R. v. G.C.* (1996), 110 C.C.C. (3d) 233 at para. 88 (Nfld. C.A.).
60 Above note 55 at para. 57.
61 Above note 25 at para. 76.
62 In *R. v. S.*, [1989] 1 N.Z.L.R. 714 (C.A.), a psychologist gave evidence of a number of characteristics presented by a child alleging sexual abuse, such as self-mutilation, lack of eye contact, and unwillingness to talk about home life. Before giving these details, she had been asked the question: "Did [the complainant] exhibit any characteristics which were consistent with what you had come to know as the characteristics of sexually abused children?" She replied: "[V]ery definitely." The Court of Appeal had some awareness of the logical flaws in this evidence and the fact that the court also needed to know how probable the evidence is if

were various Australian appellate courts.[63]

Some rationality had been regained by the time of the decision in *R. v. D.D.*,[64] a sex case where the ten-year-old complainant "delayed" two and a half years before she "complained," and where proposed expert testimony on behalf of the Crown by a child psychologist that the length of time before disclosure was not indicative of truth of an allegation because many factors and circumstances may affect the timing of complaint was held inadmissible, with the necessity requirement especially being singled out.

Since the "content of the expert evidence . . . was not unique or scientifically puzzling but was rather the proper subject for a simple jury instruction" its admission was not necessary, the Supreme Court of Canada majority held.

Previous cases dealing with delay in disclosure[65] now have to be read in light of *R. v. D.D.* A more recent case is *R. v. G.T.*,[66] where *R. v. D.D.* was distinguished and expert evidence regarding "patterns of disclosure . . . marked by delay, inconsistencies, and recantations" of abused children was held admissible or, if not, the proviso was applicable to uphold the accused's conviction. The court fell victim to an evidentiary record that made claims about patterns of disclosure, delay, and inconsistency among sex abuse victims that are not borne

---

the child had not been abused when it pointed out: "[S]ome at least of those characteristics may very well occur in children who have problems other than sexual abuse."

The politicians then acted in deplorable fashion to amend the New Zealand *Evidence Act* to expressly make admissible such worthless evidence: see Freckelton & Selby, above note 11, vol. 1, 28.670 at 2-562.

63 *F. v. The Queen* (1995), 83 A. Crim. R. 502 (N.S.W.C.A.); *R. v. C.* (1993), 60 S.A.S.R. 467 (Austl. C.A.); *J. v. The Queen* (1994), 75 A. Crim. R. 522 (Vict. Ct. Crim. App.).

64 [2000] 2 S.C.R. 275.

65 See *R. v. C.(R.A.)*, above note 51; *R. v. R.(S.)* (1992), 15 C.R.(4th) 102 (Ont. C.A.); and also *R. v. F.(D.S.)*, above note 4 at 53–54 where the court held:

> In this case, the question is whether the expert evidence was necessary to enable the jury to properly appreciate the complainant's explanation for not immediately leaving the relationship and disclosing the abuse. This involved more than simply understanding the meaning of the words used by the complainant in giving her explanation. It also involved appreciating the context in which the explanation was given; by that I mean appreciating that persons who are abused in intimate relationships may respond differently because of that relationship than they would in other circumstances.
>
> . . .
>
> Although I am inclined to think that the expert evidence admitted in this case would come within the normal experience of many jurors, I am not prepared to interfere with the decision to admit the evidence on this basis. The trial judge was obviously alive to the requirements set out in *Mohan*. She carefully reviewed the proposed evidence, the purpose for which it was being tendered and reached a considered judgment that it was admissible. I am unable to conclude that she erred in doing so.

66 Indexed as *R. v. Talbot* (2002), 161 C.C.C. (3d) 256 (Ont. C.A.).

out by any reliable research. Then, in *R. v. Page*,[67] the same court held such evidence "unnecessary" as in *R. v. D.D.*[68]

Direct violations of the credibility rule were generally rebuffed, so an expert was not allowed to testify directly that the complainant was apparently truthful, or was in fact abused by the accused or that only a small percentage of complainants lie,[69] or "that young children often will not make a disclosure at the first opportunity, as they defer doing that until they feel safe."[70] But the Supreme Court allowed expert evidence concerning the reliability of child evidence[71] and, apparently, expert evidence that children lack the motivation, the sophistication, and mental capacity to manufacture a complex fabrication.[72]

Even as courts rejected Summit's bogus expertise and wrestled uneasily with the wrongful admission of "symptom" evidence, they fell into new error, which unfortunately still currently prevails. It can be labelled the "myth-dispelling" use of social science expert evidence.[73] It is currently common in the case law,[74] but it is as scientifically invalid and logically unsound as its precursors.

---

67 [2002] O.J. No. 142 (C.A.). In *R. v. Tayebi* (2001), 48 C.R. (5th) 354 (B.C.C.A.), expert evidence on the effects of sexual abuse of children, including symptoms of sexual abuse, the significance of delayed or incomplete disclosures, and on human memory generally was allowed without objection by the defence. The appeal court seemed to approve.

68 See also *R. v. W.(W.A.)* (2001), 153 C.C.C. (3d) 56 (Alta. C.A.).

69 See *R. v. W.(A.)*, [1995] 4 S.C.R. 51, rev'g (1994), 44 C.R.(4th) 319 (Ont. C.A.); *R. v. J.(F.E.)*, above note 53; *R. v. R.(S.)*, above note 65; *R. v. Kostuck*, [1986] M.J. No. 406 (C.A.) ("children rarely lie"); *R. v. Taylor*, above note 42 (statistics on the rarity of false accusations); *R. v. T.(S.)* (1986), 55 C.R. (3d) 321 (Ont. C.A.); *Snowden v. Singletary*, 135 F.3d 732 (11th Cir. 1998): evidence by an expert witness that 99.5 percent of children tell the truth and that the expert, in his own experience with children, had not personally encountered an instance where a child had invented a lie about abuse was held inadmissible.

70 *R. v. L.A.P.* (2000), 150 Man. R. (2d) 247 (C.A.).

71 *R. v. R.(D.)*, [1996] 2 S.C.R. 291.

72 *R. v. W.(A.)*, above note 69.

73 This regrettable suggestion appears to have originated in John E.B. Myers, "Expert Testimony in Child Abuse Litigation" (1989) 68 Neb. L.R. 1 at 67–68.

74 *R. v. G.C.*, above note 59 at para. 87; *R. v. R.A.C.* (1990), 57 C.C.C. (3d) 522 (B.C.C.A.); *R. v. J.(F.E.)*, above note 53; and especially *R. v. A.K. and N.K.*, above note 25, discussed in the text. In *State (New Jersey) v. J.Q.*, above note 40, the misuse of the "Child Abuse Syndrome" to try to prove child abuse was blocked by the court. The court correctly understood the misleading nature of the rubric "syndrome" and appreciated that it is not a diagnostic device; it assumes the presence of abuse and purports to describe the reaction. However, the court did hold that evidence based upon the "Child Sexual Abuse Accommodation Syndrome" was admissible in response to, and to assist jurors in evaluating, a specific defence claim about a lack of complaint to a parent or other authority figure, by explaining the common occurrence of such features as delay in reporting or continued acceptance of abuse in these cases. In other words, to the extent that such hypothetical reactions constitute an alternative explanation for behaviour in a particular case, it is rel-

An example of this approach and reasoning is found in *R. v. A.K. and N.K.*[75] In that case, the trial judge granted leave to the Crown to call expert opinion evidence from a social worker to assist the jury in understanding the following aspects of the complainants' behaviour: delay in disclosing the abuse, inconsistent disclosures, faulty memory about alleged occurrences of sexual abuse and peripheral events, repeated involvement with the alleged abusers, and lack of detection by persons close to the complainants.[76]

The Court of Appeal held that on the record in that case "it was open to the trial judge to allow, in his discretion, expert opinion evidence on some restricted subject-matters."[77] The justification offered was as follows:

> As in many cases of this nature, the issues at trial turned on the credibility of the complainants. Counsel for the appellants concede that the above-noted features of the complainants' behaviour formed the basis of the defence's attack on their credibility and, consequently, became relevant issues in the trial. It is also conceded that the expert opinion evidence stating that certain behaviour is not uncommon in victims of sexual abuse related to those issues. Therefore, the logical relevance of this expert evidence is not disputed.[78]

This passage raises the following issues. First, the factual claim that "certain behaviour is not uncommon in victims of sexual abuse" requires data supporting that opinion. As will be seen below, in fact many claims about the behaviour of victims of sexual abuse (such as disclosure patterns) are unsupported by any reliable data and represent ideological positions taken by sympathetic, well-meaning clinicians.[79]

What is more important, it is hard to find any other example where a complainant in a particular case is allowed to justify behaviour by resort to sup-

---

evant to refute the defence's exculpatory explanation of the same behaviour. The court accepted the analysis in Myers, *ibid.* at 67–68. This approach has been limited in California: *People (California) v. Harlan*, 271 Cal. Rptr. 653 (Ct. App. 4 Dist. 1990): the myth must be identified, the testimony must be limited to dispel this myth, and the jury must be admonished that the expert testimony is not intended and should not be used to determine whether the victim's molestation claim is true; *People (California) v. Sanchez*, 256 Cal. Rptr. 446 (Ct. App. 4 Dist. 1989); *People (California) v. Bowker*, 249 Cal. Rptr. 886 at 892 (Ct. App. 4 Dist. 1988): the court held that "at a minimum the evidence must be targeted to a specific 'myth' or 'misconception' suggested by the evidence . . . . It is the People's burden to identify the myth or misconception the evidence is designed to rebut. Where there is no danger of jury confusion, there is simply no need for the expert testimony."

75 Above note 25.

76 *R. v. A.K. and N.K., ibid.* at para. 64. See also *R. v. G.T.*, above note 66.

77 *R. v. A.K. and N.K., ibid.* at para. 69.

78 *Ibid.* at paras. 106–10.

79 Another example is *R. v. P.G.*, [2009] O.J. No. 121 (C.A.).

posed patterns of behaviour of complainants generally.[80] Disclosure delays and inconsistencies in statements are routinely considered by juries without the benefit of evidence, for example, that it "is not uncommon in victims of robbery" to give inconsistent descriptions of their assailant or add fuller details with the passage of time.

Most important, it is difficult to see how this is really expert opinion evidence, as opposed to merely a factual claim. If there are data regarding the frequency of certain behaviours among complainants, the issue of "how common" is easily determined by a jury considering the relative frequencies. An expert opining "not uncommon" deprives the trier of fact of accurate information so that the trier can assess the weight of the evidence. Is "not uncommon" 60 percent or 5 percent or even 1 percent?

The court in *R. v. A.K. and N.K.* continued:

> It is argued, however, that the expert opinion evidence is of no probative value because the expert fairly conceded that the behaviour in question, although not uncommon in victims of sexual abuse, would similarly not be uncommon in cases where the complaint was fabricated. It is therefore argued that the expert evidence about those features of behaviour does not tend to prove anything and is worthless.
>
> This argument is based on the fallacy that this evidence was presented to prove that sexual abuse in fact occurred. If that were the case, the appellants would be quite correct in their assertion that the evidence would be of little, if any, probative value.
>
> . . .
>
> Rather, the expert opinion evidence that certain behaviour, such as delayed disclosure of the abuse, is not unusual in victims of sexual abuse is presented simply to prove that fact and nothing more. The same applies with respect to the other features of behaviour. The evidence is not and cannot be presented to show that the complainant is more likely to have been abused because she has not disclosed the abuse in a timely fashion or because she has exhibited some of the other forms of behaviour. Such a proposition would be untenable. It would turn features such as delayed disclosure, faulty memory, inconsistent versions, and the like into hallmarks of truth.
>
> The relevance of the evidence here is that it can provide the trier of fact with a more complete picture. For example, logic alone could lead the trier of fact to infer from the absence of timely complaint that no abuse has taken place. After all, if nothing untoward is happening to the child, it only makes

---

80 *Commonwealth v. Deloney*, 59 Mass. App. 47 at 59, 794 N.E.2d 613 at 623 (2003).

sense that she makes no complaint. And, that may indeed be the case. However, what the expert opinion evidence can show is that there are other possibilities. Mr. Fair's evidence discloses that, for several reasons, it is not uncommon for a child victim of sexual abuse to disclose the abuse sometimes only years after it has occurred. This evidence can assist by simply alerting the jury to the fact that more than one inference can be drawn from the failure to disclose the abuse at the time it occurred. Therein lies its probative value.

Much the same analysis applies to one other feature of the complainants' behaviour identified in this case, the repeated involvement with the alleged abusers. . . . Expert opinion evidence showing that, for various reasons, it is not uncommon for a child victim of sexual abuse to become repeatedly involved with an abuser can assist in rebutting this inference and is therefore relevant.

To a certain extent, the same analysis can also apply to the lack of detection by persons close to the complainants since it is somehow linked to the failure to disclose the abuse.[81]

Thus, the myth-dispelling function of this evidence seems to break down into the logic that an expert is needed to "alert" the jury "that more than one inference can be drawn from" the impugned behaviour. It is not clear why this "alert" cannot be provided by the prosecutor as a matter of argument. The answer is, of course, that it can, but proceeding in that fashion would deprive the prosecution of the advantage offered by expert evidence.

Furthermore, the logic is flawed in the following way. The "alert . . . that more than one inference can be drawn from" the impugned behaviour is rebutting a strawman argument being unfairly attributed to the defence. The defence is being treated as if it were arguing that a *bona fide* complainant would never delay, that delay or the impugned behaviour is never found among *bona fide* complainants. In such a case, evidence of the disputed conduct having been observed would of course logically be relevant. But given the myriad of possibilities and undoubted complexities of human behaviour, such a pronouncement would never be made and, if made, would be greeted with appropriate rejection by a judge or juror. A defence argument to a trier of fact along the lines of "Does it seem likely that if the complainant had been abused as she said, she would not have told so-and-so?" or "How probable is it that a person who suffered as the complainant described would remain silent for three years?" is in actuality not

81 *R. v. A.K. and N.K.*, above note 25 at paras. 107–12. In *R. v. Hughes (Ruling No. 2)*, [1998] B.C.J. No. 1699 (S.C.), the Crown was permitted to introduce expert evidence as to the reasons why victims of date rape would maintain a relationship with the perpetrator after an assault. "This was an area of inquiry where a trier of fact might be prone to make inaccurate suppositions about human behaviour."

logically rebutted with a claim that such is "not uncommon." It is only politically rebutted by having the contrary argument presented in the guise of expert opinion. The competing desired prosecutorial inference is unfairly enhanced by its presentation as expert evidence. The interpretation of such possibilities and complexities is daily viewed as within the province of a trier of fact, at least for "normal" people, so it is difficult to justify this indulgence for complainants, at least once any pretense is dropped that they are otherwise than normal.[82]

The basis for the expert's "alert" is that some unspecified number of complainants behaved in the same fashion because of the inference the prosecution seeks to be drawn, and not because of the invalidity of their complaint as the defence argues. This reasoning stands as unique in the annals of evidence. No other category of witnesses is allowed to validate merely one of several inferences by having an expert effectively testify to little more than a general knowledge of such inferences supposedly being correct in other cases.

In effect, the Court of Appeal in *R. v. A.K. and N.K.* agreed that the expert could not say: "The complainant was abused because she delayed or contradicted herself." However, the expert in effect could say: "The complainant could have been abused even though she delayed or contradicted herself." That amounts to simply the Crown's argument, validated by an expert witness, referencing other (unidentified, possibly rare, possibly inaccurately understood) cases.

Surely any lay belief that a victim will *generally* complain of being offended against as soon as appropriate is quite defensible. This common-sense inference is applied to all victims, whether they are robbed, burgled, extorted, or have their car stolen. It is also applied to persons that are punched, hit, beaten, or otherwise physically attacked. If there is some delay, a trier of fact will listen to any explanation and judge the matter accordingly. This is all viewed as matters of ordinary life well within the knowledge of lay triers of fact.

It is one thing to eliminate the normative legal rule regarding recent complaint that effectively demanded immediate complaint and was said to disallow a trier of fact from considering any delay as excusable (though in fact jurors were instructed to consider any explanation); it is another thing to claim thereafter that triers of fact are disabled from considering any delay and its explanations appropriately. In fact, at one time courts were quite express in recognizing this simple logic:

---

82 The purpose of the syndrome label — as in Rape Trauma Syndrome — was precisely to make all complainants "abnormal" and license expert evidence under the traditional rule. When the syndrome analysis did not withstand scrutiny, the courts unfortunately did not respond appropriately by disallowing such expert evidence; rather, they rationalized an illogical bending of the expert evidence rule as described in the text.

In my view, the trial judge was correct in not instructing the jury that the complainant's failure to complain in a timely fashion reflected adversely on her credibility. The significance of her failure to complain should not be the subject of any presumptive adverse inference based on now rejected stereotypical assumptions of how persons (particularly children) react to acts of sexual abuse .... *The importance to the complainant's credibility of his or her failure to make a timely complaint will vary from case to case and will depend on the jury's assessment of the evidence relevant to that failure.* In this case, the trial judge properly alerted the jury to the relevant evidence and the respective positions of the parties. *It was for the jury to decide what effect, if any, the absence of a timely complaint had on the credibility of T.S.*[83]

This view is quite different from the current prosecutorial position that failure to complain is irrelevant. In fact, the pendulum in some quarters has swung even further. Anyone who doubts the privileged evidentiary position of complainants need only consider the following from a recent appellate decision:

During submissions, a discussion took place between the court and defence counsel. Counsel was arguing that a negative inference should be taken against the complainant because she did not disclose the assault immediately. The court commented in response:

"But the literature with respect to this kind of case ... if it says anything at all, says that there is no typical response for a person who has suffered a sexual assault."

...

The accused argues that the above comments indicate that the trial judge took judicial notice of facts inappropriately. I disagree.

First, it was defence counsel who was asking the court to take judicial notice of a fact not in evidence; that is, the assumption that if a woman is sexually assaulted, she will immediately raise a "hue and cry." Counsel offered no expert

83 *R. v. M.(P.S.)*, [1992] O.J. No. 2410 (C.A.) [emphasis added]. See also *Crofts v. The Queen* (1996), 186 C.L.R. 427 at 451 (H.C.A.). The trial judge had directed the jury that "as a matter of law" the jury could not infer from the complainant's delay in reporting that the offences did not occur, based upon s. 61 of the *Crimes Act*, which abolished the doctrine of recent complaint. The High Court quashed the conviction, stating that the purpose of s. 61 was to eliminate the stereotyped view that complainants in sexual assault cases are unreliable or liars. But it was not intended to make such complainants into an "especially trustworthy class of witnesses." The jury must be allowed to weigh up the significance of any delay.

opinion to support his preconceived notion of what a person will or will not do after being sexually assaulted.[84]

This is really quite an amazing passage. Defence counsel, arguing in standard fashion the inferences that should or should not be drawn in the circumstances of the particular case regarding the conduct of a complainant claiming to have been criminally abused, is met with a rebuttal adopted from "other cases" that there is no typical response. Accepting that truth, how does it help in drawing inferences having regard to the circumstances of the particular case at bar? Is it not just a convenient rationalization to avoid drawing an unpleasant, but eminently reasonable inference where, for example, the complainant cannot explain why, if so terribly victimized, nothing followed. And if the complainant does offer explanation, what relevance do other cases have?

But the matter descends illogically from there. In the Court of Appeal, defence counsel is accused of arguing the discredited "hue and cry" doctrine and his argument is rejected because counsel failed to offer "expert evidence" to support his "preconceived notion of what a person will or will not do after being sexually assaulted." Is there now any doubt that it has become impolitic to exercise the slightest critical judgment regarding the conduct of rape complainants, that such sex offence complainants have now become completely unfettered by the rules of reality that apply to all other complainants?[85]

Besides the flawed logic, the data are unsupportive as far as the factual claim is concerned regarding child complainant reporting. One writer recently commented on this topic:

> [This] ... study of the process of disclosure by child victims of sexual abuse challenges some deeply held assumptions, and, we hope, will prove of interest to front line practitioners. One commonly held view is that most accounts of sexual abuse gradually unfold over a period of time. It is considered that few children realize the full story on one occasion, and that there is often a struggle by the child to overcome fear and reveal sensitive information. First interviews may be characterized by initial reluctance, after which the process of gradual disclosure sometimes follows. The work by Bradley and Wood calls this view into question, because the authors found that the majority of their 234 cases made partial or full disclosures during the initial investigative interview. The authors were looking for evidence that a developmental sequence of unfolding revelation of abuse was to be found, using a sourcing system specifically

---

84 *R. v. Lynxleg*, [2002] M.J. No. 352 at para. 14 (C.A.).
85 The problem continues: *R. v. Garon*, [2009] O.J. No. 24 at para. 72 (C.A.).

designed to reveal this process, if it were to have been present. Despite this they did not find gradual disclosure.

This study is important because the gradual unfolding concept has become part of the folklore among some groups. . . . Meanwhile, practitioners may well conclude that we simply do not have sufficient information to be categorical when answering the question "how do children tell?" and that the idea of gradual unfolding disclosure being the norm has not stood up to Bradley and Wood's scrutiny.[86]

The article by Bradley and Wood referenced in the above Jones editorial concludes:

> The Child Sexual Abuse Accommodation Syndrome described by Summit (1983) seems to be infrequent among the types of cases seen by child protection agencies. The present findings do not support the view that disclosure is a quasi-developmental process that follows sequential stages.[87]

There are other instances in this highly emotional context where, when facts and data came to conflict with strongly held beliefs, it was the facts that were damned while beliefs remained blessed. When a quantitative literature review published by psychologist Bruce Rind and his colleagues in the journal *Psychological Bulletin* in 1998 revealed that the correlation between child sexual abuse and later psychopathology may be considerably weaker than many researchers had supposed, Rind and his collaborators were harshly condemned by radio personality Dr. Laura Schlessinger and accused by several politicians of endorsing pedophilia, even though they were careful in their article to note that their findings could not be used to justify child sexual abuse. In addition, their article and its conclusions were formally denounced by a 355:0 vote in the United States House of Representatives.[88] This reaction is contrary to all the

---

86 D.P.H. Jones, "Editorial: Gradual Disclosure by Sexual Assault Victims — A Sacred Cow?" (1997) 20:9 Child Abuse and Neglect 879 at 879–80. See also Ceci & Bruck, above note 41 at 279: "No profile accounts for a sizable portion of these children's behaviour . . . . When the offender used aggressive methods to gain the child's compliance, children were equally as likely to disclose immediately or not at all."

87 April Bradley & James M. Wood, "How Do Children Tell? The Disclosure Process in Child Sexual Abuse" (1997) 20:9 Child Abuse and Neglect 881. See also Ceci & Bruck, *ibid.*

88 See Bruce Rind, Robert Bauserman, & Philip Tromovitch, "The Condemned Meta-analysis on Child Sexual Abuse — Good Science and Long-Overdue Skepticism" *Skeptical Inquirer* (July/August 2001) at 68. See also B. Rind, R. Bauserman, & P. Tromovitch, "Science versus Orthodoxy: Anatomy of the Congressional Condemnation of a Scientific Article and Reflections on Remedies for Future Ideological Attacks" (2000) 9 Applied & Preventive Psychology 211; B. Rind, P. Tromovitch, & R. Bauserman, "Condemnation

basic requirements of good science and valid knowledge.[89]

At the end of the day, aside from everything else, one commentator has noted the "growing trend in courts to disallow syndrome testimony in direct examination but to allow it on rebuttal to rehabilitate the witness who has been accused of delay, inconsistent accounts or recantation."[90] She responded with this incontrovertible fact: "However, these characteristics are not more scientifically reliable on rebuttal than they are on direct."[91]

---

of a Scientific Article: A Chronology and Refutation of the Attacks and a Discussion of Threats to the Integrity of Science" (2000) 4 *Sexuality and Culture* 1; Thomas D. Oellerich, "Rind, Tromovitch, and Bauserman: Politically Incorrect — Scientifically Correct" (2000) 4 *Sexuality and Culture* 67, which concludes:

> The Rind, Tromovitch, and Bauserman study of the impact of CSA among college students is politically incorrect but scientifically correct. It has a number of important implications for the research and practice communities. Among the more important is the need to stop exaggerating the negative impact of adult/nonadult sexual behavior, as suggested earlier by both Browne and Finkelhor, and Seligman. Another important implication is for conducting research that does not approach the issue of adult/nonadult sexual behavior with a political ideology as often has been the case thus far. And finally it is time to stop the common practices of (1) assuming that CSA causes psychological harm, and (2) routinely recommending psychotherapeutic intervention.

See also Richard J. McNally, *Remembering Trauma* (Cambridge, MA & London, UK: Belknap Press of Harvard University Press, 2003) at 22–26: "The Congressional Condemnation."

See also *David v. State (Alaska)*, 28 P.3d 309 (Alaska Ct. App. 2001), where a defence expert was smeared by the prosecution in cross-examination with unsubstantiated and unwarranted allegations of having abused his own children, leading to the reversal of the resulting conviction.

89 See generally Morton Hunt, *The New Know-Nothings: The Political Foes of the Scientific Study of Human Nature* (New Brunswick, NJ: Transaction, 1999).

When Profs. Loftus and Guyer set out to verify a case history being touted throughout North America as proof of "recovered memories," and after examining the real evidence demonstrated great reason to doubt there had ever been any child abuse, the treatment their research caused them to endure at the hands of their fanatical opponents can only be described as disgraceful: Elizabeth F. Loftus & Melvin J. Guyer, "Who Abused Jane Doe? The Hazards of the Single Case History — Part 1" *Skeptical Inquirer* (May/June 2002) at 24; Elizabeth F. Loftus & Melvin J. Guyer, "Who Abused Jane Doe? The Hazards of the Single Case History — Part 2" *Skeptical Inquirer* (July/August 2002) at 37; Carol Tavris, "The High Cost of Skepticism" *Skeptical Inquirer* (July/August 2002) at 41. Both parts of the Loftus/Guyer article are available online: www.csicop.org/si/online.html. Anyone who doubts the appellation "sexual abuse hysteria" should reread the above references.

90 Mary Ann Mason, "Expert Testimony Regarding the Characteristics of Sexually Abused Children: A Controversy on Both Sides of the Bench" in Ceci & Hembrooke, above note 24, c. 10 at 232. To the same effect is Lucy McGough, "A Legal Commentary: The Impact of *Daubert* on 21st-Century Child Sexual Abuse Prosecutions," *ibid.*, c. 13 at 273–75.

91 *Ibid.* at 232.

Another example of the same flawed logic is found in *R. v. F.(D.S.)*:

The evidence that the trial judge admitted was considerably narrower in its scope and its purpose than the excluded evidence. The admitted evidence was limited to the observed tendency of persons who have been abused to remain in the relationship for some time and to not immediately disclose the abuse. It was not admitted to establish that the complainant had been abused, as she alleged, but rather to put in context her explanation for not having immediately left the relationship and disclosed the abuse. The effect of the evidence was that the complainant's explanation was not as unusual as it might otherwise seem.

The difference between the excluded evidence and that admitted by the trial judge was described well in the respondent's factum, "there is a difference between saying 'people who behave this way have been abused' (a diagnosis) and saying 'people who have been abused may behave this way' (an explanation of behaviour based on clusters of observed tendencies)."

Ms. Sinclair's opinion, with respect to this evidence, was based on her own clinical experience. However, she testified that her opinion was consistent with the findings of a number of studies including a Statistics Canada survey of 12,000 women carried out in 1993, the Report of the Canadian Panel on Violence which was based on hundreds of interviews, separate studies by Dr. Murray Strauss and Dr. Richard Gells in the United States and Dr. Richard Jaffe in Canada.[92]

The court was, of course, correct in noting "there is a difference between saying 'people who behave this way have been abused' (a diagnosis) and saying 'people who have been abused may behave this way' (an explanation of behaviour based on clusters of observed tendencies)." But only the first proposition is one that is logically relevant, which is why prosecutors and clinicians tried so desperately to provide evidence that sounded "diagnostic." When that evidentiary fraud was exposed, they retreated to the second logically defensible proposition. But while logically defensible, the second proposition (unlike the first) is logically irrelevant. What relevance does that have to any issue in the criminal trial? Unless the defence is trying to assert a diagnostic negative — "people who have been abused never behave this way" — then establishing that they *may* in fact do so has no relevance. It only performs the prejudicial function of begging the prosecution's question.

---

92   Above note 4 at 90.

It should also be noted that the witness's reliance on the 1993 Statistics Canada survey on violence could easily have been debunked, because that opinion survey was as flawed a piece of work as is imaginable.[93]

The reality is that prosecutors have sought to provide sex complainants with a preferred evidentiary status as part of the ideological and political shake-up in sex abuse prosecutions that has taken place in the last three decades. In that task they have successfully enlisted the assistance of compliant clinicians opining in accordance with their personal sensitivities, in the absence of reliable data, and contrary to the rules of logic and science. Intellectual honesty would have been served by a jury instruction to the effect that such complainants are not to be judged by the standards applicable to other witnesses, and the jury is to give them the benefit of every doubt regarding delay and other behaviours that otherwise might seem surprising in one claiming to have been victimized by such a crime. To set that out is to demonstrate its unacceptability in any system of justice premised on a presumption of innocence where the benefit of doubt goes to the accused. Instead, the same result is sought to be achieved by this misuse of expert evidence and the spurious claim that juries cannot judge sex abuse complainants fairly.

The appropriate scales of judgment can be conveyed to a jury by jury instructions that openly state the normative standards that the jury is being mandated to apply. That way, any unfair biases will be exposed and appropriately debated. The matter should not be handled in this junk science fashion by the fabrication of factual claims regarding how complainants behave and the improper admission of "expert evidence" that is logically irrelevant.

If ever a myth-dispelling function for expert evidence were appropriate, expert evidence regarding eyewitness identification would be the ideal candidate. In that context reliable evidence demonstrates clearly the false beliefs entertained by juries about such evidence, accounting in part for eyewitness evidence's tremendous contribution to the legion of wrongful convictions that are known to law.[94] To disallow such evidence[95] but to allow expert evidence purporting to be necessary to banish undemonstrated mythical beliefs about sex offence complainants is puzzling, to say the least.

The best judicial word on this topic is from a Georgia appellate judge:

---

93 See John Fekete, *Moral Panic: Biopolitics Rising* (Montreal & Toronto: Robert Davies, 1994) c. 3; David Murray, Joel Schwartz, & S. Robert Lichter, *It Ain't Necessarily So: How Media Make and Unmake the Scientific Picture of Reality* (Lanham, MD: Rowman & Littlefield, 2001) at 60–64.

94 See Elizabeth F. Loftus & James M. Doyle, *Eyewitness Testimony: Civil and Criminal*, 3d ed. (Charlottesville: Lexis Law, 1997) c. 1: "Jurors' Beliefs about Eyewitness Testimony," 1–8.

95 See chapter 3, note 62 and chapter 6, note 40 and accompanying text.

Under the case law cited by the majority opinion, the proffered expert testimony regarding the profile of a paedophile was inadmissible in the instant case. However, I see little difference (in quality of evidence) between expert testimony regarding abused child syndrome, which is admissible in this state, and the type of expert testimony excluded in this case. As argued by the appellant, there is the appearance of an unlevel playing field, with the state being allowed to present such "soft science" but the defendant being prohibited from doing likewise. Evidence of "syndromes" should be greeted with caution, if not suspicion. In this age earmarked by the denial of personal responsibility, it sometimes appears that the defense strategy of choice is to formulate a new syndrome as the situation dictates. Our current legal lexicon includes such phenomena as the battered wife syndrome, the abused child syndrome, and the post-traumatic stress syndrome, and the catalogue is expanding. Recently, an attempt was made to establish an "urban survival syndrome" in a Texas murder trial, in which an expert explained that the defendant shot two unarmed men because the environment in which all three men lived had heightened his fear of the victims, who matched the profile of statistically the most dangerous men in America, i.e., inner city young black males. *Time*, June 6, 1994, p. 30. Our Supreme Court has determined that expert testimony concerning the battered woman syndrome and the abused child syndrome is admissible in Georgia, provided the expert does not state a conclusion that the victim was abused. *Allison v. State*, 256 Ga. 851, 852, 353 S.E.2d 805 (1987); *Smith v. State*, 247 Ga. 612, 619, 277 S.E.2d 678 (1981). However, that Court has not yet seen fit to question this court's resistance to adding other syndromes, such as the profile of a pedophile, to that list of admissible "soft science" evidence. See *Jennette v. State*, 197 Ga.App. 580, 398 S.E.2d 734 (1990) (expert testimony of pedophile's profile and expert testimony concerning a "lying child syndrome" held inadmissible).... Even evidence of syndromes associated with victims has met with divergent judicial treatment. Some courts have excluded such evidence where it was adduced for the sole purpose of proving the victim was abused, while admitting the same type of evidence where it was submitted to rehabilitate a witness whose credibility was attacked. *Flanagan v. State, supra* at 1113–1114. As noted above, in Georgia an expert is permitted to describe the abused child syndrome but may not conclude that the child was abused. This often results in the admissibility of such evidence depending upon a semantical distinction, in that experts are permitted to describe the syndrome and then state that the victim's behavior was consistent with that syndrome. See *State v. Butler*, 256 Ga. 448, 349 S.E.2d 684 (1986). It is difficult to explain why we should put stock in psychological evaluation and opinion with regard to syndromes pertaining to victims, yet extend no credence to syndromes or profiles relating to offenders. Perhaps the better solution would be to exclude all syndrome evidence. However, this court having no power to close the door opened by the Supreme Court, I suppose the best we can do is to continue to screen out other dubious syndromes as they are imagined and promoted by individuals who need to explain away their conduct.[96]

There is one other argument sometimes offered in support of the admissibility of such evidence that should be addressed briefly. It is the argument made, in the context of behavioural indicators of a negative nature such as drug addiction, dropping out of school, that it is somehow unfair for an accused to be able to rely upon such factors as negatively affecting the credibility of the complainant while at the same time having excluded "expert evidence" that sex abuse causes such negative sequelae.[97] It is argued the evidence is admissible for the Crown to "blunt" the accused's attack on the complainant's credibility but the argument does not withstand scrutiny.

The problem is that logically the evidence does not "blunt the defence attack," and it only appears to do so by a false analogy based upon an unacceptable presumption of guilt. This is true even if it were accepted that it can be demonstrated that the credibility deficiencies were in fact causally related to sex abuse.

First of all, their causal origin as originating from sex abuse could not *per se* blunt the attack. That would involve a claim that credibility deficiencies arising from that cause result in less impairment of credit than if caused by physical abuse or parental abandonment or whatever. So it must be that it is the human act or cause of the abuse that allows the evidence to blunt the defence attack. If the witnesses claimed their credibility deficiencies were caused by sex abuse but at the hands of some other party (other than the accused), obviously that would not blunt the defence attack. The evidence might make the witnesses objects of sympathy but their credibility deficiencies would remain "unblunted." Nor would any unfairness appear apparent.

---

96 *Gilstrap v. State (Georgia)*, 450 S.E.2d 436 at 439 (Ga. Ct. App. 1994), Andrews J., concurring in a case where profile evidence tendered on behalf of the defence to exculpate was ruled inadmissible by the appeal court.

See also Hoeffel, "The Gender Gap," above note 9, where the author reviews the background of Battered Woman Syndrome and Rape Trauma Syndrome and concludes that neither of these theories is particularly reliable. More troubling, however, is that similar theories, with greater scientific certainty, that would work to the benefit of male criminal defendants are not admissible in most courts.

97 Such an argument has been made by noted Canadian authority on the law of evidence Prof. Ron Delisle: see R.J. Delisle, "Annotation to *R. v. S.W.*" (1996) 47 C.R. (4th) 354.

Thus, what must be concluded is that this argument from unfairness or "blunting" is really saying that what blunts the defence credibility attack is that the credibility deficiencies were caused by the accused. But logically the perpetrator's identity is irrelevant. There is no logical relevance in who carried out the sex abuse and thus caused the credibility deficiencies. The perpetrator's identity is not relevant *per se*. Even if the credibility deficiencies did flow from sex abuse by the very accused, that does not diminish the credibility attack *per se* by rendering the credibility deficiencies' existence more in doubt or less credibility-affecting.

Logically, the only blunting that can be said to exist is via an "unfairness" argument: it is unfair for the accused to gain advantage from something he himself caused. On this reasoning, such cases become like the case of the accused charged with murdering his parents who pleads he is an orphan. It is this false analogy that seduces the mind. The mind is seduced because the conclusion "feels" logical by a false analogy.

The credibility-affecting factors exist and the defence is entitled to point them out to judge the accusations being made by the complainants that the accused sexually abused them — those factors exist no matter how they originated. Admittedly, those factors are not diagnostic and cannot be used diagnostically because they can arise from a variety of causes. Yet, if the obvious impression that will be left with the jury is that the sex abuse is caused by the accused, they will be impermissibly using the evidence diagnostically.

If the evidence is admitted and the jury is properly instructed it cannot use the evidence diagnostically, but can only use it to "blunt" the defence's pointing-out credibility-affecting factors, what will the jury make of that instruction? It does not diminish the existence of the credibility-affecting factors or diminish their impact on credibility. The only syllogism left is the "unfairness" approach, which assumes the accused caused the abuse that caused the factors. Again, this is "implicit diagnosticity" because the accused's having committed the abuse is a necessary inference in the logical chain of reasoning by which the evidence is used.

In the end result, it is submitted that complainant behaviours such as delay in recounting, admissions of falsehoods and retractions, lack of offender avoidance, and the inferences to be drawn therefrom are simply matters for the trier of fact as in all cases. There is no expertise involved, and facilitating a favourable inference by essentially emphasizing to the trier of fact the supposed fact that such existed in other cases should be as impermissible in sex abuse cases as it is in all other types of cases. Courts may finally be realizing this.[98]

---

98   *Gersten v. Senkowski*, 426 F.3d 588, 2005 U.S. App. LEXIS 22322 (2d Cir. 2005).

PROFILES

PROFILES ARE SIMPLY syndromes outside a medical or quasi-medical context. Like syndromes, profiles seek to diagnose or categorize based on the presence of certain descriptive features. Reference has already been made to "profile" evidence.[99] Profiles that have been considered include drug-courier profile,[100] sex-offender profile,[101] smuggler's profile,[102] battering parent,[103] power rapist,[104] even fleeing driver profile.[105] Courts have been less susceptible to profiles than syndromes as evidence of guilt and have excluded such evidence because "the use of profile evidence to indicate guilt creates too high a risk that a defendant will be convicted not for what he did but for what others are doing. . . . [The profile fallaciously assumes that] because someone shares characteristics — many of them innocent and commonplace — with a certain type of offender, that individual must also possess the same criminal culpability."[106] Regarding profile evidence,

---

99 *People (California) v. Hernandez*, 63 Cal. Rptr. 2d 769 at 779 (Ct. App. 4 Dist., 1 Div. 1997): "We believe the crime analyst's testimony is also somewhat analogous to the inherently prejudicial 'profile' evidence which was held to be inadmissible for purposes of determining guilt or innocence in *People v. Martinez* (1992), 10 Cal. App. 4th 1001." Profile evidence about an accused is inadmissible to suggest guilt of the crime charged: *Roy Dale Ryan v. State (Wyoming)*, 988 P.2d 46 (Wyo. 1999). See generally David C. Ormerod, "The Evidential Implications of Psychological Profiling" [1996] Crim. L. Rev. 863; Jane Campbell Moriarty, "Wonders of the Invisible World: Prosecutorial Syndrome and Profile Evidence in the Salem Witchcraft Trials" (2001) 26 Vermont L. Rev. 43.

100 *State (Arizona) v. Lee*, [1998] WL 268851 (Ariz. Sup. Ct. 28 May 1998); *State (Colorado) v. Salcedo*, 999 P.2d 833 (Colo. 2000); Mark J. Kadish, "The Drug Courier Profile: In Planes, Trains, and Automobiles; And Now in the Jury Box" (1997) 46 Am. U. L. Rev. 747; Tung Yin, "The Probative Values and Pitfalls of Drug Courier Profiles as Probabilistic Evidence" (2000) 5 Texas Forum on Civil Liberties & Civil Rights 141.

101 *State (Idaho) v. Parkinson*, 909 P.2d 647 (Idaho Ct. App. 1996); *Flanagan v. State (Florida)*, 625 So. 2d 827 (Fla. 1993).

102 *R. v. Cox* (1999), 170 D.L.R. (4th) 101 (N.B.C.A.).

103 *People (California) v. Walkey*, 177 Cal. App. 3d 268 (Ct. App. 4 Dist. 1986).

104 *Reichard v. State (Indiana)*, 510 N.E.2d 163 (Ind. 1987).

105 *State (Washington) v. Farr-Lenzini*, [1999] WL 5297 (Wash. Ct. App. 8 January 1999).

106 *State (Arizona) v. Lee*, above note 100, regarding drug-courier profile. The quotation expresses elegantly in this particular context the fallacy of concluding that if a person is a drug trafficker, fleeing driver, smuggler, or sex offender, he has the following characteristics. Reversing the reasoning is equally fallacious: if a person has the following characteristics, then she is a drug trafficker, fleeing driver, smuggler, or sex offender. See also *United States v. Sokolow*, 490 U.S. 1 at 13 (1989); *State (New Jersey) v. Fortin*, 178 N.J. 540 (2004); Laurence Alison *et al.*, "The Personality Paradox in Offender Profiling: A Theoretical Review of the Processes Involved in Deriving Background Characteristics from Crime Scene Actions" (2002) 8 Psychol., Pub. Pol'y & L. 115; and D. Michael Risinger & Jeffrey L. Loop, "Three Card Monte, Monty Hall, *Modus Operandi* and 'Offender Profiling':

the defence has generally been as unsuccessful as the prosecution in securing admission.[107]

However, profiles as evidence not of guilt but as some or part of reasonable or probable cause for arrest or other state action have been sometimes found acceptable, thereby raising the same issues regarding scientific reliability. An accused's test results on standardized field tests or testing by a "drug recognition officer" can be viewed as data supporting the conclusion that the accused fits the profile of the impaired driver just as an accused's demonstrating certain conduct such as purchasing her ticket with cash and deplaning last can support the conclusion she is a drug courier. The first issue is always the accuracy of the data, which involves specifying the target characteristics or test results, defining them objectively so their presence or absence is objectively verifiable, and then accurately assessing whether the target individual possesses the relevant features or test results. To the extent that profiles contemplate fuzzy or subjective qualifiers that a police officer can find at whim, or to the extent that anything and everything qualifies (a drug courier "deplanes first" or "deplanes last" or "deplanes in the midst of the passenger crowd") then the profile is scientifically meaningless.

As well, the issues of test accuracy and the base rate phenomenon disqualify profiles even for use as probable cause evidence. This is so even if 90 percent of travellers who pay with cash, deplane first, and look around furtively are in fact drug traffickers, or even if a police officer employing roadside sobriety tests is 90 percent accurate in assessing an impaired driver, unless at least 10 percent of the relevant travelling public are in fact drug couriers or 10 percent of drivers are in fact impaired. Revisiting the illustrations in chapter 4, it must be repeated that significance of a positive test result requires knowledge not only of the test's accuracy but also of the base rate of the target phenomenon.

Suppose that the target phenomenon is impaired drivers or drivers with a blood-alcohol level greater than the legal limit of 80 mg of alcohol in 100 ml of blood, or drivers with an illegal drug such as cocaine in their system, and assume that the test to be used by the officer is 90 percent accurate. As already explained, if a driver is tested and the officer concludes the test is positive then does that mean there is a 90 percent chance the driver is above the legal limit of .08 or was in fact using cocaine?

Some Lessons of Modern Cognitive Science for the Law of Evidence" (2002) 24 Cardozo L. Rev. 193.

107 *R. v. J-L.J.*, [2000] 2 S.C.R. 600. To the same effect, see *R. v. Perlett* (1999), 26 C.R. (5th) 343 (Ont. Ct. Gen. Div.). See regarding indicators of a child molester: *United States v. Fitzgerald*, 2003 U.S. App. LEXIS 23326 (4th Cir. Va. 2003).

Consider 1000 drivers. How many will be impaired/over 80/on cocaine? Let us assume 10 percent or nearly 1 in 10. A 10 percent rate of impaired drivers means that hidden throughout the 1000 drivers there are in fact 100 impaired drivers that we are trying to identify and 900 who are not impaired. The test is 90 percent accurate so if we test all 1000 drivers, of the 100 drivers that are in fact impaired, 90 or 90 percent will be correctly identified by the test as impaired (true positives) and 10 or 10 percent will be incorrectly identified by the test as not impaired (false negatives). Of the other 900 drivers that are not in fact impaired, 810 or 90 percent will be correctly identified as not impaired (true negatives). But most importantly, 90 or 10 percent will be incorrectly identified as impaired (false positives).

Thus, the total drivers identified as not impaired is 820, consisting of 810 that were correctly identified and 10 that were erroneously vindicated. More importantly, the total number of drivers identified as impaired is 180, consisting of 90 correctly identified as impaired and an equal number 90 incorrectly and falsely identified by the test as impaired. A police officer using a test that is 90 percent accurate to identify a target group or phenomenon with a base rate of 10 percent might as well flip a coin. The chances are 50:50. An equal number of incorrect identifications will be made as correct ones. The rule of thumb is simple: if the accuracy rate and the base rate total 100 percent the significance of a positive result is 50:50. If the total is less than 100 percent then false positives will exceed true positives. If the total is more than 100 percent then true positives will exceed false positives.

In considering the probative value and hence admissibility of any profile or procedure, even as screening tests, it is important to consider not only the claimed accuracy of the tests but also the base rate of the phenomenon being targeted. Absent proof of the base rate, or at least a base rate that exceeds some value that makes the test result probative by establishing that the test will in its application in the particular circumstances of the case produce significantly more true positives than false positives,[108] then the test result has no more probative value than a coin toss.[109] An evidentiary fact situation where the evidence produced is equally consistent with innocence as with guilt is surely not capable of producing probable cause.

---

108 Using R.I.D.E. program results as evidence of the base rate for impaired or "over 80" drivers results in rates rarely exceeding a fraction of 1 percent. See Alan D. Gold's Criminal Law Netletter, Issue 595 (30 June 2008), on Quicklaw in Commentary.

109 As a matter of terminology, Canadian police or expert witnesses may elaborate the accuracy rate, meaning the overall proportion of cases correctly identified, as follows: "sensitivity" (true positives); "specificity" (true negatives); "miss rate" (false negatives); and "false alarm rate" (false positives).

INDICATORS

INDICATORS ARE SIMPLY descriptive features that do not fall into the categories of profile or syndrome. However, the logic of indicators is the same as for profiles or syndromes: description leads to diagnosis. Indicator evidence is subject to the same scientific concerns regarding objectivity and the necessity to clearly indicate target phenomenon. As noted in chapter 4, breakdown in these areas was a tragic reality in sex abuse prosecutions. For the longest time, prosecution experts were prepared to state that any physical finding they considered abnormal was the product of supposed sex abuse. But what is abnormal cannot be known without an examination of what is normal,[110] and only in recent years has such basic research been done.[111] *Bona fide* researchers were shocked to find that what they had been considering abnormal was in fact statistically normal in the general population.[112] Base rate studies of nonabused children indicate that many of the findings often used to support a diagnosis of abuse are found with a high enough frequency in normals so that they do not support an opinion that abuse occurred.[113] Indicator evidence as well involves flawed logic,

---

110 For example, "Experts have identified . . . age-inappropriate sexual behavior . . . as a primary predictor of sexual abuse . . . . One of the drawbacks to making this link is defining 'abnormal' sexual activities or knowledge. For example, masturbation is common in children; thus, the issue arises as to when masturbation is so excessive as to indicate sexual abuse. Moreover, a child's heightened sexual activity may result from stimulus other than sexual abuse, such as clandestinely observing parents or others engaging in sexual activity. 'In addition, highly sexualized behavior is sometimes seen in children who are not thought to have been abused'": Susan J. Becker, "Child Sexual Abuse Allegations against a Lesbian or Gay Parent in a Custody or Visitation Dispute: Battling the Overt and Insidious Bias of Experts and Judges" (1996) 74 Denv. U.L. Rev. 75, text accompanying notes 158–65, citing Howard Dubowitz *et al.*, "The Diagnosis of Child Sexual Abuse" (1992) 146 Am J. Diseases Children 688 at 688. See *Gersten v. Senkowski*, above note 98.

111 J. McCann *et al.*, "Genital Findings in Prepubertal Girls Selected for Nonabuse: A Descriptive Study" (1990) 86:3 Pediatrics 428; J. McCann *et al.*, "Perianal Findings in Prepubertal Children Selected for Nonabuse: A Descriptive Study" (1989) 13 Child Abuse & Neglect 179; S.J. Emans *et al.*, "Genital Findings in Sexually Abused, Symptomatic and Asymptomatic Girls" (1987) 79 Pediatrics 778.

112 Debbie Nathan & Michael Snedeker, *Satan's Silence: Ritual Abuse and the Making of a Modern American Witch Hunt* (New York: Basic Books, 1995) c. 9, "The Medical Evidence" at 178–91. *R. v. O'Connor* (1995), 100 C.C.C. (3d) 285 (Ont. C.A.) is an example of a case where suspect gynecological evidence was admitted without objection at trial and upheld on appeal. *R. v. Dieffenbaugh* (1993), 80 C.C.C. (3d) 97 (B.C.C.A.) is an example of similar bad science in this area; "anal gaping" was properly rejected as expert evidence for lack of any established validity.

113 *Lillie v. Newcastle City Council*, above note 29 at para. 399: "It is important for me also to bear in mind that much attention has been given over the last 15 years or so to the scope and extent of 'normal' genital anatomy. As Dr Watkeys explained, in girls there is re-

purporting to go from description to diagnosis, and misleads triers of fact into committing the base rate "fallacy."

ARSON INDICATORS

LIKE THE SEX abuse indicators mentioned above, arson indicators are another example of bogus, scientifically unsound indicator evidence. Again the indicators have never been scientifically validated as referable in any reliable and valid way to arson fires:

> Many of the arson indicators which are commonplace assertions in arson prosecutions are deficient for want of any established scientific validity. In many instances the dearth of published material in the scientific literature substantiating the validity of certain arson indicators should be sufficient grounds to mount a challenge to the general scientific acceptability of such indicators. It is clear, from the cases, however, that arson indicators are given a talismanic quality that they have not earned in the crucible of scientific validation.[114]

Detecting traces of petroleum products can be misleadingly viewed as significant if there is no appreciation how common petroleum products are in the manufacture of common household goods.[115] The situation is such that the question has been posed: "Arson: New Frontier for Exonerations?"[116] The article describes a new Arson Screening Project launched by the John Jay College of Criminal Justice in the wake of documented instances of miscarriages of justice in arson cases.

---

cognised nowadays a wide range of attributes within the definition of 'normal' including the presence of nodules, notches, hymenal bands and adhesions."

See generally J. McCann, J. Voris, & M. Simon, "Genital Injuries Resulting from Sexual Abuse: A Longitudinal Study" (1992) 89 Pediatrics 307; McCann *et al.*, "Comparison of Genital Examination Techniques in Prepubertal Girls" (1990) 85:2 Pediatrics 182; McCann *et al.*, "Genital Findings in Prepubertal Girls," above note 111; McCann *et al.*, "Perianal Findings in Prepubertal Children," above note 111.

114 A.A. Moenssens, F.E.Inbau, & J.E. Starrs, *Scientific Evidence in Criminal Cases*, 3d ed. (Mineola, NY: Foundation Press, 1986); John J. Lentini, "Indicators of Trouble," online: www.firescientist.com/Documents/IndicatorsOfTrouble.pdf. A dated but still useful reference dealing with the issue of invalid arson evidence is Vincent Brannigan & Jose Torero, "The Expert's New Clothes: Arson 'Science' after *Kumho Tire*" (1 July 1999), online: http://firechief.com/mag/firefighting_experts_new_clothes/index.html.

115 John J. Lentini, Julia A. Dolan, & Cheryl Cherry, "The Petroleum-Laced Background," online: www.firescientist.com/Documents/Petroleum-LacedBackground.pdf.

116 Karen Franklin, "Arson: New Frontier for Exonerations?" online: forensicpsychologist. blogspot.com/2008/07/arson-new-frontier-for-exonerations.html.

In one case in Texas the death penalty resulted in a case that one arson expert described as follows: "Neither the fire that killed the three Willingham children nor the fire that killed Elizabeth Grace Belue and Gail Joe Allison were incendiary fires. The artifacts examined and relied upon by the fire investigators in both cases are the kind of artifacts routinely created by accidental fires that progress beyond flashover. The State's expert witness in both cases relied on interpretations of 'indicators' that they were taught constituted evidence of arson. While we have no doubt that these witnesses believed what they were saying, each and every one of the indicators relied upon have since been scientifically proven to be invalid. To the extent that there are still investigators in Texas and elsewhere, who interpret low burning, irregular fire patterns and collapsed furniture springs as indicators of incendiary fires, there will continue to be serious miscarriages of justice."

In another case, the accused was exonerated after a panel of fire experts working *pro bono* for the Innocence Project concluded that both fires were accidental.

Their full report is on the internet at: http://www.innocenceproject.org/docs/ArsonReviewReport.pdf

In their peer review, the fire scientists noted that many of the "indicators" of arson that were taught in fire investigation courses up into the 1990s have since been "scientifically proven to be invalid." Yet many so-called experts remain woefully uninformed on the current state of the science. Worse, others deliberately distort science, behaving "as if constant repetition would make [their false] assertion true."

The report echoes a [previous investigation] ... that found that "many of the pillars of arson investigation that were commonly believed for many years have been disproved by rigorous scientific scrutiny."

As another commentator has written,

Untold numbers of cases, both criminal and civil, were decided on the strength of fire and arson experts applying those beliefs and opining on whether a particular fire was arson or accident. Eventually, those beliefs were put to empirical tests in which buildings were set afire in ways that simulated both arson fires and accidental fires. By comparing the effects of the arson versus accidental fires on windows, walls, burn patterns, and so on, these conceptually simple experiments revealed that many of the accepted indicators of arson did not, in fact, distinguish arson from accidental fires. In light of the research findings, the field corrected its erroneous beliefs (at least as to future cases in which well-informed examiners participated). The various subfields I will focus on in this letter are in much the same sate as fire and arson investigation was before it undertook to empirically test its assumptions in order to determine which were correct and which were not.[117]

Syndromes, profiles, and indicators are simply hypotheses that provide direction for investigation. In and of themselves they are unreliable and cannot be used to prove anything. They are a start in the search for reliable and admissible opinion evidence, but only a start. Accurate data collection and proper scientific reasoning is required thereafter if there is any reliable expert evidence to arise from that beginning.

---

117 Michael J. Saks, "Remediating Forensic Science" (2007) 48 Jurimetrics 119. See J. Lentini, D. Smith, & R. Henderson, "Baseline Characteristics of Residential Structures Which Have Burned to Completion: The Oakland Experience" *Fire Technology* (August 1992) at 195.

CHAPTER 8

Science and "Consistent with" Evidence

THE LOGIC OF expert evidence is sometimes befuddled by what has become a favourite phrase of prosecution experts, especially in sex abuse cases: "consistent with." There are two ways in which this misleading phrase does harm. In the context of identification and comparison issues, the phrase accurately means an absence of difference but is erroneously taken to mean a presence of identity. In the different context of cause and effect or event and sequelae, the phrase is used to hide logically worthless tautologies or unfavourable and damaging remote probabilities. Essentially, some factor that might otherwise appear damaging to the prosecution is explained away by the expert with that turn of phrase.

Regarding identification issues, it has already been noted that the concept of "consistent with" came in for criticism for its use in the context of fibre and hair evidence adduced at one of the trials of Guy Paul Morin. One of the relevant conclusions of that inquiry was that "[c]ertain terms, such as 'match' and 'consistent with' were used unevenly in the criminal proceedings and were potentially misleading. The use of these terms contributed to misunderstanding of the forensic findings and their limitations."[1]

One of the expert witnesses who testified before that inquiry elaborated on the problems involved in this terminology in testimony he gave in a criminal

---

1   The Honourable Fred Kaufman, Commissioner, *Report of the Kaufman Commission on Proceedings Involving Guy Paul Morin* (Toronto: Ministry of the Attorney General, 1998), online: www.attorneygeneral.jus.gov.on.ca/english/about/pubs/morin at 338–43. The term "match" was also there deconstructed.

prosecution.[2] When asked if there was a "concern that the language of 'consistent with' may in fact contain a real risk of misunderstanding the true scientific
nature of the limits built into that language," he replied there was. He explained
that scientists had a clear understanding of the meaning of "consistent with"
but "that understanding is not shared by lawyers or necessarily by members of
the public ... [who] interpret consistent ... [to mean it has] some weight of
association in commonality." He further replied that scientists did not mean
there was any weight, association, or commonality and were instead conveying
"the picture that this cannot be excluded and we haven't found anything that's
different, therefore, we can't exclude it. So it's not inconsistent."

The following questions and answers from his evidence in the criminal case
give a good indication of the problems inherent with this phrase and with other
language choices:

Q. Does it necessarily convey anything about predicting an association between two objects once you conclude you haven't found a difference ... ?

A. It's not intended to do that .... [W]hen I was director of the laboratory
in South Australia ... conclusions were expressed ... in exclusionary language. So if tests are conducted and if differences are found, then the report says that it is excluded that these things were common origin. If no
differences are found, then the report says it cannot be excluded that these
things have a common origin. The additional thing that comes with that
exclusionary language that does not come with the expression "consistent
with" is that when you say cannot be excluded, that language I understand
is generally accepted by listeners as conveying something else with it which
says, well, we can't exclude it. Does that mean that there may be some possible reason why these things were not different in the test you conducted
but yet were not the same? Whereas if you express it in terms of "consistent
with", that language does not convey that sense that there might be other
explanations for the failure to find a difference and exclude.

Q. If a paint chip is taken from that wall and it's analyzed, it's tested, and
a report comes back that says this paint chip is "consistent with" having
come off that wall. Do I understand you to be saying that the average nonscientific person hearing that conclusion that it's "consistent with" coming
from the wall would assume that, that paint chip came from that wall,
whereas what the scientist is really saying when they say "consistent with,"
is that the paint chip cannot be excluded as having come from that wall?

---

2   The witness was Dr. William Tilstone. The ruling that followed is *R. v. Perlett*, [1998] O.J.
No. 6026 (Gen. Div.), Platana J.

A. That's exactly what the scientist would mean.

Q. They are not saying the paint chip came from the wall. What they're saying is, I can't tell you that it did not come from the wall?

A. That's quite correct....

Q. "Consistent with" doesn't mean coming from?

A. "Consistent with" does not mean coming from. And that's never been what it's intended to mean in scientific language. All it means is that there were no detectable differences.

   . . .

      There is an understanding in the forensic science community that the language which is used to convey conclusions is a very difficult area and must be chosen very carefully. It's been addressed in different ways. Some places and some professional organizations have tried to develop glossaries of expressions and relate every day language to some degree of scientific certainty.... I prefer to do what I've described to you and express the conclusions using non-exclusion because I believe, and the responses I've had would confer [confirm] this, that when you say that, you do invite the listener to say, well, what do you mean by that, what are the limitations that can be put on your findings, just because you used that kind of language.

   . . .

Q. Now, the language of "consistent with," does it sometimes obscure the actual weakness of a conclusion?

A. Well, again, the answer is the same.... It's because of feedback from the crime and the defence community in South Australia about their concerns about the images that were conveyed by the use of that kind of language that we made the change.

   . . .

A. Well, normally when we [scientists] say "consistent with," it really is exclusionary,... because that's what it means. It means it is not inconsistent, it is not excluded. But I'm not sure that that's the way that it's used all the time by all practitioners, and I'm pretty certain that that's not the way that it's understood by recipients of the information.

Q. So the language of "consistent with" if translated to "not inconsistent" may be understood?

A. Yes.

   . . .

Q. Let's take the word "match" because that's straight forward. If somebody says something "matches," then that quite clearly is conveying and is intended to convey an image that these things are inclusionary.

   . . .

A. Yes. The following circumstances I believe for ones where "matches" is a perfectly reasonable and appropriate language, a properly conducted fingerprint examination, a properly conducted footwear market examination, a properly and extensively [conducted] DNA test. Or if we take His Honour's example of the paint chip from the wall, if that paint chip was able to be placed back into the wall to produce a jigsaw match, then that's exactly what it is, it's a jigsaw match. And these are circumstances where really it's, I believe, quite legitimate and reasonable to use "match."

...

Q. If you were, Dr. Tilstone, to see a blood smear on the floor, and if you in your own mind had formed an investigative theory that someone might have dragged their knee through that blood stain, but there was nothing like a fibre impression that could be related to the pants or anything other than the smear, would it be appropriate in describing that smear to describe it in the context of saying ... it's "consistent with" a knee going through it?

A. Again we really are just revisiting the same issues. If there's a smear on the floor and there's an item of clothing with a blood stain on the knee, and you asked the question, could that smear have been made by the knee going through the pool of blood, then the answer is yes. But that's such a general comment that it would be dangerous to use the expression "consistent with" given all what we've explored about the differences in understanding about what it really means. If, however, there were features associated with the blood smear that where [were] physical patterns and could be related to the fabric on the clothing or, even better, some flow in the fabric in the clothing, then the language could legitimately be escalated to give a correct impression of a greater degree of certainty that that was caused. So the difference is, on the one hand, could it have caused the smear and, on the other hand, did it cause the smear. And if you want to look at the legitimate use of the word such as "match" or "consistent with," they should be pushed towards the end where the issue is, did it cause a smear, and not from the end, could it have caused a smear. But, again, if someone has used that language, the starting point has got two parts to it. One is they shouldn't, and it's generally not accepted nowadays that you do that. But the other one, you really have to ask them what they intended.

...

Q. And if they intended to convey an association ... looking at the smear without some further identifying thing, would it be a reliable conclusion about association?

A. No, it would not because there's been no testing conducted.

Thus, in cases where "consistent with" relates to identity issues,[3] what is validly being said is that there is no discernible difference between the unknown item and the known comparison. The conclusion is one of a "could be" relationship, which is not the same as an "identity" or "is" conclusion. Evidence would better be given in terms of "no discernible difference" or "not inconsistent with."

The other category of cases where "consistent with" is even more problematic concerns issues of cause and effect or event and aftermath. Unsurprisingly, such cases have commonly involved allegations of abuse. For example, in *R. v. J.(R.H.)*,[4] evidence from the Crown's expert witness about the behaviour of abused children was held admissible, along with her opinion that her observations of the female complainant were "consistent with" the girl having been sexually abused.

Two different situations arise here. In the first, the phrase is used to hide a logically worthless tautology. Simply put, everything "is consistent" with sex abuse. Immediate disclosure, delayed disclosure, or no disclosure can all be so described by a sympathetic clinician. The phrase is meaningless when it can always be applied because there is absolutely no evidentiary value to facts or circumstances for which both presence and absence have the same logical import.

In other cases, the phrase serves a slightly different function: to disguise not a tautological claim, but an improbable one. "Consistent with" is used in reference to a fact or circumstance that on the probabilities is against the proponent's hypothesis, but yet may coexist with it albeit only as a remote possibility. In such cases, the fact that probabilities favour disproof of the hypothesis is

---

3   Examples are as follows: *R. v. Cake*, [1996] B.C.J. No. 1655 (S.C.): "Later investigation revealed a 300 Winchester magnum cartridge on the shoulder portion of the road, two or three feet from the line delineating the shoulder from the travelled portion. A 300 Magnum bullet was later found in the entrails of the elk. Expert evidence concluded that it was consistent with having been part of a 300 Winchester Magnum cartridge." *R. v. Quewezance*, [1999] S.J. No. 405 (Q.B.): "I am satisfied from the nature and character of the footprint left on the door and the expert evidence which was given relating to it that it is consistent with the footwear worn by the accused and that the accused kicked in the door." *R. v. Cotter*, [1994] N.S.J. No. 142 (S.C.): "Vehicle tracks were imprinted on the grass by the side of the house on the property. The Crown's expert evidence was that these tracks were consistent with tracks made by a tandem truck and, in track measurement and width, consistent with the tandem tires of the dump truck. The defence submits that the expert could not age the grass imprints, and they could have been made by a vehicle moving several times in the same location, or even by a number of vehicles."

4   (1993), 86 C.C.C. (3d) 354 (B.C.C.A.). Other examples are *R. v. E.E.B.*, [1990] S.J. No. 365, 86 Sask. R. 243 (C.A.): "Physicians gave expert opinion evidence that the injuries were consistent with sexual abuse." *R. v. D.R.T.*, [1992] Y.J. No. 178 (S.C.): "There was expert evidence that such pattern of disclosure was consistent with sexual abuse."

hidden by the "consistent with" language. Ten straight "heads" yielded by toss-ing a coin is "consistent with" the coin being a fair one (1 chance in 2,048), but if "tails" was your winning side, that defence would sound virtually fraudulent when offered by your opponent.

The impropriety of this verbal shenanigan has even caused a clinician to remonstrate his profession for the use of this tactic,[5] calling it "an attempt to do through connotation what cannot be done through denotation. It is a state-ment designed to leave an impression that is clearly not warranted by the under-lying facts."[6]

A recent Australian case provides an excellent example of the misuse and faulty logic involved in that phrase. *Regina v. R.T.B.*[7] was an appeal from a con-viction for sex offences, which included the following excerpt of evidence:

> Dr. Jennifer Geraghty was called to give evidence. Her attention was directed to the medical history given to her by a complainant:
>
> Q. And did that history include penile penetration of the anus?
> A. It did.
>
> . . .
>
> Q. Did she state that that occurred over a period of about six months and that the last incident was then about three months previously?
> A. Yeah.
> Q. As a result of having taken that history did you examine the anal and peri-anal region of the patient?
> A. I did.
> Q. And what were your findings when you made that specific examination?
> A. The examination findings of the anal and perineal [*sic*] area were normal.
> Q. Having been given the history of penal [penile] penetration of the patient's anus are you able to express an opinion as to whether what you saw was consistent with the complaint of the child that she'd been anally penetrat-ed by a penis?
> A. The normal examination of the anus is consistent with the child's history that she had been penetrated in the anus.

5   Richard J. Lawlor, "The Expert Witness in Child Sexual Abuse Cases: A Clinician's View" in Stephen J. Ceci & Helene Hembrooke, eds., *Expert Witnesses in Child Abuse Cases: What Can and Should Be Said in Court* (Washington, DC: American Psychological As-sociation, 1998) c. 5 at 110.
6   An excellent reference debunking "consistent with" is Ceci & Hembrooke, *ibid.* at 110–11, 150, and 273. See also S.A. Newman, "Assessing the Quality of Expert Testimony in Cases Involving Children" (1994) 22 J. Psychiatry & Law 181 at 196.
7   2002 NSWCCA 104.

HIS HONOUR

Q. I'm sorry was it consistent or inconsistent?

A. It was consistent yeah.

CROWN PROSECUTOR

Q. Is that so doctor that you would not necessarily have found injury on the child if her anus had been penetrated by the penis of a male person?

A. That's correct.

The Court of Appeal had the following comments about this evidence:

> The doctor said that there was no physical indicator of such an occurrence. The import of her evidence was that there would not necessarily be any such indicator. No doubt evidence of this character will often be appropriate in order to ensure that a jury does not speculate about the absence of medical evidence. Where (as here) the evidence has limited materiality, consideration should be given to alternative ways in which the issue might be handled.

Perhaps an example will demonstrate what is logically deplorable about the foregoing facile acceptance of this type of forensic evidence or its equivalent (and perhaps why the judge "stumbled" over what the expert's answer had been, as if he could not believe his ears).

A complainant says the accused was standing three feet away from him, holding a gun. The complainant looked away, and then claims he heard a shot and thought he felt himself struck. At issue is whether the accused in fact shot the complainant; that is, aimed at and fired at the complainant. The accused denies any shooting.

First, the obvious thing to do would be to physically examine the victim for any signs of bullet holes. Such physical evidence would go a long way towards establishing the disputed act. But suppose the complainant's entire body is devoid of any bullet holes. The accused would obviously rely on such negative evidence to establish the lack of any shooting, and locate the claimed sound and feeling of being struck in the complainant's imagination or untruthfulness.

Could the prosecution then call an expert to testify that the lack of a bullet hole is "consistent with" being shot at three feet (on the theory that there are some really bad shots or lucky victims)? First of all, if it did, the witness's evidence would probably be given as "not inconsistent" to acknowledge that it was an improbability or a "long shot" that was being contemplated. "Not inconsistent" is reserved for improbabilities while "consistent" carries a connotation of reasonable probability.

Second, such expert evidence would be excluded as unnecessary because any ordinary person has a sense of the probabilities involved in the situation. The chances of an unintentional miss at close range are within the common stock of knowledge. Both sides are quite capable of arguing the issue without any expert evidence being necessary.

To return to the sex abuse context, expert evidence such as that in the above example should really be nothing more or less than accurate and reliable evidence of probabilities or patterns supposedly outside the common stock of knowledge. It is to inform the trier of fact of otherwise unknown probabilities.

A layperson has no idea of the probabilities of normal findings in the anal area three months after regular incidents of penetration. Without that knowledge, it is impossible to determine whether the absence of findings has any significance, such as the absence of a bullet hole supposedly fired at three feet as opposed to a shot at half a kilometre.

If Crown experts, in keeping with this reasoning, gave objective and reliable evidence regarding probabilities based upon sound data, there could be no complaint. But that is not what happens.

First, there are not as many sound data on a lot of these issues as there should be because of the hysteria that blankets the area and the damnation visited on researchers that come to politically incorrect conclusions.[8] As a result, the conclusions can and are founded on ideology and speculation in preference to the admission of agnosticism that would be appropriate.

Second, "consistent with" is used in preference to the more intellectually honest "not inconsistent with" to disguise the low probability of the scenario being favoured and avoid instigating the further questioning that might expose the cover-up.

In the example above, the evidence should have gone along the following lines (the questions can be implied from the answers):

A. Even though I found no physical signs in the anal region whatsoever, I do not believe that is necessarily inconsistent with the allegation of anal penetration.

A. Of course the lack of findings is completely consistent with such acts never having taken place.

A. But I believe it is also not inconsistent with the acts having taken place.

A. I have the following data that show that in some cases where anal penetration occurs, such as is alleged here, that three months later the anal

---

8   See notes 88 & 89 in chapter 7.

region looks perfectly normal: (data are set out so they can be examined and verified and validated).

A. I agree that according to the data in only about 3% of the cases was there a complete absence of any physical signs. So I agree that it is a rare situation. So I have to agree that according to the data, absence of any physical signs is much more consistent with no such penetration. I agree that in saying the lack of findings was "consistent" with the allegations being true I really meant it was "not inconsistent" in the sense that in a rare case, a very small percentage of cases, it is possible to find such a situation.

In other words, Crown experts should be testifying to the actual probabilities and not covering up with the intellectually dishonest device of talking about consistency whereby the actual low probabilities are being disguised. When evidence incriminates, Crown experts have no problem asserting, for example, that digital penetration rather than a diaper rash is "far more consistent" with the observed physical signs. But when the evidence exculpates because it is highly consistent with innocence and only remotely consistent with guilt, it is unfairly hidden by the expedient of dropping the adjectives and discussing consistency as if it were an all-or-nothing concept.

Where the evidence is obviously exculpatory, such as an absence of physical or other sequelae, the proper questions should go as follows:

Q. If the allegations were true, would you have expected to see some physical signs?

A. Not necessarily.

Q. On what do you base that opinion? With what probabilities?

The triers of fact should be informed of the respective probabilities to form their own opinion of whether, as in the shooting example, the accused shot and missed or in fact never shot at all.

In a case where if the offence was committed it would be probable (though not certain) that certain sequelae would obtain, it is unfair to deprive the accused of the fact that the probabilities are in his favour by the expedient of talking only in terms of the dualism consistent or inconsistent.

If it is a reasonable inference that if an act is done its reasonable and probable consequences will follow, then it is equally a reasonable inference that if those consequences have not appeared, then the act was not done.

An accused is entitled to the benefit of the reality that if what is claimed was done, it would have left results. In fact, the absence of evidence is usually what is crucial for an innocent accused. When the issue is whether an act was done or not, logically what other evidence can exist that something was not done than the absence of its probable consequences? This word game utilizing "consistency" should not be allowed to incapacitate the ability of physical reality to appropriately and justly controvert evidentiary claims.[9]

If a jury is entitled to utilize the common-sense inference that from an act one can infer its usual and probable consequences, then an accused is entitled to invoke the related logic that from the absence of the usual and probable consequences it is a common-sense, reasonable inference of the absence of the act.[10] Prosecution witnesses should not be allowed to utilize "consistent with" to prejudice an accused. As one English court put it, "Whereas 'inconsistency' was often probative, the fact of consistency was quite often of no probative value at all."[11] The gamesmanship implicated by such a language device is most definitely not "consistent with" the proper role of an expert.

9   Unfortunately the gambit continues to appear: *R. v. Garon*, [2009] O.J. No. 24 at paras. 21 & 22 (C.A.) at paras. 21 & 22.
10 Unlike the fallacies earlier described — see text after note 67 in chapter 4 — this is the permissible reasoning called "denying the consequent."
11 *R. v. Puaca*, [2005] EWCA Crim 3001.

CHAPTER 9

Science and Social Science Evidence

ISSUES OF EXPERT evidence can also arise where courts try to obtain and consume expert evidence on their own, without the assistance of an expert witness. This has become an issue because in the market expansion of social science evidence, its purveyors have discovered the legal doctrine of judicial notice.

A prominent attempt to enhance the use of social science evidence in general relies on a categorization of the types of "facts" that courts must find.[1] Using a taxonomy of "social fact" (or adjudicative facts: facts important only to the immediate parties to a dispute) and "social authority" (legislative facts, or facts used to help courts decide questions of law and policy), supplemented by "social framework," authors Monahan and Walker argue for a categorization of the evidentiary requirements for each as follows:[2]

- Social science research that bears on an adjudicative fact is governed by the normal rules of evidence. The precedential value of social science used in this way is limited to the methodology of the social science (e.g., the use of standard deviation analysis to establish a *prima facie* case of employment discrimination).
- "Social authority" evidence and "social framework" can be obtained outside the normal rules of evidence.

---

1   J. Monahan & L. Walker, "Social Authority: Obtaining, Evaluating and Establishing Social Science as Law" (1986) 134 U. Pa. L. Rev. 477.

2   As summarized in Judge R. James Williams, "The Use of Social Science Evidence" (undated, Dartmouth, Nova Scotia). ·

The mechanism proffered for this "obtaining outside the normal rules of evidence" is the doctrine of judicial notice. Aside from mandatory recognition of laws and subordinate legislation, judicial notice usually applies to "adjudicative facts," to use the above terminology; that is, facts that concern the immediate parties.[3] However, in addition, as another author put it, "the doctrine of judicial notice of legislative facts allows Courts development and interpreting the law to take judicial notice of the society within which the law operates."[4]

The rationale offered is that this broad and potentially far-reaching utilization of judicial notice that allows judicial notice of social "context" is necessary for appellate courts, especially as they are called upon to address important public issues where determining the law will require an "understanding" of the social environment and reality. The necessity for such "social framework" evidence has become a popular buzzword,[5] especially in the highly politicized

3   Utilizing the doctrine, courts can accept facts that are "indisputable and notorious," such as geographic locations: *R. v. Zarelli* (1931), 55 C.C.C. 314 (B.C.C.A.); *R. v. Purcell* (1975), 24 C.C.C. (2d) 139 (N.S.C.A.); *R. v. Bednarz* (1961), 35 C.R. 177 (Ont. C.A.); *R. v. Cerniuk* (1948), 1 W.W.R. 653 (B.C.C.A.); mechanics of the breathalyzer machine: *R. v. Walters* (1975), 26 C.C.C. (2d) 56 (N.S.C.A.): must blow into tube attached to machine; availability of legal aid services: *R. v. Cobham* (1994), 118 D.L.R. (4th) 301 at 309–10 (S.C.C.); but not the workings of laser beam speed devices: *R. v. Waschuk* (1971), 1 C.C.C. (2d) 463 (Sask. Q.B.). However, in *Joliette (City) v. Delangis* (1999), 141 C.C.C. (3d) 445 (Que. C.A.), it was held that the court could take judicial notice of the fact the laser beams can be used as a device to measure the speed of the vehicle. In general, as stated in *R. v. Potts* (1982), 66 C.C.C. (2d) 219 (Ont. C.A.), "it is nevertheless clear that a trial court is not justified in acting on its own personal knowledge of or familiarity with a particular matter, alone and without more."

4   David M. Paciocco, "Judicial Notice in Criminal Cases" (1997) 40 Crim. L.Q. 35 at 47. For those overly enthusiastic about this doctrine, the same author has accurately noted (*ibid.* at 59):

    There is nothing simple about the doctrines and theories of judicial notice. At its core the concept confounds scholars, lawyers and jurists alike. We have yet to even identify adequately when a Court is taking judicial notice and when it is not, or to accept, or reject that all judicial reasoning is a species of judicial notice.

5   See generally J. Monahan & L. Walker: "Judicial Use of Social Science Evidence after *Daubert*" (1995) 2 Shepard's Expert and Scientific Evidence 327; "Social Facts: Scientific Methodology as Legal Precedent" (1988) 76 Cal. L. Rev. 877; "Judicial Use of Social Science Research" (1991) 15 Law & Hum. Behav. 571; "Social Science Research in Law: A New Paradigm" (1988) 43 Am. Psychol. 465; "Social Authority: Obtaining, Evaluating and Establishing Social Science in Law" (1986) 134 U. Pa. L. Rev. 477; "Social Frameworks: A New Use of Social Science in Law" (1987) 73 Va. L. Rev. 559; and by Neil Vidmar, "Evaluating Expert Scientific Evidence" (5 November 1999), ADGN/RP-093 at para. 74*ff* (on Quicklaw in Commentary).

context of family law.[6] But even in the criminal law context, there are examples. In *R. v. Edwards Books & Art Ltd.*,[7] it was said:

> I do not accept that in dealing with broad social and economic facts such as those involved here the Court is necessarily bound to rely solely on those presented by counsel. The admonition in *Oakes* and other cases to present evidence in *Charter* cases does not remove from the Courts the power, where it deems it expedient, to take judicial notice of broad social and economic facts and to take the necessary steps to inform itself about them.

The Supreme Court has had no difficulty in taking judicial notice regarding the dangers and effects of drinking and driving[8] or the social problems posed by prostitution and the activities of pimps.[9] There are other examples.[10]

The Monahan and Walker argument for "social framework" as a widespread ticket of admission for social science "evidence" that trumps the usual rules of evidence demonstrates a faith in social science that may be extremely unwarranted.[11] Even a minimal examination of the social sciences raises concern that they are more "social" than "science." It is all too easy to disguise political ideology and advocacy in pseudo-scientific garb and urge its acceptance as "evidence" by judges and juries. The dangers of allowing unrestrained availability of social science resources are very real, especially if the crucial protections that flow from strict adherence to the methods of science are not fully operational.[12]

---

6 Justice C. L'Heureux-Dubé, "Making Equality Work in Family Law" (1997) 14 Can. J. Fam. Law 103; Justice C. L'Heureux-Dubé, "Re-examining the Doctrine of Judicial Notice in a Family Law Context" (1994) 26 Ottawa L. Rev. 551.

7 [1986] 2 S.C.R. 713 at 802.

8 *R. v. Penno*, [1990] 2 S.C.R. 865 at 881–82; *R. v. Ladouceur*, [1990] 1 S.C.R. 1257 at 1279–81. See also *R. v. Bonin*, [1989] B.C.J. No. 108 (C.A.), regarding judicial notice of drinking and driving risks.

9 *R. v. Downey*, [1992] 2 S.C.R. 10.

10 See *R. v. Keegstra*, [1990] 3 S.C.R. 697 ("our collective historical knowledge of the potentially catastrophic effects of the promotion of hatred"); and *R. v. Seaboyer*, [1991] 2 S.C.R. 597 (historical attitudes and beliefs regarding rape complainants). In *United States of America v. Saad*, [2004] O.J. No. 1148 (C.A.), Moldaver J.A. did his own Internet research regarding the drug known as "ecstasy."

11 Some commentators have specifically argued that *Daubert* requires independent research by judges: Michael E. Keasler & Cathy Cramer, "Appellate Courts Must Conduct Independent Research of *Daubert* Issues to Discover 'Junk Science'" (2006) 90:2 Judicature 62.

12 Paciocco, above note 4 at 52 notes: "[A]lthough the 'incontrovertibility' requirement for judicial notice of adjudicative facts does not apply strictly in the context, the use of literature in making social context determinations is fraught with difficulty and must be undertaken with caution."

Furthermore, concerns must exist about the ability of judges to intelligently consume such materials on their own without the benefit of critical commentary.[13] There have been some unfortunate precedents. In *R. v. Askov*,[14] the Supreme Court incorporated empirical data and social science research into determining the appropriate length of time it should take a matter to proceed to trial so as not to violate subsection 11(b) of the *Canadian Charter of Rights and Freedoms*. Very shortly thereafter, in *R. v. Morin*,[15] the Court again utilized empirical data from social science research to alter the *Askov* benchmarks.[16]

In a case where the Supreme Court of Canada adopted the "power imbalance" theory to invalidate apparent sexual consent in certain contexts,[17] it referred to an article representative of the genre by a Professor Coleman,[18] which, in the Court's words, "identified a number of types of relationships, including that of a teacher and student, in which a power dependency relationship is inherent." This reference was echoed in other cases[19] without any independent analysis. The reader may be forgiven for interpreting this as if it were a descriptive statement suggesting that Professor Coleman has some research and data showing this power imbalance in fact, showing that teachers inevitably can manipulate their students and render them incapable of acceptable decision making. Examination of Professor Coleman's article shows no such evidence. Rather, what is clear is that Professor Coleman simply subscribes to an ideology wherein such a power imbalance is a *given*. It is disappointing that the Supreme Court of Canada so uncritically bought into that ideology.[20] Episodes like this

---

13   Kenneth R. Foster & Peter W. Huber, *Judging Science: Scientific Knowledge and the Federal Courts* (Cambridge, MA: MIT Press, 1999) at 148–50.

14   [1990] 2 S.C.R. 1199.

15   [1992] 1 S.C.R. 771.

16   See Carl Baar, "Criminal Court Delay and the *Charter*" (1993) 72 Can. Bar Rev. 305 at 306, 334, & 333, respectively: Prof. Baar opined that *Askov* was based upon an "incomplete understanding of the material before it" and that in *Morin*, the Court acted on "erroneous social facts." He noted that it would have been far preferable to avoid the "inaccuracy of a do-it-yourself approach" by having the matter scheduled for rehearing with all parties and intervenors given an opportunity to present evidence.

17   *Norberg v. Wynrib*, [1992] 2 S.C.R. 226 at 255.

18   Phyllis Coleman, "Sex in Power Dependency Relationships: Taking Unfair Advantage of the 'Fair' Sex" (1988) 53 Alb. L. Rev. 95.

19   *R. v. Saint-Laurent* (1994), 90 C.C.C. (3d) 291 (Que. C.A.); *R. v. G.M.* (1992), 77 C.C.C. (3d) 310 (Ont. C.A.); *R. v. Matheson* (1999), 44 O.R. (3d) 557 (C.A.); and *R. v. Audet* (1996), 106 C.C.C. (3d) 481 (S.C.C.).

20   This "inherent power imbalance" position has its fundamental (and seminal) pronouncement in the infamous Mackinnon-Dworkin critique of all heterosexual activity in our allegedly patriarchal society. Consent is obviously not a meaningful concept for someone for whom rape and intercourse "are difficult to distinguish": Dan Greenberg & Thomas

(which have still not been undone) raise issues about *ex parte* judicial consumption of social science materials.

The utility of an adversarial examination of purported social science information has been noted by the Supreme Court. In *R. v. Corbett*,[21] Dickson C.J. referenced the scientific inadequacy of social science research at hand (namely, jury studies) as follows:

> The dissent in the Court of Appeal of British Columbia relied heavily upon two sociological studies which purported to demonstrate that jurors are incapable of distinguishing between evidence that goes to guilt and evidence that

H. Tobiason, "The New Legal Puritanism of Catherine Mackinnon" (1993) 54 Oh. St. L.J. 1375 at 1422, n.281, and see generally *ibid.*, especially section C, "The Problem of Consent and Coercion." Mackinnon's definition of consent, whereby it can be negatived by "coercion" — "even something like love" — is an example of "the fallacy of persuasive definition" (implicitly infusing a general term with a contingent and rhetorically convenient meaning); see also Elfrieda Schroeder, "Catherine's Wheel: Mackinnon's Pornography Analysis as a Return to Traditional Christian Sexual Theory" (1993) 38 N.Y.L. Sch. L. Rev. 225 (and references therein to Mackinnon's work); Cathy Young, "The New Madonna/Whore Syndrome: Feminism, Sexuality and Sexual Harassment" (1993) 38 N.Y.L. Sch. L. Rev. 257.

Because of women's place in society, according to Mackinnon and Dworkin, there is in fact no such thing as a valid "consent" by women in our society. This bizarre concept of consent, to put it mildly, is obviously erroneous to all but the most ardent radical feminists, and like other unacceptable doctrines, it has tried to survive by mutating into a more palatable form. Trying to limit the alleged power imbalance to specified professions or social roles may make the concept superficially more palatable, but it does not make it more valid.

The inherent power imbalance ideology also has another equally nefarious point of origin: Freudian psychoanalytic theory. The Freudian construct of "transference," as vacuous as any of Freud's ideas, is often invoked in aid of the power imbalance construct as if this rubric explained, as opposed to merely labelled. Coleman is a follower of Freudian therapeutic relationship cant: see Phyllis Coleman, "Sex between Psychiatrist and Former Patient: A Proposal for a 'No Harm, No Foul' Rule" (1988) 41 Okla. L. Rev. 1 at 4ff. Someone who traces an "aspect of transference to the Oedipus complex" is obviously not a commentator in whom anyone can have any degree of confidence regarding ideas of substance.

In Patricia M.L. Illingworth, "Patient-Therapist Sex: Criminalization and Its Discontents" (1995) 11 J. Contemp. Health L. & Pol'y 389 at 399–400, the author in restrained terms debunks the transference ideology as a basis for denying consent. She then goes on to debunk Coleman's "power imbalance" argument as well: *ibid.* at 401–2.

See also Sheppy Young, "Getting to Yes: The Case against Banning Consensual Relationships in Higher Education" (1996) 4 Am. U.J. Gender & L. 269 for an excellent discussion of these issues (though that author is unwittingly gullible regarding the Freudian transference cant). It is a real shame that references such as these were not brought to the attention of the Court before it so unwittingly bought into Coleman's position.

21 [1988] 1 S.C.R. 670.

goes to credibility. Those studies have been analyzed with great sophistication by the intervener, the Attorney General of Canada, and the scientific method of the studies has been cast into doubt. Moreover, the Attorney General of Canada refers to other sociological and psychological studies that call into question the conclusions of the data relied upon by Hutcheon J.A. in dissent. It is not possible to undertake a complete analysis of all these studies for the purposes of this judgment, but the conflicting results and the inherent limitations of such investigations should cause the Court to be wary of relying upon the data adduced by the appellant before the Court of Appeal.[22]

Therefore, if this utilization of social science information by means of the doctrine of judicial notice does develop into a relatively frequent occurrence, simple fairness and the requirements of good science demand that the materials be made fully available to the parties and an opportunity for comment and criticism be allowed before judicial acceptance and reliance take place. As one commentator noted, "[t]he problems of fairness to the parties are generated in the silent use of facts judicially noticed. Without disclosure prior to the decision, the parties must guess at the Judge's appreciation of how the world turns and will not have the opportunity of displaying contrary data to support a competing view."[23]

If a court feels that further research is required and further information is necessary for a decision, the parties must have an opportunity to participate in the court's obtaining and utilization of such materials. This is simply what justice requires, not to mention the additional reliability of the decision making that will be fostered.

---

22 *Ibid.* at 693, para. 40.
23 R.J. Delisle, Annotation to *R. v. R.D.S.* (1997), 10 C.R. (5th) 1 at 7.

CHAPTER 10

Problematic Procedural Issues

THE *VOIR DIRE*

UNLESS THE SUBJECT of agreement by the opposing party, an expert witness must first be qualified as such upon a *voir dire* regarding qualifications.

> In some cases it may be possible to rule on the admissibility of the proposed evidence on the basis of counsel's submissions alone. However it may at times prove necessary to hold a *voir dire* in order to properly consider all relevant factors. Where the trial is before a jury and the questions of admissibility cannot be clearly determined in a summary fashion, it may indeed be prudent to scrutinize the evidence during the course of a *voir dire* before admitting it. While in some cases the ruling can be made early in the proceedings, in other cases, it may be only later in the trial that the value of the proposed evidence can be properly assessed.[1]

Whether the *voir dire* is done in the absence or presence of the jury will depend upon the nature of the proposed evidence and expert and any prejudice that might be occasioned to the adducing party by an unsuccessful application. It is generally done in the presence of the jury when only qualifications are in issue since the jury is entitled to hear such evidence in any event as relevant to its assessment of the weight of the evidence. If the witness is qualified as an expert, the evidence heard on the *voir dire*, both in chief and cross-examination, will

---

1   *R. v. A.K. and N.K.* (1999), 27 C.R. (5th) 226 (Ont. C.A.).

be useful to the jurors in determining weight, and if the witness is not qualified, generally no harm is done. Of course, if an unsuccessful attempt to qualify the witness will not be harmless to one or other party in the particular circumstances, a request can be made to hold the *voir dire* in the jury's absence.

The party tendering the witness has the onus to demonstrate admissibility. The tendering counsel adduces evidence in chief on the *voir dire* regarding the witness's qualifications and the areas of proposed expert testimony. The opposing party has the right to cross-examine the witness regarding the issues on the *voir dire*, including qualifications.[2]

HEARSAY EVIDENCE

THE RELATIONSHIP BETWEEN the hearsay evidence rule and expert opinion evidence remains somewhat problematic. It is clear that expert evidence can be based on technically hearsay evidence, as it will almost inevitably be, but it is also clear that expert evidence does not render hearsay evidence admissible.[3]

Courts have stated that an expert opinion can be based on a *mélange* of admissible and inadmissible information, although there must be some admissible evidence presented to establish the factual foundation on which the expert opinion is based.[4]

Further, the expert can describe both the admissible and the inadmissible information that he has relied on to explain the foundation for his opinion to the trier of fact. The inadmissible information is received solely to enable the trier of fact to understand and assess the expert opinion. It cannot be relied on to support the truth of the facts it asserts.[5]

Also in a jury trial, the judge must warn the jury that the more the expert relies on inadmissible information, the less weight may be given to the opinion. The Supreme Court of Canada stated in *R. v. Abbey*[6] that although an opinion based on inadmissible information may be admissible, "[b]efore any weight can be given to an expert's opinion, the facts upon which the opinion is based must be found to exist ... through properly admissible evidence."

---

2   See generally Robert White, *The Art of Using Expert Evidence* (Aurora, ON: Canada Law Book, 1997) at 40.
3   *R. v. Mathieu* (1994), 90 C.C.C. (3d) 415 (Que. C.A.), aff'd [1995] 4 S.C.R. 46.
4   *R. v. Abadom* (1982), 76 Crim. App. R. 48 (C.A.); *R. v. Moase* (1989), 51 C.C.C. (3d) 77 (B.C.C.A.).
5   *R. v. Lavallee*, [1990] 1 S.C.R. 852; *R. v. Babcock* (1984), 16 C.C.C. (3d) 26 (Alta. C.A.).
6   [1982] 2 S.C.R. 24 at 39.

Logical consistency is not a hallmark of these disparate pronouncements. The best one can say is that the expert opinion is viewed as having a separate existence from its factual underpinnings, so that the former can be technically admissible even if the latter is inadmissible hearsay. However, though admissible, it will be of no weight. How weightless evidence is nevertheless admissible has never been made clear.[7]

PRESENTING THE EXPERT EVIDENCE

THERE IS A certain preferable logical development to the direct examination and cross-examination of expert witnesses. First, the expert is introduced and her involvement in the case — the issue on which she is going to opine — is explained. How the witness came to be retained and the purpose of her evidence is brought out.

It is generally useful at the outset to make clear the issue that is going to be addressed in evidence, at least in summary form, so the trier of fact does not have to wait until the end of the evidence to hear its essence. Thus, it should be brought out that the witness will be providing an opinion "on the accused's mental state at the time of the killing" or "what the accused's blood-alcohol level was at the time of the driving," even if the actual opinion is postponed until after the following areas are dealt with.

The witness's qualifications relevant to the particular area in issue should be brought out to emphasize the credibility of the opinion. Specific expertise presented in a pleasant manner is preferred. An endless repetition of degrees, publications, professional memberships will dull the interest of the keenest judge or juror. Articles directly on point, relevant practical experience, any qualifications lacked by the opposing expert, and previous court appearances should especially be emphasized.

Next in logical order is the opinion itself. After the opinion, any underlying theory should be set out to assist the trier's understanding. The theory or underlying principles are the logical link between the data or investigation carried out and the opinion reached.

If the foundational facts are not in dispute, they can be expressed by the expert witness without special qualification. But if they are in dispute, then the expert witness is in effect assuming or hypothecating those facts in forming his opinion. To keep clear the logic of the situation, the device of the hypothetical question is utilized. The expert witness is questioned by the examiner along the

---

7   *R. v. Fontaine*, [2005] M.J. No. 230 (C.A.).

lines of "Assuming that ..." followed by the facts the examiner hopes will be accepted.[8]

After the opinion and theory have been explained, the expert can be taken in detail through the investigation and resulting data and any calculations performed. The data should be presented in a comprehensive and understandable fashion. Any assumptions made will also be set out at this point. The scientific principles involved in general and in particular should be set out, with references, as well as the premises relied on. If testing is involved, issues of methodology should be described, explained, and justified.

Facts or information obtained first-hand should be so delineated, and any special techniques utilized explained and justified. Facts or information from other sources should be described and explained. Any potential sources of reliability can be identified and protections taken described, including protections against falsification. If an opposing expert has or will be giving contrary opinions, it is useful at this point to differentiate the other expert's theory or assumptions or, rarely, data, to explain the divergence of opinion.

The witness should be prepared to testify in plain language, avoiding long speeches, and using examples and analogies that will be persuasive to the trier of fact. Visual aids may be useful. If the testimony covers a lot of ground, internal summaries at various points will be a useful repetition of important points and allow listeners to recognize a change of subject matter.

Since expert evidence is an opinion, a conclusion, its assessment requires complete knowledge of the facts and principles leading to it.

> Before a Court can assess the value of an opinion it must know the facts upon which it is based. If the expert has been misinformed about the facts or has taken irrelevant facts into consideration or has omitted to consider relevant ones, the opinion is likely to be valueless.[9]

In some cases, the expert witness may be able to testify to such matters, such as pathological findings or physical examination results from personal knowledge. In other cases, the expert witness has only hearsay knowledge of foundational facts. Then the foundational facts must be proved by admissible evidence from other witnesses, though they can be assumed by the expert during his testimony.

---

8   See generally Earl J. Levy, *Examination of Witnesses in Criminal Cases*, 4th ed. (Toronto: Carswell, 1999) c. 14, "The Expert Witness" at 293–306.

9   *R. v. Turner* (1974), 60 Crim. App. R. 80 at 82 (U.K.C.A. (Crim. Div.)). See generally Levy, *ibid.* at 289.

The examination in chief will generally conclude with an effective and (you hope) memorable restatement of the opinion.

CROSS-EXAMINATION OF EXPERT EVIDENCE

CROSS-EXAMINATION OF EXPERTS requires first and foremost a knowledgeable counsel, educated through reading and studying the subject matter, especially all the relevant articles and other items listed on the expert's résumé. Counsel must also be educated by her own expert witness.

If the witness has published in the area relevant to the issues at trial, counsel must carefully review these publications to see if the witness has expressed opinions that are contrary to what the witness is expected to express at trial. If the witness has not published in the area relevant to the issues at trial, this point should be stressed in the cross-examination.

All expert witnesses should be fully researched in the legal databases, such as Quicklaw, to locate prior cases or decisions in which their names have been mentioned. Other online databases, such as newspapers, can also provide important information or even quotations or comments by the witness that may be of use. Communication with other counsel involved in previous cases in which the witness has testified may secure transcripts of previous testimony of the witness, which may provide valuable materials for cross-examination.

An interview with an opposing witness is invariably a useful exercise. A good expert witness will make clear the limitations and qualifications of his opinion. A bad expert witness will say things that with investigation and reflection can be extremely useful in undermining his credibility.

Areas of attack in cross-examination[10] include first of all the witness's credentials. Any missing credentials or credentials lesser in status than one's own expert's credentials should be stressed. A telling argument will always be if the qualifications of the other side's expert in the area in question are far less impressive than that of your own expert's qualifications. It will also tell against credibility if the witness has overstated or misled the court as to her qualifications. Further, the importance of *relevant* credentials should not be overlooked. If the majority of the expert witness's expertise is in a field unrelated to one or more of the issues upon which she has been called to testify, that fact should be emphasized. One author wrote:

---

10   See generally Levy, *ibid.*, c. 14, "The Expert Witness" at 306.

It is common for prosecutors deliberately to mislead juries by introducing testimony of the over-qualified expert, thereby lending specious dignity to a questionable case.

If asked by his family physician to go to the Mayo Clinic for the simple purpose of having his blood pressure taken, any juror would instantly and instinctively object to such absurd medical overkill. The Mayo Clinic is no better qualified to take one's blood pressure than is the average nursing student. Yet, that same form of overkill frequently appears impressive and logical when performed by the prosecution in a criminal case.

. . .

Accordingly, two fundamental questions to be considered by the defense lawyer faced with a prosecution expert should be:

1. To what degree, if any, is this witness's education relevant to the opinion which he will render in this case?
2. On what scientific principles does he rely, and at what stage of his training was he familiarized with the principles?

It is sometimes very effective to force the witness to concede before the jury that his impressive statement of qualifications was almost completely irrelevant to the opinion which he rendered, thereby demonstrating to the jury that in a very real sense it has been "conned" by the prosecution.[11]

Cross-examination can also bring out favourable information. An honest expert witness will concede appropriate points.

The witness's credibility can be attacked by challenging her impartiality if grounds for such challenge exist. Fees being paid and her history of testifying are relevant matters.

In cross-examination, omissions may render an expert witness vulnerable, such as omissions to perform certain tests or omissions to carry out her investigation in accordance with applicable standards.

Obviously, cross-examination of the witness will test the validity of the opinion if the assumed facts, or some of them, are not borne out, or if other additional facts are found. Cross-examination may consist of changing the information or data upon which the opinion is based. Assumptions can be questioned and changed. Relevant facts may be challenged and changed, or the dependence

---

11   Melvin B. Lewis, "The Expert Witness in Criminal Cases: General Considerations" (undated, unpublished paper) at 7–8, reproduced with permission in Mark J. Mahoney, "Materials on Examination of the Expert Witness" (Ontario Criminal Lawyers' Association for the Program "Experts and Junk Science," Toronto, 5 April 1997).

of the opinion on other testimony to supply crucial facts emphasized. Finally, the techniques or theories used by the expert witness can be challenged.

It is especially important to examine all references that a witness claims as support for crucial principles of the science involved. Counsel will soon learn how often the references do not support the proposition put forth, or are distinguishable, or have their conclusions couched in much more modest or restrained terms, or are even being misunderstood by the witness. Nothing should be assumed or taken for granted if an expert witness's evidence matters.

As well, the trier of fact will have to decide that the "facts" are as hypothesized for the opinion evidence to have any value. If the trier of fact finds facts materially inconsistent with the hypothetical question, the opinion becomes useless.

The most important general aspect of cross-examination will be to utilize the general principles involved in the scientific method to demonstrate any and all available methodological and logical problems involved in the evidence given.

THE USE OF WRITTEN AUTHORITIES

REFERENCE WORKS SUCH as books and articles are hearsay when they are being relied on to provide accurate information. An expert witness can refer to, and even quote from, other authorities while testifying in chief so long as he adopts the opinions contained in those authorities as his own by expressing his agreement with them, and thus adopting them as his own.

The expert can be cross-examined using reference materials such as texts, articles, and studies, but only where the expert witness acknowledges that the works being used are authoritative.[12] Where the witness acknowledges the authority of the work, if she adopts the opinions of the author, such opinions become part of the expert's evidence. Where the witness acknowledges the authority of the work but rejects its conclusions, she can be asked to explain why, and her responses can be of relevance in assessing the credibility of the opinion being offered.

The use of authorities in cross-examination even if the expert does not recognize their authority has sometimes been misunderstood. The rule in some American jurisdictions allows that, so long as the reliability of the work is established independently or by judicial notice, it can still be used in cross-examination. However, in Canada, an expert unfamiliar with the authorities in his field cannot be confronted with them. This has been misinterpreted to make "ignorance into bliss" for expert witnesses. It does not.

---

12   *R. v. Conroy* (1993), 84 C.C.C. (3d) 320 (Ont. C.A.). See generally Levy, above note 8, c. 14, "The Expert Witness" at 314–23.

An expert witness's lack of familiarity with the authoritative texts, periodicals, research papers, or other publications in the field in issue is (and certainly should be) a serious blow to his credibility. An expert witness unfamiliar with the authoritative works in his field can be confronted with that very fact as a measure of his lack of expertise. Such a witness should be clearly pinned down as to his lack of familiarity with the leading references. Then, evidence can be adduced that no competent expert in that field would suffer from such unfamiliarity; that any competent expert would be familiar with, and acknowledge, such authoritativeness. The expert witness's ignorance can thus be made into a damning credibility deficiency.

An ingenious example of cross-examination on "leading authorities" has been reported as follows:

> I had occasion to hear such a cross-examination many years ago when I was in Court waiting for my case to be called and listening to a criminal trial in which an experienced Defence counsel was cross-examining a handwriting expert who had been called by the Prosecution. The cross-examination went something like this:
>
> Q. Are you familiar with the leading texts in your field?
> A. Yes, I think so.
> Q. In particular are you familiar with Patterson on Forged Documents?
> A. Yes
> Q. When was the last time you had occasion to consult Patterson's book?
> A. When I was working for the R.C.M.P. on a case in Ottawa. I checked it out of their library.
> Q. What about Ligner on Handwriting Analysis?
> A. Yes I am familiar with that work.
> Q. When was the last time you had occasion to read Ligner?
> A. I don't remember but certainly within the last five years.
> Q. Do you have a copy of Ligner in your library?
> A. Not now, but I did when I worked for the R.C.M.P.
> Q. Are Patterson and Ligner authoritative in your area of expertise?
> A. Yes
> Q. Would it surprise you to know that I made up the names of these authors and books this morning?
> A. (pause) I guess it would . . .[13]

---

13   Harvey Spiegel, "Attacking the Defence Expert's Qualifications" (Paper presented at the Fall Conference of the Ontario Trial Lawyers Association, Toronto, 7–8 November 1997).

STATUTORY EVIDENTIARY PROVISIONS

PROVINCIAL EVIDENCE ACTS, the *Canada Evidence Act,* and the *Criminal Code* contain statutory provisions relevant to expert witnesses.

One type of provision limits the number of experts that a party can call without leave of the court. These provisions, of which the *Canada Evidence Act*[14] is an example, generally limit the number of experts a party may call to five unless leave to call more is granted by the court. However, a breach of the section seems inconsequential.[15]

Another type of provision allows expert evidence to be given by documentary evidence. An amendment to the *Criminal Code*[16] (in force 23 September 2002) adds subsections 657.3(3)–(7), which provide for notice of expert testimony and set out the consequences if notice is not given.

Notice of expert testimony has to be given by prosecutors and defence at least thirty days before the beginning of the trial or within such other period fixed by the court. The notice has to include the name of the proposed expert witness, a description of the witness's area of expertise, and a statement of the witness's qualifications. A copy of any report prepared by the expert or, if no report has been prepared, a summary of the opinion expected to be given by the witness, has to be provided to the other side — in the case of the prosecutor within a reasonable period before trial and in the case of the defence not later than the close of the case for the prosecution.

When a party calls an expert without having complied with the notice requirements, the court shall grant an adjournment of the proceedings to the party that requests it to allow her to prepare for cross-examination of the expert witness; order the party that called the expert witness to provide the other party and any other party with a copy of the report, or where it does not exist, a summary of the anticipated evidence, so as to allow for preparation for cross-examination; and order, where appropriate, the recalling or calling of any witnesses.

Even when a party has complied with the notice provisions, the court may — where a party has not been able to prepare properly — adjourn the proceedings, order that further particulars be given of the evidence of the proposed witness, and order the calling or recalling of any witness for the purpose of giving testimony on matters related to those raised in the expert witness's testimony.

---

14 R.S.C. 1985, c. C-5, as amended, s. 7.
15 *R. v. Vincent* (1963), 40 C.R. (3d) 365 (Man. C.A.).
16 R.S.C. 1985, c. C-46.

DISCLOSURE ISSUES WITH EXPERT REPORTS

IN *R. V. STONE*,[17] the Supreme Court of Canada considered whether the trial judge erred in compelling defence counsel to disclose to the Crown a copy of an expert report in circumstances where defence counsel commented with respect to the anticipated evidence of the defence expert in his opening address to the jury.

The Court held disclosure was properly ordered because defence counsel had waived privilege in the contents of the report by his conduct of the trial. That was the limited basis of the decision. However, the Court in *R. v. Stone* went on to enunciate a more general proposition that merely by calling an expert witness to testify, the defence thereby waived all privilege and had to turn over to the Crown the reports from the expert, including any prior inconsistent statements by the accused, no matter how inconsequential they were with regard to the psychiatric opinion.[18]

Although the law of privilege is beyond the scope of this book,[19] it should be kept in mind that in general, privilege applies to experts retained as part of the defence function, and also that privilege applies to communications and not to information, so that even if a third party acquires the same information from an external source, a solicitor-client privileged communication remains privileged. To the extent that *R. v. Stone* appears to have created a broad exception to privileged reports merely because the expert witness is called to testify, it also stands for the proposition that there is little good and much harm that flows from obtaining such reports. Of course, the expert witness should carefully document the foundational facts upon which his opinion is based and be prepared to fully and completely convey them to opposing counsel during a pretrial interview or courtroom questioning, as well as to the court, but there seems little to be achieved by defence counsel securing a detailed report in advance of trial.

R. v. Stone also provides the valuable caution that defence counsel should do her utmost to ensure there are no significant inconsistencies between the expert's information and other defence evidence, for obvious reasons.

Finally, the importance of pretrial interviews of expert witnesses for the opposing party cannot be overestimated. The fact that "there is no property in a witness" applies with greatest force to an expert witness, whose credibility is

---

17 (1999), 24 C.R. (5th) 1 (S.C.C.).

18 See also *R. v. Frechette*, [2000] B.C.J. No. 373 (S.C.).

19 See the U.K. case *R. v. Davies*, [2002] EWCA Crim 85, holding that privilege barred the Crown from subpoenaing as a witness a psychiatrist retained by the defence.

founded upon a presumed neutrality and an agenda of assistance to the trier of fact. For an expert witness to refuse to be available to the opposing counsel for an interview in advance of trial can and should lead to adverse comment. Such an interview with any competent expert witness is an invaluable source of information to assist counsel in preparing the best cross-examination that the facts will allow.

CONFLICTING EXPERT EVIDENCE

IT IS NOT unusual for expert witnesses to disagree. *R. v. Parnell*[20] considered the proper jury directions to be given in a case of conflicting experts:[21]

> The proper direction to be given in a case of conflicting expert evidence is summarized in a case summary and comment in *R. v. Platt*, [1981] Crim. L.R. 332. In that case, two pathologists, one called by the prosecution and the other for the defence, had expressed differing opinions as to the maximum time between the infliction of certain injuries and the brain death of the victim. In relation to the conflicting doctors, the jury was directed "You have to decide whose evidence you prefer." Allowing the appeal from a conviction for manslaughter, the Court of Appeal said, in summary, at p. 333:
>
> > The only safe way of directing the jury was either to tell them that before they accepted the opinion of the prosecution's pathologist they must feel sure that he was correct, or else to tell them that they were to assume that the [page 364] defence pathologist was right and, therefore, to approach the case on the other evidence solely and not base their approach on the pathologist's evidence at all. Unfortunately the judge had done neither but had asked the jury to decide which of the two bodies of medical evidence they preferred. In the extraordinary circumstances, that was a misdirection and the conviction would be quashed.
>
> In cases of competing expert evidence, it is not proper to limit the jury by asking whose evidence is preferred or who had the better opportunity to observe. It is correct to point to the latter, as a factor only, to be considered in resolving the question whether the Crown has proved guilt beyond a reasonable doubt. See *R. v. Laverty (No. 2)* (1979), 47 C.C.C. (2d) 60 at p. 62, 9 C.R. (3d) 288.

---

20 (1983), 9 C.C.C. (3d) 353 (Ont. C.A.), leave to appeal denied 7 February 1984.
21 *Ibid.* at 355.

Thus, it is misdirection to leave the jury to simply select between the opposing experts. Rather, the jury is to be directed by telling it either it must be sure before it accepted the opinion of the prosecution's expert that he was correct, or else the jury could approach the case by assuming that the defence expert was right and then consider the case on the other evidence solely and not base its approach on the prosecution expert's evidence at all.[22]

---

22 See also *R. v. Anderson*, [2000] 1 V.R. 1 (Vict. C.A.), regarding conflicting evidence whether wounds were self-inflicted or not. The jury had to be satisfied beyond a reasonable doubt that the incriminating opinion was correct.

CHAPTER 11

Proposals for Change

THERE ARE THREE changes that should now be compellingly obvious that would go a most substantial way towards ensuring the reliability and validity of expert opinion evidence offered in court.

USING SCIENCE AS A PRACTICAL LITMUS TEST FOR "EXPERTS"

SINCE THE CRUCIAL discriminating factor between good and bad expert opinion lies in methodology and not in content, knowledge of that methodology, as opposed to knowledge of any particular content, becomes the obvious litmus test to initially separate the good from the bad. Scientific literacy can, in fact, be used as the basic test to discriminate real experts from junk scientists. Knowledge of the methods of science can and should be used to determine in effect who is worth listening to in a courtroom.

The issues for all proposed experts could become:

+ Are they scientifically literate?
+ Do they know and appreciate the scientific method?
+ Are they aware of illogical reasoning?

It is true that passing this test does not guarantee an absence of junk science: prominent and knowledgeable scientists can believe in astrology and worse. But failing that test — being scientifically illiterate — virtually ensures the presence of junk science. It means the witnesses' purported knowledge almost certainly arises from their imagination or ideology or some other unreliable source, but not from reality because they are illiterate with regard to reading reality.

The significance of impressive-sounding credentials must be properly translated into an inquiry into the depth of the witness's knowledge about to "really and validly know" — scientific literacy, and not just an abdication of that judgment by relying on an apparently impressive educational background.

Applying this test ensures that witnesses allowed to pass into the evidentiary arena will at least be speaking the right language of science, so that their knowledge can be measured by appropriate standards and found wanting or not. For this reason, the initial content of any forensic scrutiny by knowledgeable lawyers is increasingly turning to an exploration of the witness's scientific literacy,[1] and this is why scientific literacy is an excellent guide to the appropriate test for the requisite judicial gatekeeping function regarding expert evidence as well.

USING SCIENCE AS A SOURCE FOR EXPERT EVIDENCE *PER SE*

THE SYSTEMATIC KNOWLEDGE described in this book should be recognized as a legitimate area for expert evidence in its own right. It meets all the requirements of expert evidence, but unfortunately is not commonly known —that is a serious reflection on society. This source of knowledge is extremely relevant, highly reliable, and absolutely necessary to ensure quality expert evidence in our courtrooms, and those same referenced books show an abundance of qualified experts quite familiar with the scientific method.

The second change I would recommend is the increased use of science framework evidence when other expert opinion evidence is sought to be adduced, to critique the proposed evidence and expose its failure to meet the standards of science, if such be the case. Instead of, or in addition to, a defence expert to dispute the merits of the substance of the fingerprint identifier's conclusion, an expert scientist should testify about the methodological flaws in fingerprint identification, its disguised subjectivity, its unproved assumptions, the potential for various biases to operate, and, in short, its unscientific and potentially unreliable nature.

---

1   *R. v. Olscamp* (1994), 95 C.C.C. (3d) 466 (Ont. Ct. Gen. Div.); *R. v. Kavanagh*, [2001] EWCA Crim 140.

An example of such an approach[2] is found in *R. v. Perlett*.[3] In this murder case, it was technically not expert evidence that was in issue, but rather evidence as to the observations of witnesses regarding an odour of gunpowder.

The evidence in issue involved "experiments" or tests conducted by the police to determine whether an odour of gunpowder should or should not have been detected by witnesses. The defence called expert evidence to describe the failings in the police test procedures.

> This is a motion by the defence to exclude evidence of what counsel have jointly referred to as the gunsmoke odour tests.
>
> . . .
>
> The information in general in the motion materials indicates that on March 22, 1996, an evening of double homicides, eight shots were fired in the residence occupied by the two deceased and the accused Mr. James Perlett, that four shots were fired upstairs and four shots were fired downstairs. No time of the firing of the shots was established. However, the police arrived within five minutes of receiving the 911 call to attend at the residence. During the course of their immediate investigation, no witnesses made any note of the presence or absence of any gunsmoke odour.

The Crown relied on the witness's nondetection of odour as probative of the falsity of the accused's story and hence inculpatory regarding the accused's guilt. For this logic to apply, however, the Crown had to show that the witnesses, if the accused's story were true, should have detected gunsmoke odour; hence, the police "tests."

> On May 7th, 1997, a series of tests was conducted in the same residence in an effort to determine how long the smell of gunsmoke would remain in the air after discharge of a firearm. Efforts were made to duplicate the physical set-up of the residence as it was on March 22, 1996: the same residence obviously was used; the same officers attended for the tests as had attended at the residence at the time of the homicides; the same type of ammunition was used; shots were fired in approximately the same location in the residence as the officers had been given information; the officers followed the same route within the residence as they had on March 22, 1996.
>
> Some problems with the police testing procedures were obvious:

---

2   Although not an example of such evidentiary use, clearly in the same spirit are the comments in *R. v. Corbett*, [1988] 1 S.C.R. 670 of Dickson C.J., who referenced scientific inadequacy in the context of jury studies. See extract in text at note 21 in chapter 9.

3   [1998] O.J. No. 6026 (Gen. Div.).

Other aspects had significant differences: no attempt was made to approximate the same inside or outside temperatures; the residence was furnished differently; the residence had been painted; a different type of weapon was used although a similar .22 calibre class of handgun; one of the officers involved in the test on May 7th had a nasal condition which he did not have March of 1996; no attempt was made at that time to determine the aspect of airflow and, in particular, air or heat registers.

Sergeant Maule, who was responsible for conducting the tests on May 7th, stated that the tests were not intended to be scientific but purely investigative. He acknowledged in cross-examination that, subsequent to that test, he determined that there were many factors which should have and could have been taken into account to increase the reliability.

Therefore, following the tests of May 7th, 1997, a second series of tests was conducted on March 4th and 5th of 1998. That date was chosen because the outside air temperature was then approximately the same as it had been on March 22nd of 1996. In an effort to further replicate the conditions of March 1996, furniture was placed in the residence in the same locations as it had been in March of 1996 although not all of the exact same furniture was used.

There were differences between the March 1996 and March 1998 tests. Without specifying all of the differences, I note the following: The deceased obviously were not in the room; bedding and personal items were no longer in the room; walls in the bedroom had been painted and many other areas in the residence had been painted; there were differences with respect to the location of ashtrays and the presence of cigarette butts; an attempt was made to put the windows and doors in the same open or closed position as in March of 1996; however, no effort was made to duplicate the effect of a broken glass window in the outside door.

. . .

The tests essentially consisted of shots being fired in the residence into a bucket filled with sand. The two officers waited outside for 20 minutes, then went into the residence to determine if they could smell gunsmoke odour. On March 4th, 1998, one smelled nothing, and the other detected a faint smell at the base of the stairs.

A second series of similar tests was conducted on March 5th, 1998, with the same officers following the same general procedure. They waited 15 minutes before entering the residence. At that time they detected different smells. One could not say it was gunsmoke. The other officer said he first smelled gunsmoke in the kitchen, more going up the stairs and a continuous odour going down the hallway to the master bedroom where the deceased had been sleeping. On completion of that test, doors and windows of the house were opened for eight minutes. A second test consisting of the same firings was done. The officers waited ten minutes on entering the house. Both detected gunsmoke odour on entering the kitchen which, although variable between the two officers, remained present and got stronger as they made their way up the stairs toward the master bedroom. The evidence is that the ten minute period was selected as the time-span from the 911 call to the first officer arriving at the scene was five minutes, and that time-span was doubled.

It was in response to that proposed evidence that the defence called an expert witness, one admitttedly inexpert regarding firearms, but extremely expert regarding the ways of good science:

Doctor William Tilstone was called by the defence on other motions.... He was acknowledged by the Crown to be an expert in the field of Forensic Science qualified to give opinion evidence on (1) identifying describing the general principles of scientific testing and (2) to offer an opinion on what distinguishes reliable forensic testing from unreliable testing.

The defence adduced from Dr. Tilstone's evidence about good science and bad science, and why the police "tests" fell within the latter category:

He was . . . asked:

Do these tests and the observations and results form a reliable scientific basis to draw any conclusion about the correctness of the hypothesis?
Doctor Tilstone clearly acknowledged that he is not a firearms expert. However, he raised a number of issues of concern to him. Without reviewing here all of the issues he raised, his opinion on the hypothetical is that no scientific conclusion can be drawn on the basis of this type of testing. He further noted that human cognitive studies are extremely difficult to replicate. His ultimate opinion is that the testing described can clearly not be characterised as true scientific tests.

. . .

The concluding and all encompassing submission of defence, as I understand it, is that there are numerous flaws in the way this testing was carried out; that both scientific witnesses agree it cannot be considered as valid scientific testing; that in any event the subsequent testing is incapable of any inferential connection to the date of the offence; further, that even though it ought not to be categorized as valid scientific testing, the evidence ought to be excluded as its probative value is outweighed by its prejudicial value. Again the argument is that it is far too unreliable to be placed before a jury since it cannot assist them in their fact finding process. In sum, counsel says it cannot be relevant because it is unreliable and unnecessary and cannot be placed within the category of proper science.

Ultimately, the court held as follows, based upon this evidence as well as comparable evidence from a Crown witness who agreed with the defence expert concerning the weaknesses in the "experimental" evidence:

> The threshold test for the admission of any evidence is relevance. I find the evidence in this case to be unreliable and unnecessary. Therefore, it is not relevant to assist the jury. Its probative value is minimal, and the potential for prejudice is significantly higher. Evidence relating to the experiments carried out May 1997 and March 1998, therefore, should be excluded.[4]

APPOINTING A SCIENCE DEVIL'S ADVOCATE

AS MENTIONED PREVIOUSLY, various reforms have been suggested to help the law cope with the burgeoning volume of expert evidence. All have their positive features, but also their drawbacks. For example, the suggestion for neutral court-appointed experts to eliminate the perceived inevitable partisanship and motivational bias on the part of the parties' experts may simply replace party allegiance with "own theory" allegiance.

I would suggest a third reform based upon science's major lesson: truth lies by engaging in a dedicated search for disconfirmation. The strongest establishment of a proposition comes not from marshalling evidence in support, but from the inability to marshall evidence to refute; not from all the arguments in favour, but from the lack of cogent arguments against.

Research on group decision making shows that the best decisions come not from a group brainstorming, but from a group that appoints one of its members to argue against its conclusions, pointing out weaknesses and overlooked problems. There is also a famous historical precedent: the Catholic Church's *advocatus diaboli*, or Devil's Advocate.

The Devil's Advocate was a Roman Catholic official whose duty was to examine critically the evidence on which a demand for beatification or canonization rested, to ensure a correct decision. Similarly, I suggest that improvement of expert evidence lies not in a court appointing its own experts, but in a court appointing a Science Devil's Advocate to testify regarding the scientific merit of the parties' expert evidence.[5]

---

4   *R. v. Perlett, ibid.* at para. 31

5   This may or may not differ from the proposal in Andrew Roberts, "Drawing on Expertise: Legal Decision-Making and the Reception of Expert Evidence" [2008] Crim. L. Rev. 443 at 461–62 of a court-appointed "expert advisor" because Roberts is unclear as to the scope of the "advisor's" office. It is hard to argue with Roberts' conclusion: "Satisfactory reform

This approach falls wholly within the scientific spirit of disconfirmation and reliance on vindication of the ways of good science, while leaving the initiative for the substance of the expert evidence to the parties where it belongs. Instead of the court becoming simply another party with a better expert, the actual parties to the litigation provide the expert evidence but the court has an independent assessor and insurer of the quality of that evidence in accordance with the scientific method.

The court-appointed Devil's Advocate would examine and critique the expert evidence to be presented by the parties. That report would be available to the parties in advance of the proceedings. Any criticisms could be reflected in better preparation or alteration of the expert evidence to be presented in court, or the parties could decide to stand pat and dispute the Advocate's conclusions and opinions. Instead of the scientific issues being debated implicitly and decided out of the reach of the parties in the court's decision, the scientific issues would be expressly and knowledgeably considered and debated in advance of the final decision, providing the court with the best-quality basis for a decision.

The court would not only have the views of the parties' experts to assess, but also the assistance of an expert critique by the Devil's Advocate to inform and assist that assessment, as well as the parties' responses and further consideration of the issues raised. The court's decision is more likely to become the best possible judgment in that environment than if the court only has the opposing experts' evidence to consider. The important added element is that the court is not only being informed by expertise as to the substance of the expert forensic issue, but is also being expertly informed about what — if anything — is wrong with the opinions being put forth regarding the substance of the expert forensic issue.

CONCLUSION

THERE CAN BE little doubt that the law's consumption of expert evidence will grow, if not accelerate. Concerns about junk science have brought home to the law the important insight that how we know, not what we know, is the key to real knowledge. This basic rule of science is the law's only reliable guidepost.

What is important is that the law demand of experts that they provide references to the data on which they rely, the theories and assumptions being

of the law may depend on an acknowledgement that the reception of expert evidence requires the use procedures [*sic*] which differ fundamentally from those through which law testimony is received" (at 462).

utilized, and can demonstrate logical reasoning based thereon. If the methodology by which the opinion was reached cannot be completely and transparently made clear, including examination of the underlying data, then there is something very wrong with the "experts" and their approach to knowledge. In short, courts should demand that their expert witnesses be as scientific as possible. Anything less creates a grave risk of allowing valueless or erroneous pseudo-science to exist.

The reforms suggested here further the ends of science. Allowing witnesses to be questioned on their scientific literacy, and disallowing witnesses that cannot be relied on to form their opinions on an acceptable basis because they do not know how to do so, would, in and of itself, constitute a substantial step in the correct direction. Engaging Devil's Advocates to examine and report on proposed expert evidence would carry the law even further towards scientific literacy and ultimately to justice.

I hope that in the future, expert opinion evidence in our courtrooms will continue to grow more and more congruent with the lessons and demands of science. That approach will further the ends of justice immensely. As has been quoted earlier in this text, "Science is what human beings have learned to keep from fooling ourselves." I would add: "Making expert witnesses respect the rules of science is what will keep them from fooling judges and juries."

Table of Cases

Index

About the Author

ALAN D. GOLD practises criminal law at the trial and appellate levels and has appeared as counsel before all levels of courts in Ontario, as well as in other provinces, and in the Supreme Court of Canada. He is certified by the Law Society of Upper Canada as a Specialist in Criminal Litigation and was the first Chairman of the Criminal Litigation Specialty Committee. In 1993, Mr. Gold was inducted into the American College of Trial Lawyers. He received the G. Arthur Martin Award for Contribution to Criminal Justice in November, 1997. He is a past President of the Ontario Criminal Lawyers' Association. Mr. Gold is a Bencher of the Law Society of Upper Canada. He has written and edited numerous works dealing with criminal law, and is a regular speaker at conferences and media commentator. The first edition of *Expert Evidence in Criminal Law: The Scientific Approach* was awarded the 2005 Walter Owen Book Prize, awarded by the Foundation for Legal Research to the author of a book which represents an outstanding new contribution to Canadian legal literature.